# STANDARD GUIDE TO

# BRITISH

## SPORTS CARS

SPW990

## JOHN GUNNELL

©2004 Krause Publications

Published by

An F+W Publications Company

700 East State Street • Iola, WI 54990-0001
715-445-2214 • 888-457-2873
www.krause.com

Our toll-free number to place an order or obtain
a free catalog is (800) 258-0929.

Library of Congress Catalog Number: 2004100741

ISBN: 0-87349-757-0

Designed by Brian Brogaard, Kim Schierl

Edited by Tom Collins

Printed in the United States of America

# ACKNOWLEDGMENTS

## Marque reviewers:

| | |
|---|---|
| Alvis | Wayne Brooks, North American Alvis Owners |
| Connaught | Jason Wenig, The Creative Workshop, Dania Beach, Florida |
| Dellow | Jim Harvey, "Dellow Developments" |
| Doretti | Thomas Householder |
| Elva | Roger Dunbar |
| Fairthorpe | John Allan, Tony Hill, Charles Armstrong-Wilson, The Fairthorpe Registry |
| Frazer-Nash | James Trigwell |
| Gordon-Keeble | John Follows |
| Healey | Bill Emerson |
| Jowett | Edmund Nankivell and Jowett Club Owners, United Kingdom |
| Lea-Francis | Robin Sawers |
| Marauder | Barry Kensett |
| Morgan | Norbert Bries |
| Panther | George Newell and Panther Club members, United Kingdom |
| Peerless | Jon Nolan and members of the Peerless-Warwick Club of Great Britain |
| Reliant | Geoff Eldridge |
| Singer | Peter McKercher |
| Sunbeam | Bob Hamilton (1950s Alpine), Steve Laifman and William Spear (1960s Alpine and Tiger) |
| Turner | Stephen Agins and Russell Filby, Turner and TVR Club of North America |

## Auto image and marque literature assistance:

Stephen Agins, Agins Communications, *Fort Lee, NJ.*

Aston Martin Media, Mark Gauntlett, *Aston Martin Lagonda Ltd., Gaydon, Warwick, UK*

Dick Dance, *Waupaca, WI*

The Frazer-Nash Archives, *Coxon House, Henley on Thames, UK*

Gordon-Keeble Owners Club, *Brackley, Northants, UK*

Heritage Classic Motors, Edward Gibson, *Beverly Hills, CA*

Lea-Francis Club, *French's, Long Wittenham, Abingdon, Oxon, UK*

McLaren Media, *Woking, Surrey, UK*

Bruno Meier, *Rheinfelden, Switzerland*

North Shore Sportscars (Morgan), *Lake Bluff, IL*

Riley Motor Club of South Australia, *Parkside, South Australia*

Wheels on Paper, Rod Laing and Bev Fane, *Christchurch, New Zealand*

## Owner submissions:
*Professional images*

| | |
|---|---|
| Tom Glatch | Brookfield, Wisconsin, USA |
| David Gooley | Paramount, California, USA |
| Bob Harrington | Burlington, Ontario, Canada |
| Greg Hertel | Toronto, Ontario, Canada |
| Kris Kandler | Krause Publications, Iola, WI, USA |
| Richard Langworth | Contoocook, New Hampshire, USA |
| Andrew Morland | Glastonbury, Somerset, United Kingdom |
| Jonathan Stein | Reading, Pennsylvania, USA |
| Thomas Touw | Abbekerk, Holland |
| John Wheater | Market Weighton, York, United Kingdom |

Bob Harrington

# CONTENTS

# Frazer-Nash

# Gordon-Keeble

# Healey

# HRG

# Jaguar

# Jensen

# Jensen-Healey

# Jowett

# Lea-Francis

# Lotus

# Marauder

# Marcos

# McLaren

# MG-T

# MG-A,B, & C

# MG-Midget

# Morgan

# Nash-Healey

# Panther

# Peerless

# Reliant

# Riley

# Singer

# Sunbeam

# Triumph-TR Series

# Triumph-Spitfire/GT

# Turner

# TVR

# Resources

Peter McKercher

*The 1937 Singer Nine is proudly restored and graces the streets of Ottawa, Ontario, Canada's national capitol.*

# An Exciting Heritage

Sydney Allard, the Morgan family, Rod Clarke, John Gordon and Jim Keeble. Just a few of the enterprising people who gave their talents to British sports cars. Each car reflects their viewpoints about what a car could be.

And names like Jaguar, Daimler, Austin, MG and Standard-Triumph represent another portion of British car making— the corporate planning and large manufacturing capacities. North American buyers have had much to choose from if they've been interested in British sports cars. Whether it's a stately Alvis, a racing Elva, a world car like the McLaren F 1, a head-turning Aston Martin or a tough little Dellow, British car buyers often become dedicated backers of a particular marque. It's as if they wear their car like a favorite shirt. Some of these cars have been—and continue to be—made by the weathered hands of veteran craftspeople or the willing hands of a today's generation of apprentices. Body parts have been pounded and shaped by them using the same tools, turning wheels, and bucks their grandfathers used to shape earlier models. British sports cars always have been much more than practical or utilitarian vehicles. Driving, enjoying and competing often have spurred creation of these cars. Sport driving has engendered bonds between drivers and machines for generations in England.From the earliest days of motoring, British cars have competed on tracks like Brooklands, entered in endurance courses like Le Mans, endured the extremes of Alpine and desert road rallies, or climbed muddy hill courses. The men and women who were responsible for the various cars included in this book often were unique. Some were visionaries. Others were bottom-line oriented. And still others were hopeless romantics. They shared a love for getting behind the wheel and make their idea a roadworthy reality. Racing driver Rod Clarke was the force behind the Connaught. The Allards

were from a family of Ford dealers and enjoyed cramming powerful engines into light cars and driving them as fast as possible. Donald Healey raced and won with Triumph Glorias in the 1930s and gave his name to many sports cars for the rest of his career.

This book attempts to convey the enjoyment of their raw power, the rush of open air, hanging on in a taut curve and the vista of the open road ahead in top gear. Whether you're a Peerless purist, a Marauder maven, or a true fan of TVRs, this book hopes to help you appreciate your favorite car even more.

sAnd if you've never had a chance to drive a British-made car, this book will help teach you what the excitement is all about. Highly individual, radically risk taking, refined as a rare bottle of Jamesons and unique as bobbies, Big Ben and Shakespeare, British cars stand out wherever they go.

Plunge into the heritage. We've made the trip more interesting with a steady mix of British and American automotive terms throughout the book. So if your carburettor is petrol-lean, the spanner is in the boot, the accumulator is charged and the RoStyles are spinning, you'll jolly well feel right at home whether you're in Butte or Calgary, Christchurch or the banks of the Thames.

During the production of this book, British automotive icon Peter Morgan passed away. Mr. Morgan personified all that made his Morgan cars special, and all that makes collecting British sports cars fun and interesting. We dedicate the book to him, a symbol of all those whose ideas, toil and talents made every British sports car in this book something interesting and special.

Enjoy the read! And as you explore these pages, may it be a heart-pounding experiece that brings a smile to your face.

*John Gunnell*
*Jan. 19, 2004*

*The Bentley Le Mans, a stately reminder of early British racing cars.*

This 1936 Singer has a famous racing name—the Le Mans Speed Special.

David Campbell

*This angle beckons drivers to take the road in this 1937 A.C. sports roadster.*

Dick Dance Collection

*Aston-Martins and Lagondas were assembled with care at this plant in 1951.*

# A.C.

Bob Harrington

# 1954-1963 Ace

The A.C. factory at Thames Ditton, Surrey, (near London) had a reputation for sedate, rather old-fashioned models, but A.C. Cars, Ltd. introduced its modern Ace sports car at the October 1953 London Motor Show. This car established the company's reputation worldwide. A.C. owners Charles and Derek Hurlock saw John Tojeiro's sports-racer, fell in love with it and bought production rights from him.

The Ferrari-inspired two-seater, rode a ladder-type chassis made up of three-inch diameter tubes. It had independent wishbone-and-leaf-spring suspensions at both ends. One Tojeiro had a race-tuned Lea-Francis engine, while another used a 2-litre Bristol power plant. Articulated axle shafts were employed with a differential bolted to the parallel steel tubes that made up the car's frame. The chassis had minimal unsprung weight at the rear axle.

A.C. folks decided to build both the chassis and a racy body at its own plant. The first production Aces were delivered in 1954. A.C. switched to cam-gear steering and raised the headlamps to meet international requirements. Al-Fin brake drums and the aluminum body reduced weight.

Long known for quality, A.C. suddenly promoted "Exciting performance, thrilling speed, beautiful styling." A 1991-cc (121.5-cid) single-overhead-cam in-line six with solid lifters provided power. With a 65 x 100-mm (2.56 x 3.94-in.) bore and stroke, the five-main-bearings monobloc engine featured an aluminum block and head (with cast iron cylinder liners). With a 7.5:1 compression ratio, it developed 85 bhp at 4500 rpm and 105 lbs.-ft. of torque at 2750 rpm. Three SU carburetors with automatic easy-starting devices were employed. A six-branch manifold merged into twin pipes to keep exhaust back pressure to a minimum. A double roller chain operated the cams.

A.C. fitted a Moss gearbox with overall gear ratios of: (1st) 12.34:1, (2nd) 7.21:1, (3rd) 4.98:1, (4th) 3.64:1, and (rev) 12.34:1. Twin parallel chassis tubes held the suspension and differential, while tubular outriggers carried the light body. Tube-type shocks were mounted at an

*A bright red 1958 A.C. Ace roadster is captured in road course action.*

angle between the frame and lower wishbones. Open shafts extended from the fixed hypoid spiral-bevel differential to the drive wheels. The standard rear axle ratio was 3.64:1.

The Ace had a 90-in. wheelbase and measured 151.5 in. from end to end. It was 59.5 in. wide and only 49 in. high. The 5.50 x 16 tires were mounted on Dunlop center-locking wire wheels. A 50-in. tread was used front and rear. The racy and aggressive-looking front end displayed a large, semi-circular grille opening with a recessed insert featuring wide-spaced crosshatching. Small, round parking lights stood below the built-in headlamps on the fender tips.

"Your comfort is our first consideration," said a sales brochure. "Snug-fitting bucket seats really hold you firm."

The stark cockpit was fitted with leather upholstery over Dunlopillo filling. The doors had map pockets and the steering wheel was adjustable. Small bumperettes were placed outside the grille opening for protection.

The $3,200 Ace weighed just 1685 pounds. Available extra-cost equipment included a Radiomobile radio, a heater, a Fram bypass oil filter, a passenger grab handle, overrider-type bumpers, stone shields for the gas tank and battery, a second spare wheel and tire, twin-coil ignition, twin fuel pumps and alternate gear ratios. The Ace could accelerate from 0-to-60 mph in just 11.4 seconds and did the standing-start quarter mile in 18 seconds. It had a top speed of 100-103 mph and got 18 miles-per-gallon fuel economy—which wasn't shabby in 1954!

The 1955 Ace continued with little change, except under the hood. The compression ratio was boosted to 8.0:1 with an accompanying increase of 90 horsepower. There was a $600 price jump. The $3,800 price tag included a telescopic steering column, a spring-type steering

wheel, adjustable bucket seats, a leatherette-covered dashboard with Smith instruments, dual exhaust pipes with individual headers, dual wind-tone horns, and a Lucas electrical system.

The 1956 Ace roadster was little changed. An electrical overdrive transmission became optional and the P.O.E. price jumped to $4,495. Front disc brakes became available a year or so later. Standard body colors for 1956-1957 models were black, red, maroon, bright blue, green, off-white, and cream. The leather upholstery came in black, red, maroon, green, beige, grey/blue, or grey. A horsepower boost gave the 1958-1959 A.C. Ace 102 bhp. The Moss gearbox was replaced by new Triumph TR3A gears inside an A.C. housing. The list price was $4,799, but U.S. buyers could pick up their cars for $3,985 stateside. Worldwide Import Company, Los Angeles, was the company's American distributor.

A removable hardtop became an extra-cost option and a curved windshield was available. Another new option was a cowl that covered part of the radiator to cut air drag. It boosted top speed to 120 mph.

The basic Ace roadster production continued with little change in 1960 and 1961. Even the listed P.O.E. price remained the same. Things changed drastically in 1962 when A.C. turned to the Ford Zephyr six as an available option. And in the U.S., ex-race driver Carroll Shelby was turning the six-cylinder Ace into a V-8 Cobra.

The A.C. 1991-cc, 102-hp alloy six remained the base engine, but the optional Zephyr in-line six came in a broad range of horsepower ratings from 90 (SAE) all the way to 170.

This 2553-cc (155.7-cid) overhead-valve engine featured a cast-aluminum block and head. It had an 82.55 x 79.5-mm (3.25 x 3.13-in.) bore and stroke, solid valve lifters, four main bearings, and three SU HD6 carburetors.

The last British-built Aces were made in the spring of 1964 with a smaller, Cobra-like grille. According to factory records, the production of A.C. Ace models (not counting Ace-Bristols) over the 10-year period between 1954 and 1963 was only 220 units.

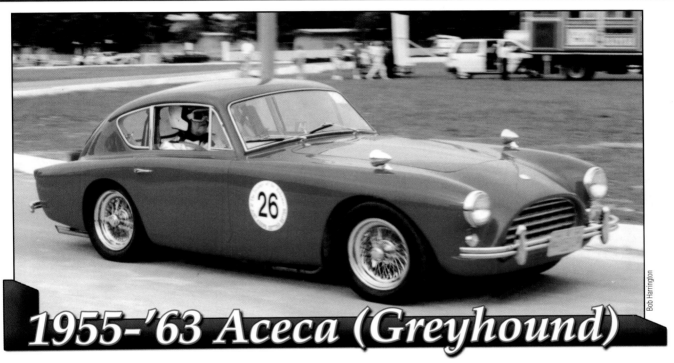

Bob Harrington

# 1955-'63 Aceca (Greyhound)

A.C. Cars, Ltd. of Thames Ditton, Surrey, England, introduced the Aceca coupe in October 1954. The car's name was pronounced "Ay-See-Kuh." Essentially, it was a fastback version of the same company's Ace roadster. The automaker said it was designed for "the discerning motorist who requires closed bodywork."

Considered a new-for-1955 model, the Aceca featured a composite steel-tube-and-ash body framing with aluminum paneling. This construction combined strength and lightness. The coupe's frontal appearance was similar to that of the Ace, but in profile the roofline and small rear side windows were reminiscent of the 166 and 212 Ferraris.

The influence of Italian designers was much greater in the coupe than in the roadster. Instead of a rounded, roadster-like rear end, the coupe had squared-off rear fenders that looked almost like tailfins when viewed from the side.

The coupe used the same 1991-cc single-overhead-cam in-line six as the Ace roadster. It incorporated an aluminum block and head. With an 8.0:1 compression ratio and triple S.U. carburetors, the solid-lifter, five-main-bearings engine developed 90 hp at 4500 rpm and 105 lbs.-ft. of torque at 2750 rpm. Attached to the engine was a four-speed manual gearbox with a floor-mounted shift lever. A 3.64:1 final drive ratio was used. Top speed was in the 102-103-mph range. The Aceca

*The 1959 A.C. Aceca coupe was attractive and fast!*

could move from 0-60 mph in as little as 13.4 sec.

Bishop cam-gear steering was employed in the Aceca. The independent front suspension had transverse leaf springs and dual wishbones. The rear suspension, also independent, was of similar design. Girling hydraulic brakes with Al-fin drums were used front and rear. The coupe was designed on the roadster's 90-in. wheelbase, but it was two inches longer (153.5 in.) in overall length. It was also three inches higher (52 in.) and one and a half inches wider (61 in.). Naturally, this made the Aceca heavier. It weighed in at 1,840 lbs. — 155 more than the roadster. The coupe retained the open car's 50-in. front and rear tread, as well as its Dunlop center-lock wire wheels and 5.50x16 tires. Like its Ace cousin, the Aceca coupe got a new electrical overdrive transmission as optional equipment in 1956. Front disc brakes became available a year or so later. A.C. produced only about five cars per week in mid 1956 and few were Acecas. Michell and Pauli, of Los Angeles, was the American distributor at this time. The Port-of-Entry price for the coupe climbed to $5,549, from $4,500 the previous year. Other than the above, there was not much product change in the Aceca. Worldwide Import, Inc., of Los Angeles, became A.C.'s American distributor starting in 1958. Twelve added horsepower and a gearbox swap were the major news that season. The same changes were made to the Ace roadster. List price for the fastback was now up to $5,649.

During the first two years of the '60s, Aceca coupe production continued with little change. The price remained at $5,699. Starting in late 1959, A.C. also offered a 2+2 coupe called the Greyhound, primarily for the British home market. Priced at $6,699, the Greyhound "saloon" had a flatter grille than the Aceca, as well as built-in recessed running lights and a hood air scoop.

With a stretched 100-in. wheelbase, the Greyhound was 180 in. long, 53 in. high and 65.25 in. long. It came with a 125-hp version of the A.C. six-cylinder engine, as well as the more powerful Bristol engine option. Other differences from the Aceca coupe included a 4.1:1 final drive ratio and a coil spring suspension.

Road testers found the Greyhound capable of top speeds in the 108-120 mph range and reported that it could move from 0-to-60 mph in 19 seconds. These cars did not sell well and were rarely seen outside Great Britain.

Production of the basic Aceca coupe carried over into 1960 and 1961, but drastic changes started in 1962 when A.C. offered the Ford Zephyr six as an option. A.C.'s own 1991-cc, 102-hp alloy six remained the base engine, but the Zephyr powerplant cranked up a lot more horsepower — up to 170. The last British Acecas were made in the spring of 1964 and had smaller, Cobra-like grilles. According to factory records, the production of A.C. Aceca coupes (not counting those with Bristol engines) was 150 cars over 11 years. As you can imagine, these were uncommon cars and they are even rarer to find today.

# 1967-1973 289/427

Production of a British version of the Cobra, with its own distinctive appearance, continued into 1973. Two versions were offered, one powered by the 289-cid small-block Ford V-8 and another with Ford's 428-cid "Interceptor" V-8 under the bonnet. A fixed-head fastback coupe also joined the earlier drophead coupe in the model lineup. Total production of these cars from 1965 to 1973 was about 28 convertibles (including 427s) and no more than 58 coupes. The 1967-1973 models used the same Hi-Po 289 V-8 employed in 1966 models, but the 428-cid (7014-cc) engine was brand new. This overhead-valve engine had a cast-iron block and head. With a 4.13 x 3.98-in. (104.9 x 101-mm) bore and stroke, the 428 offered 10.5:1 compression and developed 345 bhp at 4600 rpm and 462 lbs.-ft. of torque at 2800 rpm. Other specifications were the same as the 1966 version with the 427, except that 205 x 15 radial tires were available. These cars had a 140-mph top speed and the 428s did 0-to-60 mph in about six seconds.

Produced only in limited quantity and priced quite high, the 427/428-powered A.C.s were the final sport offerings from the long-lived firm. A.C. continued to produce three-wheelers for invalids until 1976, then turned to making trailer bodies. Early in the 1980s, a few dozen 3-litre coupes with a mid-mounted Ford V-6 were made. The company was then bought by Scottish businessman Brian Angliss in 1984. He renamed it A.C. (Scotland) Ltd., but it folded after producing a handful of automobiles. An Ace for the Eighties even appeared in prototype form at the 1986 British International Motor Show in Birmingham, England.

Carroll Shelby and his Shelby-American organization remained active long after the demise of the Cobra, turning out special high-performance models for major domestic automakers, including Shelby Dodge Daytonas in the 1980s.

A great many Cobra replicas have been marketed, some similar to the original, others not. Some used fiberglass bodies, and some carried a 428- or 429-cid Ford V8. The Cobra "Mk IV," built by Auto Kraft Ltd., was claimed to be an exact replica, using original tooling and equipment. That company operated inside the old Brooklands race course at Weybridge, Surrey, in England. The firm began by repairing and restoring "real" Cobras, then obtained permission to use the "Cobra" trademark and ship cars to the U.S., to be sold by Ford dealers. The latest ones had a 305-cid (5.0-litre) V-8 engine, as used in Mustangs, and appeared to be identical to the last Cobra 427.

OCW Archives

# 1966-'68 A.C. Frua

**R**ather than merely import Cobras back from the United States, A.C. turned out its own version of a V-8 roadster, one that seemed to be intended more for grand touring than competition. A prototype appeared at the London Motor Show in late 1965, and the car went on sale during 1966. Styling of the new drophead coupe (and subsequent hardtop coupe) was markedly different from the earlier Ace or the current Shelby Cobra. A low, flat grille gave a distinctive front-end appearance and there were wraparound parking lights below the headlamps.

The two-seater body was created by Frua (in Italy) and a 427-cid Ford V-8 provided the power. The car's overall appearance was similar to the Maserati Mistral (also done by Frua). Underneath, A.C. used a parallel-tube chassis like that of the updated (Mark III) Shelby Cobra, but it was longer and designed more for softer riding qualities. Buyers could choose between a four-speed manual transmission or a Ford three-speed automatic transmission. The car also had four-wheel disc brakes and center-lock wire wheels.

Construction of the 1966 A.C. was a multi-step process, with the engine coming from Dearborn, Michigan, the chassis built in Great Britain, and the body made in Italy. Final assembly work was done in Italy, then the entire car was shipped back to England for testing and inspection.

A version powered by a 289-cid Ford V-8 also was sold in

*The A. C. 427/428 drophead featured distinct design by Frua of Italy and Ford V-8 engines.*

Europe. It used a Mark III Cobra chassis, similar to that used in 427 Cobras.

The 289-cid (4727 cc) V-8 was Ford's "Hi-Po" version with a 101.6 x 72.8 mm (4.00 x 2.87-in.) bore and stroke, 10.5:1 compression ratio and a single four-barrel carburetor. It produced 271 bhp at 6000 rpm and 312 lbs.-ft. of torque at 3400 rpm.

The 427-cid (6997-cc) V-8 had a 107.6 x 96 mm (4.24 x 3.78-in.) bore and stroke, 11.1:1 compression ratio and a dual Carter four-barrel carburetors. It generated a ground-shaking 425 bhp at 6000 rpm and 480 lbs.-ft. of torque at 3700 rpm.

Some sources indicate that only 55 cars were built, 27 with the smaller Ford V-8 and 28 with the larger Ford 427. Other sources say that 29 of the 427 roadsters were made.

A 90-in. wheelbase chassis was used with the smaller engine, while the 427 model had a 96-in. wheelbase. Overall length was 166 and 174 in., respectively. The height and width of the larger-engined car were 51 in. and 67 in. A 54-in. tread was used up front, 53 in. in the rear.

Tires were big 8.15 x 15s mounted on the center-locking wheels. Rack-and-pinion steering was featured. The suspension used wishbones and coil springs front and rear.

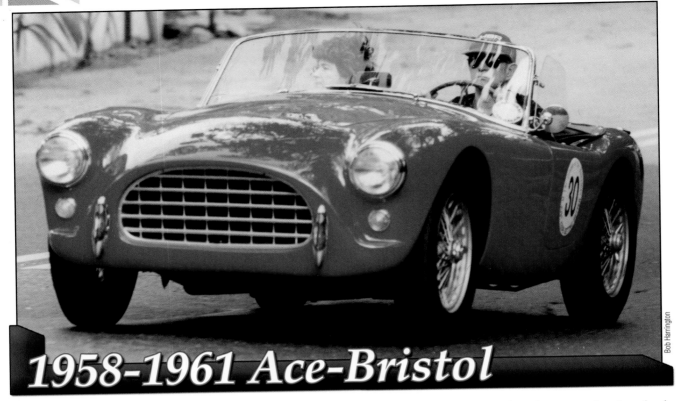

Bob Harrington

# 1958-1961 Ace-Bristol

Starting in 1958, those who weren't satisfied with the power and performance of the basic Ace or Aceca—or who wanted an engine that didn't date back to 1919—were given another choice. A Bristol 2-litre six was made available as an option. Cars with this power plant under their bonnet were referred to as A.C.-Bristols, as if they were a separate marque.

The Bristol six wasn't exactly new. It was based on the 1933-1937 BMW six. Ken Rudd, a British race driver, built the first A.C.-Bristol and the factory was impressed enough to offer the combination to the car-buying public. Bristol models were announced around April 1956 and first shown in the fall of the same year. By the following spring, they were in production. They were more powerful and more suitable to race-tuning, but appearance-wise, the "Bristols" were almost identical to the A.C.-engined roadster and coupe.

Bristol had obtained rights to the engine design and built it for other automakers. Instead of an overhead cam, this one was of overhead-valve design with semi-spherical combustion chambers. The Bristol engine had a 66-mm bore and a rather long 96-mm (2.60 x 3.78 in.) stroke. It had an 8.5:1 compression ratio. Three downdraft Solex carburetors supplied fuel to the four-main-bearings solid-lifter engine.

In standard B-type (100B) form, it produced 105 bhp at 4750 rpm and 123 lbs.-ft. of torque at 3750 rpm. An optional D-type (100D2) engine was even more powerful. It used a 9.0:1 compression ratio, which upped horsepower to 120 at 5750 rpm and torque to 122 lbs.-ft. at 4500 rpm. All A.C.-Bristols used a four-speed gearbox. An optional Laycock de Normanville overdrive worked in second, third and fourth gear. Because the Bristol engine added few pounds, the added performance came with little loss of fuel economy.

John Bolster, writing in *AutoSport* magazine, declared that for "sheer pleasure of driving, this is one of the best sports cars I have ever

*The A.C. Bristol roadster has been turning heads since 1962.*

driven." That article added that the Ace-Bristol "holds the road at least as well as any Continental car."

The Ace-Bristol roadster had a $5,549 price tag and weighed just 1,685 lbs. The fastback coupe version (Aceca-Bristol) was $6,549 and 1,840 lbs. Most chassis and technical specifications were similar to those of the Ace and Aceca, but the Bristols rode on 5.50 x 16 Michelin X tires. Top speed was 115-117 mph and 0-to-60 mph took 9.1 seconds in the Ace-Bristol and 10.3 seconds in the Aceca-Bristol. The Bristol D-type did 0-to-60 in 7 to 8 seconds and ran the quarter mile in 16 seconds. Even at that, fuel economy was 18+ mpg.

During 1958, the Bristol engine continued to be available in the Ace and Aceca in various states of tune ranging from the basic 105 hp to as much as 130 hp. On Bristol models, the overall gear ratios were unique, 11.42:1 in first, 7.13:1 in second, 5.05:1 in third and 3.91:1 in fourth. The standard final drive ratio was also 3.91:1.

Production of the Bristol-powered models continued in 1960-1961, when the Ace sold for $5,699 and the Aceca cost $6,599. In the latter year, Bristol announced that its new 407 model would use the Chrysler hemi-head V-8 instead of a six. That meant A.C. was about to lose its source for optional power plants. At the time, this announcement rocked the racing world because Bristol-powered A.C. models were consistent winners in sports-car competition. *Sports Cars Illustrated* magazine reported that the A.C.-Bristols "thoroughly dominated Class E competition in American racing." Approximate total production between 1957 and 1964 was 466 Ace-Bristol roadsters and 169 Aceca-Bristol coupes.

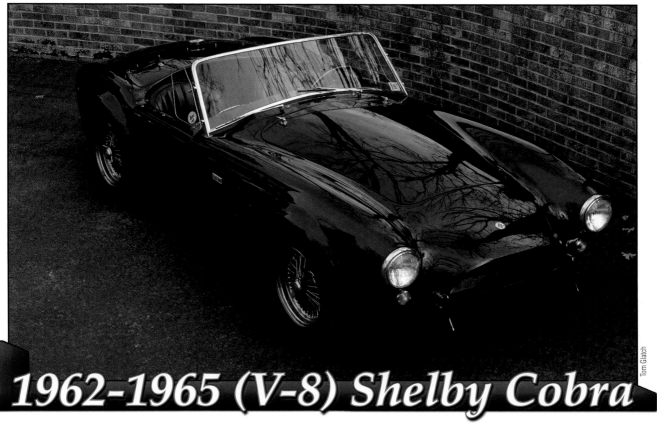

Tom Glatch

# 1962-1965 (V-8) Shelby Cobra

**R**eferred to as the A.C. in Britain, the V-8 powered version of the Ace roadster, built from 1962 until 1965, adopted the Cobra name in the U.S. The cars were known as either Shelby-A.C. Cobras or just Shelby Cobras.

The Cobra concept sprung from retired Texas race car driver Carroll Shelby, who was aware A.C. Cars Ltd. had lost sourcing of the Bristol six. In September 1961, Shelby sent an airmail letter to A.C. proposing to continue production of the Ace chassis for a special Shelby sports car to be powered by an American V-8. At the time, Shelby was unaware that Ford would soon release a new lightweight, thinwall cast, small-block V-8 for its mid-size Fairlane.

Charles Hurlock, one of the brothers who owned A.C., answered Shelby's letter. Hurlock expressed interest in Shelby's scheme if a suitable engine could be found. That same month, Shelby learned about Ford's new 221-cid small-block V-8. He wrote to Dave Evans at Ford and outlined his sports car concept and the need for a suitable V-8. Evans bought into the idea and immediately called Shelby to say he was sending him two of the new V-8s.

The first car, minus engine and transmission, was air freighted to Shelby's shop in Venice, California, on Feb. 2, 1962. According to Shelby, the Cobra name came to him in a dream in which the named appeared on the front of the car.

"I woke up and jotted the name down on a pad which I kept by my bedside — a sort of ideas pad — and went back to sleep. Next morning when I looked at the name 'Cobra,' I knew it was right." The car was also known as the "260 Roadster" based on its horsepower rating. Less than eight hours after that first car arrived, a 260-cid Ford Hi-Performance V-8 and a Borg-Warner four-speed transmission were bolted in. Shelby and his buddy Dean Moon (the inventor of Moon discs) then test drove the car.

Operations at the Shelby-American shop on Princeton Drive in Venice began the next month and Shelby hired Ray Geddes, a Ford finance business school graduate, to coordinate the program with the Dearborn automaker.

Part of Geddes' role was to downplay Ford's involvement to reduce their product liability concerns. By April 1962, the CSX 2000

*An A.C. in muscle form. The sensational Carroll Shelby modified 1964 A.C. Shelby Cobra.*

(Carroll Shelby Experimental 2000) was introduced to the public for the first time at the New York Auto Show. It was put on exhibit at the Ford booth wearing a special Pearlescent Yellow paint job applied by famed customizer Dean Jeffries. The car drew sufficient dealer orders to finance production of the Cobra.

Shelby put members of the automotive press in the car as quickly as possible. CSX 2000 was even repainted a different color for each road test, so the writers thought more cars were being produced. The road tests and promotional efforts paid off. *Sports Car Graphic* (May 1962) called the Cobra's acceleration "explosive." By May, a second car was shipped by air from England to New York and Ed Hugas installed the drive train in Pittsburgh, Pennsylvania. The third car, sent to Los Angeles, became the first competition version. Cobras did well in racing, as they weighed a ton less than competition-prepped Corvettes.

Production was slow at first, as Shelby-American extensively re-engineered the A.C. The first 75 Cobras had the lightweight Ford 260-cid (4.2-litre) V-8 engine. Then the 289-cid (4727-cc) V-8, with a basic rating of 271 bhp, was used. This engine produced up to 370 bhp in race tune. Ford insisted that "Powered By Ford" decals be put on the valve covers below the "Cobra" name.

The Ace's tubular chassis was stiffened somewhat and a limited-slip Salisbury-type axle was added. Four-wheel disc brakes were also installed. The steering gearbox had to be tilted a bit to fit over the V-8 engine. The Cobra's appearance wasn't much different from that of the Ace, except that flared wheelarches were needed to fit over its larger tires.

Quite a few other engineering changes took place over the next years. After the 125th car, for instance, rack-and-pinion steering replaced the old cam-gear setup. The Cobra's Borg-Warner four-speed gearbox was fully synchronized. Smith instruments were used for early models, after which Stewart-Warner gauges were installed.

The 260-Cobra was initially priced at $5,995 and weighed in at 2,100 pounds. Shelby-American built 75 copies of the 260 Roadster in 1962-1963, but only 51 of the 289-powered models. Specifications were very much like those of the Ace, although the Shelby sat lower to the ground at 45 in. high. It was also slightly wider at 61 in. and had a wider track (53.25-in. front/52.5-in. rear). The 260 Roadster offered a choice of 6.50 x 15 or 6.75 x 15 tires. Buyers of 289 Roadster could pick between 7.35 x 15 or 8.5 x 15 radials.

Road tests reported a 0-to-60 mph times in the 5.2- to 5.5-second with range and quarter-mile acceleration between 13.8 and 13.9 seconds. In August 1962, although only eight cars had been built, Shelby-American homologated the Cobra with the Federation Internationale de L'Automobile (FIA) as a GT III car in the over-2-liter class. This meant that 100 cars had to be built that year. On Oct. 13, 1962, driver Bill Krause piloted the first competition Cobra in the "Los Angeles Times Grand Prix." Krause took the lead on lap nine, but broke a rear hub. Shelby-American's Phil Remington soon started working with Halibrand to come up with new wheels.

Although originally intended for sale solely in America, Shelby Cobras were marketed in Britain, as well as the U.S., starting in 1964. Some had the earlier 260- and 289-cid V-8s, but those with the 427-cid big-block also were available.

During 1965, coil springs and wishbones replaced the original transverse leaf springs. The original Ace chassis was abandoned in favor of a special frame with larger-diameter tubes, spaced farther apart. Because so much work was done to the car at the Shelby facility in California, Cobras are generally viewed as American cars, even though their bodies came from England.

*The 1951 A.C. sports tourer was streamlined and ready for the road in this publicity photo.*

*A rather sedate A.C. drophead coupe (convertible) echoes British refinement.*

# ALLARD

Dick Dance Collection

# 1946-1949 J1/K1

**S**ydney Allard sold motorcars at his family's Ford dealership in London during the 1930s, but he also loved trials racing. In 1929, at age 19, he was already racing three-wheel Morgan Super Sports at Brooklands, with minimal success. By 1936, following some early tries at rallies and hillclimbs with flathead Ford racing cars, he built his first Allard Special. Its shortened Ford V-8 coupe chassis and running gear held a portion of a Type 57 Bugatti body. The Special performed well in hillclimbs, rallies and trials. Over the next few years, until war broke out, Allard built 11 more Specials. All were powered by either Ford V-8 or Lincoln Zephyr V-12 engines.

After the war, Allard's family kept the Ford dealership running, but Sydney formed the Allard Motor Co. In January of 1946 he announced his first postwar car. This J1 two-seat racer featured a Ford flathead V-8 and Ford transmission mounted in a special chassis. The J1 was produced at a new plant in Clapham (not far from central London).

Instead of Ford's customary—and wagon-like—front suspension, Allard used an independent suspension designed by Leslie Bellamy. It combined a split front axle with a conversion of the Ford transverse leaf spring setup. Only 12 J1s were built before the somewhat more successful K1 came out.

The K1 was a postwar car, although it was essentially the same as Allard's J1, which originated before the war. The K1 had a six-inch longer wheelbase. Under the hood was a nearly-stock British 221-cid Ford V-8 with a 7.0:1 compression ratio that was rated at 85 hp. A few K1s used the more powerful 239-cid V-8 from the Canadian Mercury. This engine had a 7.5:1 compression ratio and developed 95 hp at 3600 rpm or, in some cars, 100 hp. Both were three-main-bearing engines with solid valve lifters. In traditional Allard style, the stock transverse-spring front axle was split to become an independent swing axle. At the rear was a torque tube with a "live" beam axle held by a transverse leaf spring. The K1 frame was made for Allard by Thomsons of Wolverton and used stamped-steel channel sections.

*This is the rare 1949 Allard J 1 competition roadster.*

The car's steel body panels were attached to a wood framework.

With a squarish grille using vertical bars that appeared to roll down the curvy nose, the 2,460-lb. K1 had a rather homemade look. Its front and rear fenders were separate. All K1s were right-hand-drive cars. A handful (possibly three) of the 151 K1s built arrived in the United States, although it was never officially offered for sale in America.

According to *Autocar* magazine, the early postwar Allard had "roadholding and stability which allow an enthusiastic driver to throw it about as he pleases." Describing entry into the driver's seat The Motor noted that one was "immediately impressed by the way in which appearance has been blended with the requirements of the fast driver." Of the car's potential, the editors added: "What appear to be impossible speeds can be safely maintained without the slightest sign of skidding." The Allard K1 rode on a 106-in. wheelbase and had an overall length of 168 in. It was 71 in. wide. With standard 6.25 x 16 tires mounted, the K1 had a 56-in. front tread and 50-in. rear tread. The transmission was a three-speed manual type with synchros on second and third gear. Up front was the split-swing-axle independent front suspension, with a beam axle, torque tube and transverse leaf spring used at the rear. Lockheed drum brakes were used all around.

Top speed in the K1 was 92-93 mph and 0-to-50 mph took 11.5 seconds. It could do the quarter-mile in about 20 seconds on a wet road.

Among their many racing victories in the early postwar years, Allards won the Lisbon Rally in 1947 and 1949, took five awards in the 1947-1948 Alpine Rally and won the Team Trophy (and two others) in the 1949 Monte Carlo Rally.

A total of seven Allards were built in 1946, 173 were sold in 1947, 432 sold in 1948 and 265 sold in 1949, but not all of them were J1s and K1s.

Dick Dance Collection

# 1950-1951 J2

Although early postwar Allards were well received in Great Britain, Sydney Allard wanted to make inroads into the United States market for sporty semi-racers. "Specially designed for the American competition motorist," said promotional copy for the updated J2, a car that helped him to achieve his goal. The idea for the J2 resulted from a trip Allard made to America. Riding the same 100-in. wheelbase as the J1, the new car did well both in the marketplace and on the racetracks of the world.

Customers could choose from a variety of engines including a 239-cid flathead Ford V-8, a 140-bhp Ford V-8 with an "Ardun" overhead-valve conversion. The Ardun kit for the flathead Ford V-8 engine came from Zora Arkus-Duntov of New York City, who later became famous as chief engineer of the Corvette.

Operating with pushrods and rocker arms, the kit produced an engine similar to early Chrysler "Firepower" Hemis. The Ardun option was abandoned after the first few dozen J2 models, but the Chrysler Hemi or the famous Cadillac OHV V-8 were made available. Allard's price list noted that the wide selection of engines was offered "to permit the enthusiast to fit his own particular choice of motor, hopped-up or otherwise."

Although the J2 was a competition car, it was also capable of road touring. Allard made it available with either left- or right-hand drive. A small vertical-bar pentagonal grille sat in a curvy protruding nose. The engine-turned instrument panel contained a five-inch speedometer and tachometer, oil-and-temperature gauge, ammeter, fuel gauge and fuel switch. The body had bolt-on rear fenders and cycle-style front fenders, separate headlights and tiny round taillights.

Though basic in appearance and engineering, the J2 was quick. Top speed with a Cadillac V-8 was reported as 110 mph, although some enthusiasts claimed they made 130 mph. With the same engine, 0-to-60 mph took 5.5 seconds and the quarter-mile was covered in just 16.3 seconds, which was literally unheard of at the time.

Highly modified Cadillac V-8 Allards reached 250 bhp with twin

*When Allard is mentioned many people think of the classic J2.*

carburetors, special camshafts and racing heads. These cars could to go from 0-to-100 mph in as little as 12 seconds.

The J2 displayed an unmistakable race-car look. As Allard's brochure suggested, it had "just about everything for the speed man." The J2 was available as chassis assembly only weighing 1,950 lbs. and costing $2,237. The J-Type engine was an additional $568. This was the 239-cid (3917-cc), 95-100-hp three-main-bearings, cast iron Canadian Mercury L-head V-8. Solex racing-type carburetors were fitted, along with an oil-cooler radiator.

Early J2 buyers could opt for the Ardun heads or even order a competition model with a version of the Canadian Mercury engine that was bored out to 266.8 cid for 120 hp at 3800 rpm. The Allard body added $560 to the car's price. With the 331-cid, 160-hp Cadillac V-8 installed, total price ran about $3,995. The 331-cid Chrysler "Firepower" Hemi upped output even more — to 180 hp at 4000 rpm. Both of these OHV V-8s also added hydraulic valve lifters

From front to rear, the J2 was 148 in. long. Measuring 63 in. wide, it had a 56 in. front and 52-in. rear tread: The car's disc wheels carried 6.00 x 16 tires. Allard stuck with a three-speed manual transmission with synchronizers on second and third gears. A 3.54:1 rear axle was employed. The front suspension was similar to the J1/K1 type, but at the rear, a De Dion axle with quick-change differential and coil springs was used. The brakes were 12-in. Lockheed with Al-Fin front and rear drums. Designed chiefly for racing, the car carried a 26-gal. fuel tank with reserve tank.

A total of 305 Allards were sold during 1950 and 337 the following year, but not all of these were J2s. At least 21 cars went to American buyers in 1950 and 42 in 1951. The U.S. distributor was Moss Motors Ltd., of Los Angeles, California.

Dick Dance Collection

# 1950-1952 K2

**S**leeker in appearance and a bit more rounded than the earlier Allard K1, the reworked K2 two-seater Sports Tourer could easily be identified by the trio of Buick-style "portholes." They decorated the sheetmetal alongside a small bonnet that sat far back from the grille. The bonnet carried an air scoop and short hood straps. A pentagonal grille with vertical bars–shaped like that of the J2—replaced the K1-style "waterfall" grille. Round headlights were mounted low in the "clamshell" fenders.

The roadster's cut-down doors had a gracefully-curved upper edge. The rear end reminded some observers of the Jaguar XK-120's tail. Short, horizontal bumperettes were used at all body corners, front and rear. Standard equipment included high-compression aluminum cylinder heads, a floor-mounted gearshift lever, a racing-type fly-off hand brake, a windshield, and all-weather equipment.

Although basic, the cockpit was actually less austere than that of the previous two-seater. It was similar in design to the interior of four-passenger Allard models. A fabric curtain behind the seat gave access to a small luggage area. Leather bucket seats faced a telescoping steering wheel. Rubber bags in the seat cushions were inflatable for a custom fit. The dashboard displayed seven gauges strung out across its entire width and including a tachometer.

Both right- and left-hand drive models were offered. The frame components were stamped by Thomsons of Wolverhampton, while

*Americans enjoyed the styling, and choice of engines in the K2 Allards.*

powertrains and axles again came from Ford. Four engines were available: the 221-cid flathead Ford V-8, a 239-cid Mercury flathead V-8, an Ardun modification of the 221-cid Ford (140-bhp) or a bored-out 266.8-cid Mercury engine with aluminum heads. This Allard stuck with a live rear axle, transverse leaf springing and a split-type front axle with two coil springs.

Speed equipment, although created by Allard, was based on U.S. components, which simplified servicing in America. A considerable number of K2s found their way to buyers in the States.

The K2 Roadster was priced at $2,739 without an engine or $3,094 with the standard 221-cid, 85-90-hp engine. This L-head V-8 carried a single downdraft carburetor. Other specifications included a 106-in. wheelbase, 168-in. overall length, 62-in. height and 72-in. width. The wheels were bolt-on stamped-steel discs with 6.25 x 16 tires. The transmission was of the same type used on other Allards linked to a 3.78:1 rear axle.

The independent front suspension employed split I-beam swing axles with coil springs. At the rear were transverse leaf springs. The brakes were 12-in. Lockheed units with Al-Fin drums.

Dick Dance Collection

*The 1953 Allard JR was built for speed and seems to be in motion standing still.*

Bob Harrington

# 1952-1954 J2X

The classic J2X was Allard's competition-type roadster. Perched on a 100-in. wheelbase, the J2X came in either standard or Le Mans form and was available with Chrysler, Lincoln or Mercury engines, as well as the Cadillac V-8 that became its most famous power plant.

The appearance of this improved model was about the same as that of the former J2, although the spare tire was now mounted on the right side of the car, rather than in a compartment at the rear. The suspension was also the same as J2's, but the front radius rods were now of the "leading" (rather than "trailing") style.

The "X" suffix in the model name stood for "extended," which indicated that the frame was lengthened by six inches to accommodate the radius rods, even though the wheelbase remained at 100 in. The engine was moved forward, too.

Most J2X models had a Chrysler or Cadillac ohv V-8 engine, but some carried the standard 239-cid (3.9-liter) flathead Mercury V-8. Many cars had the optional center-lock, knock-off wire wheels.

The standard J2X had a custom-built, aluminum, two-seater body with cycle-style front fenders and aerodynamic windshield. It was largely a racing model, as opposed to the touring-style J2. The more costly LeMans edition had a completely different look, with an aerodynamic body. Following the usual Allard layout, a split front axle was used while the rear axle was a DeDion type and coil springs were featured all around. Optional on both types of bodies were a full-width windshield, wire wheels and a top.

The standard J2X roadster with the 239-cid V-8 was priced at $3,480. It weighed 2,150 lbs. Prices for the 200-lb. heavier LeMans version were a bit higher. Production of both models for 1952-1954 amounted to just 83 cars. Engine specs were the same as for K3s with similar engines, but the horsepower ratings were slightly different: 140 at 4000 rpm for the 239-cid Merc engine, 160-235 for the Chrysler V-8 and 190-250 for the Cadillac V-8.

The 331-cid (5420-cc) Cadillac overhead-valve V-8 had a base 7.1:1 compression ratio, but could be had with compression as high as 8.25:1. Its "standard" brake horsepower rating was 210 at 4500 rpm.

*The dashing 1952 Allard J2X is at home in racing action.*

Torque was 322-330 lbs.-ft. at 2200-2700 rpm. Hydraulic valve lifters were also fitted to this motor.

Chassis specs included a 155-in. overall length, 44.5-in. height, 68-in. width, 6.00 x 16 standard tires and 56-in./52.5-in. front/rear tread measurements. A 3.27:1 rear axle was fitted. Girling hydraulic drum brakes with Al-Fin drums were used to stop the beast.

The complete LeMans type body cost $280. Other options included: Full-size windshield with wipers and hood ($123.20); five fitted wire wheels with hubs and caps ($224); additional spare tire sidemount ($27.72); tonneau cover ($31); oil cooler radiator ($19.27); a set of fitted Dunlop "Road Speed" tires and tubes ($95.35); luggage carrier ($47.60) quick-change rear end ($28); oil temperature gauge ($14); Le Mans type headlamps and stone guards ($36.40); 8000-rpm tachometer ($15.40); Le Mans type racing mirror ($17.92); 40-gallon fuel tank ($56); Cadillac modification and kit ($140), and Chrysler modification and kit ($168).

A J2X in proper tune could hit 120 mph. The 320-hp Chrysler-powered version went 0-to-60 mph in just 7.9 seconds and others reported figures as low as 7.2 seconds.

The factory rating for 0-to-50 mph was 6.8 sec. and the quarter-mile was covered in just 16.7 sec.

Rumors of a merger between Allard and Chrysler were rampant at this time, including suspicion of a fast, compact, lightweight, and low-cost car that would use the Dodge Red Ram V-8 engine and transmission. Although production officially continued through 1959, only about seven additional cars were built after 1954, including a Mark II version of the Allard Palm Beach convertible.

Until his death in 1966, Sydney Allard worked on sunroofs, dragsters and ambulance conversions.

Much later, in the early 1980s, production of a J2X replica, powered by a Chrysler V-8 engine began in Canada.

Legendary actor Clark Gable once owned this 1953 Allard K3 "Palm Beach" roadster.

A Cadillac-powered British hot rod—also known as the 1951 Allard—in racing competition.

# ALVIS

Pete Amsler

# 1948-'58 TB14, TB21 & TC 108G

A lvis made expensive, up-market cars in small numbers from just after World War I until 1967. The firm was founded in 1919, in Coventry, England, by T.G. John, a one-time naval architect. The company that bore his name got its start by building engines and carburetor castings. With the assistance of G.P.H. de Freville, the company soon designed a power plant for Alvis' first motorcar, called the 10/30.

Designations for Alvis models were based on RAC (Royal Auto Club) horsepower ratings. This was calculated with a formula relating to just the bore area. Since British road taxes were based on rated horsepower, small-bore long-stroke engines predominated. On Alvis models, the numbers were often preceded by an "S" for sports or a "T" for touring, followed by another letter indicating the car's sequence in the particular model's production span. This system was not used consistently and sometimes totally different engines had similar dimensions. The Alvis name itself didn't stand for anything, but was thought to have nice ring to it.

Large sports cars appeared early in the company's history. While the regular 10/30 with its 1.5-liter four-cylinder engine managed 60 mph, a Super Sports version was designed to go faster. It featured a ducktail profile that became an Alvis tradition.

In 1923, an Alvis 12/50 with an overhead-valve four-cylinder engine won the Junior Car Club's 200-mile race at Brooklands, hitting 93.29 mph. Two years later, an experimental front-wheel-drive race car fared well in hillclimbs, but a production version launched later in the decade lacked sales appeal even with a 100-mph top speed.

The first Alvis six, the Silver Eagle, arrived in 1928. Like all Alvis motorcars, its body came from a separate coachbuilder. During the late 1920s, front-wheel-drive Alvis racing cars (with independent front suspension) made a strong showing on many European courses.

Late in 1931, the new Speed Twenty arrived, carrying a 2.5-liter six-cylinder engine and capable of 90 mph. Longer and lower than

*The well preserved 1950 Alvis TB 14. Alvis ads appealed to those who expressed individuality.*

prior Alvis models, the Twenty was compared by some to the famed SS1 from Swallow (Jaguar). On the technical side, an all-synchromesh gearbox arrived in 1934, along with independent front suspension, both for the first time on a British car.

More powerful models with up to 170 hp in racing trim and 100-mph top speeds came later. In 1940, a total of 108 automobiles came out of the Alvis factory, but World War II intervened. During the 1941 "Coventry Blitz," Nazi bombers made a direct hit on the Alvis factory, destroying the plant, all machinery, and all company records. Later on, engineers recreated blueprints for every Alvis model based on parts removed from cars that were brought into the factory for servicing.

After the war, Alvis came back with incredible resilience to play a significant part in the postwar automotive industry in Britain. The first product, in 1946, was the TA 14, a car derived from the 12/70. It was offered with a choice of saloon or drophead coupe bodies, but a TB14 sports roadster would also emerge in 1948.

The company's distributor in Belgium was aggressive and many cars that he sold carried sporty bodies. These models formed the basis of the TB 14, a sports version with a body made by AP Metalcraft. Many TB14s were left-hand-drive cars. The 14 was the first Alvis chassis to offer this option to boost sales overseas.

The TB14 sports car, with its cut-down doors, had styling that differed from that of the TA14, although both used the same chassis. The grille did not follow the traditional Alvis format, since the car was aimed at the enthusiast market. The Sports Roadster sold for $2,795 at the factory and about 100 were made through 1949.

The TB14 had a 108-in. wheelbase and 174-in. overall length. Under the bonnet was an 1892-cc (114.4-cid) overhead-valve four-

*This silver Alvis TB 21 can be found today in New Zealand.*

cylinder engine with dual carburetors that generated 68 hp at 4000 rpm. Its top speed was about 84 mph. The engine drove through a four-speed synchromesh transmission to a 4.30:1 rear axle. Top speed was 80 mph, a bit higher than that of the TA14.

A series of 3-liter models streamed from the Alvis factory between 1950 and 1957. The first was the 1950 TA21, which rode a new 111.5-in. wheelbase chassis with independent front suspension and Girling hydraulic brakes. It carried a 2993-cc 90-hp six-cylinder engine with a single Solex carburetor and dual exhaust manifolds. Twin S.U.

carburetors were soon made standard and were retrofitted to many cars. Most models looked old-fashioned with their upright profiles and a vertical-style grille reminiscent of prewar models, but another Sports Tourer was made available–and was probably the last true sports car that Alvis produced.

While custom coachwork was not common in the postwar era, Hermann Graber, of Carrosseries Graber in Switzerland, did several very sporty bodies for the TA 21. In 1951, a factory Sports Touring model arrived. Naturally, it was called the TB 21 and it was offered

*This green Alvis TB 21 represents a proud British carmaking tradition.*

OCW Archives

*The 1948 Alvis was a typical offering of a carmaker that stressed grace and quality.*

through 1953. It used the body that AP Metalcraft made for the TB14 with the normal Alvis radiator. About 20 TB21s were made and it came with both single and dual S.U. carburetors.

By 1956, Alvis realized that it needed a more modern car. Using the chassis from the TC21/100 and a two-door coupe body designed by Carrosseries Graber (of Switzerland) and built by Willowbrook firm, a new TC 108G model was built in limited quantities. With its more modern lines and a 100+ mph top speed, this sporty four-place car attracted interest, but only about 16 left the coachworks.

Expanded production resumed during 1958, as a result of an agreement between Alvis and Mulliner Park Ward. The English body building firm—a Rolls-Royce subsidiary—built a pair of two-door bodies based on the Graber design, a closed saloon and a convertible, which had some sports car attributes. In 1965, after Alvis was taken over by Rover, a mid-engine V-8 sports car was also proposed, but that prospect faded away and auto production finally ceased in late 1967.

After auto production ceased, Alvis focused on military vehicle production with vehicles like the Stalwart, Scorpion, and Stormer. Today, after many periods of restructuring, Alvis Group is the United Kingdom's leading manufacturer of armored fighting vehicles.

# ARNOLT-BRISTOL

Dick Dance Collection

# 1955-1959 Arnolt-Bristol

If Chicago imported-car and accessory dealer S.H. "Wacky" Arnolt hadn't also served as vice president of the Bertone coachbuilding firm in Italy, it's likely that neither the Arnolt-Bristol roadster nor several other low-production hybrid sports cars would have existed.

By 1952, Arnolt had already built a rebodied Arnolt-MG on a T-series chassis. When he attended that year's London Motor Show, Arnolt had another idea in mind. He spoke with executives of the Bristol Aeroplane Company, which had formed a Car Division in 1947, about building a wildly different body for their automobile chassis. After a visit to the plant in Bristol, Wiltshire, he bought a Bristol 404 platform with running gear and shipped it off to Milan, Italy, for a new body. A prototype of the complete car appeared at the London Show in November 1953. Later, the completed vehicles were shipped from Italy to Illinois for sale to eager buyers.

Immodestly billed as "the world's most distinguished sports car," the internationally-created Arnolt-Bristol was designed to blend racing-car speed and agility with flowing Italian design. This resulted in a motorcar certain to tempt the most discriminating connoisseur. "American ingenuity," explained the brochure, "envisioned this dashing sports car. British engineering skill and Italian artistry helped to bring it into being." A 1958 ad for the stripped-down Bolide, in racing trim, promised "a round-the-clock sports car, as much at home at the supermarket or country club as on the race course." Arnolt's multinational operation continued to produce race-winning sports cars for the next eight years.

Both the Bolide and Deluxe models were characterized by a collection of swoopy curves, led by a pinched-look front end. Most Arnolt-Bristols were roadsters, but it's believed that two fastback coupes were made.

The basic Bolide roadster initially cost $3,995, but the price was soon raised to $4,245. It wore a cut-down windshield and had no top

*Arnolt-Bristol promoted their coupe and convertible with post cards in 1954.*

at all. An extra $750 bought the DeLuxe version, adding such niceties as bumpers and side curtains. A pair of coupes was also made and these two rare cars had wind-up windows.

At the front of the Arnolt-Bristol, the headlights were inset into low air openings alongside an oval center grille. Tiny round parking lamps in recessed nacelles were placed farther outward. The round taillights were also recessed. The deep-cushioned, "anatomic" bucket seats had armrests alongside and the interior was upholstered in crushed grain Connolly leather in colors described as "harmonizing." However, the austere Bolide roadsters were upholstered in synthetic leather. An open parcel compartment was contained in the dashboard and featured a full complement of gauges including a tachometer and clock.

With careful tuning, Arnolt got the standard Bristol two-liter six-cylinder BS1 sports-racer engine (related to the prewar BMW 328's six) to deliver extra power. Specifications of the overhead-valve BS1 Mark II in-line six included a 66 x 96-mm (2.598 x 3.779-in.) bore and stroke, a 1971-cc (120.23-cid) displacement, a 9.0:1 compression ratio, 130 bhp at 5500 rpm and 128 lbs.-ft. of torque at 5000 rpm. The four-main-bearings motor had a cast iron block with an aluminum cylinder head, solid valve lifters and triple Solex Type 32 B.I. multi-jet downdraft carburetors.

The car's brakes and transmission came from the 1953 Bristol 403 model. All models were poised on a 96.25-in. wheelbase, with the roadster measuring 167 in. overall. The convertible and coupe were about 4-1/4 in. longer. At 44 in. height, the roadster was just under a foot lower than the other body styles. Front/rear tread measurements were 51.86 and 54 in., respectively. Michelin 5.50 x 16 tires were used. The four-speed manual transmission had gear ratios of 11.4:1 in

**ARNOLT CONVERTIBLE**

*Dick Dance Collection*

*Top down and ready for the open road was the 1954 Arnolt-Bristol convertible.*

first, 7.12:1 in second, 5.04:1 in third, 3.9:1 in fourth and 11.27:1 in reverse. A 3.9:1 rear axle was standard.

The company claimed an extremely high power-to-weight ratio of one horsepower for less than 14.7 pounds for the Competition model. Four roadsters later had a 283-cid, Corvette V-8 installed, instead of Bristol's inline six.

Rack-and-pinion steering was employed in Arnolt-Bristols. Up front was a suspension featuring twin wishbones with transverse leaf springs. The rear suspension combined a live axle with radius arms and longitudinal torsion bars. Hydraulic drum brakes were used at all four corners. A 12-volt Lucas electrical system supplied the juice.

Because Arnolt-Bristols were essentially hand-built cars, the specifications of any two similar cars may vary a bit—or a lot. Early models carried steel disc wheels, but center-locking wire wheels were added later.

A total of 142 Arnolt-Bristols with serial numbers 404X3000 to 404X3141 and engine numbers 205 to 342 were built. The total included five Bolides, 135 Deluxe roadsters and the two Deluxe coupes, which were priced at around $5,995. Naturally, exact prices, weights and specifications tended to vary on a car-by-car basis. Unfortunately, 12 of these great cars were destroyed in a warehouse fire in Chicago.

The Arnolt-Bristol had a top speed in the 107-120 mph range and did 0-to-60 mph in about 10 seconds. The quarter mile took 17.5 seconds at 85 mph. Racing success came early, with one car, driven by "Wacky" himself, winning the 2-litre class at Watkins Glen. Arnolt-Bristols also won their class at the Sebring 12-Hour race in both 1955 and 1956. They continued winning races into the 1960s. At Sebring in 1955, the Arnolt-Bristol team was the only one to finish intact. It earned two trophies for team performance. Arnolt-Bristols also took 1st, 3rd and 6th place in their class in the 1960 Sebring race. By late 1955, Arnolt had seven U.S. dealers, in addition to his main outlet in Chicago. He died in 1960, but the last car was built in 1964, using leftover parts from the bin.

# ASTON-MARTIN

Andrew Morland

# 1948-1950 DB1

**A**lthough the first true Aston-Martins weren't produced until 1919, the name dates back to 1913 and the partnership of Robert Bamford and Lionel Martin, a sportsman and auto enthusiast, in a dealership handling Singer motorcars. The two men wanted to build a sophisticated racing car and the resulting "special" was named for the Aston Clinton hillclimb. It was powered by a 1.4-liter Coventry-Simplex L-head four-cylinder engine and used a Bugatti-designed 1908 Isotta-Fraschini racing chassis. The hillclimb, at a site just outside London, had been run by Singer automobiles. Lionel Martin's surname became the second part of the new car's title.

Similarities to Bugatti persisted when the first production Aston Martins were built in 1919 (although none were sold until two years later). A Coventry-Simplex engine capable of speeds above 70 mph was under the bonnet. Early in the 1920s, Aston broke 10 world records and began making strong showings in nearly every type of competition. An Aston nicknamed "Bunny" took five world records at Brooklands.

In 1924, the firm was taken over by the Charnwood family, who experienced financial woes within a year or so. "Bert" Bertelli and W.S. Renwick tried to save the company, initiating what would turn into a string of ownership changes. In 1927, a new Aston Martin two-seater arrived. It was built at the Feltham facility in Middlesex. Instead of a Coventry-Simplex engine, this one used a new 1.5-liter four with single overhead camshaft. Overall, however, its design was nothing special. By 1930, only 30 of these revised Astons had been built.

As sales began of the low, four-seat International sports model, company ownership wound up in the hands of W. Prudeaux Brune. He didn't last long either, turning over control in 1932 to Sir Arthur Sutherland.

*The beautiful Aston Martin DB 1 drophead coupe was designed by Frank Feeley.*

Adopting a 73-bhp engine in 1934, the Aston Martin was capable of reaching 80 mph. One of the most striking models of that era was the two-seat Ulster racer, noteworthy for its cycle-style fenders, long tail and outside exhaust manifold.

A new 2-liter model with a 1949-cc engine came in 1936 and a Sports Tourer was offered. A "Speed" edition won the 1938 Leinster Trophy. A year later, the new "Atom" model designed by Claude Hill on a multi-tube space frame began to emerge, but the war postponed serious development.

Unlike many British firms that hurriedly resumed production after World War II, Aston Martin couldn't seem to get started. In 1947, industrialist David Brown bought the company, bringing with him some badly-needed funds. Brown, who'd formerly manufactured gears and tractors, also bought Lagonda—a purchase that included access to a new dual-overhead-camshaft six-cylinder engine. Brown's initials were used for the DB series of Aston Martin sports cars.

Aston's first postwar model was the DB1. This car was based on the Atom design by Claude Hill and offered in drophead coupe (convertible) or saloon (coupe) models. Chassis serial numbers ranged from AMC/48/1 to AMC/50/15 and no more than 15 were built. Some sources put production at 13 drophead coupes and one saloon.

The car's name stood for the new company owner's initials and the fact that this was the first model built. It was also called the Two-Litre Sports, by virtue of its two-liter, four-cylinder engine, which produced

90 hp. A box-section, multi-tube space frame chassis was used, with coil springs all around.

The DB1's standard four-seater convertible body was designed by Frank Feeley, who, while with the Lagonda company, had designed not only the 1930 V-12 models, but also the latest 2.6-liter Lagonda sedan. The DB1's three-section grille, which had a large center segment flanked by two small outer grilles at the base (all with vertical bars), was suggestive of the shape that would be used on later Aston Martins. The curvaceous bodyside displayed sweeping, sculptured lines from front to rear. The front fenders swept downward into the door, meeting bulging rear fenders. Stylish rear fender skirts left the knock-off wire wheel hubs exposed.

The DB1's in-line, overhead-valve four-cylinder engine had a cast-iron block. An 82.55 x 92-mm (3.25 x 3.62-in.) bore and stroke gave it a displacement of 1970 cc (120.2 cid). With a 7.25:1 compression ratio and twin S.U. carburetors, it put out 90 hp at 4750 rpm. Top speed was 85-95 mph.

The DB1 was built on a 108-in. wheelbase, measured 176 in. long and 67.5 in. wide and had a front and rear tread width of 54 in. In standard format the 5.75 x 16 tyres were mounted on wire wheels. An independent front suspension featured coil springs with trailing arms and an anti-roll bar. At the rear was a live axle with coil springs, radius rods, and a Panhard rod. Drum brakes were used all around.

DB1 was built in a plant at Feltham, Middlesex, England. It was introduced in September 1948 and discontinued by May 1950. The costly-to-build car was not a profitable product, but David Brown was planning to introduce the new Lagonda twin-cam six-cylinder engine in another model and the DB1 was considered an interim, temporary offering. Its low production makes it one of the rarest and most difficult examples to restore and maintain, especially since the engine was never used in any other model.

A special lightweight, two-passenger DB1 sports racer driven by St. John "Jock" Horsefall and Leslie Johnson won the 1948 Belgian Spa 24-Hour race.

OCW Archive

# 1950-1953 DB2 & DB3

Aston Martin achieved success with the DB2, which bowed in May 1950 and lasted until April 1953. Three prototype fastback coupes entered the 1949 Le Mans 24-Hour race. Two had the DB1 four-cylinder engine and one was powered by the new Lagonda six. Soon afterward, an Aston earned third place at Belgium's Spa 24-Hour race. The DB2 went on sale the next year, with the 2580-cc Lagonda engine and a new multi-tube chassis offering two bodies. Ads in U.S. publications promised: "To Delight the Fast Car Enthusiast."

These first "real" Aston Martins—the first produced fully under David Brown's stewardship. A DB2 was closer to a competition car than a road car. The closed two-door saloon (fastback coupe) arrived first, followed by the drophead coupe (convertible). Styled by Frank Feeley, both body styles carried two passengers and were sleeker and faster than the DB1.

The two body styles were "...luxuriously appointed and

*Even snow cannot take away the sporting allure of this green 1951 Aston Martin DB 2 convertible.*

immaculately finished." They came with wraparound front and rear bumpers and inside was a 17-inch spring-spoke steering wheel, a map reading light, leather-covered panels, upholstered Dunlopillo seats and a folding center armrest. Round instruments on an aircraft-styled panel included a tachometer and clock. Right-hand drive was standard. Windshield washers became standard equipment by 1952.

Initial models wore a three-piece grille with vertical bars, and air intakes outboard of the license plate to help cool the brakes. During 1951, the grille changed to a one-piece design but retained the overall shape. Wider at the bottom, it set a motif that would become an Aston Martin trademark. A small air scoop stood ahead of the windshield. Separate parking lights were installed and the fastback coupe had a small backlight.

Early Aston Martins carried their chassis number on a cowl-mounted plate on the right-hand side. And it was stamped on the upper right top frame tube, just ahead of the firewall. The prefix LML was followed by digits indicating the year the car was released for sale. An engine number suffix, identical to the serial number, was stamped on the timing cover or the right front engine mount. The prefix LB6B for the engine was followed by digits indicating year of release for sale. DB2 chassis serial numbers ranged from LML/50/5 to LML/50/406, but early team and development cars were numbered LMA/49/1 to LMA/49/4. DB2 engine number prefixes varied by horsepower: LB6B for 105-hp, LB6E for 116-hp, LB6V for the 125-hp Vantage engine, VB6B for later Vantage engines, and VB6E for the export version.

The DB2's American debut took place in 1950, at the British Motor Show in New York City. Initial DB2 prices were $6,050 for the 2,662-lb. drophead coupe and $5,950 for the 2,500-lb fastback. Aston Martin built 97 of the open cars and 309 coupes. Ten DB3 racing cars were manufactured as well.

By 1953, the DB2 drophead coupe's price dropped $100, while the closed car increased by the same amount. A total of 409 to 411 DB2 models were built during the full 1950-53 production run, including three Graber drophead coupes. Approximately 62 Aston Martins were sold in the U.S. in 1953 and 24 in 1954.

The DB2's 2.6-liter, twin-cam in-line six-cylinder engine was designed by W.O. Bentley, who had worked as Lagonda's technical director since 1935. It used a cast-iron block and had a 78 x 90-mm bore and stroke giving it a 2580-cc displacement. The valves were actuated directly via thimble tappets, eliminating the need for adjustment. Hemispherical combustion chambers were formed into the cylinder head. The four-main-bearings engine delivered 105-107 hp at 5000 rpm and 125 lbs.-ft. of torque at 3000 rpm. Early in 1951 an optional Vantage engine was introduced.

David Brown industries built the four-speed transmission used in the DB2 and it was available with either a floor- or column-mounted gearshift lever. The lightweight multi-tube steel chassis evolved from the DB1 design and carried a handcrafted aluminum-alloy body with a hinged front clip that tilted forward for engine access. The body was moored on Silentblock mountings. Early models had twin gas caps below locking filler doors in each rear fender, which opened from inside the car. Only one gas filler was used in 1951 and later.

The DB2 chassis had a 99.25-in. wheelbase, while the DB3 racecar's 93-in. wheelbase was shorter. Overall lengths were 162.5 in. and 159.5 in., respectively and it was 53.5-in. high, 65-in. wide and had a 54-in. front and rear tread. Most DB2 production cars had 6.00 x 16 tires mounted on Dunlop center-lock wire wheels. A 3.77:1 ratio rear axle was standard. Worm-and-roller steering was fitted. The independent front suspension featured coil springs, trailing links and an anti-roll bar. The independent rear suspension combined a live axle with coil springs, radius rods, and a Panhard rod. Girling hydraulic drum brakes were fitted.

David Brown's enthusiasm for speed made the Aston Martin DB2 a knockout performer. The new car was capable of 110-117 mph, while the Vantage engine upped top speed to 122-125 mph. It took 12.4 seconds to reach 0-to-60 mph with the base six and 10.8 with the Vantage option. Quarter-mile time for the stock DB2 was 18.5 seconds. Aston Martin literature at the 1952 Paris Salon called the DB2 "the race-bred luxury sports car," adding that "speed is built into its every line; exhilaration is there for the most enthusiastic sports driver." A later American ad described the car as: "Like a piece of precious sculpture."

Aston's involvement in motor racing explained the release of the 125-hp Vantage engine. A lightweight version of the DB2 fared well at Le Mans and won its class at the Italian Mille Miglia race. The DB3 racer on a tubular chassis with 140-hp engine and a DeDion rear end came in 1951. Later versions carried a larger 2922-cc twin-cam engine that produced 162 hp.

Aston Martin won its class at the 1951 LeMans and finished third, fifth, seventh and tenth overall. Astons also won their class at the 1951 and 1952 Mille Miglia, 1951 International Alpine Trial and 1951/52 Silverstone International Production Car Race. The DB3S race car, built in small numbers for "road" use starting in 1953, had a shapelier body on a short wheelbase and could hit 150 mph. It was victorious in eight 1953 racing events it entered.

Tom McCahill, the famed automotive writer at *Mechanix Illustrated*, praised the Aston's comfort. Veteran road-racer Phil Hill, writing in *Motor Trend*, called the DB2's steering "fantastic . . . the best cornering car I've had. I have never driven a car that tracks as straight and as comfortably as the Aston." Hill claimed: "...furnishings are Rolls-Royce-like."

OCW Archive

# 1953-1957 DB2-4 & DB3S

The Aston Martin factory in Feltham, Middlesex, produced the DB2 model all the way through April of 1953 and built the last DB3 race car about a month later. In October 1953, the DB2 was superseded by the DB2-4, which stayed in production until October 1955. The DB2-4 (or DB2/4) looked similar to its predecessor, but offered 2+2 seating and a hatchback rear end. It came standard with the high-compression Vantage engine, which cranked out 125 hp and helped maintain the performance reputation of the new Aston Martin, even though it was more than 200 lbs. heavier.

Inside the DB2-4, semi-bucket front seats folded forward and inward, giving access to the rear. The DB2-4 marginally qualified as a 2+2, but squeezing people in the back seats required a good shoe horn. The rear compartment was intended only for "occasional" use, although Aston Martin promoted the DB2-4 as a car "for speed and comfort on long distance touring."

Its plusher cockpit included two-speed windshield wipers, trafficators (turn signals) and an octane selector. A radio was optional. Once again, the David Brown four-speed manual gearbox was installed. A drophead coupe (convertible) and sports saloon (coupe) were offered but the latter body style had a one-piece windshield, instead of the divided glass used earlier.

The sloping rear end now held an outward-hinging panel that incorporated the rear window. It lifted up to allow outside access to the storage compartment. It was a top-hinged hatchback, something new for a sports car.

Aston Martin's coupe bodies were now built by H.J. Mulliner and Sons at Birmingham, a company best known for creating Rolls-Royce coachwork.

A small bulge in the coupe's rear roof line allowed some headroom for the back-seat passengers. A smaller gas tank rode above the spare tire and the luggage area grew considerably larger. The rear seat back folded forward to form a rubber-ribbed flat floor.

*The 1955 Aston Martin DB 2/4 was advertised as a blend of speed and comfort.*

The Mk II DB2-4 was introduced in October 1955 and lasted though August 1957. Its larger-displacement engine produced 140 hp. Other DB2-4 Mk II features included a hood air scoop and side vents for interior ventilation, a fly-off hand brake (next to the gearshift lever) and a gas cap inside the trunk. Flashing turn signals had replaced the early semaphore-style trafficators.

Also new for 1955 was a Tickford-built notchback coupe. The English body builder was located at Newport Pagnell and also produced the DB2-4 convertible. This notchback coupe had a conventional hood and front fenders, rather than Aston Martin's tilt-forward nose. By 1955, chrome trim was added to the fluted rubber on door sills. The Mk II version had a chrome strip.

Another version of the DB3 racing model was produced from May 1953 through December 1956. This car included a high-output version of the 2922-cc twin-cam six-cylinder engine. Using triple carburetors, this power plant delivered either 180 or 210 bhp. The DB3's wheelbase was only 87 inches, a foot shorter than the DB2-4. The DB3S was more streamlined than the DB3, with upward-bulging fenders front and rear. A total of 19 sports-racing versions of this car were built.

DB2-4 chassis numbers started at LML/501 and ran to LML/1065, while the numbers AM300/1100 to AM300/1299 were found on Mark II versions. Different prefixes were used to denote the different engines: TDB2-4 for the base six, VB6E for the 2.6-liter Vantage six and VB6J for the 2.9-liter DB3S race-type cars. In 1953, the 2,635-lb. DB2-4 fastback sold for $5,950 Port of Entry in the United States, while the slightly heavier drophead coupe was $6,295. The Mk II option added $45 and a "road" version of DB3S racer sold for 3,684 pounds in Great Britain. The DB3S tipped the scale at only 2,052 lbs. Production included 566 DB2-4 drophead coupes, 139 Mk

II 2+2s, 24 Mk II dropheads, 34 Mk II notchback coupes and 30 DB3S competition coupes (11 of which were for racing). Mk II production also included two Spider models with bodies built by Touring.

Base engine in the DB2-4 was the in-line, dual-overhead-camshaft six-cylinder Vantage mill with 78 x 90-mm bore and stroke and 2580-cc displacement. It had an 8.16:1 compression ratio, solid valve lifters and twin variable-jet S.U. carburetors helped it produce 125 hp at 5000 rpm and 144 lbs.-ft. of torque at 2400 rpm.

The Mk II version was bored to 83 mm with the same stroke, upping horsepower to 140 at 5000 rpm and torque to 178 lbs.-ft. at 3,000 rpm. A 165-bhp version of the Mk II engine, with 8.6:1 compression also became optionally available. Standard in DB3S competition coupes was the dual-overhead-cam 2922-cc (83 x 90-mm bore and stroke six with an 8.6:1 compression ratio and 180 hp at 5500 rpm. It carried three Weber carburetors or three Solex carburetors with race-tuned, 210-220 hp versions available.

Dimensions for the DB2-4 included a 99-in. wheelbase, a 169.5-in. overall length, a height of 53.5 in., a width of 65 in., and a 54-in. front and rear tread width. The DB3S racecar was 153.8 in. long, 41 in. high, and 58.8 in. wide. It was available with different tread widths.

DB2-4 standard equipment included 6.00 x 16 tires mounted on Dunlop center-locking quick-change wire wheels. The DB2-4's four-speed manual gearbox had ratios of 10.9:1 in first and reverse, 7.38:1 in second, 4.96:1 in third, and 3.73:1 in fourth. It was linked to a 3.73:1 rear axle and available conversion gearsets gave 4.1:1 and 3.5:1 axle ratios. Steering, suspension, and brakes were the same as in the past.

Top speed was 111 mph for the DB2-4, 120 mph for the Mk II, and 135-150 mph for the DB3S, depending on state of tune. Accelerating from 0-to-60 mph took 12.6 seconds in the DB2-4, 11.1 seconds in the Mk II, and just 6.6 seconds in the race car. The DB3S won 15 international racing victories, including the Sports Car World Championship.

Bob Harrington

# 1957-'59 DBMk III/Mk IIIB

**A**ston Martin's DB2-4 designation was dropped, but the Mk II version of the company's first 2+2 coupe was carried over in early 1957 before the new DB Mk III arrived. The "A" version of this new model bowed in March 1957. Later the same year, the "B" type—with Girling front disc brakes as standard equipment—superseded the A type.

A man named John Wyer had been appointed Aston Martin's general manager in 1957 and he began to place added emphasis on export sales. Early models of the DB Mk IIIA were intended strictly for the export market—primarily the United States. The DB Mk IIIB remained in production and continued to be offered by numerous importers in this country until July 1959. Fourteen DBR racing models were also built between 1956 and 1960.

U.S. distributors for the marque included J.S. Inskip in New York City; S.H. "Wacky" Arnolt of Chicago, Illinois; Ship and Shore Motors in West Palm Beach, Florida; Kjell Qvale's British Motor Car Company

*The 1959 Aston Martin DB Mk III graces any gathering of fine cars.*

of San Francisco, California; and the Peter Satori Company of Pasadena, California. In Canada, Pimbley Brothers and Bud and Dyer handled the marque.

Both a fixed-head coupe and drophead coupe were offered in the Aston-Martin DB Mk III lineup, but the drophead's convertible top (or "hood" in English terminology) had a more upright look than before. A new radiator grille displayed a tightly-meshed crosshatch pattern, but carried on the traditional overall shape. Tiny round parking lights stood below the headlights.

Taillights that had first been used in the Humber Hawk were mounted on slightly restyled Aston Martin fenders. They now ran the full depth of the back fenders. Inside, a new instrument panel, designed by Frank Feeley, put all of the gauges in a hooded panel directly in front of the driver, instead of toward the center of the dashboard as before.

The chassis number range for both the 1957 DB Mk IIIA and DB Mk IIIB was AM300/3A/1300 to AM300/3/1850. For 1958-1959 versions, the numbers started with AM300/3/140L. The prefix DBA was used for the 162-hp engine, DBB for the 180-hp engine, DBD for the 195-hp engine and DBC for the rare 214-hp engine. The 1957 fastback listed for $6,995 and weighed 2,850 lbs. In 1958-1959, the price of this model increased to $7,550. The drophead coupe stickered for about $8,190.

A total of 550 DB Mk IIIs were produced from 1957 to 1959, plus one competition model with a 214-hp engine. Of these, 140 units were sold in the United States, a number that represented a higher percentage of total sales than in the past. As part of expanding its U.S. operations, the British automaker established a facility in San Leandro, California, near San Francisco.

A primary feature of the DB Mk III was its more powerful 2922-cc six-cylinder engine that made 162 hp at 5500 rpm and 180 lbs.-ft. of torque at 4000 rpm. With optional dual exhausts, output rose to 178 hp in 1957 models and 180 hp in 1958-1959 models.

Known as the DBA (1957) or DBB (1958-1959) engine, this solid-lifter, four-main-bearings powerplant had a stiffer block, a stronger crankshaft and larger valves than the previous engine. Two variable-jet S.U. carburetors and a 12-volt electrical system were fitted as standard equipment.

The DB Mk IIIB could also be had in two triple-carburetor versions (with Weber or S.U. carburetors) producing 195 hp and 202 hp. The standard DB Mk III recorded a top speed of 119-120 mph. Acceleration from 0-to-60 mph required 9.3 seconds, while the quarter mile took 17.4 seconds.

Three transmissions were available: the standard four-speed manual gearbox, optional Laycock de Normanville overdrive unit (which was quite popular) or a Borg-Warner three-speed automatic. A variety of competition options were available including a close-ratio gearbox, an engine oil cooler, a competition clutch and suspension and an oversized (33.6-gal.) fuel tank.

At 99 in., the DB III's wheelbase was unchanged from that of the DB2-4, but overall length grew two inches to 171.5 in. The newer car's height increased to 54 in., although body width remained at 65 in. and tread was also unchanged at 54 in. front and rear. Standard again were 6.00 x 16 tires on wire wheels. A 3.77:1 ratio rear axle was standard. Steering and suspension specs were basically untouched, but Girling front disc brakes were optional at first and later were standard on the DB Mk IIIB.

In 1958, Prince Philip of Great Britain gave Aston Martin Lagonda his Royal Warrant of Appointment. That bestowed the right to display his coat of arms on the cars and for company letterheads to read "Motorcar Manufacturers by Appointment to His Royal Highness."

Andrew Morland

# 1960-1963 DB4GT/Zagato

"In this year of triumphant Aston Martin achievement," said Aston Martin's October 1959 Paris show brochure, "the David Brown Aston Martin DB4GT. Embodying the lessons of 10 years of endeavor on the most arduous race circuits of the world, this new Gran Touring model is designed to provide for the most critical of high-performance car owners—a culminating experience of really fast motoring."

Evolved from a short-chassis DB4 driven by Stirling Moss in 1959, the DB4GT came out late in 1959, as a 1960 model. It was described by *Sports Car Graphic* as a "race car in luxury clothing." Truly a semi-racing model produced in limited quantites for go-fast enthusiasts, the new car was smaller and lighter than a regular DB4. Its wheelbase was 93 in. and its overall length was 171.75 in., although height, width and tread width were the same as for regular DB4s. The doors were shorter, the

*The lines of the Aston Martin DB 4 Zagato are unforgettable.*

cockpit was smaller and it came with no back seat.

Built of 18-gauge magnesium alloy panels, the DB4GT's body carried on the graceful lines of the regular DB4, but featured a more rounded front end with recessed headlights hidden behind aerodynamic, see-through covers that blended into the fenders. Only 75 production versions of the DBGT were built between 1960 and 1963, but a few more cars were made especially for racing teams.

Under the hood was a new version of the 3.7-liter twin-overhead-cam six with a high-lift camshaft, larger valves and a 9.0:1 compression ratio. This engine was fed gas by three dual-choke Weber 45DCOE4 carburetors. It produced 302 hp at 6000 rpm and 240 lbs.-ft. of torque at 5000 rpm. Dual ignition was standard, using twin distributors and two spark plugs per cylinder. A "Powr-Lok" limited-slip differential was included, with a choice of five axle ratios.

Transmission gear ratios for the DB4GT were 2.49:1 in first, 1.74:1 in second; 1.25:1 in third, 1.0:1 in fourth, and 2.43:1 in reverse. A choice of five rear axle ratios was provided: 2.93:1, 3.31:1, 3.54:1, 3.77:1, or 4.09:1. Steering, chassis and body construction were overall similar to regular DB4 features, but a larger 36-gal. fuel tank with a quick-action filler cap was added.

Standard DB4GT equipment included a wood-rimmed steering wheel on a column that was adjustable for rake and length, Girling four-wheel disc brakes and 6.00 x 16 Avon Turbospeed tires on Borrani 5K x 16 center-lock wire wheels with light alloy rims.

The fully-adjustable seats had light alloy tubular frames contoured to the driver and passenger. A DB4GT could accelerate from a standstill to 100 mph and brake back down to zero in 20 seconds. Top speed was

142 mph, 0-to-60 mph took 6.4 seconds and quarter-mile acceleration was in the 14.5-second range. The GT coupe carried a $12,500 price tag and weighed only 2,706 lbs.

The DB4 Zagato was a special version of the fastback coupe built by the Zagato company in Italy. It was even lighter in weight than the DB4GT. This was intended to make it more competitive in racing. Only about 19 were built starting late in 1960. Although the body was built and installed in Italy, final assembly and painting took place at Newport Pagnell in England. Bumpers were available only on special request.

The Zagato engine was the same twin-cam in-line six found in other DB4s, except with a 9.7:1 compression ratio that boosted brake horsepower to 314 at 6000 rpm and torque to 278 lbs.-ft. at 5000 rpm.

This car sold for $13,500 in 1960 and $14,250 in 1963. Its all-out top speed was 153 mph; 0-to-60 mph took 6.4 seconds and quarter-mile acceleration took 14.5 seconds.

Tom Glatch

# 1963-1965 DB5 & Volante

The Aston Martin DB5 was introduced in mid-1963 and remained in production until September 1965. It was a refined and improved version of the DB4 and became one of the best-known Aston Martin models after actor Sean Connery drove one in his role as James Bond in the motion picture "Goldfinger.".Also making the marque better known here was the fact that Aston Martin-Lagonda opened up new offices in King of Prussia, Pennsylvania, in May 1964.

Both the fixed-head and open bodies were done by Turin in Italy, using the Superleggera design principle introduced with the DB4. Headlamps on the hardtop coupe went behind sloping covers, while the convertible's headlamps were exposed. A detachable steel hardtop was optional for the convertible.

Again the familiar in-line, twin-cam six grew, this time getting a 4-mm wider piston bore and 3995-cc displacement. An even more powerful Vantage engine option came along by the fall of 1964. The seven-main-bearings Aston Martin engine continued to use an aluminum alloy block and cylinder head. With an 8.9:1 compression ratio and triple S.U. carbs 282 hp was delivered at 5500 rpm.

Torque was advertised as 288 lbs.-ft. at 3850 rpm. The optional Vantage engine, with three twin-choke Weber 45DCOE9 carburetors, developed 314 hp at 5750 rpm. This engine became standard equipment in Volante models.

At first, DB5 buyers had a choice of four different transmissions,

*Many recognize the Aston Martin DB 5 thanks to the James Bond movie "Goldfinger."*

the standard David Brown four-speed manual, the same gearbox with overdrive, a ZF five-speed manual or an automatic. By mid-1964, the four-speed and overdrive were dropped and the five-speed became standard. Its fifth gear was an overdrive ratio. Overall gear ratios: were 10.18:1 in first, 6.57:1 in second, 4.59:1 in third, 3.73:1 in fourth, 3.11:1 in fifth, and 12.35:1 in reverse. Fifth gear was actually a 0.83:1 overdrive.

Production of the DB5 with 3995-cc six-cylinder engine continued into 1965, when the DB5 convertible got quarter bumpers to replace the former full-width design. An extra oil-cooler air intake was added below the license plate and convertibles took on the "Volante" name (which would remain into the 1980s). In 1965, a dozen DB5s were even converted to shooting brakes (station wagons) by the Harold Radford firm of London.

Early Port of Entry prices in the United States were $12,775 for the 3,233-lb. coupe and $13,650 for the convertible. In 1965, the coupe price went to $12,850 and the ragtop to $13,750. A total of 1,021 DB5s were made between 1963 and 1965 and included 886 coupes, 123 convertibles, and the 12 Shooting Brakes.

The DB5 shared the DB4's 98-in. wheelbase and was 180 in. long overall. It was also 53 in. high and 66 in. wide. The front tread was 54 in. and the rear tread was a ½-in. narrower. The 6.70 x 15 tires rode on center-lock wire wheels with chrome spokes.

A 3.31:1 rear axle was standard, but other ratios were available. Steering, suspension and brake specifications were similar to the Aston-Martin DB4 models

A 22.8-gal. fuel tank was fitted.the DB5 had a top speed of 141 mph. It moved from 0-to-60 mph in 8.1 seconds and did a quarter mile in 16.0 seconds.

# 1965-1970 DB6 & Volante

The Aston Martin DB6 was introduced in late 1965 and remained in production until July 1969, when the Mk II version debuted. The Mk II remained in production until November 1970. Larger and plusher than its predecessor, the new Aston DB6 also had a somewhat less of a sporty image. It was a longer car with a longer wheelbase, but its chassis was otherwise the same as that of the DB5. The stretch job on the chassis provided more space in the rear passenger compartment.

DB6 body construction combined aluminum body panels with an ordinary steel floor and inner panels. The frontal appearance was similar to that of the DB5, with a low-mounted air scoop for oil cooling. From the cowl rearward, a considerable change in design took place. The DB6's roof line was taller and its wraparound windshield was taller and more upright.

Although the fixed-head coupe was again of a fastback design, the rear quarter windows swept upward, rather than downward. The old tapered tail was replaced by a squared-off Kamm-style back end. The doors held the quarter windows, and quarter bumpers went on each corner. Standard DB6 fittings included a radio, electric windows, air conditioning, adjustable shock absorbers, a heated rear window, and a power antenna.

A Volante drophead coupe (convertible) arrived about a year after the DB6 fixed-head coupe. Rumor had it that the open cars were constructed on leftover DB5 chassis. They had a new power top and the Vantage engine and Borg-Warner automatic transmission were no-cost options. Power steering became optional for the first time on an Aston.

No change in engine design was done and the DB6 continued to utilize the 3995-cc, 282-hp all-aluminum dual-overhead-camshaft in-line six with 8.9:1 compression and triple S.U.s. The 325-hp Volante engine with three twin-choke Weber 45DCOE9 carburetors was fitted in drophead coupes and optional in fixed-head coupes. Later coupes came with an optional fuel-injected engine and featured flared rear wheel openings.

Riding a 101.75-in. wheelbase, the DB6 stretched 182 in. overall and stood 54.5 in. tall and 66 in. wide. The chassis and suspension were also of the same design used under DB5s, but the new Salisbury-type 3.73:1 rear axle was mounted in a different position. A "Powr-Lok" limited-slip differential was now standard, as were chrome wire wheels. Transmission coices included the five-speed manual gearbox or the Borg-Warner automatic.

Initially, the 3,250-lb. fixed-head coupe sold for $15,400 in the United States. The Volante drophead coupe cost the same. A half-dozen Shooting Brakes were made by Radford and sold for an undetermined price. Production of the other body styles between 1966 and November 1970 was reported as 1,321 coupes and 140 convertibles.

Jonathan Stein's authoritative book *British Sports Cars in America 1946-1981* says 1,750 DB6s were made in all. Just a trickle of cars made it to the United States in the later 1960s. Eighteen cars were sold here in 1967 and 20 in 1968. Total imports are put at 166 vehicles for the run.

Though less of a true sports car, the DB6 was no slouch when it came to going fast. Top speed with the Volante engine was in the 140-148 mph bracket and European versions were capable of 150 mph with the base engine and 161 mph in Volante format. Zero-to-60 mph with the Vantage engine took 6.5-6.7 seconds and the quarter-mile took just 14.5-15.4 seconds at 94 mph.

By 1966, Aston Martin's relationship with the coachbuilder had faded away after the Italian firm's financial collapse. In addition, demand for costly automobiles was declining in Great Britain. Car and Driver called the DB6 "one of the most attention grabbing cars on the road," and said that "everything on the car has been beautifully made," but faulted its noisy engine, handling and hard steering.

Heritage Classics

# 1967-1973 DBS & Vantage

T he Aston Martin DBS—introduced in October 1967 and remaining in production until 1973—was the last of the company's six-cylinder cars. To mark the appearance of this all-new model, Aston Martin dropped its practice of adding a number to the "DB" prefix and called it the DBS. Much of its running gear and chassis were shared with the previous DB6.

Styling of the DBS was handled by William Towns, who created outstanding designs for both a fixed-head coupe and a new Lagonda sedan. The Lagonda design proposal was not accepted, but Towns' fastback coupe became the Aston Martin DBS.

Though it was similar in basic appearance to the DB6, the new DBS displayed a more angular look. Early DBS models had quad round headlamps flanking a full-width eggcrate grille that had mainly horizontal strips, with vertical divider strips. On the instrument panel, seven round dials sat in a shrouded oval panel, ahead of the driver. A drop-head coupe (convertible) was not offered in the DBS series.

Space was available under the DBS hood for a V-8 engine, but that would not arrive until 1969. Initially, the engine bay held the same power plants available for the DB6: either the base 282-hp twin-cam six with twin S.U.s or the 325-hp Vantage six with triple Webers. AE-Brico fuel injection was on the options list, but because of its reputation for unreliable performance, the system had few takers.

At 3,760 lbs., the DBS weighed considerably more than its predecessor, but since it got no power boost to compensate, its performance dwindled quite a bit. Top speed was 140 mph. With the optional Vantage engine it did 0-to-60 mph in 8.5 sec. The quarter-mile took 16.3 sec.

Like the DB6, the DBS grew in wheelbase. It had a 102.75-in. stance. However, at 180.5 in., it was actually a bit shorter in overall length. It was lower (54.5 in.) and wider (72 in.) than the DB6 and also had wider (59-in.) front and rear treads.

Larger 8.10 x 15 tires were mounted on the DBS's center-locking wire wheels.

Up front, the new car featured the same front suspension used under the DB6, but the rear got a new De Dion axle arrangement with

*Dual headlights give a distinct look to this green 1969 Aston Martin DBS V8.*

Watt linkage, trailing arms and coil springs. Four-wheel disc brakes were fitted.

In the United States, the DBS came with a $16,850 price tag, which may partly explain why only 787 were made between 1967 and 1973. The price climbed to $22,000 for later cars equipped with the new V-8 engine.

DBS coupes could be ordered with this V-8 — a light-alloy, 5.3-litre dohc V-8 — as well as the traditional six starting in 1969. The Aston Martin-built V-8 actually had made its debut on the racetrack in 1967. It was virtually a hand-built engine. Aston Martin never released a horsepower rating for the early V-8, stating simply that its power output was "sufficient." Various sources estimated that it had at least 350 hp. Later versions topped 400 hp.

Power steering became standard equipment in 1969. Buyers who didn't want the ZF five-speed manual gearbox got a Chrysler-built three-speed TorqueFlite rather than the old Borg-Warner automatic transmission. Standard equipment included air conditioning, power brakes, power steering, a wood-rimmed dished-spoke steering wheel, and a radio.

Larger GR70VR15 Pirelli Cinturato radial tires on ventilated cast alloy wheels were used. Price for the six-cylinder model rose to $17,900. The Vantage and V-8 models were even more. Models with the V-8 were not commonly available in the United States until 1971 or 1972.

The new V-8 engine had a 90-degree, dual-overhead-camshaft design incorporating a light alloy block and aluminum heads. With 100 x 85-mm bore and stroke measurements, it displaced 5,340 cc. Other specifications included a 9.0:1 compression ratio, five main bearings and Bosch mechanical fuel injection. When the V-8 was attached to the ZF five-speed manual gearbox, the ratios were 2.90:1 in first, 1.78:1 in second,

1.22:1 in third, 1.00:1 in fourth, and 0.845:1 in fifth. The standard final drive ratio for V-8s was 3.54:1 with the ZF or 3.31:1 with TorqueFlite automatic transmission.

The DBS V-8 had a top speed of about 160 mph. It could do the standing-start quarter mile in 14.3 seconds. Early factory claims for the European DBS V-8 included a top speed of 170 mph, and 0-to-60 mph in 5.7 seconds. Production of the six-cylinder DBS halted in July 1973, with subsequent Astons carrying a V-8 engine.

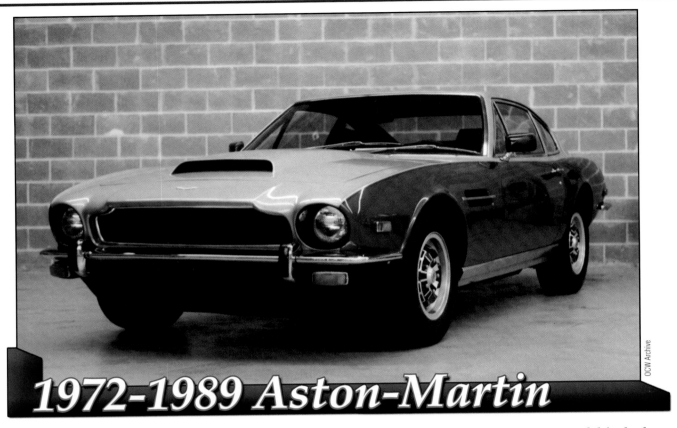

OCW Archive

# 1972-1989 Aston-Martin

By 1972, David Brown sold his interest in Aston Martin to a firm called Company Developments, Ltd. With the departure of Brown, the "DB" prefix was dropped. The six-cylinder DBS was restyled and renamed the Aston Martin Vantage. This car had single headlamps and a narrower grille with a tight crosshatch pattern of black mesh. The 325-hp engine became standard and fuel injection was abandoned.

The DBS V-8 was renamed the Aston Martin V-8. At the same time, it got the sixes' new single-headlamp nose (replacing the former quad setup) and the narrower black-mesh grille. In addition, a hood bulge replaced the former scoop. In 1973, the V-8 was fitted with a quartet of Weber carburetors. Later yet, an improved version of Bosch's fuel-injection system would replace the carburetors.

Production of the DBS twin-cam six ceased in mid-1973, leaving only the V-8 to carry on after that. For about six months during 1974-1975, no Astons at all were built, as the company scampered to find funds and people needed to keep the company going. By 1976, when Aston Martin's new Lagonda sedan entered production, the base price for the V-8 coupe rose to $33,950.

Horsepower of the V-8 coupe got a boost in 1977, going up by a claimed 15 percent. In the same year, a Vantage V-8 joined the lineup, wearing a deep front air dam (with cooling slots), a blanked-out grille, large Cibie driving lamps ahead of the grille, a rear lip spoiler and big Pirelli P7 tires.

The initial rating of the Vantage engine was an estimated 400 hp. It had revised cam profiles and larger intake valves and carburetors. Vantage models were built only to order and only with manual gearboxes. In June 1978, a Volante convertible was added, but not until two years later could it be ordered with the Vantage engine option.

Standard Aston Martin V-8 equipment included a front passenger

*The Aston Martin V-8 series was graceful in both convertible and coupe form.*

footrest, reclining front bucket seats, a contoured rear seat with folding armrest, Sundym glass, power windows, and an electrically-heated rear window. Also included in late-1970s models was Coolaire air conditioning and a Blaupunkt electronically-controlled stereo radio with cassette player. In 1976, the massive four-door Lagonda saloon joined the Aston Martin coupe, but it was not a sports car.

Prices kept climbing and by 1979 rose to 52,250 for the fastback coupe, $55,700 for the Vantage coupe, and $71,835 for the Volante convertible. A total of 262 Aston Martins (all models except the Lagonda) were built in 1977, 280 in 1978, 266 in 1979, and 203 in 1980. Approximately 39 Volante convertibles were sold in the United States in 1980.

The 325-hp V-8 standard engine and the 400-hp Vantage option had no major changes, but there were minor variations in other specifications over the years related to bumper changes, tire revisions and other factors. By 1980, overall length was up to 183.8 in. Vehicle heights also increased very slightly to 52.5 in. for the V-8 and 54 in. for the Volante. Overall width and tread widths were unchanged. The Aston Martin V-8's cast alloy wheels carried GR70 x 15 or 235/70VR15 radial tires and Vantage models had 255/60VR15 radials.

Production of Aston Martin coupes and convertibles continued through the 1980s without major alterations. Official specifications for horsepower and torque from the two versions of the 5340-cc V-8 engine were not released at this time, but U.S. versions were considerably de-tuned. By 1982, prices for the Vantage coupe and Volante convertible were into the six-figure range ($101,000 and $115,000, respectively), while the V-8 coupe sold for a "modest" $96,000. A total of 149 Aston Martins were produced in 1981, 138 in 1982, 145 in 1983, 170 in 1984, and 180 in 1985. The two coupes were about $2,000 less with automatic transmission.

Top speed of the carbureted V-8 model was 145 mph in 1980 and the Vantage V-8 raised this to 170 mph. Zero-to-60 took 6.2 seconds with the base engine and .8 seconds less with the Vantage power plant. By this time, the handful of Aston Martins sold in the United States each year were distributed from New Rochelle, New York. A man named Victor Gauntlett took control of the Aston Martin company in 1984.

Production of Aston Martin's coupe and convertible continued into 1988 without major alterations and the Volante convertible remained into the 1989 model year. By this time, the convertible came in Volante ($183,000) and Vantage Volante ($197,000) models and the latter had a particularly aggressive look with its front air dam, rear spoiler, side skirts, flared wheel arches, and large round auxiliary lights mounted within the front panel's bright surround molding. Its interior displayed burr walnut, hand-stitched Connolly leather and Wilton carpeting.

Late in the 1980s, the Zagato firm of Italy was scheduled to build 50 coupes and 25 convertibles, using special bodies with aero-shaped undertrays. With a modified and more potent Vantage engine, the two-seat Zagato could accelerate from 0-to-60 mph in 4.7 seconds. Aston Martin announced that it could hit 185 mph. Styling features of the alloy/reinforced-polyester body included a large hood bulge and large rectangular quad headlamps. A total of 65 Aston Martins (all models) were sold in the U.S. in 1988.

By 1989, the 5340-cc twin-cam V-8 was running a 8.0:1/8.3:1 compression ratio and four dual-choke Webbers or fuel-injection. European editions were rated for 309 hp at 5500 rpm. With the Vantage option, power increased to 403 at 6200 rpm or an estimated 432 hp in the 50 Zagato coupes which could do 185 mph flat out.

Ford Motor Company bought a three-quarter interest in the Aston Martin company in September 1987, three years after it had been taken over by Victor Gauntlett, who continued as chairman. A Volante served James Bond well in the movie, "The Living Daylights," just as earlier Aston Martins had been driven by Sean Connery as he portrayed the famous Ian Fleming character.

Andrew Morland

# 1989-1994 Virage

**D**isplaying a distinctive wedge shape, the Aston Martin Virage featured a hand-formed aluminum body on a box-section steel frame. Its body design was the work of Ken Greenley and John Heffernan and featured uniquely angular styling. Although curved in the profile view only, it conveyed a more rounded look than the Aston Martin V-8.

The car had a front-engine, rear-drive layout. It included a low cockpit, aero-style flush glass, the absence of chrome, and the use of only a few insignias. New, flush-style rectangular headlights gave the car a wider look. The exhaust pipes fit into chassis niches. An underbody tray, like that used on the Vantage Zagato, added to the Virage's clean, unified appearance. There were no loose pieces hanging below the car.

The introduction of the Virage took place in October 1988 at the Birmingham (England) International Motor Show. Co-designer Heffernan said that it was created as the "evolutionary successor" to the DB series and the more recent V-8. Aston Martin had 50 orders for the Virage before it was even introduced in England, with sizable deposits plunked down. It finally went on sale there in 1989, but did not reach the United States until later.

*The V-8 powered Aston Martin Virage was introduced in the 1980s.*

In January 1990, the Virage bowed stateside at the North American International Auto Show in Detroit, Michigan. It arrived there amid great fanfare, trumpets, and smoke. Company chairman Victor Gauntlett pointed out that it had not been de-tuned for sale in the States and stated that Americans now would "know how a real Aston Martin feels." Only a few Americans knew the feeling, of course, since production was low and sales were miniscule.

Under the new car's hood was an unusually handsome engine. It had plates covering the spark plug valleys, detailed cam covers for each cylinder head and a brass plate on the engine to identify its assembler.

Engine development work at Callaway Engineering, in Old Lyme, Connecticut, was directed by Tim Good. Callaway was best known for its Twin-Turbo Corvettes and had started on the Virage project in 1987. Experiments there included conversion of an existing Lagonda V-8 and the manufacture of prototype parts. Final development took place at the Aston facility in England. The original aluminum engine block was retained, but it was fitted with all-new 16-valve heads.

The 5340-cc dual-overhead-camshaft, 32-valve V-8 had a 100 x 85-mm bore and stroke, a 9.5:1 compression ratio and a Weber-Marelli fuel-injection system. It developed 330 hp at 6000 rpm and 350 lbs.-ft. of torque at 4000 rpm. Running on no-lead gasoline with a catalytic converter, the Virage was described as "one of the most powerful environmentally-friendly cars in the world." Unlike earlier Astons, it could be sold in the same form worldwide, without re-tuning for specific countries. Performance figures for the automatic transmission model put top speed at 155 mph and 0-to-60 mph acceleration at six seconds flat.

The Virage chassis was also outstanding. It was designed in concert with the Cranfield Institute of Technology Finite Element Analysis Department, a leader in British aerospace technology. Considerable aluminum was used in its construction to save weight, especially in the suspension and brake systems.

The front suspension incorporated upper and lower control arms, coil springs, an anti-roll bar, and Bilstein gas shock absorbers. At the rear was a De Dion axle with Watt linkage, trailing arms, coil springs, and Bilstein gas shock absorbers. Disc brakes (vented in front and solid in the rear) were used at all four corners.

Poised on a 102.8-in. wheelbase, the Virage ran 186.5 in. in overall length, stood a mere 52.0 in. high and measured 73 in. wide. It had a 59.4-in. front tread and a 59.9-in. rear tread. The car's 255/60VR16 Avon Turbospeed radial tires were mounted on 8J x 16 aluminum alloy wheels.

Virage interior highlights included Crimson Connolly leather trim on the seats, doors, and console and Wilton floor carpets. The heated seats had a memory adjustment that also adjusted the outside rearview mirrors (which were also heated). Naturally, all of this came for a price and in the United States the Port of Entry tarriff for the 3,947-lb. Virage was $200,000.

The Aston Martin Lagonda Ltd. factory was still located in Newport Pagnell, Buckinghamshire, England, but Aston Martin Lagonda of North America, Inc. had relocated to Stamford, Connecticut.

The company returned to motor racing in 1989 with its AMR1, which finished in eight of its 10 outings and ranked sixth overall in the World Sports-Prototype Championship. The race car was powered by a 6.3-litre version of the Virage engine, which delivered more than 650 hp. By 1991, the Virage coupe's price tag went up to $241,500. In 1992, a convertible version known as the Virage Volante was placed on sale. The following year, you could get an Aston Martin "shooting brake" or station wagon in England, but not in the United States. There were no changes in models or specifications for 1994 and in 1995, no cars were imported.

Andrew Morland

# 1993-1998 DB7

The Aston Martin DB7 made its debut at the 1993 Geneva Motor Show. It was downsized from previous models and the transition worked well. In terms of production, the DB7 became the most successful Aston Martin of all time. A production record was clinched on July 1, 1998, when a Pentland Green Volante convertible--the 2,000 DB7 made--was built (the record previously belonged to the DB6). The 4,000th DB7 was put together on February 16, 1999.

Voted "One of the Most Beautiful Cars in the World" by an independent panel of Italian artists, sculptors, photographers, and graphic designers, the DB7's popularity was no surprise. Its elegant, flowing lines were the work of Scottish designer Ian Callum, who had worked as a senior designer for Ghia coachbuilders of Turin, Italy.

A classic 2+2 front engine, rear-wheel-drive, British sports car, the original DB7 employed a 24-valve 3.2-litre in-line six that

***The Aston Martin DB 7 series is well known for its beauty and sophistication.***

developed 335 hp. A single Eaton supercharger with bypass valve and liquid intercooler was fitted to the engine. It also included a Ford EEC V engine management with sequential fuel injection, an EDIS distributorless ignition system and a fully-catalysed exhaust system. A close ratio five-speed all-synchromesh manual transmission or a four-speed electronically-controlled automatic were available with this engine. Behind it was a 3.5:1 ratio limited-slip differential.

The coupe was joined by the Volante convertible model in 1996. Both featured twin air bags, side-impact beams, full on-board diagnostic equipment and a comprehensive range of luxury and safety features as standard equipment.

To create the convertible, every panel behind the B-pillar had to be reworked, the fuel filler had to be relocated and a longer, flatter trunk (boot lid) was incorporated into the car's design. The rear bumper also had to be extended to meet U.S. safety regulations.

Individual components and assemblies were installed in each DB7 by hand, while a series of sophisticated quality control systems were used to complement the skills of the craftsmen who are responsible for the production of DB7. Power-assisted rack-and-pinion steering was fitted and cruise control and a climate-control system were both standard.

Wheelbase for the DB7 was 102.0 in. It was 186.0 in. long, 48.0 in. high, and 72 in. wide, with a 59.8-in. front track and 60.3-in. rear track. The DB7 used independent suspension systems at both ends. Up front was a double wishbone design incorporating anti-dive geometry, coil springs, monotube dampers, and an anti-roll bar. Double wishbones incorporating longitudinal control arms, coil springs, monotube dampers, and an anti-roll bar supported the rear.

The front brakes were ventilated steel discs, 284 mm in diameter, with alloy four-pot calipers. 305-mm ventilated steel discs with sliding aluminum calipers and a drum-type hand brake were at the rear. A Teves antilock-braking-activation system was incorporated. Ultra-low-profile Expedia 245/40 ZR18 Bridgestone radial-ply tires, developed specially for the car and tuned to the DB7 suspension, provided exceptional ride comfort and road holding. They were mounted on unique 8J x 18 lightweight aluminum alloy wheels.

The interiors of both the coupe and the Volante were trimmed with Connolly hide upholstery, deep-pile carpet, and burr walnut on the fascia panel and center console. Many color and trim combinations were offered to buyers of the coupe or Volante.

Green was used on about 35 percent of the cars leaving the new Aston Martin factory in Bloxham, Oxfordshire, England (where Jaguars were built previously). The second most popular color (25 percent) was blue, followed by silver (12 percent). In 1997, the price of the DB7 coupe was $80,000.

The DB7 was designed and developed with the assistance and support of Sir David Brown, who owned Aston Martin from 1947-1972. Like Brown's earlier cars, the DB7 was fast with both manual and automatic transmission models capable of speeds in excess of 160 mph and 5.7-second 0-to-60 mph acceleration.

Ford, which had purchased part ownership in Aston Martin-Lagonda, contributed to the development of the DB7. The composite materials used for sections of the body and the on-board diagnostic equipment were developed in co-operation with Ford Advanced Vehicle Technology. Full use was made of Ford Research Centers and proving grounds in Europe and the United States during the car's 1-million mile test program.

A complete range of special performance parts, first designed for a special DB7 GT project, was made available via the company's 89 sales and service specialists located in 31 countries throughout the world. They include AP racing ventilated anti-lock disc brakes, adjustable front and rear suspension systems, five-spoke magnesium alloy road wheels, traction control, a catalysed competition exhaust system, and a range of custom-made body panels designed to complement and accentuate the classic lines of the Aston Martin DB7.

In a coach work competition organized by the Worshipful Company of Coachmakers and Coach Harness Makers to celebrate the centenary of the British Motor Industry, an international panel of design judges named the Aston Martin DB7 as its "Dream Choice."

Bob Dover, chairman and chief executive of Aston Martin Lagonda, described the the DB7 models as "undoubtedly the most sophisticated and technologically advanced Aston Martins ever to be introduced." According to Motor Trend, the manually-shifted DB7 was capable of accelerating from 0-to-60 mph in 5.4 seconds and did the standing-start quarter mile in 14.37 seconds. The coupe, with a top speed of 171 mph, was 16 mph faster than the Volante convertible.

Aston Martin Media

# V12 Vanquish

Designed by Ian Callum, the V12 Vanquish was introduced by Aston Martin in April 2001 at the New York International Auto Show and was immediately labeled the venerable automaker's new flagship bearer. The Vanquish, which relied on such styling cues as its familiar front grille, resembled the memorable DB series cars, especially its familiar grille shape. Yet the car also was a 21st century leader with technology such as Formula I-inspired fingertip electronic controls for the six-speed transmission. Aston Martin claimed gear changes were possible in less than the blink of an eye—250 milliseconds. Powering the V12 Vanquish was a 48-valve, 6.0-liter 460-hp V-12 engine. The engine featured all-alloy twin overhead camshafts and a sophisticated Visteon twin PTEC system that controlled fuel injection, ignition and diagnostics. The engine was developed with the technical assistance of the Ford Research and Vehicle Technology Group.

Reviewing the V12 Vanquish, *Canadian Automotive Network* writer Alex Law wrote: "To the list of the most desirable cars in the world we must add the Aston Martin V12 Vanquish. The Vanquish will cost more than your house if you live in Montreal or Toronto or Vancouver and more than your block if you live anyplace else in the country." The price for the V12 Vanquish was set in the 180,000 Pounds Sterling range when it was new or $320,524 at current exchange rates. A rare used example recently was priced at $340,000. A carbon fiber central transmission tunnel forms a spine for the Vanquish. "Super-plastic-formed" aluminum skin panels are fixed to the Vanquish by hand.

"The main body structure," wrote V12 Vanquish reviewer Law, "uses carbon-fibre, extruded aluminum and composite materials bonded together to form a central monocoque safety cell with additional…energy absorbent zones at both front and rear."

*The V12 Vanquish continues the stylish tradition of Aston Martin sports cars.*

The V12 Vanquish is available in either two or 2+2 seating configurations. Among the choices potential buyers are asked to make in addition to body color are choosing the shade of Connolly hide upholstery, a satellite navigation system and pre-programmed lighting and windshield wiper systems.

Those choices aren't made from a catalog. Potential buyers visit the factory at Newport Pagnell, Buckinghamshire, England!

The V12 Vanquish rode on 255/40 ZR 19 front and 285/40 ZR 19 rear tires designed exclusively by Yokohama for the Aston Martin. The Vanquish had disk brakes on all four wheels, as well as independent double aluminum wishbone suspension front and rear with coil springs, monotube dampers and anti-roll bars. A limited slip differential and electronic traction control were added to the rear axle on later models.

"This is the most dynamic, technically advanced and sophisticated new model ever to be introduced by Aston Martin," said Aston Martin's chief executive Ulrich Bez in 2001. "It will provide exhilarating performance with impeccable handling and is a true driver's car." The V12 Vanquish accelerates from 0-to-100 km/h ( 62 mph) in just 5.0 seconds and produces 400 lb. ft. of torque at 5000 rpm with its 460 bhp engine. The V12 Vanquish had a 107.6-inch wheelbase, was 186.6 inches long, 76.9 inches wide, and 52.7 inches high. It weighed just over 4,000 pounds.

Production of the V12 Vanquish continued through 2003 with a limit of 300 cars per year.

# AUSTIN-HEALEY

Bob Harrington

# 1953-1956 100-4

The brochure distributed at 1953 motor shows announced the first Austin-Healey was for "the enthusiast who wants quality." It suggested the new British sports car was aimed at: "…the skilled driver who wishes to practise the exciting art of fast motoring." The car was the product of two different companies.

The Austin Motor Co. Ltd., of Longbridge, Birmingham, England, traced its roots back to at least 1895, stemming from the Wolsley cars produced by Lord Herbert Austin. The first Austin-built car was made in 1906. During the late 1940s, Austin became known to Americans as a major British small sedan producer.

Donald Healey Motor Co. Ltd., of The Cape, England, a much smaller company, evolved from his racing and engineering experiences in the '30s. Healey was also technical director at Triumph. After the World War II, his Warwick shop turned out Riley-powered sports cars, most notably a model called the Silverstone.

In 1952, the British Motor Corporation (which was producing Austins) held a competition for a design of a new Austin-based sports car. Donald Healey's "100" won. Healey's prototype received an award at the 1952 Earl's Court (London) motor show and was earmarked for manufacture. Before production began at Longbridge, Birmingham, Leonard Lord, head of BMC, renamed the car "Austin-Healey." Two examples were hastily assembled to appear at the 1953 International Motor Sports Show in New York City. The model went into production in the spring of 1953, selling in Britain for 1323 pounds. Austin-Healeys—reasonably priced, attractive, tough, and with a well-proven engine—quickly became popular in America.

The Austin-Healey's "envelope" style two-seater body, with its beautifully smooth and flowing lines, was welded to the frame. Bodies were later built by Richard and Alan Jensen at their West Bromwich facility. They worked from a Donald Healey design, modified by the Tickford. The shell-shaped grille was made up of thin vertical bars.

*The 1954 Austin-Healey 100-4 leads the way in this racing action.*

Small round parking lights stood directly below the built-in round headlights. The outer fender halves of the aluminum body were quickly removable for repairs. Tiny round taillights were just above the bumper. The lid on the full trunk had exposed hinges. The shallow trunk held a remarkable amount of luggage.

Standard equipment included a heater, disappearing top, "Perspex" detachable side curtains, and a one-piece, fold-back windshield. There was minimal ground clearance, especially with the car's low-slung exhaust system. The instrument panel held an adjustable steering wheel, a 6000-rpm tachometer and a 120-mph speedometer. Bucket seats were provided for the driver and passenger, and the passenger seat was shaped to hold the rider in position through hard cornering. The gas filler nozzle was inside the trunk.

Beneath the bonnet was an in-line, overhead-valve four-cylinder engine, the same one used in the unpopular Austin A90 Atlantic, a drophead coupe. Sales of the A90 Atlantic had never reached expectations and plenty of their engines were on hand to slip into Austin-Healeys.

The three-main-bearings, solid-lifter engine had 87.3 x 111.1-mm bore and stroke measurements and displaced 2660 cc. With a 7.5:1 compression ratio, it developed 90 hp at 4000 rpm and 144 lbs.-ft. of torque at 2000 rpm. Twin S.U. H4 carburetors were fitted and top speed was in the 103-111 mph bracket. Acceleration from 0-to-60 mph took about 10.5 seconds and quarter-mile times ranged from 17.5-18.5 seconds.

Austin provided a competition kit on special order. The engine could gain 15 percent more power by boosting compression, installing a special camshaft, and modifying the carburetion and ignition.

Riding a 90-in. wheelbase, the Austin-Healey stretched 151.5 in.

long. It was 49 in. high and 60 in. wide with 48.8/49.5-in. front and rear tread measurements. The standard 5.90 x 15 tires were mounted on center-locking wire wheels with knock-on hubs. Larger 6.00 x 15 tires were optional. Burman cam-and-lever steering was used.

Coil springs and a torsion-bar-type anti-roll bar were used in front. At the rear was a rigid axle with semi-elliptic leaf springs and anti-sway bar. Girling hydraulic drum brakes were standard. Options included higher axle ratios and Alfin brake drums.

The transmission also came from the Austin A90. A Laycock de Normanville overdrive unit was added, which operated on second and third gears. Overdrive was activated at 40 mph when the dashboard-mounted switch was turned on. Overall gear ratios without overdrive: 9.28:1 in first, 5.85:1 in second, 4.125:1 in third, and 20.53:1 in reverse. Ratios with overdrive engaged were 7.00:1 in first, 4.42:1 in second, and 3.12:1 in third. A 3.66:1 rear axle was used on cars without overdrive, while those with it had a 4.125:1 overall gear ratio.

"It's Really That Good," trumpeted the *Motor Trend* road test in November 1953. One of the magazine's editors noted it was "light and short, making it easy for both the sports car enthusiast and the housewife to drive." Handling was "…good enough for even the most ardent driver."

The 100-4 carried a P.O.E. price of $2,985—about what a Buick Century convertible sold for. It weighed just 2,015 lbs. BMC was able to make and sell 10,688 of them from 1953 to 1955. More than half of all Austin-Healeys were shipped to the U.S. and were distributed through Austin Motor Company, Ltd. in New York and San Francisco.

Don Healey drove one to a record-breaking 142.636-mph speed over a measured mile at the Bonneville, Utah, Salt Flats. Brochures and ads claimed over 100 "Class D" records were broken for both speed and endurance. One Austin-Healey, modified for high altitude, averaged 122.03 mph over a 2,000-mile run. A stock example averaged 104.3 mph for 24 straight hours.

Except for the substitution of a four-speed gear box late in 1955, the Austin-Healey continued much the same for 1954 and 1955. These are known as BN2 models and also were $2,985.

Late in 1955, the 100M arrived. Priced at $3,275, it was fitted with the 110-hp "LeMans" engine modification kit. A racing model called the 100S ("S" standing for Sebring) was also developed and sold for $4,995. Its stripped-down aluminum body wore no bumpers and its modified 132-hp engine wore a Weslake cylinder head. Disc brakes were used all around.

In addition to the 10,688 copies of the original BN1 version made between 1953 and 1955, Austin-Healey produced 3,924 of the BN2s, 1,159 of the 100Ms and 50 of the 100S competition roadsters. A 100S placed third at the Sebring 12-Hour Race in 1954. A streamlined evolution of the same car, carrying a 224-bhp supercharged engine, hit 192 mph on the Bonneville Salt Flats.

Tom Glatch

# 1956-1959 100-6

**R**arin' to go," read the ads for the new Austin-Healey 100-6, "either in competition or just for a family holiday spin." The copywriters promised the "maneuverability and eager response of this powerful, road-hugging thoroughbred is so fast and sure (that) you'll wonder if it's reading your mind." The six-cylinder 100-6 was introduced in August 1956 and made its public debut in September. Initial production took place at the Austin plant in Longbridge, Birmingham, England.

The 100-6 had a longer wheelbase than earlier A-Hs. Two tiny back seats, suitable mostly for children, were added. Changes were also made to the cockpit and trim elements. A new horizontal oval-shaped grille, which came almost to a point at its outer ends, was dominated by horizontal bars separated by three vertical members. A winged insignia stood just to the rear of the grille, ahead of the bonnet (hood) which now incorporated an air scoop.

To improve weather tightness, a fixed windshield was used and rubber channels were added to the windshield pillars to mate with rubber flanges on the side curtains. The folding top had a larger plastic back window. The revised doors had locking outside handles. On the inside was a padded dashboard with an armrest between the two front

*The rare Austin-Healey BN-2 100-M was produced in 1956.*

seats. An adjustable steering column was used again. The car's battery was mounted in the trunk, along with the spare tire, leaving little room for luggage. The gas filler nozzle was mounted on the rear deck instead of inside.

The new 2639-cc engine was a cast-iron, overhead-valve, in-line six with a four-port cylinder head. It had a 79.4 x 88.9-mm bore and stroke. Running an 8.25:1 compression ratio and carrying twin S.U. model H4 carburettors, the four-main-bearing motor developed 102 hp at 4600 rpm and 142 lbs.-ft. of torque at 2400 rpm.

Displacement was actually a tad less than the earlier four-cylinder power plant, while the car was heavier. As a result, the performance of the four-port six-cylinder engine was slightly lower than the earlier four. A six-port edition of the cylinder head would come along later to rectify this.

Behind the engine was a four-speed gearbox. Overdrive was optional. A 3.91:1 rear axle was standard equipment. Suspension and brakes were of the same basic designs used for earlier A-Hs. Top speed was about 104 mph. Acceleration from 0-60 mph took 12.9 seconds, while 18.9 seconds was required for the standing-start quarter mile.

Perched on its 92-in. wheelbase, the 100-6 measured 157.5 in. end to end. It was 49 in. high, 60.5 in. wide and had a 48.8-in. front tread and 50-in. rear tread. The standard 5.90 x 15 tires could be mounted on ventilated pressed-steel disc wheels or optional knock-off wire wheels. Priced at $3,195, the 1956 A-H 100-6 (BN4) roadster tipped the scales at 2,436 lbs. Hambro Automotive Corp., of New York City, was the Austin-Healey distributor by this time. Between August 1956 and March 1959, a total of 10,826 of the BN4 versions were made.

Due to its popularity with U.S. buyers, assembly work for the six-cylinder model had to be shifted to the MG plant at Abingdon-on-Thames by the fall of 1957. And by 1958, Austin Healey sales in the States were running in the 5,446 bracket. Production of Austin-Healey 100-6s with the four-port engine continued, but a new six-port cylinder head was also made available. With the new head, an 8.7:1 compression ratio and twin S.U. HD6

carburetors, it made 117 hp. The hotter head featured six separate ports for intake and exhaust and was mated to a new cast-aluminum intake manifold. The carburetor throats and valves were also larger.

A two-seat model became available again in 1958. It was known as the BN6 and was offered concurrently with the BN4 2+2 model. Styling changes were minimal. The rear half of the plastic window in the car's side curtain now slid forward instead of rearward. The standard versions of the Austin-Healey had disc wheels and offered only two options: a heater and tonneau cover.

Deluxe versions included wire wheels, turn signals, a heater, a telescopic steering column, a tonneau cover, and overdrive. A hardtop was optional.

The new base BN4 roadster sold for $2,919, while the deluxe version remained at $3,195. For BN6 editions, the prices were $3,087 for the standard Sport Roadster and $3,389 for a Deluxe version.

A total of 4,150 two seaters were made in 1958-1959. Production of six-cylinder BN4 and BN6 Austin-Healeys continued into 1959.

Tom Glatch

# 1958-1961 Bug-Eye Sprite

**A**fter discussing the idea of a diminutive, back-to-basics sports car with Donald Healey in 1956, British Motor Corporation (BMC) chairman Sir Leonard Lord commissioned Healey to design such a vehicle. The idea was to create a model that dipped into many existing BMC parts so manufacturing costs could be kept as low as possible. Lord wanted to market a car at a lower price than the $2,300 MGA roadster, so the two models would reach separate audiences, rather than competing for the same buyers.

Production of the Austin-Healey Sprite began in mid-1958. Although Donald Healey and his sons began development work in Warwick, the design was finalized and produced by the MG factory in Abingdon-on-Thames. The car was largely aimed at the American marketplace and 24,148 were imported to the United States between 1958 and 1960. Major distributors in the U. S. included Hambro Automotive Corp., of New York City and two firms located in

*Called it the "Bug Eye" or the "Frog Eye," the Austin-Healey Sprite Mk I.*

California.

The Sprite name had actually been used on a prewar Riley, but the postwar Austin-Healey version was all new and became the first British sports car to feature unibody construction. Because of the cute protruding headlights on its hood, the car was affectionately known as the "Bug-Eye" in the United States and the "Frog-Eye" in Great Britain. The tiny two-seater shared its engine, gearbox and suspension with the little Austin A35 sedan. The steering was donated by the Morris Minor 1000.

A rather small oval grille identified the $1,795 Sprite. It featured a tight crosshatch mesh surrounded by a heavy bright molding. A small round emblem stood just to the rear of the grille. For engine access, the entire front end (including fenders) hinged upward. No external trunk access was provided, but the seats folded down to permit access to the storage space. The cockpit was basic, but nicely finished. It included a leather-covered dashboard and leather upholstery. The doors were hollow to provide storage space and included provisions for attaching sliding side curtains. A tachometer was optional and a detachable hardtop became available before long.

The Sprite's ultra-light 1,316-lb. shipping weight was a plus when it came to performance, because the overhead-valve four-cylinder in-line engine was small, too. The Austin power plant had a 62.9 x 76.2-in. bore and stroke that gave it a 948-cc displacement figure. Running an 8.3:1 compression ratio, solid valve lifters and two S.U. model H1 carburetors, the Sprite engine could propel the little car to 80 mph. Zero-to-60 mph took 20.2-20.9 seconds and the quarter mile took 21.6-22.5 seconds.

The three-main-bearings power plant was rated for 42.5 hp at 5000 rpm and 52 lbs.-ft. of torque at 3300 rpm.

Mounted behind the engine was a four-speed manual transmission with a floor shifter. This was another Austin A35 item. The gearbox had ratios of 15.3:1 in first, 10.0:1 in second, 5.96:1 in third, and 4.22:1 in fourth. At the rear was a low-geared 4.22:1 axle.

The car's tight rack-and-pinion steering system, brakes and rear axle were pirated from the Morris Minor. Up front were upper and lower A-arms with coil springs. Double trailing links with quarter-elliptic leaf springs and lever-type shock absorbers were fitted at the rear. With an 80-in. wheelbase and 132.6-in. overall length, the Sprite stood just 49.8 in. high and was a mere 53 in. wide. Tread widths were 45.8 in. up front and 44.8 in. at the rear. The disc wheels held tiny 5.20 x 13 or 145SR13 tires.

A total of 129,354 Sprites of all series were produced from 1958 to 1971, but the Bug-Eye model was available only until the early part of 1961 when it was replaced by a new Mk II model. First-year output was 8,279 units. An additional 21,566 Bug-Eye Sprites were produced in 1959 and 18,665 were made in 1960.

Production of 1961 models is known only for the two styles combined. Only a few options were offered for the Bug-Eye Sprite, but they came in handy. Available extras included a heater for $55.75, a tachometer for $13.75, a windshield washer for $6.25 and a tonneau cover for $19.95.

Sprites held their own in a number of sports-car racing classes and were especially popular with amateur drivers because of their affordability. Even aftermarket racing equipment was available at the low end of the price range.

However, even well-heeled drivers like actor Steve McQueen raced them. McQueen drove his car at Sebring in 1962, where he met Donald Healey.

Kris Kandler

# *1959-1967 3000*

In spring of 1959, the big Austin-Healey got a new 2912-cc engine. BMC rounded displacement up to the next hundred to come up with the 3000 model designation. Three variations of the new car—BN7 two-seat Deluxe Roadster, BT7 four-seat Sport Roadster and BT7 four-seat Deluxe Roadster—were offered at prices of $3,371, $3,051 and $3,371, respectively. The BN7 model turned out to be the rarest and only 2,825 examples were made from 1959 to 1961. In the same time span, 10,825 BT7s were built.

Austin-Healeys continued to feature an oval-shaped grille opening, but switched to a grille insert with multiple, closely-spaced, vertical bars. As before, small round parking lights stood directly below the round headlights and the hood carried an air scoop with short vertical bars decorating its front edge. Pointed round taillights were positioned just above the rear bumper, with smaller round lenses mounted higher

*One of the memorable examples of the Austin-Healey is the 1967 3000 series.*

up on the rear deck lid. As before, the trunk lid had exposed hinges.

Similar in overall configuration to the engine it replaced, Austin-Healey's new in-line six had bore and stroke measurements of 83.3 x 88.9 mm. With 9.1:1 compression, the 3000 developed 124 hp at 4600 rpm and 162 lbs.-ft. of torque at 2700 rpm. The engine had four main bearings, solid valve lifters, twin S.U. HD6 carburetors and a 12-volt electrical system. It could power the 2,465-lb. roadster to 115 mph. That made it more than 10 mph faster than the 100-6 model. The horsepower ratings would grow over the next eight years, eventually reaching 148 hp.

With a top speed of 112-115 mph, the 3000 was a fast car. It could go from a standing start to 60 mph in 11.4 seconds and do the quarter-mile in 17.9 seconds. K.N. Rudd (Engineers) Ltd., of England, marketed a modification kit with three S.U. carburetors on a special intake manifold. This setup gave the 3000 a considerable boost in horsepower and torque.

Visually and dimensionally, the new 3000 was very similar to the 100-6 that it replaced in mid-1959. The wheelbase remained at 92 in., the overall length hung in at 157.5 in., and the 49-in. height and 60.5-in. width measurements were also unchanged. Only the front (48.75-in.) and rear (50-in.) tread widths changed slightly. Standard throughout the model run were 5.90 x 15 tires. A four-speed manual transmission was mated to a 3.91:1 rear axle. Overdrive was optional. Cam-and-peg type steering was employed and the front suspension combined wishbones with coil springs up. At the rear was a rigid axle and semi-elliptic leaf springs. The 3000 had front disc and rear drum brakes.

Production of the original 3000 continued into 1961, when it was replaced by a Mk II version. As before, both two-passenger and 2+2 seating arrangements were available. Prices remained the same as in 1960. For the full Mk II model run from 1961 to early 1962, production came to only 355 BN7 Deluxe Roadsters and 5,096 of both BT7 styles combined.

Little change was evident on the 3000 Mk II's body, but the 2912-cc six now carried three S.U. HS4 carburetors. As a result of this revision, the engine produced 132 hp at 4750 rpm and 167 lbs.-ft. of torque at 3000 rpm. Road performance showed little if any improvement from the change and the triple-carb setup lasted only one year. The gearshift linkage was also modified.

During 1962, the BJ7 version of the big Austin-Healey 3000 Mk II was revised to include a curved windshield and roll-up windows. It was now considered a convertible. The triple S.U. setup was replaced by dual S.U. H6s that actually produced slightly better acceleration. Magazine road testers put the 0-to-60 mph time at 10.3 sec. and the quarter-mile acceleration time at 17.1 sec. DeLuxe models had such extras as wire wheels, an adjustable steering column and a tonneau cover.

The serial number—located on right side of firewall—clearly indicated the model by the first five symbols in the sequence. Two-seat roadsters had numbers starting at HBNMK/13751, while four-seat roadster numbers started with HBTMK/13751 and convertible numbers were HBJ7L/17551 and up. The BN7 and BT7 models carried over in the early part of the 1962 model year had slightly raised prices: $3,420 for the two-passenger Deluxe Roadster, $3,120 for the four-passenger Sport Roadster and $3,438 for the four-passenger Deluxe Roadster. Production of these early-year cars was counted with that of the 1961 models.

When the BJ7 convertible arrived in mid-1962, it was offered as a base four-passenger Convertible for $3,231 and as a Deluxe version of the same model for $3,535. The convertibles were about 115 lbs. heavier than roadsters and a total of 6,113 were made from 1962 to 1964.

Production of the Austin-Healey 3000 Mk II four-passenger convertible continued with little change into 1963-1964 with very modest changes. Starting on Jan. 31, 1964, a new 3000 Mk III was produced. This revision added more luxurious interior appointments, including a wood fascia and a center console between the front seats. There were a number of significant technical refinements, too. The output was boosted to 150 hp. In late-1964, a "phase two" version got chassis modifications including a switch to radius arms at the rear axle.

The Mk III was the quickest of the Big Healeys. With 150 hp at 5,250 rpm and 173 lbs.-ft. of torque at 3000 rpm, it had a top speed of about 120 mph. Zero-to-60 mph took 9.5 seconds and the quarter-mile could be covered in 17 seconds. Standard equipment included an adjustable steering wheel, heater, windshield washers, a four-speed manual transmission (with overdrive) and front disc brakes. Power brakes became standard in the 1966-1967 models and air conditioning was optional, but there were very few changes overall. Mk III serial numbers started with HBJ8/25315 and engine numbers—located on the left side of the block—had a 29K prefix. The Mk III carried a $3,565 price tag and was a popular attraction in the showroom. A total of 17,712 were produced from 1964 to the end of 1967 and 16,322 were "phase two" editions.

The 3000-series Austin-Healeys did well in competition, especially rallies, taking wins in Alpine events in 1961 and 1962. There were additional victories at the Liege-Rome-Liege runs in 1960 and 1964 and at the Austrian Alpine rally in 1964.

Norbert Bries/ Northshore Imports

# 1961-1964 Sprite MkII

Around July 31, 1961, a totally new Austin-Healey Sprite replaced the original "Bug-Eye" version. Called the Sprite Mk II, the second-generation model was much more conventional in its design, although still quite diminutive. Its restyled body featured a squared-off front end. The rectangular grille opening had a mesh insert with a crosshatch pattern. Rectangular parking lights, with rounded top edges, were positioned below the headlights, which were round and mounted in the fender tips in the usual manner.

Also designated model AN6, the new Sprite Mk II remained a small (and lovable) two-passenger roadster. Its $1,868 price tag was increased from that of the Bug-Eye, but only by $73. It also gained 134 lbs. and tipped the scales at 1,450 lbs.

Austin-Healey chose to bolt the front fenders on this car into position. A rear-hinged hood that raised in the traditional fashion replaced the previous flip-up-style front end. The rear body styling was also updated with squarer lines, larger taillights, and a lockable trunk lid. To make it more weather-tight, the folding top now featured a metal-back overlap joint along the windshield. Sliding plastic side windows were fitted for the same practical purpose. The bucket seats were upholstered in plastic.

The Sprite remained a unibody car and stuck with a front-engine, rear-drive layout. It was perched on an 80-in. wheelbase and measured just 137.25 in. long. It was a mere 49.8 in. high and 53 in. wide with tread measurements of 45.8 in. front and 44.8 in. rear. The four-speed manual gearbox was linked to a 4.22:1 rear axle.

Steering was rack-and-pinion, front suspension was upper and lower A-arms with coil springs, and the rear suspension featured double trailing links with quarter-elliptic leaf springs. Disc brakes were fitted up front with drums at the rear. Size 5.20 x 13 tires were standard.

Under the bonnet (what we call the hood) was the same in-line, overhead-valve 948-cc four-cylinder engine used in the Bug-Eye Sprite,

*The Austin Healey Sprite Mark II was a popular small roadster.*

but with a modest horsepower increase resulting from a higher 9.0:1 compression ratio and additional improvements. It was now rated for 46 hp at 5500 rpm and 53 lbs.-ft. at 2750 rpm. The other engine modifications included valve train revisions and the use of two large-throat S.U. HS2 carburetors.

Test drivers reported a top speed of 86 mph for the 1961 Sprite Mk II. Zero-to-60 mph took about 19.3 sec. and the quarter mile could be covered in another two seconds. Production for Bug-Eye and Mk II models combined, in 1961, totaled 10,059 units.

For most of the 1962 model year, the Sprite Mk II was unchanged, but in the fall, the original 948-cc four-cylinder engine was replaced by a 1098-cc version having a 64.6 x 83.7-mm bore and stroke. It produced 56 hp at 5500 rpm and upped performance slightly. Top speed was now 88 mph, 0-to-60 took 16.8 seconds, and the quarter mile could be done in 21 seconds flat. The new engine also helped to increase sales and raised production to 12,041 units.

In 1963, the price of the Sprite Mk II rose about $7, but there were few other changes in design, equipment or specifications. An S/S version of the Sprite was described in Hot Rod magazine during 1963. It was produced by the Donald Healey Motor Co. and used the 948-cc engine with a three-quarter Healey cam and Sebring cylinder head. Production tapered off to 8,852 cars in 1963.

On Sept. 1, 1964, a new Sprite Mk III model arrived. The unchanged Mk II continued to be available until that time and the production total for both cars lumped together was 11,157. It's likely that most of these were Mk IIs, although the improved Mk III may have accounted for the annual increase.

# 1964-1967 Sprite MkIII

The Austin-Healey Sprite Mk III became available on Sept. 1, 1964. It was essentially a new-for-1965 model, but in some states, early examples may have been registered according to calendar year and titled as 1964 models. The new Sprite's soft top came with a collapsible frame that could be completely removed. The car's curved windshield was carried within another chrome frame. The wraparound-style front and rear bumpers held standard overriders. British Motor Corp. described the car as "A winner on—or off— the track. Economical. Fast. Fun." Standard colors included Tartan Red, Riviera Blue, Old English White, Dove Grey, British Racing Green, and black. On the options list were a heater, a tonneau cover, and white sidewall tires.

Roll-up side windows and hinged "butterfly-style" vent windows were added. The wheels were of a new design and the cockpit took on additional amenities with a restyled fascia, a restyled parcel shelf and angled instrument dials. Otherwise, the appearance was similar to that of the Mark II, with large vertical taillights and a rectangular-mesh grille. Locking doors and a lockable trunk, the latter with 11.5 cubic-foot cargo capacity and a lay-flat spare tire, were other improvements. The Mk III had a Port of Entry price of $1,888 and weighed all of 1,566 lbs.

While the size of the three-main-bearings engine stayed the same, horsepower rose from 56 to 59 at 5750 rpm and torque was rated 62 lbs.-ft. at 3250 rpm.

Twin S.U. HS2 semi-downdraft carburetors delivered fuel to the engine. Top speed was reported to be 101 mph. The Sprite Mk III could accelerate from 0-to-60 mph in 12.3 sec. and covered the quarter mile in 18.8 sec.

The Sprite Mk III retained the Mk II's 80-in. wheelbase and 136-in. overall length. Other measurements were also the same as on the Mk II including front and rear tread widths, even though the rear suspension was converted to semi-elliptic leaf springs. The front suspension stayed with wishbones, coil springs and lever type shock absorbers. The four-lug, ventilated pressed-steel wheel discs were fitted with tiny 5.20 x 13 tires.

The four-speed manual transmission had gear ratios of 3.20:1 in first; 1.916:1 in second; 1.357:1 in third and 1.00:1 in fourth. A 4.22:1 rear axle was used again. As usual, the front brakes were discs, with drums at the rear.

A total of 7,024 Sprites were produced in 1966 and 6,895 were made in 1967. Some of the latter group may have been Mk IVs.

# 1967-1970 Sprite MkIV

Production of the Mk III Sprite continued with little change in 1966 and 1967. At some point during the latter year, a new Mark IV model arrived. With the Mark IV version came a larger 1275-cc four-cylinder engine that generated 65 hp. That engine was essentially a de-tuned version of BMC's Mini-Cooper 'S' power plant and was sufficient to give the Sprite a top speed around 95 mph. Upping the power meant upping the price, which climbed to $1,995, but the weight decreased to only 1,512 lbs.

The new power plant had a 70.6 x 81.3-mm bore and stroke. Everything else remained just about the same, down to the dual S.Us. It had 65 hp at 6000 rpm and 72 lbs.-ft. of torque at 3000 rpm. The car could now do 0-to-60 mph in 12.3 seconds and the quarter mile in 18.8-19.1 seconds.

For its final three years on the U.S. market, the little Sprite got a new negative-ground electrical system, a safety-type dashboard and an exhaust emission system. In 1969, new side safety marker lights were added to the cowl on imported models. These changes were relatively

*This Mark IV Austin Healey Sprite is a well-preserved late '60s roadster.*

pricey and hiked the window sticker up to $2,050. Surprisingly, the car lost 10 lbs. in the modernization process. New options included a front anti-roll bar, wire spoke wheels, and an oil cooler.

The last Sprite Mk IVs sold were called Austin Sprites and the "Healey" name was dropped. Production totals were 7,049 Sprites in 1968, 6,133 in 1969 and 1,280 in 1970. Imports to the U.S. ceased in 1970, but an additional 1,022 Sprites were built in England in 1971.

From the beginning in 1958 until the end in 1970, a grand total of 129,354 Sprites was manufactured. Of that number, 79,338 were produced in the restyled MkII thru Mk IV formats. In 1968, the British Leyland company was formed. The MG Midget, which was nearly identical to the Sprite, and which usually sold better, also continued to be produced until 1977.

# BERKELEY

Tom Glatch

# 1956-1959 328

Created by Laurie Bond, designer of the 1949 Bond minicar, the Berkeley took the sports car concept down to its tiniest dimensions. Bond's objective was to create a sporty car that was cheap to buy and run, but performed with enough spirit to appeal to enthusiasts. He did his work at the request of Charles Panter of the Berkeley Coachwork Company, Ltd., a builder of house trailers in Biggleswade, Bedfordshire, England.

Body construction was of a unitized three-piece design. The body and frame were made of resin-bonded molded fiberglass with aluminum bulkheads and three crossmembers. A steel sub-frame was provided for drivetrain and suspension components. Since Bond Minicar Works was already accustomed to working with fiberglass, it seemed logical to use that new material in making the Berkeley.

The Berkeley's initial appearance was at the London Motor Show in the fall of 1956. In England, the car sold for the equivalent of $1,064. It looked like a sports car with its crosshatch-pattern oval grille under a crease at the front of the nose, but it was tiny. A round ornament was placed ahead of the nearly horizontal hood. The headlights were deeply recessed into long nacelles.

To get an idea of the car's diminuative size and weight, the fender tops were just 25-in. high and one man could lift the back end of the 616-lb. roadster right off the ground. At $1,600 Port of Entry in the States, a Berkeley cost nearly as much as some ordinary-size sports cars like the Austin-Healey Sprite.

As a result, only a modest number of Berkeleys ever found their way to the U.S. California was the biggest market here. Only 3,000 were made in total between 1956 and 1960.

Berkeley standard equipment included a 120-mph speedometer, a fuel gauge and an ammeter, but no temperature gauge. The driver and passenger seats had no conventional adjustment and no provision was made for a heater. A tiny rumble seat for (small) children could be mounted in the space ordinarily filled by the spare tire. During its first

*This 1958 Berkeley roadster is one of the earliest to reach American shores.*

two years on the market, the Berkeley 328 came with either an Anzani or Excelsior vertical-type, air-cooled twin-cylinder engine. The engine was tranversely mounted ahead of the front axle. The 322-cc Anzani engine had a 60 x 57-mm bore and stroke, an 8.5:1 compression ratio, an Amal carburetor and dual exhausts. It produced 15 hp at 5000 rpm. The Excelsior engine was known as the "Talisman Twin." It had a 58 x 62-mm borte and stroke. A 7.4:1 compression ratio was standard, but an 8.2:1 option was offered. It also featured an Amal carburetor and dual exhausts and its output was rated 18 hp at 5000 rpm.

The front-wheel-drive Berkeley featured a three-speed motorcycle-type transmission with chain drive to three-plate disc clutch. A gate-style gearshift lever moved in a progressive (forward-and-back) pattern —like that of a motorcycle—with neutral positions between gears, as well as a main neutral. The 5.27:1 ratio standard final drive was by duplex chain and steel sprocket.

In automobile specifications books, the Berkeley's measurements sounded like typographical errors. The wheelbase was 70 in., overall length was 123 in., the height was 41 in., and it was only 50 in. wide. The tread width was 44 in. front and rear. Michelin 5.20 x 12 tires were standard equipment. Burman worm-and-nut steering was featured. Independent front a rear suspension systems featured twin wishbones with combined coil springs and shock absorbers up front and swing axles with combined coil springs and shocks at the rear. Girling supplied the all-drum brakes.

Although cars sold in England switched to a larger three-cylinder engine during 1957, two-cylinder Berkeleys with Excelsior engines were shipped to the U.S. after that time. The home-market models had nicely faired-in headlamps, but certain state laws in the U.S. outlawed these and some imported Berkeleys arrived with tacked-on headlights.

A top speed of 60-70 mph was claimed for the original Berkeley and reports said it could move from a standstill to 50 mph in about 30.6 sec. The factory also promoted 60-mpg fuel economy.

Berkeley of America, Inc., in New Haven, Connecticut, was one of the biggest Berkley distributors in the U.S. Other distributors were located in Pensacola, Florida; Hollywood, California; and Lubbock, Texas.

Alan Wagner

# 1958-1959 Sports 500

Ads of 1958 promised Berkeley buyers "vivid acceleration" and "boundless capacity for fun." A Berkeley, they said, "generally requites the sportsman's love for a fine machine." A larger two-stroke engine was released to create the Sports 500 model. This line offered a new hardtop coupe and a roadster. The open car was priced at $1,745 and weighed 725 lbs. The closed coupe was $95 additional and weighed more. A Foursome version of the roadster, with a 78-in. wheelbase and 131-in. overall length, was able to squeeze in four passengers.

New features included unique, thinly-upholstered seat cushions that rested on wide rubber bands and easily adjusted to the rider's weight. A Siba Dynastart-combined starter and generator was used in the 12-volt electrical system. An ammeter replaced the former ignition-warning light. By 1959, sliding windows were added to the side curtains.

The new 500 engine (actually 492 cc) had the same bore and stroke as the previous engine, but added a third cylinder to get the

*A yellow 1959 Berkeley SE 492 roadster looks perfect in the sunshine.*

extra displacement. This vertical engine was air cooled and had a 7.5:1 compression ratio. Three Amal carburetors were fitted. The factory advertised 30 hp at 5500 rpm and 35.4 lbs.-ft. of torque at 3500 rpm.

Road testers at the time praised the tiny sports car's handling, noting that virtually no roll was evident in turns, yet the ride was quite comfortable. Approximately 551 Berkeleys were imported and sold in the U.S. during 1958, while 361 found customers here in 1959.

With the new three-cylinder engine, the top speed of the Berkeley went up to 65-75 mph. It could now go from 0-to-50 mph in 14.4 seconds and the standing-start quarter-mile could be done in 22.4 seconds. A Berkeley Sports 500 won its class at the 1959 Mille Miglia and also at the Monza 12-Hour Race, beating Abarths in the process.

# 1960 B95/B105 & QB95/QB105

The 1960 Berkeley B95, B105, QB95 and QB105 models were the final automotive products of Berkeley Ltd., of Biggleswade, Bedfordshire, England. The B prefix indicated cars with the shorter, 70-in. wheelbase used on earlier Berkleys, while QB models were built on a 178-in. wheelbase chassis.

A considerably larger 692-cc four-stroke powerplant with more than double the horsepower of the original 1956 Berkeley 328 was used in cars with the "95" suffix, which stood for the factory's "claimed" top speed. This was an air-cooled, vertical overhead-valve twin made by Royal Enfield. It had a 70 x 90-mm bore and stroke, a 7.5:1 compression ratio, and an Amal monobloc carburetor. It developed 40 hp at 5500 rpm and 43 lbs.-ft. of torque. Cars with the "105" suffix got a version of the same engine with an 8.0:1 compression ratio and 50 hp at 6250 rpm that the factory suggested could propel the Berkeley to 105 mph.

"Docile, easily handled . . . for town use, the QB95 becomes a really fast and safe sports car when opened up on clear roads," said factory literature describing the 1960 Berkeley for its appearance at the 1959 Turin (Italy) Auto Show. The car was introduced in Europe during 1959, but as is often the case with imports, took a bit longer to arrive in the United States. American advertisements promoted it as "The world's lowest-priced all-sports car."

The tiny roadster's appearance actually changed somewhat for its final season. It now sported a square grille with six horizontal bars and a sizable hood bulge. The rear tires protruded beyond the rear fenders.

A pair of pointed round parking lights on each side stood below headlights that were slightly recessed at the bottom. The front fenders rolled sharply inward, below the parking lamps, leaving a large gap alongside the nose section.

Inside, a pair of deep, well-sprung bucket-type seats were upholstered in Vynide. Other features included a locking trunk lid, a one-piece curved windshield, and Hardura plastic carpets. Standard equipment included a large parcel tray, door pockets, side screens, aluminum alloy wheel discs, and a tool kit. Available body colors were red, light blue, dark green, Old English White, and yellow. Upholstery came in either red or light brown.

B models were 127.5 in. long and QB models stretched 133.5 in. bumper to bumper. Both were 46 in. high with 5.5 in. ground clearance. Width was 50 in. for Bs and 54 in. for QBs. Both used a 46.25-in. front tread, a 46-in. rear tread, and Michelin 5.20 x 12 tires. The floor-shifted, cable-activated Albion four-speed gearbox had overall gear ratios of 13.7:1 in first, 8.62:1 in second, 5.95:1 in third, 4.31:1 in fourth, and 14.05:1 in reverse. It was attached to a multi-plate Albion clutch. Standard final drive ratio was 2.23:1 (by duplex chain and steel sprocket). Other technical specifications were just about unchanged from earlier Berkeleys.

The B95 carried a Port of Entry price of $1,595 ($37 higher on the West Coast) and weighed just 784 lbs. The QB95 was $200 pricier and weighed an additional 56 lbs. A total of about 3,000 Berkeleys were sold between 1956 and 1960. Berkeley reportedly planned to produce a full-size sports car called the Bandit in 1960, but only one prototype was made. Berkeley ceased production that year after a proposed merger with the makers of the Bond car fell through. The main distributor was Berkeley Motor Cars Ltd., Los Angeles, California. Despite the factory's claim of 95- and 105-mph top speeds for the 95 and 105 models, the true top speed of both was about 85 mph. Zero-to-60 mph took 14 seconds and 50 miles per gallon of fuel was possible.

# BRISTOL

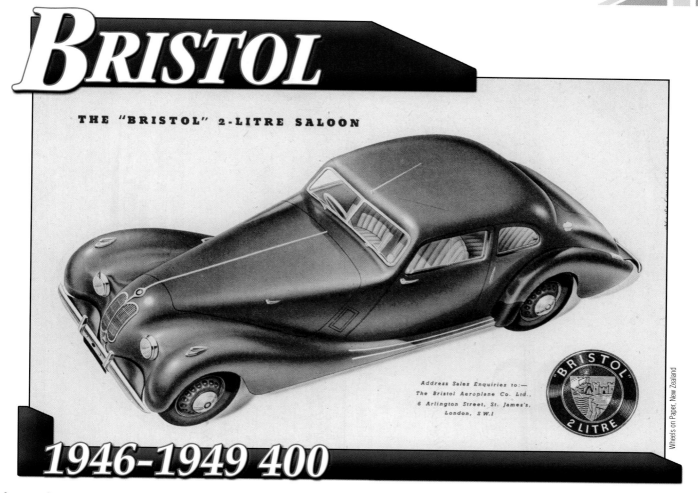

THE "BRISTOL" 2-LITRE SALOON

Address Sales Enquiries to:—
The Bristol Aeroplane Co. Ltd.,
6 Arlington Street, St. James's,
London, S.W.1

BRISTOL 2 LITRE

Wheels on Paper, New Zealand

## 1946-1949 400

The Bristol Aeroplane Company Ltd. of Filton, Bristol, England, started to produce aircraft in 1910. The company always wanted to build cars and bid unsuccessfully for Aston Martin when it went through one of its periodic bankruptcies in 1925. During World War II, Bristol produced over 14,000 aircraft. After the war, the firm realized that diversification into automaking was essential.

Bristol's Board of Directors wisely decided to base the initial product on existing technology and obtained ownership of BMW designs as war reparations. After inspecting what was available, Bristol decided to combine the excellent engine of the sporty BMW 328 with the advanced rear torsion bar suspension of the BMW 326 and a body somewhat similar to the BMW 327 coupe, which offered more interior room and better aerodynamics. Body construction featured aluminum alloy body panels on a steel frame.

The car-buying public anticipated something special from the aviation giant and the results surpassed all expectations. The BMW components were substantially improved in design details and material quality and this commitment contributed to Bristol's reputation as a car for the connoisseur. During the marque's first decade, Bristol further developed lightweight, aerodynamic bodies and was also known for incorporating advanced—and thoughtful—features.

Introduced in 1946, the Bristol 400 was a meticulously engineered four-seat coupe that established the company's reputation as a sporting gentleman's car. Based on prewar BMW principles it was nevertheless built to demanding aviation standards by artisans taken from the parent aircraft company.

The *Autocar* opined that, "the buyer obtains a connoisseur's car, attractive to look upon, comfortable to ride in and a constant delight to handle."

**The BMW-powered 1948 Bristol enjoyed the rich heritage of Bristol aircraft making.**

Often wrongly thought to be a twin overhead camshaft engine due to its unique cross-pushrod design, the overhead-valve in-line six was a development of the BMW 328. It had a 66 x 96-mm bore and stroke and 1971-cc displacement. With solid valve lifters, a 7.5:1 compression ratio and three S.Y.U. carburetors, it developed 80 hp at 4200 rpm and 96 lbs.-ft. of torque at 3000 rpm. The engine was capable of pushing the 2,537-lb. coupe to 95 mph and moving it from 0-to-50 mph in 10.3 sec. The quarter mile took 19.7 seconds.

The Bristol rode a 114-in. wheelbase and measured 183 in. long end to end. It was 59 in. high and 64 in. wide. The 52-in. front tread was two inches narrower than the rear tread. The transmission was a four-speed manual with synchromesh on all but first gear. The gear ratios were 4.3:1 in first, 2.17:1 in second, 1.3:1 in third, 1.1:1 in fourth, and 3.44:1 in reverse. The freewheeling first gear allowed its selection on the move, without double clutching, making the 400 a popular contender in rallies and other sporting events of the time.

A 3.44:1 rear axle was standard. Rack-and-pinion steering was used. The front suspension used transverse leaf springs with upper wishbones. At the rear was a live (rigid) axle with lateral links, an A-bracket and longitudinal torsion bars. Lockheed hydraulic drum brakes were used all around.

The Bristol 400 was introduced in 1946 and production of the model continued into 1949, although the company's new 401 was out by that time. A Type 400 took first place in the Touring category at the 1948 Belgian Circuit de la Sarthe race and a first in the 2-liter class at the Polish Rally.

OCW Archive

# 1949-1955 401/402/403

Introduced during 1949, while the 400 was still being produced, was the new Bristol 401 with a $6,950 price tag. In addition to offering five more horsepower, it had an advanced streamlined body developed in Bristol's own wind tunnel. To reduce weight, Bristol licensed the new "superleggere" coachwork, developed by Carrozerie Touring (Italy), that used a framework of light tubes over which aluminum panels were fixed.

The 401 incorporated other innovations. The four- or five-passenger fastback body even boasted flush-opening push-button doors. Sales brochures noted that conventional protruding door handles presented a "potential threat to clothing."

The inside door releases were concealed beneath the leather trim. More push buttons allowed the hood to be opened from either side or removed in seconds for service access. The trunk, fuel filler, and concealed spare wheel tray were also push-button operated, while the bumpers were styled as part of the body and had impact-absorbing rubber mounts.

Derived from the 401, a small number of 402 convertibles were built. Although lacking in elegance with the top in position, the complicated top folded away completely to give a clean, graceful profile that attracted such movie stars as Stewart Granger and Jean Simmons. Under the hood of both cars was the same two-litre in-line six-cylinder engine used in the 400. It featured an aluminum cylinder head, hemispherical combustion chambers, and inclined overhead valves. The engine's brake horsepower rating was 85 at 4500 rpm. It developed 107 lbs.-ft. of torque at 3500 rpm. Triple Solex downdraft carburetors replaced the triple S.U.s. The engine was again linked to

*The Bristol 401 with a Bristol bomber—a symbol of England in World War II.*

a four-speed gearbox. The gear ratio was changed to 16.77:1 in first, 8.37:1 in second, 5.51:1 in third, 3.9:1 in fourth, and 13.43:1 in reverse. The overall gear ratio was also changed to 3.90:1.

The drivetrain combination was strong enough to allow Bristols to run in "top class" rally events during 1949 an the Bristols invariably ranked in the top four spots. In 1951 Tony Crook, racing driver and later owner of Bristol Cars, set an amazing one-hour average speed record of almost 105 mph—an achievement beyond the ability of the other saloon cars running engines more than double the Bristol's size.

The 401 shared the 400's wheelbase, but was seven inches longer, an inch higher and three inches wider. It had a 51.75-in. front tread and 54-in. rear tread. The standard 4.5J16 bolt-on "easy clean" disc wheels were shod with either Dunlop 5.50 x 16 or Michelin 5.75 x 16 tires.

Bristols were available with either right- or left-hand drive. The box-section chassis had four crossmembers and an integral rear floor structure. Lockheed hydraulic brakes were used, along with a cable-operated "fly-off" hand-brake. A foot pedal operated the "one-shot," built-in chassis lubrication system. Telescopic shock absorbers were used. Standard equipment included a radio and a touring kit with spare parts.

In 1949, Bristols took third place overall at the Monte Carlo Rally; second in the Sicilian Targa Florio road race and first in the touring category of the Tuscany Cup. The 401 had a top speed of 93-96 mph.

*A 1950 Bristol 402 drophead shows its natural grace.*

It could do 0-to-60 mph in 14.1 to 17.8 seconds. Going a quarter mile from a standing start took 19.9 seconds.

Similar in appearance to the former 401, but identified by silver enameled front grilles and model badges on the rear bonnet edges, the Bristol 403 two-door saloon was introduced in May 1953. Mechanically, the new $5,600 car was substantially improved with larger inlet valves, an upraked camshaft and a fully-counter-balanced crankshaft allowing an extended rev range and an 18 percent jump in horsepower to 100 at 5000 rpm. It developed 117 lbs.-ft. of torque at 3500 rpm. The last Type 403s built in 1955 had the 100B2 engine used in the Type 405, which generated 105 hp at 5000 rpm and 123 lbs.-ft. at 3750 rpm.

The 403's polished walnut dashboard held a tachometer and a full compliment of gauges in stylized square surrounds. Two large glove compartments and a rear window blind operating remotely from the driver's seat were typical 403 refinements.

The addition of a front anti-roll bar improved handling of the 2,670-lb. Bristol and Alfin aluminum brake drums improved its stopping ability.

Autosports tester John Bolster wrote, " I recorded it as one of the few really great cars that I have handled." Some later examples adopted a shorter gearshift lever with remote linkage.

Chassis and technical specifications for the 403 were mostly the same as those for the 401 and 402 models. Top speed was about 100 mph. Acceleration from 0-to-60 mph took about 15 seconds.

Andrew Morland

# 1953-1956 404

While the Type 403 continued the earlier 401 look, the new Bristol 404 (which first appeared late in 1953) was a completely different 2+2 coupe with a smoother, more modern design. The $8,000 two-seat fastback soon became known as the "Businessman's Express" due to its quick acceleration and top speed beyond 110 mph. Considerably smaller than earlier Bristols, the 404 rode a 96-in. wheelbase and weighed a light 2,262 lbs.

Bristol built the 403 body using steel and light alloy panels over a steel and laminated ash (wood) framework. A dark, recessed, mesh-pattern grille looked almost like a plain hole in the front of the car. The headlights were moved to a conventional location in the fenders, as opposed to the narrow-set installation in the 401, 402, and 403 models. Small round amber parking lamps went below the headlights and the hood sported an air scoop. At the rear were small tailfins and round taillights: two red and two amber-colored. Fog lamps were optional.

British versions of the 404 had a central spotlight, while export models usually substituted twin auxiliary lamps above the front bumper. The left front fender held an opening for the spare tire, while a matching hatch on the right fender covered the battery and electrical parts. Standard equipment included a heater and windshield washer.

Brochures promoting a drophead coupe (two-passenger convertible) version of the 404 were distributed at the London Motor

## The 110-mph Bristol 404 series was nicknamed the "Businessman's Express."

Show in fall 1953, but probably no more than one example—built by E.D. Abbott—was produced.

The same BMW-derived in-line six-cylinder Bristol engine was used in the 404, but with a higher 8.5:1 compression ratio. Brake horsepower was rated 105 at 5000 rpm and torque was 123 lbs.-ft. at 3750 rpm.

Top speed was 110-115 mph and 0-to-60 mph came in 12.3 to 13.5 seconds.

The Alfin front brake drums were made of light aluminum. An optional 100C engine, delivering 125 hp, was available for competition use. A sales brochure for the sport coupe noted that the 404 "combines the performance of a competition car with the docility and dignity of a town carriage."

The shorter-wheelbase Bristol 404 naturally had a shorter 171.25-in. overall length. It stood 55.5 in. high and was 68 in. wide.

Tread measurements were 52.4 in. up front and 54 in. at the rear. Dunlop or Michelin X 5.75 x 16 tires were mounted on the 4.5J16 bolt-on disc wheels. The 404 remained in production until 1956. In the later years of production, the price fell a bit to about $6,370.

Andrew Morland

# 1954-1958 405 Drophead Coupe

A four-door saloon version of the Bristol 404 called the 405 debuted in 1954. It was built on the 114-in. wheelbase previously used for the 401, 402 and 403 models. The 405 saloon remained in production into 1958. It was a sporting car, if not a true sports car. In addition to the saloon, a two-door drophead coupe was offered. This convertible built by E.D. Abbott Ltd. (of Farnham) was certainly more of a sports car. Its top, when folded, fit flush into a compartment. The side windows held ventipanes.

The front end appearance of the 405 was similar to that of the 404. A Laycock de Normanville (electrical) overdrive was standard, working only on fourth gear. Noting the car's "sleek lines [and] wondrous collection of unusual features,"     called the 405 "a deluxe sedan with true sports car performance and handling."

The convertible model provided 405 buyers with true sports car looks as well. The engine used was the same one found in Type 404 Bristols, except that some of the final models had a Type 406 engine.

Standard equipment in the 2,782-lb. drophead coupe included a heater with demister, a windshield washer, leather-trimmed sliding front bucket seats, a four-inch speedometer, a tachometer, and a map reading light.

*In the late 1950s, Bristol offered the 405 series—pictured in a drophead version.*

Ten body colors were offered, including: Reef Blue, Hungarian Green, Copper Beech, Peach, Brown, Torch Red, Midnight Blue, Deep Grey, Ash Grey, Off White, and black. Those were complemented by nine choices of upholstery colors. Major options included a radio and fitted suitcases in the drophead.

With a 189.25-in. overall length, the 405 stood 57.5 in. tall and measured 68 in. wide. The tread measurement was 52.4 in. up front and 54 in. at the rear. Mounted on the 4.5J16 bolt-on disc wheels were either 5.75 x 16 Dunlop or 6.00 x 16 Michelin tires.

The front-engine, rear-drive layout was retained. The drive moved through a floor-shifted four-speed manual transmission. Gear ratios were the same as in the 1954-1957 Type 404 with addition of 0.78:1 overdrive. A 4.22:1 ratio rear axle was used. The steering, suspension and brakes were the same as on earlier models, except that Dunlop front disc brakes were used on the final 405 models. Body construction featured aluminum alloy panels on a steel and laminated ash frame.

# 1958-1961 406

After several years of offering a short-wheelbase coupe and a long-wheelbase saloon (sedan), Bristol switched to a long-wheelbase two-door coupe in 1958. This would be the last Bristol with a BMW-derived in-line six under its hood.

Instead of being a fastback coupe, the Type 406 was a notchback style, with a more modern and conventional appearance. The tailfins were less pronounced and the twin taillights, on each side of the back panel, were mounted in a diagonal pattern. Back-up lights stood alongside the license plate. The quarter windows were considerably larger than those used in the 404. Although the basic grille shape was similar to the 404 and 405 type, the 406 used a brighter pattern of horizontal bars and the nose itself had less of a frontal bulge. Round parking lights were positioned below the single, fender-mounted headlights. The new model tipped the scale at a trifle above 3,009 lbs. and was heavier than earlier Bristols.

While the overhead-valve engine had new 69 x 100-mm bore and stroke dimensions and grew in displacement to 2216 cc, it developed the same 105 hp. However, the power peak came at a lower 4700 rpm range. Bristol advertised 129 lbs.-ft. of torque at 3000 rpm. The engine continued to incorporate solid valve lifters, four main bearings, and triple Solex carburetors.

Half a dozen special 406 models had lightweight coupe bodies built by Zagato. They weighed just 2,469 lbs. Under their bonnets were specially-tuned engines with a 9.0:1 compression ratio that delivered 130 hp at 5750 rpm. Although quite startling in appearance, these rare cars were capable of hitting 125 mph.

Once again, the six-cylinder powerplant drove through a four-speed manual gearbox with overdrive. The suspension was similar to that used on earlier models, except that a Watt linkage was now used to position the rear axle. Disc brakes were also standard at all four wheels.

At 60 in., the body was taller than before and the car's 68 in. width made the interior roomier. Zagato coupes were only 55 in. high and 63 in. wide, which made them tighter fitting inside. The front and rear tread dimensions (53 in. and 56 in.) were larger.

The front fender compartments continued to hold the spare tire, battery, and windshield-washer fluid container. Standard tires were 5.75/6.00 x 16 Dunlops or Michelins or 6.00H-16 Dunlops.

The price for the 406 coupe at the Bristol Aeroplane Company Ltd. factory in Filton, Bristol, England, was $8,386.

The Zagato coupe price was not released, but must have been substantially more. Top speed for the standard Bristol was about 105 mph and, as mentioned above, Zagato coupes were about 20 mph faster.

Production of both the Type 406 coupe and the 406 Zagato coupe continued into 1961. The production total of the coupe was only 292 units in four calendar years, not counting the six Zagatos that were made.

BRISTOL 407 5·2

*automatic transmission—evolved in concert with the power unit—has three forward speeds, selected by illuminated push-buttons on a facia panel. The body of the 407, externally and internally, maintains traditional Bristol standards of general excellence derived from a combination of classical and modern coach-craft techniques. The 407 five-point-two has an elegance and comfort that belie its potential for high-average long-distance travelling with minimum fatigue for driver and passengers. Disc brakes, servo-assisted on all four wheels exemplify the many high-performance component features which, in conjunction with expert use of the finest materials, result in a car of rare quality.*

Wheels on Paper, New Zealand

# 1961-1963 407

Bristol had designed an alternate six to replace the aging BMW derivation, but for cost reasons, went another route. In 1961, the company abandoned the six-cylinder powerplant and turned instead to a Canadian version of the Chrysler "Hemi" V-8. This engine became the heartbeat of the new Type 407—a model introduced during 1961.

Although similar in appearance to the Bristol 406, the 407 got a lower hood line with little of the bulginess that marked the earlier model. A large shield insignia decorated the dark-patterned grille insert, which had a round emblem above it. Body construction on the new car featured aluminum body panels on a steel frame.

**As the 1960s dawned, Bristol took the shapely form of the 407 series.**

The new five-main-bearings power plant was built by Chrysler to meet Bristol's requirements and was somewhat unique. Instead of Chrysler's usual hydraulic valve lifters, this engine had solid lifters. The displacement was unavailable anywhere else in the Chrysler lineup. It had a 98.5 x 84.1-mm bore and stroke, which added up to 5130 cc. With a 9.0:1 compression ratio, it developed 250 hp at 4400 rpm. Torque was rated 340 lbs.-ft. at 2800 rpm. A Carter four-barrel carburetor was used. The enormous horsepower boost made this the fastest, heaviest Bristol yet.

The new power plant drove through a modified, Chrysler-built, three-speed TorqueFlite automatic transmission. A 3.31:1 ratio axle was standard and a 3.07:1 axle was optional. The front and rear brakes were 11.25-in. discs.

At long last, Bristol abandoned the old transverse-spring front suspension, replacing it with a modern arrangement of dual, unequal-length control arms, coil springs, and an anti-roll torsion bar. The advantage of replacing the former rack-and-pinion steering with a Marles cam-and-roller setup was less evident, but much needed with the big, heavy V-8 under the hood.

At the rear was a rigid (live) axle with lateral links, Watts linkage, a Torque link and longitudinal torsion bars.

The 407 retained the traditional 114-in. wheelbase, but grew to 199 in. in overall length. It was 60 in. high, 68 in. wide, and had front and rear tread measurements of 53 in. and 54.5 in., respectively. Dunlop 6.00-H16 tires were mounted on 5K16 wheels.

Tipping the scales at 3,585 lbs., the Bristol 407 had an all-out top speed of 122 mph. It could do 0-to-60 mph in just 9.9 seconds and the quarter mile took 17.4 seconds.

A total of 300 cars were made. During the run of the 407, the Bristol company was sold to Anthony Crook and Sir George White.

# 1963-1965 408

S tyling changed significantly when Bristol replaced the 407 coupe with the 408. The basic type of body construction was unchanged, but the 408 had an entirely different grille with a wide, rectangular shape. It carried horizontal bars and inset driving lights. The grille also tapered forward slightly at the top, giving the car a much more angular appearance.

The Type 408 had rounded rectangular parking lights and signal lights. They were set into flat panels, at the front of the fenders, below the single round headlights. Rather than looking like a short lid, as on prior models, the new flat bonnet extended all the way to the grille.

Stuffed below the bonnet of the majority of 408s was Chrysler of Canada's 313-cid (5130-cc) overhead-valve V-8. It had a 3.88 x 3.31-in. (98.5 x 84.1-mm) bore and stroke, a 9.0:1 compression ratio, five main bearings, solid valve lifters and a Carter four-barrel carburetor. It was rated for 250 hp at 4400 rpm and 340 lbs.-ft. of torque at 2800 rpm. Very late examples of the Type 408 (called Mark 2s) used Chrysler's 318-cid V-8.

Two body side trim strips were used on the Bristol 508, instead of just one, but the lower strip stopped halfway back on the door. The roof

*The Bristol 408 Zagato V-8 featured exotic-looking Italian styling.*

line was also flatter than before. Tall, single taillights resided along the rear edges of the quarter panels, just below little vestiges of tailfins.

The new model carried a $12,000 price tag and weighed in at 3,585 lbs. It was built on a 114-in. wheelbase chassis with an overall body length of 193.5 in. The car stood 59 in. high and was 68 in. wide. Tread measurements were 53 in. up front and 54.5 in. at the rear. Bristol again used 6.00H16 Dunlop tires on 5K16 disc wheels.

The 408 retained Bristol's traditional front-engine, rear-drive layout. Chrysler's three-speed TorqueFlite automatic was used once again. At first, Bristol customers who admired the sophisticated high revving six-cylinder engine and manual gearbox were wary of the V-8 and automatic transmission combination, but one drive was enough to convince the skeptics. A 3.31:1 rear axle was standard. Suspension, steering and brake specifications were about the same as those for the 407.

Production of the 408 coupe continued into 1965.

Andrew Morland

# 1965-1967 409/410/411

The appearance of the Bristol Type 409 changed little from that of the 408 model, but under the hood was a slightly larger 318-cid (5211-cc) Chrysler V-8, sourced from the automaker's Canadian branch. In England, the 409 coupe listed for the equivalent of $11,261, but the Port Of Entry price in the United States was probably well over $12,000.

The 318 continued to use five main bearings, overhead valves, solid valve lifters, and a cast-iron block and cylinder head. It had a 3.91 x 3.31-in. (99.3 x 84.1-mm) bore and stroke. With a 9.0:1 compression ratio and four-barrel Carter carburetor the 318 produced 250 hp at 4400 rpm and 340 lbs.-ft. of torque at 2800 rpm.

Although neither horsepower nor torque got a boost over 313, stronger performance was reported. Bristols were now said to be able to hit 130 mph and break nine seconds in a 0-to-60 mph sprint. Improved weight distribution, with the larger engine sitting farther back in the chassis than its predecessor, may have made a difference. The coupe's shipping weight was 3,527 lbs.

A revised TorqueFlite automatic transmission (now in a lighter weight alloy housing) allowed holding the car in second gear for quicker acceleration. The rear axle ratio was also changed to a standard 3.07:1. Revised springs gave a softer ride. Four-wheel disc brakes continued, but the new ones were supplied by Girling, not Dunlop. A Mark 2 edition of the 409, with power steering, emerged in the fall of 1966.

The Bristol 410 was introduced in 1967 with an at-the-factory price of $11,094. It had a similar appearance to the Type 409, except that the headlights were slightly recessed and no longer shared a flat panel with the rectangular parking and signal lights directly below them. Power steering was standard and air conditioning was optional. Acrylic body paint replaced the former enamel. Both body side trim strips extended nearly the full car length. They met each other at both the front and rear.

Instead of American-style push-button controls for the Chrysler TorqueFlite automatic transmission, a floor-mounted gear shift lever was used.

As before, Girling disc brakes were installed on all four wheels, but the 410's system had two separate circuits for "fail-safe" operation. Suspension modifications improved the Bristol's handling, but retained the former basic layout of front coil springs and rear torsion bars.

*The Bristol 410 two-door saloon was part of the look-alike 409, 410 and 411 series.*

A drop in tire size from a 16- inch to 15-inch diameter also helped handling. Production of the 410 coupe continued into 1969, when it was replaced by the Type 411.

Bristol changed a few details in the early 411, and subsequent editions would change even more in appearance. Only a short upper body side trim strip was used, extending from the front wheel opening, barely halfway along the door. Another tiny strip at the same level ran only a few inches above the rear wheel. Farther down, twin bright strips reached between the front and rear wheels. Both windshield and backlight rake angles became slightly steeper in this version. Vertical tail lamps were similar to prior models, but squared off at the top and bottom, rather than rounded. As before, backup lights stood alongside the license plate.

Except for suspension and drivetrain modification over the years since the 400 was introduced, the basic box-section platform, and squarish body (evolved from a prewar BMW design) had changed remarkably little.

Under the hood, though, came yet another major change: a switch from the 318-cid Chrysler hemi V-8 to a 383-cid Chrysler wedge-head engine. The bigger engine added plenty of horsepower and torque, quickening 0-to-60 mph acceleration time to seven seconds and boosting top speed to near 140 mph.

The 383 cid (6277 cc) had a 4.25 x 3.37-in. (107.9 x 85.7-mm) bore and stroke. The compression ratio was raised to 10.0:1. The new engine was rated for 335 hp at 5200 rpm and 425 lbs.-ft. of torque at 3400 rpm. As usual, the big V-8 drove a Chrysler TorqueFlite three-speed automatic transmission. Size 185VR15 tires were now standard.

While the 411 designation remained through 1976, no less than six variants were sold. A Series 2 version arrived in late 1970, with wider wheels and a self-leveling rear suspension. Then, in 1972, the Series 3 edition sported four big (seven-inch) round headlamps, each pair mounted side by side, instead of the former combinations of headlamps and large driving lamps. The full-width oval grille opening, with a dark squarish insert, encompassed all those headlamps. Amber park/signal light lenses were down in the bumper. Instead of a trim strip along the upper bodyside, a narrow paint stripe ran from the leading edge of the front fender to halfway back along the door. Four exhaust outlets emerged from the back end.

In 1974, came yet another version: the Series 4, with a 400-cid Chrysler V-8 and a restyled rear end. This 6556-cc engine had a 4.34 x 3.375-in. bore and stroke, but compression was lowered to 8.2:1. Its output was rated in net horsepower and net torque, 264 SAE net hp at 4800 rpm and 335 lbs.-ft. at 3600 rpm. Following the Bristol Series 4 came a short-lived Series 5, with little change evident.

OCW Archives

# 1976 and Newer Bristol

The Series 412 four-seat convertible moved Bristol right up to date in 1975. It was styled by Chairman Tony Crook's long-term friend Gianni Zagato and represented a total break with Bristol tradition.

Bristol again used the Chrysler 400-cid V-8. Despite tighter emission regulations, the new car continued to offer 140-mph performance. A huge 22-cu.-ft. trunk and a versatile two-part soft top with massive roll hoop emphasized practicality. The forward and rear top sections could be opened separately. For winter use, a hardtop was available. Frameless windows motored down one inch electrically to allow the doors to open—a Bristol innovation that has since been copied by many others. The 412 retained its predecessor's exceptional roadability and *Motor* magazine wrote, "The result is handling that belies the car's size and compares favourably with any car in the World."

By 1976, a series of fuel crises prompted Bristol to replace the 400-cid Chrysler V-8 with the lighter 312- and 360-cid small-block V-8 in the 412 Series 2 model. What the car lost in performance (which wasn't much) was more than made up for in improved handling and fuel efficiency.

The last Bristol styled by long-term chief stylist Dudley Hobbs, the 603 also appeared in 1976 as an update on the four-seat theme. Using the lighter 312-cid Chrysler V-8, it introduced a thoroughly modern exterior and interior design that improved passenger accommodations. To maximize fuel economy, a two-barrel carburetor was used, along with an economy low-stall torque converter.

For Bristol customers who valued power above economy (which was most of them), the 603S sported a performance four-barrel

*This blue Bristol 600 looks great, even on a rainy British day.*

carburetor, a larger 360-cid Chrysler V-8 and a high-performance torque converter. As had become a Bristol tradition, it offered shock absorbers that were adjustable to suit the owner's taste.

The 603S offered the silence and comfort of a Rolls Royce with the performance of a contemporary Aston Martin. As on the "E" model, air conditioning was standard, along with electrically-adjustable front seats. The hand-brake enjoyed its own separate calipers and a self-leveling suspension was standard at the rear.

The 412 and the 603 models were further improved over time, retaining their calm, dignified exteriors, while including such exciting models as the turbocharged Brigand and Beaufighter, the fastest accelerating four-seaters in the world at the time.

Current Bristols—like the Blenheim 3 and Blenheim 3 "S" —continue to provide the company's hallmark mix of dignified, aerodynamically superior coachwork, aluminum hand-made body work, exceptional finish, and cosseting luxury, combined with remarkable performance, roadholding and handling capabilities.

In 2001, the first of the company's new two-seater Fighter models was delivered. This supercar featured a 525-hp V-10 and could do over 200 mph.

Its performance capabilities were combined with a stunning aerodynamic body and gullwing doors. All Bristols are built to order and no more than 150 are sold worldwide each year to ensure exclusivity.

# CONNAUGHT

Jason Wenig/ The Creative Workshop

## 1948-1956 Connaught

Known mainly for race cars, the Connaught Engineering (Continental Cars Ltd). was located in Send, Surrey, England. The firm produced a handful of sports roadsters in the late 1940s and early 1950s. Connaughts were actually created by Rodney Clarke, who was well known as a race driver and Bugatti owner. Early examples were raced by Clarke himself, along with Kenneth McAlpine. Chief draftsman C. E. "Johnny" Johnson also played an important role in the Connaught's development.

Building Connaught sports cars was a parallel story of exciting car development and constantly struggling to find financial backing. Lack of corporate support led to the demise of the Connaught. The last Connaughts were built for racing only. By 1957 even that end of the business was abandoned, although the very last car wasn't completed until two years later.

The Connaught used an aluminum alloy body on a tubular steel frame. Like many low-production sports cars, it was available with a choice of engine tunes. Early in its production, Connaught used the "Iron" Lea-Francis four-cylinder engine and later used both the 2.0 litre aluminum Lea-Francis and, later, the 2.5 litre Alta engine late in the Connaught's production lifespan. Lea-Francis engines were extensively modified as they were turned into Connaught power plants.

For example, they were usually converted to dry sump lubrication and used four Amal carburetors. In some cases, Hilborn fuel injection systems were attached instead. When the engines were modified to Connaught specifications, they produced 6,000 rpm.

The Connaught-modified, three-main-bearings, 1767-cc Lea-Francis four-cylinder engine was tuned to deliver much more than its original 70-hp.

The Lea-Francis engine was an overhead-valve, in-line four with solid lifters and a 75 x 100-mm bore and stroke. Connaught's standard-tune job had an 8.5:1 compression ratio. The hottest version of the engine had a 9.5:1 compression ratio and 140 hp – twice its original output.

*Connaughts were created by British race car driver Rodney Clark.*

The Connaught street cars had traditional front-engine rear-drive chassis layout and a 99-in. wheelbase. They were 147 in. long and 59.5 in. wide and had a maximum tread width of 52.5 in. A 4.55:1 ratio rear axle was used. Early cars had semi-elliptic leaf springs up front, but parallel wishbones and independent torsion bars were used beginning in 1951, when chassis supplier Lea-Francis changed its system. At the rear was a de Dion suspension and driveline system. Hydraulic drum brakes were fitted front and rear. Size: 6.00 x 16 tires were standard.

Some Connaughts, like the L3 and B series had faired-in headlights while many sported cycle fenders. A small horizontal oval grille was used with a trim strip extending back along the hood from the grille's center. The entire front end (hood, fenders, etc.) hinged forward for engine access. The basic car weighed just 2,165 lbs. An unusual design feature of the Connaught A series was the so-called "McGuffin box," an air intake and carburetor enclosure on the right side of the cars.

The Connaught sports/racing car debuted at the Silverstone racecourse in June 1949. The first road-going model appeared in the following year. As reported in *Motor Trend* late in 1950, Connaughts were "hand finished, one at a time." The magazine called the roadster a "thoroughbred machine."

In 1955, Tony Brooks raced a B series Connaught to victory in the Syracuse Grand Prix. It was a first for a British racing team and created a lot of attention, especially since the British beat a team of Maseratis. Even this impressive Grand Prix win couldn't convince corporations to back the Connaught cars.

Approximately 27 Connaughts were produced from 1949-1953. The hottest of these cars had a top speed in excess of 122 mph. Models included the A, B, and L Series as well as the AL, L3/SR, and the AL/SR. The "SR" stood for "Sports Racer."

# DAIMLER

Andrew Morland

# 1954-'55 Conquest Roadster

P erhaps best known for stately and dignified motorcars in the early postwar years—including limousines built for the British royal family—the Daimler has a long and notable history that reaches back to the earliest motorcars.

Gottlieb Daimler, a German, was one of the early developers of the internal combustion engine for automotive use. As early as 1888, Frederick Simms purchased the rights to that engine, intended for marine applications in Great Britain. Horseless carriages followed in 1896, leading to a broad line of Daimler examples that were built at the company's plant in Coventry, England.

Daimler produced the first British-built four-cylinder automobile in 1899. Over the next 15 years, until the beginning of World War, Daimer issued more than 40 different models. Royal patronage began at the turn of the century.

King Edward VII, an early motoring fan, took a particular liking to Daimlers. Many engineers who went on to careers at other firms learned their trade at the Daimler works. In 1910, Daimler was purchased by Birmingham Small Arms Company (BSA), a name that would later establish itself in the motorcycle arena and would build their own line of cars until 1939.

By the 1920s, Daimler had a long-established reputation for quiet, elegant and refined motorcars. In addition to four- and six-cylinder models, the company turned out a Double-Six chassis in the late 1920s.

It carried low-slung Park Ward coachwork and was powered by a 7-liter, 150-hp sleeve-valve V-12. Other smaller-displacement Daimler V-12s also used the sleeve-valve configuration. Daimler was among the first automakers to adopt the Wilson self-shifting transmission, with preselector and fluid coupling, making it standard in 1932. A year

*A 1956 Daimler Conquest roadster—the sports car of British royalty.*

earlier, Lanchester had joined with Daimler to produce lower-priced family cars as a complement to the posh limousines and saloons. Sleeve valves gave way to overhead-valve powerplants by 1936, including a series of straight eights. A few examples in the 1930s were of a more sporting nature, some wearing rather dramatic coachwork.

A simpler model lineup emerged after World War II, starting with the expected saloons (sedans) and limousines, powered by in-line six- and eight-cylinder engines. In 1954, came something completely different—the Conquest roadster. Rakish, tail-finned and wearing cut-down doors, the Conquest served as a startling companion to the more sedate Daimler models.

When the first Conquest—a saloon (or four-door sedan)—arrived in 1952, its announcement was timed to coincide with the Coronation of Queen Elizabeth II. The model name suggested something different about the newest Daimler, but it wasn't until the roadster version arrived, in 1954, that the extent of change was really evident. Described as "an entirely new concept in motoring," the new roadster had conventional Daimler styling up front, but a sharply wraparound windshield, cut-down doors, cut-away rear-fender openings, a long rear end, and tacked-on-looking tailfins. The open two-seater was intended to appeal to younger, more sport-minded customers, whereas Daimlers in general were targeted at the affluent elderly.

A 2.5-liter 100-hp "high-speed" six-cylinder engine provided the power. Like other Daimlers, the Conquest roadster used the familiar Daimler preselector gearbox. The desired gear was selected in advanced by moving a small lever on the steering column. Then, as the clutch pedal was depressed, the gears shifted automatically. Standard roadster colors were Red with Cream upholstery, Ivory with Red upholstery, Silver with Blue upholstery, and Powder Blue with Red upholstery. The roadster had a folding top, side curtains, a leather-covered instrument panel, chrome fittings, leather seat upholstery, and full-width door pockets. Fog lamps mounted on the front fender apron were available. The roadster's top speed was a bit in excess of 100 mph.

Under the roadster's bonnet was a special version of the Conquest saloon's overhead-valve, in-line six. It had the same 76.2 x 88.8-mm bore and stroke and 2433-cc displacement, but the compression ratio was changed from 6.6:1 to 7.75:1 and it had twin S.U. carbs, rather than a single carburetor. As opposed to the saloon's 75 hp, the roadster produced 100 hp at 4600 rpm. It had four main bearings and solid valve lifters.

Perched on a modest (for Daimler) 104-in. wheelbase, the Conquest stretched 177 in. bumper-to-bumper. At 55 in., the roadster was 10 in. lower than the saloon. It was also a half inch wider (66 in.) A 52-in. tread width was used front and rear. The standard 6.70 x 15 tires were mounted on bolt-on disc wheels.

The front-engine, rear-drive roadster's overall gear ratios were 14.32:1 in first, 8.24:1 in second, 5.48:1 in third, 3.73:1 in fourth, and 19.43:1 in reverse. A 3.73:1 rear axle was used on the open version only. The steering system was of the cam gear type. Up front were laminated torsion bars, with a rigid axle and semi-elliptic leaf-type rear springs. Daimler-Girling hydromechanical drum brakes were used.

With a top speed of just over 100 mph, the roadster was a fast car in its day. It could accelerate from 0-to-50 mph in 10.6 seconds and it covered the quarter-mile in 20.3 seconds. Motor Trend reported that the Conquest roadster was designed and built in just six weeks. Part of Daimler's purpose for introducing the roadster was to attempt to capture a few more sales in the United States.

In 1955, a hotter Century model joined the basic Conquest saloon. It was powered by the same 100-bhp version of the 2433-cc six-cylinder engine used in the roadster. A drophead coupe (with conventional doors rather than the roadster's cutdown design) was also continued and a fixed-head (hardtop) variant of the roadster also became available later.

The 1955 instrument panel had inlaid woodwork. The upright curved vertical-bar grille had a broad, bright surround molding. Built-in headlights stood at the front fender tips, with the parking lights mounted in long housings atop the fenders. As before, the roadster had a sharply-curved wraparound windshield with a thin framework and prominent tail fins. Approximate prices at the factory in England were $3,000 for the Conquest and $3,316 for the Conquest Century.

Dramatic it may have been, but the Conquest roadster lasted for less than two seasons or so in the Daimler lineup. The model was dropped before the 1956 model year began.

# 1956-1957 Conquest Drophead

The dramatic Conquest roadster was dropped after 1955, but Daimler offered a drophead coupe with a similar profile and made it available into 1957. Both 75- and 100-hp versions of the 2.5-liter six-cylinder engine were available in this regal ragtop. A third passenger could sit sideways, in the rear seat, while front passengers had bucket seats. Standard equipment included a leather-covered instrument panel with a tachometer, plus genuine leather upholstery.

Factory prices in 1956 were about $2,985 for the Conquest saloon, $3,282 for the Conquest Century, $5,278 for the 104, $6,420 for the 4.5-liter, and $7,820 for the DK400 limousine. The drophead coupe was a fairly hefty machine that weighed in at 3,150 lbs.

The 2433-cc overhead-valve in-line six used in the drophead coupe was shared with the Century model only. It had a 7.75:1 compression ratio and dual S.U.s. This engine was rated for 100 hp at 4400 rpm and 130 lbs.-ft. of torque at 2500 rpm.

Buyers could substitute the base version of the same power plant, which had a 7.0:1 compression ratio. It generated a lower 75 hp at 4000 rpm and 124 lbs.-ft. of torque at 2000 rpm.

Like the roadster, the drophead coupe was on a 114-in. wheelbase. Overall length was 178 in. It was slightly lower and wider than the closed cars. Cars with the base engine topped out at around 81-88 mph, but those with the Century six could do over 90 mph.

An automatic transmission became available for the first time for the 1957 model year, but the traditional preselector gearbox and fluid transmission also remained available. Otherwise, changes were minimal.

Andrew Morland

# 1959-1964 SP250

"Nimble as a kitten in town traffic, yet the highway is the true domain of the SP250," said Daimler's sales pitch for a rather unique new model. "With the exhilaration of its power, you get the confidence of feather light handling, positive disc braking and impeccable cornering."

The full-fledged sports car—the Daimler SP250— was announced in 1959, initially under another name. The powerful, V-8-engined roadster lasted through 1964, even though Jaguar—which was also headquartered in Coventry, England—took over the Daimler Company Ltd., during 1960.

While most Daimlers would soon become badge-engineered versions of the Jaguar XJ6, XJ12 and Mk X, the SP250 remained a real Daimler until its demise in 1964. The last true Daimlers were built three years later. By 1983, the Daimler name was no longer even used, except in Great Britain.

In 1959, Daimler surprised many people by veering from its traditional big saloons (sedans) and limousines and turning to a two-seat sports car. Appearing at the New York Auto Show in spring 1959 (suggesting the car's major target market of American sports-car fans), the two-seater was initially called the Dart.

Since Chrysler's Dodge Division happened to be introducing a new compact with the same name at about the same time, threats of legal action caused Daimler to adopt the SP250 monniker.

The SP250 was certainly distinctive looking. Styling features of the low front end included a prominent "V" as part of the grille. It was set in front of an insert with a crosshatch (eggcrate) pattern. The front fenders had a swooping shape and the domed hood tapered down between the protruding headlights. Heavily-sculptured body lines were evident on the rear fenders, which had pronounced fins.

The SP250 had a fluted, wide-oval grille and flaunting rear tail fins. Its fiberglass body was a first for Daimler. Standard colors were Jet Black, Royal Red, Racing Green, and Ivory. The upholstery was done in tan leather. Wind-up side windows were installed, while the quickly-erected fabric top had transparent quarter windows.

*Photographer Andrew Morland is the proud owner of this 1964 Daimler SP250.*

Adjustable front bucket seats wore genuine cowhide trim. The padded control panel contained large, quickly-read instruments. A short, rapid-shift type gear lever worked the four-speed transmission, which was synchronized on the top three ratios (with provision for optional overdrive). Standard equipment included a tachometer, an ashtray, a lockable glove box, and a full-width front bumper.

To a large degree, the SP250 was an evolution of the earlier Conquest roadster, but it probably wouldn't have come about if not for the development of Edward Turner's new V-8 engine. Turner, a BSA motorcycle designer who'd become Daimler's managing director in 1957, created a compact 2548-cc overhead-valve V-8 that featured a motorcycle-like valve configuration and hemispherical combustion chambers. It produced 140 hp at 5800 rpm and 155 lbs.-ft. of torque at 3600 rpm. That was far more torque than any other Daimler engine ever offered. The five-main-bearings power plant had solid valve lifters and twin Model HD6 S.U. carburetors.

The car's four-speed manual gearbox was similar to that used in the Triumph TR3A with overall gear ratios of 10.49:1 in first, 6.24:1 in second, 4.41:1 in third, and 3.48:1 on fourth. Second thru fourth gears were synchronized. Overdrive and automatic transmissions were available options. The gearbox was linked to a 3.58:1 ratio hypoid-bevel rear axle carried by semi-elliptic leaf springs.

A separate steel chassis, similar to that of the Triumph TR3A, supported the SP250's fiberglass coachwork. The chassis had a 92-in. wheelbase and 160.5-in. overall length. The car was 50.25 in. high and 60.5 in. wide. A 50-in. tread was used up front and the rear track was two inches narrower. The press steel disc wheels held standard 5.90 x 15 tires, but narrower 5.50 x 15 rubber was optional.

Cam-type steering was featured. The TR3A-type suspension used long/short control arms with coil springs up front and the rigid axle with semi-elliptic leaf springs at the rear. Four-wheel Girling disc brakes handled the stopping chores.

The SP250 was introduced at a price of $3,900. It had a 2,900-lb. curb weight. Port-of-Entry prices in the United States soon fell to $3,702 (or $4,075 for a hardtop model). Later, the tarriff rose to $3,995 and $4,245, respectively. Some early SP250 bodies were prone to overflexing. Nevertheless, the car was fast. It could do 120 mph and was able to hit 60 mph in about 10 seconds.

Major options included a detachable hardtop, overdrive, and a Borg-Warner automatic transmission. Five knock-on wire wheels sold for $100. Ace disc wheels for the standard bolt-on wheels were another extra. Whitewall tires added $50.

Also available was an ajustable steering column, a leather-covered steering wheel, a front bumper, a rear bumper (in place of standard twin overriders), a tonneau cover, a reserve gas tank and switch, a heater and demister, a cigar lighter, windshield washers, exhaust pipe finishers (extensions), fog lamps, passing lamps, a badge bar, a fan cowl (for tropical conditions), twin safety belts, a trickle-charger socket, a radio (and antenna), and fender mirrors.

The SP250 had a top speed of 120-123 mph. Accelerating from 0-to-60 mph took 9.7-11 seconds. The driver could reach 100 mph, from a standing start, in just 28.9 seconds. The quarter mile required 17.8 to 18.2 seconds.

Daimler's sales of two-seater cars never approached anticipated levels and the SP250 never turned a profit.

A restyling was proposed, but abandoned. Two improved SP250s were built, with little appearance change.

In 1961, the "B-Specification" was phased in. It came with with standard equipment that was formerly optional (heater, bumpers, adjustable steering column). It also had a stiffer body.

A subsequent "C-Spec" car, appearing two years later, added a heater and trickle-charger socket as standard equipment.

A small number of later model SP250s had a fixed hardtop.

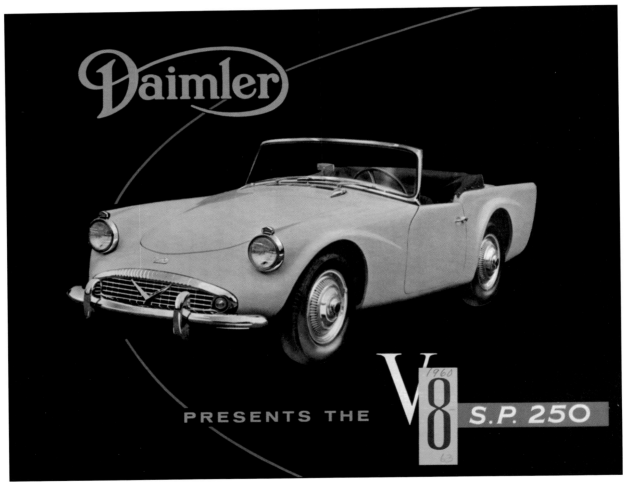

*Daimler history is linked with the SP250 in this brochure.*

# DELLOW

Bob Harrington

# 1947-1959 Dellow

Named after highly successful British sporting trial drivers K.C. Delingpole and R.B. Lowe, this car came out in 1947, but was practically unknown in the United States until the mid-1950s. The Dellow was designed specifically for sporting car trials--competitive events that take place in rough-terrain areas. Trial drivers try to drive up hilly, marked courses. The driver attempts to complete the course without hitting marker poles, stopping or traveling outside course boundaries.

The winner has the least marks scored against him or her. Each car has a driver and a "bouncer" (passenger)--a navigator and who moves his or her body weight to maintain traction. Usually, the events are run on private lands by local car clubs.

To be successful, trials cars must have exceptional maneuverability, good traction, high ground clearance and good low-to-mid-range torque. The Dellow—which one publication described as "a cross between a spritely four-wheeled car and a kangaroo"—was well suited to its purpose.

Delingpole, owned Delson and Company, a bolt, screw and fastener manufacturer. Their race tuning and sports car preparations soon became more prominent, as did their Wade-Ventor supercharger agency. And they sold H. R. G. sports cars, which Delingpole enjoyed driving.

The trial car, built by Dellow Motors Ltd. of Alvechurch, Birmingham, was largely designed around British Ford components. The first dozen cars actually were converted Ford Tens. Those 12 cars represented about 10 percent of Dellow's total annual production.

The original two-seater Dellow Mk I had a short 84-in. wheelbase and a 31-hp engine. The Mk I, produced for less than a year, had a definite prewar appearance with separate headlights and a split-oval

## Advertising called owners "Dellow Fellows." They enjoy racing the 1952 Mk IIM.

upright grille. Narrow, large-diameter 4.50 x 17 tires gave the car the high ground clearance it needed to avoid pounding the chassis in the "off-road" trial excursions.

Under the bonnet was Ford's 1172-cc in-line, L-head four with a 63.5 x 92.5-mm bore and stroke. It came standard with a 6.16:1 compression ratio and was rated for 31 hp at 4200 rpm. The engine used solid valve lifters and a single S.U. carburetor.

The Mk I was 136 in. long, 55 in. wide and had a 45-in. track at both ends. A 5.5:1 ratio rear axle was used. An A-shaped tubular chassis used quarter-elliptic leaf springs in the suspension, but Dellow later switched to coil springs. Bodies were aluminum alloy.

Early Dellow buyers provided their own parts, which were reconditioned and used to build their car. By 1950, Ford components were used.

An "A" version of the Mk II Dellow debuted in mid-1951, followed by a "B" edition in 1953. The Mk II had a slightly shorter wheelbase and 16-inch tires were substituted for the earlier 17 inch type. The rear suspension was changed to coil springs.

The English auto magazine *The Motor* described the Mark II Dellow as a "sporting marque with an excellent competition record." Dellow also introduced a four-seat Mk III mounted on a longer 94.5-inch wheelbase with coachwork by Radpanels Ltd. They built a Mark IV prototype powered by a 1508-cc engine.

Specifications for the four-place car were similar to the two seat

Mk II. In 1953, English prices for Dellow models were 448 pounds for the Mark II and 498 pounds for the Mark III. A desirable option for both models was a Marshall-Nordec supercharger. A combination of 5.00 x 16 or 5.50 x 16 tires was used.

The next version was the Mk IIC, which had a stronger engine, but looked similar to the earlier "A" and "B" models. The four-seat Mk III also continued in production through 1954. In mid-1954, a new Mark V joined the original Dellow. It was more rounded in appearance and sported an oval grille.

The Mk V featured faired-in front fenders that appeared almost cycle-like, adding to its racing-car look. Headlights were mounted separately and the doors were hinged at the front. The body extended almost in a horizontal plane and was unable to carry spare tires like its predecessor.

A vast choice of body colors was available on Mk Vs, including British Racing Green. The semi-bucket seats were upholstered in leather and had a solid (single) backrest. Turn signal lights were standard. The Mk V instrument panel held a tachometer and speedometer. The canvas top incorporated a Plexiglas wraparound back window. The Mk V Dellow carried the more potent 36-hp version of the British Ford engine with a 7.6:1 compression ratio and twin S.U. carburettors. "It's really a man's car," declared *Motor Trend*, one that "doesn't give a hoot for styling trophies."

The magazine added that a Dellow was: "...really a small hairy beast that is at its best charging thru woods, over hills and across swamps." And it added: "...driving a Dellow is more like wearing a car than sitting inside one."

Advertising showed a smiling cartoon character in a semi-airborne Dellow climbing a hill with the heading: "The Fellow in the Dellow."

The Mk V was larger than the Mk I/Mk II style cars. It had an 84-in. wheelbase and a 140-in. length, while the height, width and front and rear track all measured 54 in. Coil springs were used in both the front and rear suspensions. Mechanical brakes and a three-speed floor-mounted gear shifter were used.

The first Dellow to reach the American market—a Mk II model — arrived in 1954. According to *Motorsport* magazine, it wound up with an employee of Republic Aviation. "Dellow is a driver's car," the magazine said, noting that it delivered "somewhat the same sort of enjoyment that the first ride in the old MG TC provided," while "handling and roadability was much like the Morgan . . . cornering at high speeds is phenomenally flat and precise."

Most Dellows exported to the U.S. and other countries had the same size tires front and rear, as well as left-hand drive. Only about a dozen Dellows made it to the U.S. between mid-1955 and mid-1956. One of the first cars brought into the U.S. was raced. Dellow importer Alec Tarpinian came close to winning the 1.5-liter hill climb at Manchester, New Hampshire. Dellows were imported by London Motors of Edgemere, Long Island, New York and Light Car Motors of Los Angeles, California.

Top speed for a Dellow Mk II was 70-80 mph, while the Mk V could hit 89 mph. The lower-powered model took 13.7 seconds to hit 60 mph from a standing start, while the Mk V did 0-to-50 mph in 13.3 seconds. A Rootes-type supercharger was available.

By 1956, the company name had changed from Dellow Motors Ltd. to Dellow Engineering Ltd. The final Mark VI model carried a $2,050 price tag and featured a full-width fiberglass body, a split windshield and all-weather gear. This 1,300-lb. car rode on smaller 13-in. wheels. Standard and Stage 1 (high-tune) versions of the Ford four-cylinder engine were offered. Production of the "C" version of the Mk II also continued into 1957. It was priced at $1,900.

The Dellow marque disappeared in 1959. The company was a victim of its desire to produce the sophisticated Mark VI rather than sticking with the original scheme of a specialized trials car.

*The silver Dellow Mk V-B flashes its form as it competes in its racing class.*

# DORETTI

Andrew Morland

# 1954-1959 Doretti

I n 1935, Sir William Lyons, head of the Swallow Coachbuilding Company, in Walsall, Staffordshire, England, founded Jaguar's predecessor . . . SS Cars Ltd. Swallow Coachbuilding Company then turned to making motorcycle sidecars.

Following World War II, the firm came under new ownership and switched to aircraft work. Its sidecar operation was taken over by another company called Tube Investments Ltd. The success of the Standard-Triumph Motor Company, Ltd.'s TR2 sports car, after its 1952 debut, prompted Swallow to take a stab at the sports-car market. It was aiming especially at American customers who were buying sports roadsters. Before making the Doretti, Swallow actually produced sporty versions of the Austin Seven and Wolseley Hornet production cars.

The $3,295 Doretti—the name was inspired by a daughter of Triumph's American importer, who was actually named Dorothy—was announced in January 1954. The Port of Entry price was later cut to $2,980 with wire wheels or $2,905 with disc wheels. Though differing considerably in appearance from the TR2, it carried a conventional Triumph engine, gearbox and front suspension.

Sitting atop a box-section tubular steel chassis, the two-seat roadster's flat-sided twin-skin body consisted of steel inner panels and doors and an aluminum alloy outer shell. The conventional body styling included fully rounded wheel openings and a lid-type front-hinged hood. The rectangular grille opening, slightly rounded at the top, contained five horizontal bars with a bright surround molding.

Small round parking lights stood directly below the headlights. A horizontal body side trim crease ran along the cowl and onto the doors (extending to a point near the doors' trailing edges). The doors were taller than those on the TR2, eliminating the "wind whipping"

*Swallow Doretti owners are proud of their well-designed, classic roadsters.*

associated with that model.

Leather upholstery, carpeting and a punched-aluminum steering wheel with a laminated wood rim were found inside the Doretti. A set of instruments and controls were symmetrically mounted in the center of the dashboard, but the speedometer sat ahead of the passenger. A laced-on leather cover trimmed the padded dashboard and continued over the door tops. A removable strapped-in suitcase on a shelf behind the seats matched the seat upholstery and could hold at least a change of clothing.

Standard equipment on the Doretti included side curtains, a tonneau cover and a heater. Most examples shipped to the U.S. had optional wire wheels mounted in place of the standard disc wheels. For competition use, aero-type screens could be ordered in place of the detachable windshield. Bumper overriders were added for 1955.

A four-speed manual gearbox and a hydraulic clutch were standard equipment. Overdrive (operating on fourth gear only) was a $145 option. The 1991-cc Triumph in-line, overhead-valve four had an 83 x 92-mm bore and stroke. It produced 90 hp at 4800 rpm. The three-main-bearings, solid-lifter engine ran an 8.5:1 compression ratio and carried twin S.U. carburetors. Top speed was over 100 mph and 75-90 mph was a typical touring speed. The Doretti—or Swallow Doretti—could accelerate from 0-to-60 mph in 13.7 seconds and run through the quarter mile in 19.2 seconds at 72 mph.

Perched on a 95-in. wheelbase, the Doretti measured 156 in. from bumper to bumper. The car stood 48.5 in. high and was 61 in. wide.

Its maximum tread width was 48 in. Disc wheels with hubcaps and 5.50 x 15 tires were standard. A 3.7:1 ratio rear axle was used. Swallow relied on wishbones and coil springs up front, with a rigid axle and semi-elliptic leaf springs at the rear. Lockheed hydraulic drum brakes appeared front and rear.

Triumph ads in U.S. publications during 1954 advised readers to see and test drive the fabulous new Doretti. An American sales brochure promised "elegance without peer . . . A hand-finished car, in the aristocratic tradition."

That same year, Walt Woron of *Motor Trend* noted that few cars tested by that magazine had "created as much interest or drawn so much attention as the new Doretti."

Dorettis were produced through 1955 (followed by about 16 built after the factory closed). Production continued until at least as late as 1958 and total output even included one or two coupes. In the United States, Dorettis were distributed by Standard-Triumph Motor Co., Ltd., of New York City, Cal-Sales, Inc., of Gardena, California and Southeastern Motors, Inc., of Hollywood, Florida. Unfortunately, sales never took off, partly because of the car's high price.

Some experts claim the Doretti was heavier and slower than a TR2 and others (especially in America) insist it was quicker. A serious injury to company head Sir John Black, while he was at the wheel of a Doretti, contributed to the car's demise. In 1956, the company was sold and the limited-production roadsters were soon forgotten.

*This Swallow Doretti is the 112th produced and can be found in Caldwell, Idaho.*

*The Doretti crest found on Bob Carpenter's car.*

# ELVA COURIER

Bob Harrington

## 1958-1966 Elva Courier

The name of the British-built Elva Courier had French and Spanish origins. Builder Frank Nichols took it from "Elle va," meaning "she goes." "Go" is what Elva did, both on the track and on the street. Couriers became popular in the United States, and intial sales were limited to exports only. Even before the Courier arrived, the Elva was: "...better known in the U.S. than in Europe," according to *Sportscar Quarterly*.

Race driver Nichols, who'd handled Ford Special and Lotus cars, finished his first Elva sports-racer early in 1955. Built from scratch without blueprints, it sold immediately. Powering the car was a 1072-cc English Ford engine with an overhead-valve conversion and Standard suspension.

Observers noticed the Elva at its first race and Nichols quickly formed Elva Engineering Co. Ltd. at Bexhill-on-Sea, Sussex, England, to produce duplicates called Mark Is. The prototype Mk I used a rigid Austin A35 rear axle and a Wolseley engine. A subsequent Mark 1B switched to a wishbone-style front suspension. Next was the Mark II, which carried a De Dion rear end. A Coventry Climax engine replaced the Ford engine.

A string of wins by an Elva in the United States built up domestic interest in the Elva. American sales success helped Elva finance a new factory to turn its own parts for subsequent cars. American Elva distributors included Continental Motors Ltd., in Washington, D.C. and Southwestern Motors, in San Diego, California.

The Courier was Elva's first streetable car. It arrived in 1958, the result of a suggestion from the car's main American importer. The first version was the $2,745 Mark I, followed by the Mark II, which sold for $2,895. The Courier could be driven on the street and raced on weekends. The streamlined two-seat fiberglass body had a full-width windshield and wraparound bumpers. A simple air intake between the bumper segments served as a rudimentary grille. No door handles were evident. The body had squared-off rear wheel openings. It had leather bucket seats.

Couriers used the MGA (British Motor Corporation's standard four-cylinder), transmission, and rear axle. The three-main-bearings

*Elvas are best remembered for their competitive presence on race courses.*

engine was an in-line four with overhead valves. It had a 73 x 88.9-mm bore and stroke and 1489 cc's of displacement. With an 8.3:1 compression ratio and twin S.U. carburettors it developed 72 hp at 5500 rpm and 77.4 lbs.-ft. of torque at 3500 rpm. A 1588-cc variant with a 75.4 x 88.9-mm bore and stroke was used in the Mark II.

The Courier had a 90-in. wheelbase, was 154 in. long, 46 in. high and 59.5 in. wide. The front tread was 50.3 in. and the rear tread was 50 in. Standard tires were 5.20x14s. The Courier used a ladder-type frame, unlike the racing Elvas. The front suspension, with twin tubular wishbones, Woodhead-Monroe coil springs, and Armstrong shocks all came from the Triumph 10.

The transmission was a four-speed manual with overall gear ratios of 13.2:1 in first, 8.6:1 in second, 5.6:1 in third and 4.6:1 in fourth. It drove to a 3.73:1 rear axle. Steering was rack and pinion. At the rear was a rigid axle with twin parallel trailing arms, a track bar and leaf springs. Lockheed drum brakes were used all around.

*Road & Track* described the Courier's ride as "definitely firm." The engine was mounted low and far to the rear, giving 50/50 weight distribution and a low hood. Ground clearance was under four inches, but the high rear end allowed a fair amount of luggage room.

"Despite its scalding performance," said *Sports Cars Illustrated*, "the Elva is perfectly suited to normal every-day driving." Its engine "is lightly stressed and therefore non-temperamental." Top speed was in the 97 to 105 mph range, 0-to-60 mph could be achieved in nine to 12.4 seconds and the quarter mile could be covered in 18.2 to 19.9 seccends.

Elva continued to sell a competition model that used the 1100-cc Coventry Climax engine. Archie Scott-Brown used it to set a new class record at Brands Hatch and won several American events. This Mark 3 had a cut-down, wraparound windshield flowing into tiny door windows (with curved upper edges), and a huge hump behind the driver. Viewed as a Lotus rival, its streamlined body had a small unadorned grille opening at the end of a long protruding nose. The front suspension was Triumph TR, while the rear end was a De Dion type with coil springs. The aluminum body rode a light tubular space frame. Under the racing car's bonnet was the 83-hp Coventry Climax engine, which gave a top speed of about 130 mph.

For the Mark 4 competition model, Elva swapped the De Dion axle for a fully independent rear suspension with swing axle, coil springs and transverse radius arms. The Coventry Climax engine sat farther back in the chassis. The Mark 4 sold for $5,875 and weighed just 810 lbs.

Quite a few Couriers raced, including one driven by Mark Donohue, who later became a champion at Indy and elsewhere. A Mk 5 competition model replaced the Mk 4 in 1959. In 1961, Elva's managing director announced the company had built 140 front-engine Formula Junior single-seaters, with BMC or Auto Union engines. About 80 of those were exported to the U.S.

Unfortunately, the main American importer didn't pay off all the loans he'd taken out to buy cars. At times, he offered customers free service, so their cars would be in the dealership when the bank auditors visited. Eventually, he went to prison without paying for the cars he'd accepted. Elva founder, Frank Nichols, put the company into liquidation in 1961. After the original company folded, Elva Cars Ltd. was formed that same year to continue race car production. Couriers were turned out by Trojan Ltd., of Croydon, Surrey, best known for their Heinkel-powered three-wheeled vehicles.

A Mark III edition appeared late in 1962 in both a fixed-head coupe with reverse-angled back window and open two-seater forms. In 1962, the open sports model was 701 pounds and the coupe was 723 pounds. In England, both were available in kit form. Power came from the BMC four, then a 76.2 x 88.9-mm bore and stroke and 1622-cc cylinder displacement. This larger engine ran an 8.9:1 compression ratio, developed 90 hp at 5000 rpm and 105 lbs.-ft. of torque at 3000 rpm. Twin S.U. carburettors were fitted.

The final Mark IV Elva Courier had an independent rear suspension. Inboard rear disc brakes were added in 1963. The T Type Spyder (roadster) wore a low, tightly-crosshatched, wide oval grille and recessed headlamps. Exposed front hinges were used for the hood. The roadster also had wind-up windows. Some testers complained about difficulty erecting the soft top and the extreme offset of the car's pedals.

Power came from a 1.8-liter MG or 1.5-liter Ford Cortina GT engine. Both were overhead-valve, in-line fours with solid valve lifters. The three-main-bearings MG motor had an 80 x 88.9-mm bore and stroke and 1798-cc displacement With 8.8:1 compression and twin S.U.s, it gave 98 hp at 5400 rpm and 110 lbs.-ft. of torque at 3000 rpm. The Ford engine had five mains, an 81 x 73-mm bore and stroke, 1498 ccs and 9.0:1 compression, but only 83.5 hp at 5200 rpm and 97 lbs.-ft. of torque at 3600 rpm. One two-barrel Weber carburettor was fitted. A tuned Ford-Cosworth engine also was available.

A Mark III ad noted it "Goes to 105 mph . . . eagerly, sleekly, safely." *Popular Imported Cars* recommended a Mk IV Courier for those who "yearn for…sports cars…as suntan specials with…hot acceleration, steering you had to pay attention to and a pleasant exhaust boom."

When Trojan Ltd. took over Courier in 1962, Nichols focused on race cars. These included a Mk 6, Mk 7 (available with Cosworth-Ford engines) and Mk 8 (with engines from 1.0 to 2.0 liters, the latter from BMW and Porsche). The 160XS was a roadgoing version of the Mk 8 racer, but only three were built in 1964. The GT160 prototype had hidden headlights and a 185-hp engine. Two interesting Elvas were considered in 1964. The Elva Sebring, based on a Sebring racing version, had a 140-hp engine, light chassis, and wide magnesium alloy wheels. Only five were reportedly produced. Another special Elva never left the planning stages. It was designed to use a Chevrolet V-8 engine in a GT body. Frank Nichols assumed consultant duties with Trojan until 1965, when Elva was taken over by Ken Sheppard Customised Sports Cars Ltd. No significant vehicle production took place after that time. A new BMW-powered coupe was announced, but only prototypes were ever built.

The Courier was built in miniscule numbers until 1969. Couriers

with the 1489-cc BMC four-cylinder engine accounted for the majority of the company's output and most were exported. About 400 were produced between 1958 and late 1961. "Despite successes in SCCA production racing," said *Car and Driver* of the Mk IV Elva Courier in 1966, the "MG-engined sports car hasn't caught on beyond a small claque of devotees." Elva remained on American import car lists into 1967, though regular production ceased in 1966. All remaining Elva parts were purchased in 1969, but no further cars were built. By 1973, the Elva name was gone.

*Elva played up the translation of its name— "She Goes"—in advertising.*

# FAIRTHORPE

*Fairthorpe*

FOR FABULOUS ACCELERATION

ZETA

ELECTRON

WONDERFUL ROAD HOLDING
BRAKING AND SHEER SPEED

ELECTRON
MINOR

LIVELY — LOVELY

Wheels on Paper, New Zealand

# 1954-1976 Fairthorpe

Fairthorpe Ltd., of Buckinghamshire, England, was established in 1954 by Air Vice-Marshal D.C.T. Bennett. The company was a competitor in the minicar and kit car markets in the 1950s and 1960s and was a pioneer in fiberglass auto body construction. Fairthorpe started in the aircraft industry and began making cars in 1955. Bennett made several coupes, called the Atom, powered by front- or rear-mounted BSA motorcycle engines. His initial sports model was the Electron roadster, which came along in 1956. It used the overhead-cam Coventry Climax in-line four. This 1098-cc engine produced 84 hp and gave the 995-lb. Electron a top speed in the 116 mph range.

The Electron's fiberglass body had recessed headlights, a curved windshield, rounded wheel openings and exposed door hinges. A very low oval grille opening contained only a single vertical bar with large air intake gills at the cowl. Obviously, the $2,850 sports car had an excellent power-to-weight ratio, which aided its performance and made it economical to operate.

The Electron was on an 82-in. wheelbase and had just seven inches of car-to-ground clearance. It was 144 in. long and stood 46 in. high and 60 in. wide, with a 48-in. tread width. A four-speed manual transmission was fitted. Front and rear suspensions combined swing

*The Fairthorpe Zeta, Electron and Electron Minor graced the 1961 brochure cover.*

axles with coil springs. Rather large 5.20 x 15 tires were specified. Handling was outstanding.

By 1957, Fairthorpe had a distributor in the United States. Paul Pollard & Associates, of Los Angeles, California, sold the new-for-1958 Atomata coupe, the Electron, and a new, even smaller sports car dubbed the Electron Minor that also arrived in 1958. The two-seat Electron Minor roadster had an 81-in. wheelbase and a diminutive 120-in. overall length. It originally was powered by a 948-cc four-cylinder Standard Ten engine that produced 38 hp at 5000 rpm and 49 lbs.-ft. of torque at 4750 rpm. It carried twin S.U. carburettors and could hit 90 mph at top end, while delivering 55 mpg fuel economy. More than 700 Electron Minors were made from 1957 to 1973. The 1958 Electron Mk II was essentially unchanged except for the addition of front disc brakes. The two-seat roadster again came with a standard 1098-cc (67-cid) Coventry Climax engine, but three optional engines were avaiable: a 1.5-liter 141-hp Coventry Climax FPF, a 1.5-liter 145-hp Butterworth, and a modified 1172-cc Ford.

The Electron Minor had no significant changes for 1959, but the Electron was upgraded to Mk III tune with compression boosted from 9.8:1 to 10.5:1. This raised output from 84 to 93 hp and top speed to 120 mph. Prices at the factory in England in 1960 were $1,355 for the Electron Minor and $2,175 for the Electron Mk III.

One interesting Fairthorpe was the Zeta roadster. The tiny open car, which resembled the earlier Rockette, could be equipped with Ford Zephyr or Triumph TR 3 engines and some sources say it could reach speeds of 120 mph or more.

The Fairthorpe factory was relocated twice during the early 1960s, and additional U.S. distributors signed on. They included Martin M. Fuss, of Tucson, Arizona; Town and Track of Detroit, Michigan; and Bob Martin Auto Sales of Delmar, New York. Production of the Electron Minor model ceased in 1963, but other Fairthorpes remained in production into the 1970s. However, interest among U.S. buyers faded away early in the 1960s.

In 1963, Fairthorpe introduced a plastic-bodied Electron EM III roadster that rode on a tubular ladder frame. It carried an 1147-cc Triumph Herald engine delivering 63 hp (later 67 hp). There were also Mk IV, Mk V, and Mk VI editions of the Electron that used a 1296-cc Triumph Spitfire power plant rated at 75 hp. From 1962 to 1965, a Rockette sports model was produced. It had an 88-in. wheelbase and a 1596-cc Vitesse (the Standard/ Triumph S6) six-cylinder engine. The Rockette evolved into the TXGT coupe of 1967-1968, which had a 1998-cc six-cylinder engine rated at either 95 or 104 hp.

The TX GT had its roots with Air Vice-Marshall Bennett's son, Torix, who designed a car called the TX1 to demonstrate a trailing link and transverse rod rear suspension system. Interest in the design study car influenced moving the TX GT from concept to production. Another fixed-head coupe—the TX-S—arrived in 1969. Under its bonnet was a 112-hp version of the 1998-cc S6 that was good for a top speed of 115 mph. Perhaps the ultimate Fairthorpe—the 140-hp TX-SS coupe—was produced in 1969.

TX-series Fairthorpes had a more conventional appearance than earlier models and looked more like a boulevard sports car than a racer or a prototype. The TX-SS had back-slanted door and rear quarter windows and a sharp, fastback-shaped rear end.

Enthusiast Barry Gibbs formed a group known as the Fairthorpe Owners Club in 1960. Over the years, it became the Fairthorpe Sports Car Club and was expanded to include other types of fiberglass-bodied kit cars from the 1950s and 1960s.

The FSCC is based in England, but has members and cars throughout the world. The club relies on Marque Registrars to supply technical advice and support for their particular make of vehicle. It publishes a monthly newsletter and holds local meetings around the UK. For information, contact Tony Hill, 9 Lynhurst Crescent, Hillingdon, Middlesex UB10 9EF or e-mail webmaster@fairthorpescc.co.uk.

# FRAZER-NASH

Bob Harrington

# 1948-1957 Frazer-Nash

Chain gang was the term given by Frazer-Nash fans to early examples of the marque. Archibald (Archie) Frazer-Nash, had worked on the chain-drive GN cyclecar. Frazer-Nash and Ron Godfrey, later of HRG fame, founded GN. Archie left in 1922 when they disagreed over the direction the company was taking. Frazer-Nash soon formed a company to modify GNs for racing purposes.

His first order of business was to buy surplus parts from the GN company and he then turned out a handful of chain-driven Frazer-Nash editions of the cyclecar. Little more than the body came from the new company.

The first true Frazer-Nash arrived in 1924, initially offered with a Plus-Power 1.5-liter engine. Later it was powered by Anzani, Meadows, Gough, and other engines. The cars performed handily in hillclimbs and other race events. One special supercharged race version of a Frazer-Nash was capable of 135 mph. In 1927, control left the hands of Captain Archie Frazer-Nash. H.J. Aldington, who'd been part of the company all along, took over and remained in charge through the postwar decade.

A total of 350 Frazer-Nashes were produced by 1939, with 39 built in 1934 alone. The car was always a limited-production automobile and attracted stalwarts who fancied the basic, cycle-fendered bodywork and its primitive drivetrain and suspension.

Frazer-Nash comforts were few, but traction was great with the chain drive. Top speeds reached as high as 90 mph. Both four- and six-cylinder engines were used. Aldington acquired rights to the German BMW in 1934 and began to import Frazer-Nash-BMWs, including the appealing model 328.

Designed by Fritz Fiedler, who'd worked on the BMW 328 powerplant, the postwar Frazer-Nashes abandoned the prewar chain drive, but used Bristol engines and transmissions housed in a new chassis with 4-inch diameter steel tubes, transverse-leaf front suspension and torsion bars for the rear section.

*You can almost hear the roar of this Frazer-Nash coming toward you.*

Postwar Frazer-Nash models came in more than a dozen different varieties, from the first 1948 competition edition to the final Continental of 1956-1957. With the exception of the BMW V-8-powered Continental and a four-cylinder prototype built in 1952, all postwar Frazer-Nashes were powered by the BMW-based Bristol six-cylinder engine. Output ranged from 85 hp to 150 hp. The range of body styles included open roadsters, closed and drophead coupes, and single-seat racing cars. Each Frazer-Nash automobile was built to order and there was no standard type or strict specifications. Frazer-Nash variants included the Competition, also known as the High Speed model. Others included the Mille Miglia, the Single-Seater, the Targa Florio, and the Le Mans coupe.

The best known postwar Frazer-Nash was the $6,850 Le Mans Replica edition, of which 34 were made. Named after a Competition model that won third place at the prestigious French race, it had a stark, prewar-race-car look. According to a U.S. sales brochure, the hand-built competition two-seater was "guaranteed a replica in specification, performance and construction of the Frazer Nash which was so successful at Le Mans." Separate headlights were mounted high, alongside a narrow grille. An insignia was placed in the top of the bright surround molding. The headlights and "mudguards" (fenders) easily detached.

The cowl and hood of the Le Mans Replica were loaded with grillework and a leather belt held the hood in position. Straight exhaust pipes stuck out the side of the cowl. The bucket-type seats were upholstered in leather. Tubular main body hoops and a subsidiary framework for the aluminum body were welded to the chassis. The maker said that this provided, "exceptional strength and rigidity."

Standard equipment included a tonneau cover and twin aero windshields. Body colors were offered to the customer's choice. A "one-shot" chassis lubrication system was operated by pressing a foot pump.

Early examples offered two versions of the Bristol six--an overhead-valve in-line engine with four main bearings and solid valve lifters. The bore and stroke measurements were 66 x 96 mm, giving a 1971-cc displacement. An 8.5:1 compression ratio was standard, with 9.5:1 optional. In milder tune the motor produced 110 hp at 5250 rpm and 121 lbs.-ft. of torque at 3750 rpm. The optional version was good for 120 hp at 5500 rpm and 125.5 lbs.-ft. at 4500 rpm. Both used triple Solex downdraft carburetors. A later Mk II version was also made available with up to 132 hp.

Specifications for the $7,850 Mille Miglia model were similar to those of the Le Mans model, except that box-section extensions in the main tubular chassis members passed under the rear axle instead of sweeping over it to permit an even lower body profile.

The Mille Miglia's envelope-style body had built-in headlights, a protruding grille, and a surround molding rounded at the top. Two tiny aero windshields were installed. The body had full wheel openings plus an air scoop in its hood.

The Fast Roadster had a fully faired, full-width body with a 16-gal. gas tank mounted on upward extensions of the frame immediately behind the seats. This allowed the rear of the body to be used as a trunk. The spare wheel was fully enclosed in a front fender.

Large running lights stood inboard of the built-in headlights. The hood was a lid, not covering the entire top of the front end. The sloping windshield was made of curved glass. A traditional Frazer-Nash radiator design was made up of vertical bars. Color schemes were the customer's choice. Seats and cockpit trim were upholstered in leather. The dash included both a 5-inch tachometer and speedometer.

A 90-hp version of the Bristol six-cylinder engine powered the roadster and was hooked to a four-speed manual gearbox. The roadster body was also available on a competition chassis.

Riding a longer (108-inch) wheelbase than its mates, the Foursome Cabriolet model carried an 85-bhp version of the Bristol engine. *Autocar* described it as "undoubtedly one of the most attractive convertibles yet seen." All of the wheels were partially enclosed, giving a very sleek look.

Introduced in 1952, the Targa Florio came in Gran Sport and Turismo forms. A 1953 Frazer-Nash Le Mans Replica was the first British car to win the 35th Targa Florio, beating a Ferrari and Maserati. The Targa Florio roadster featured all-weather protection that included a raked and curved windshield, a three-point top and Perspex side

windows. Actor Errol Flynn bought a Targa Florio for his wife and posed for publicity stills.

*Autocar* noted that it was "as easy and comfortable as a convertible and remarkably warm even when the outside temperature is below freezing." The Targa Florio had a hood scoop and used different grilles than the Mille Miglia.

The Targa Florio Gran Sport was identical in specifications to the Le Mans Competition model, with three tubular steel body hoops welded to the main chassis members. It used thinner metal for the body than the Turismo, which accounted for its weighing only 1,710 lbs. The Targo Florio's Dunopillo seats were upholstered in leather.

Seats, steering column rake, height, and foot pedal positions could be adjusted to suit the customer. Plastic three-quarter panels in the soft top were standard. Under the Turismo's hood was a 100-bhp version of the Bristol six-cylinder engine, while the Gran Sport's six delivered 132 hp.

The modern-looking Sebring was introduced in 1954 and differed from most other Frazer-Nash offerings in front end design. It had a wide radiator-grille opening with large, recessed horizontal bars set into a low nose. The headlights were built into the curving fender tips. The hood (actually just a lid) held an air scoop.

The Sebring engine was basically the same Bristol power plant used in other models, except that it had an 8.8:1 compression ratio and developed 140 hp at 5750 rpm. The Le Mans name was used again on a 1954 $7,500 coupe.

The sleek fixed-head coupe looked like the Sebring roadster, and included a pentagonal grille opening.

The 1956 and '57 Frazer-Nash Continental coupe was the rarest, and last, of the company's postwar models. It was powered by a BMW V-8 engine in a choice of three displacements 2430 cc, 2580 cc or 3168 cc. Horsepower ratings ranged from 120 to 173. Its appearance was similar to the Sebring and Le Mans coupe.

Bristol Motors, Inc., of New York City, handled U.S. distribution of Frazer-Nash models. *Autocar* declared the Frazer-Nash showing at Le Mans "a significant performance."

Frazer-Nashes continued their tradition of success in international competition. A Le Mans Replica won the first Sebring 12-hour race in the U.S., in 1952. Promotional material referred to Frazer-Nash as "The Competition Car for the Owner-Driver," adding that it could be "Raced As Sold."

According to Frazer-Nash Archive trustee James Trigwell, 13 of the 84 post-war Frazer-Nash cars were exported to the United States, including five Le Mans Replicas, four Targa Florios, three Mille Miglias, and one Le Mans coupe.

*A pair of veteran Frazer-Nash cars is a rare site today.*

*1952 Targa Florio owned by actor Errol Flynn*

Frazer-Nash Archives, UK

*1950 Le Mans Replica*

Frazer-Nash Archives, UK

*1954 Le Mans Coupe*

Frazer-Nash Archives, UK

# GORDON-KEEBLE

Wheels on Paper, New Zealand

## 1964-1967 Gordon-Keeble

For a time in the 1950s and 1960s, the idea of dropping a big American V-8 into a European chassis was thought to be the way to go with sports car development and a way to lure American customers in mind.

Gordon-Keeble Ltd., of Eastleigh, Hampshire, England, figured an Italian-styled body on a British chassis with a Corvette V-8 under the hood might just be even more irresistible to Americans. It seemed like doing this the right way might create a Ferrari rival. A good idea, perhaps; but the target buyers for the Gordon-Keeble managed to resist, just as they resisted the somewhat similar Peerless GT a few years earlier.

Immediately after the collapse of the Peerless 2+2 coupe project, John Gordon pondered the blend of a British chassis, a body design by Italy's Bertone, and a 283-cid, 4.6-litre Corvette engine. A four-door, steel-bodied prototype with a space frame, De Dion rear axle, and four-wheel disc brakes was developed. Journalists praised the prototype, but the project couldn't quite get moving.

Retired racing driver Jim Keeble, who became a garage owner, decided to rebuild a Peerless coupe and replaced the Triumph 2-litre engine with a Buick Special 215-cid V-8. Keeble's engine swap got the attention of Jim Keeble, who believed there was a niche market for a new car with a larger engine. Wearing a handsome Bertone-styled body, the vision of the two men evolved into the 1964 Gordon-Keeble, a close-coupled coupe that offered quick locomotion and good handling. Though handsome, the body design dated back to 1960. That fact, a crippling industrial strike, and an unrealistically low selling price all contributed to failure. Only a few Gordon-Keebles reached the United States at the time, though an active owner's club emerged in Britain by 1970.

Built on an essentially handmade chassis, the Gordon-Keeble GT coupe wore a fiberglass body from Williams & Pritchard, with hardtop styling and large rear quarter windows. Quad round headlamps were installed, with each pair on a slight angle. Round parking lights sat below the headlamp pairs. A fine crosshatch pattern on the wide grille was dominated by horizontal strips--initially with six vertical dividers and later with four. The hood contained a small faux air scoop. Vertical-style taillamps stood in slightly finned back fenders, alongside a sloping

*The Gordon-Keeble was a graceful sports car from England that wasn't well known in North America.*

deck. The dual gas filler caps was just to the rear of the back window. The Gordon-Keeble mascot was an overview of a tortoise surrounded by laurel leaves.

The car's chassis was welded together from many one-inch square-section steel tubes. To maintain silence, the spaces between the tubes were filled with foamed plastic for insulation. An undersheet of alloy metals also was used. Under the hood was a 300-bhp, 327-cid Chevrolet V-8 engine matched with a Warner four-speed manual gearbox. One Chevrolet extra Americans were used to, Powerglide automatic transmission, was not available.

Dunlop disc brakes on all four wheels used separate front and rear master cylinders, plus two separate vacuum servo units. The De Dion rear axle tube passed behind a Salisbury differential, with two trailing links on each side of the chassis and a transverse Watt linkage. Coil springs handled suspension chores, front and rear. According to Gordon-Keeble expert John Follows of the Gordon-Keeble Owners Club of Great Britain, Jim Keeble had intended to develop a Mark 2 version of the GK1. His intention was to include rack-and-pinion steering, a five-speed transmission, anti-roll suspension bars front and rear, a limited slip Salisbury differential and an upgraded interior that would have included wood and leather appointments.

The Gordon-Keeble was called the GK1 model. Later, Sholing-built versions labeled a series the IT (International Touring) model.

Standard GK1 equipment included a radio, fire extinguisher, reclining seats, front seat belts, two-speed wipers/washers, and electric windows.

In England, the GK1 cost 1,934 pounds (Sterling) plus 967 pounds (Sterling) UK tax. The IT version, produced later, cost 3,626 pounds (Sterling).

The Gordon-Keeble was indirectly involved in another effort. In 1968, a car called the DeBruyne, named after its American entrepreneur John de Bruyne, was crafted from the original Gordon-Keeble body. Both the Gordon-Keeble and the DeBruyne cars faded into history.

# HEALEY

Bob Harrington

# 1949-1954 Healey

**B**est known in America for the popular Austin-Healey and the Nash-Healey, Donald Healey worked on sports cars for two decades before hooking up with the British Motor Corporation (BMC). In the 1920s, he was a top European rally driver. In the 1930s, Healey became technical director for Standard Triumph, working on projects including Riley and Invicta rally racers.

Immediately after World War II, Healey started Donald Healey Motor Co. Ltd. at Warwick, England. With minimal financing in hand, he made extensive use of components from other manufacturers in his cars. The first Healey appeared in January 1946. A variety of Healey models appeared in the next few years with bodies from British coachbuilders Tickford, Abbott, Duncan, Westland, and Elliot.

Fergus Motors of New York City advertised the 1949 Healey drophead sports model as a "symphony in comfort, speed and roadability. Through traffic at 15 mph or over the pike at 115 mph . . . the Healey is again first in sports car circles." The model shown had a diamond-shaped vertical-bar grille, with headlamps alongside, low on the nose, and running lamps at fender tips.

The Healey models included true sports cars like the Silverstone, sporty roadsters and drophead coupes (convertibles), four-passenger fixed-head coupes, and even sport saloons. All could hit at least 100 mph, but the Silverstone was capable of reaching 110 mph.

The sports car bowed in summer 1949, but it gained scant attention in America. Bill Frick and Briggs Cunningham added a Cadillac V-8 and a De Dion rear axle to a Silverstone and finished second in the 200-mile Palm Beach road race in January 1950.

A Nash Ambassador six-powered Silverstone finished fourth at Le Mans in 1950. Other Healeys did well in the Alpine Trial, the Targa Florio, the Mille Miglia, and the Belgian 24-Hour race. A Healey sport sedan averaged over 100 mph for one hour at Montlhery, France, streaking through the "flying mile" at 110.8 mph.

Sporty Healey models included the Westland roadster, the Duncan sports, the Tickford sport saloon, and the Sportsmobile drophead coupe. Standard equipment included leather upholstery, polished walnut interior woodwork, provisions for a radio and heater, a spare tire and tools in a compartment below the luggage area, a 120-mph

*The Healey Silverstone lived up to its British race course namesake.*

speedometer, and a tachometer. Some Healey models were built as late as 1954.

The Silverstone was a true sports car, with a name that stemmed from the new British Grand Prix race course. "Race-and-ride" Healeys had taken the Royal Automobile Club prize there in 1949.

Few vehicles looked more like racing cars. Instead of the smooth, "semi-envelope" body used on other Healeys, the Silverstone switched to a projectile shape. With separate cycle fenders, an old-fashioned rectangular windshield, and cut-away doors, it was a handsome sight. An air scoop was placed near the front of the small horizontal hood.

A fully rounded rear end held the spare tire in a horizontal position, tucked into a slot, where it served as a back bumper of sorts. Not a bad idea, since the Silverstone had no regular bumpers at either end. A gas filler was on top of the deck.

Buick-style rectangular "portholes" ran along the Silverstone's cowl. The body, built by Abbey Panel & Sheet Metal Company, included a folding top and removable windshield.

Intended as a lightweight, functional race car that could also tour, the Silverstone offered only minimal weather protection and weighed nearly 500 lbs. less than other Healeys. Built mostly by hand, it was costly at $3,995. The bodies weren't always extremely durable, especially in hot and damp climates. The tough chassis and drivetrain of the 2,075-lb. car held up well.

A supercharged Silverstone climbed to $4,650. A total of 105 Silverstones were built, along with 676 other models. Slightly more than half of the Silverstones were "E" types with upgraded interiors.

The three-main-bearings power plant used in most Healeys was an overhead-valve, 2.4-liter in-line four similar to the Riley RM series engine. It had an 80.5 x 120-mm bore and stroke and 2443-cc displacement. With a 6.9:1 compression ratio, it developed 104 hp at 4500 rpm and 132 lbs.-ft. of torque at 3000 rpm. Twin S.U. carburetors were utilized. About two dozen of the last Healeys made were powered by a 3.0-liter six borrowed from the Alvis model TA21. This in-line engine had solid valve lifters and twin S.U.s like the four. With an 84 x 90-mm bore and stroke, it displaced 2993 cc. It was rated at 106 hp at 4200 rpm and 150 lbs.-ft. at 2500 rpm.

Early Healeys rode a box-section platform with a 96-in. wheelbase. Trailing arms and coil springs made up the front suspension, which included an anti-roll bar. At the rear was a "live" axle with a torque tube, radius arms, and coil springs. Later the wheelbase grew to 102 in. Overall length was 168 to 180 in. depending upon the model. The sports car was 55 in. high and 63 in. wide. Tread widths were 54 in. up front and 53 in. at the rear. The perforated steel disc wheels wore either 5.50 x 15 or 5.75 x 15 tires, with larger sizes optionally available. A four-speed manual transmission with overall gear ratios of 12.76:1 in first, 7.542:1 in second, 4.963:1 in third, and 3.5:1 in fourth was fitted to the Silverstone. A 3.50:1 rear axle was standard with the four and a 3.77:1 axle was used with the six. Cam-type steering was employed.

It's likely that no more than a half-dozen Silverstones were imported into the U.S. when they were new. Approximately four Healeys of any type were sold in the U.S. in 1948, seven in 1949, seven more in 1950, and just two in 1951.

After the Silverstone ended its 1952 production run, the company developed and built about 50 Healey Hundreds with an Austin 2660-cc 90-hp engine. *Automobile Topics* called it "a very fast everyday road car, of superior refinement and with exceptionally fine handling qualities." The magazine reported acceleration from 0 to 60 mph in 10.5 seconds and an 18-second quarter-mile. Priced at 850 pounds in England and about $3,000 here, it quickly evolved into the Austin-Healey 100 under Sir Leonard Lord of Austin. Donald Healey enjoyed cruising on waterways as well as highways. In the 1950s, Healey Marine produced fine wooden boats. Shells were built at a furniture factory near Bridgeport in Dorset, then were shipped to Warwick where BMC 1500 cc or 1600 cc engines were installed. Later, Healey became an influential director at the Jensen auto company where the two-liter Jensen-Healey bore his name and sports car heritage.

*The Healey Silverstone almost seems to be racing right off the page .*

# HRG

John Gurnell

# 1946-1956 HRG

HRG stood for E.A. Halford, Guy H. Robins, and H.R. Godfrey (whose initials also happen to be "HRG"). While most European automakers could hardly wait to move into the modern era after World War II ended, HRG Engineering, Ltd. of Tolworth, Surrey, took a different tack. Founded in 1935, the firm produced less than three dozen stark, down-to-business sports cars before the hostilities broke out.

Most postwar HRGs simply carried on the prewar design. A modern roadster, called the Aerodynamic, was introduced, but when it failed to attract favorable attention (especially in the United States), HRG returned to the traditional sports car arena.

The company's first car had been a basic two-seater with a 58-hp Meadows 1.5-liter, four-cylinder overhead-valve engine. It was capable of hitting 90 mph. Soon, a more powerful Singer 1.5-liter overhead-cam engine was substituted. HRG's early racing successes included a second-place-in-class finish in 1937 at the famous Le Mans course in France. A total of 25 HRGs of the 1.5-liter class were built before World War II, along with eight companion 1100 models that carried a smaller, 1074-cc Singer overhead-cam engine. These were rough-looking, rough-riding sports cars with superior cornering abilities that made up for the lack of amenities.

The HRG two-seaters that appeared after the war looked nearly identical to the pre-war cars with separate fenders, a square upright appearance, cut-away doors, and austere interiors. Assembled largely by hand, with bodies crafted by various coachbuilders, HRGs also had prewar-type mechanical brakes and primitive suspensions with rigid axles and leaf springs at both ends.

A fold-flat windshield sat atop the aluminum, two-door body, which rode low to the ground with a ground clearance of 6.5 in. The 1100 had a 99.75-in. wheelbase and measured 142.5 in. long. It carried a smaller engine than the larger 1500 model, which had a 103-in. wheelbase and 144-in. overall length (except for the Aerodynamic

***The car produced by the team of Halford, Robins and Godfrey was known simply as the HRG.***

model, which was a foot longer). Both prewar-style cars were similar in appearance. The early 1500 model had a Port of Entry price of about $2,450. Later, this rose to about $2,800.

An Aerodynamic version of the 1500 was also built—until 1950—on the same narrow prewar style chassis. It had a streamlined full-width "envelope" body and a full set of outriggers to attach the body to the frame. This roadster failed to find many buyers. The few that were sold tended to deteriorate over the years, but when they were new, they fared well in competition.

HRG allowed many variations from standard equipment, such as different wheel sizes, different fender shapes, an extra spare tire, and interior modifications to suit the specific driver. As in prewar years, the engine sat well back in the frame. Both early engines were overhead-cam in-line fours with three main bearings. The smaller had a 60 x 95-mm bore and stroke and 1074-cc displacement. With a 7.75:1 compression ratio and twin side-draft S.U.s, it generated 40 hp at 5100 rpm. The larger 1496-cc engine—a modified Singer power plant—had 68 x 103-mm bore and stroke dimensions. It ran a 7.0:1 compression ratio and put out 65 hp at 4800 rpm.

During 1948, half a dozen HRGs entered the French Alpine Rally, taking home several prizes. Sales did not improve and only 40 cars were sold in 1948. The HRG's rally and racing success continued and eventually included two class wins at the 1949 Le Mans race. Despite such victories, deliveries slipped to just 11 by 1950.

In 1951, a different 1496-cc engine with a 73 x 89-mm bore and stroke was used. The compression ratio was a higher 7.5:1, but it still peaked at 65 hp at 4800 rpm. This engine had two downdraft carburetors and developed 77 lbs.-ft. of torque at 2800 rpm.

All models used a four-speed manual gearbox and had similar prewartype suspension and braking systems. Near the end of production, Girling hydraulic brakes became an option. A small 10.8-gal. fuel tank was fitted and rear axle ratios varied by model. The 1100 came with a 4.55:1 rear axle, while the 1500 offered the choice of that ratio or 4.00:1. The 100 was capable of a 75 to 80-mph top speed while the 1500 could do 90 to 100 mph. The early 1500 did 0-to-50 mph in 11.2 seconds. Late-production 1500s could move from 0-to-60 mph in 13.5 seconds. Quarter-mile acceleration times were 21.6 seconds for the 1100 and 19 to 20.4 seconds for 1500s.

In 1953, a new Singer-based 1100 WS model appeared. It had a shorter-stroke four-cylinder engine. Only about a dozen of these were produced. For 1955, HRG had high hopes for its modernized Mark II sports car, which featured an alloy body on a tubular frame and a twin-cam engine that developed more than 100 hp.

Its curvacious and contemporary race-car styling included oversize wheel openings.

The Mark II was expected to sell for around $4,000 in the U.S., but only two or three were built.

Between 1946 and 1956, HRG built approximately 49 of the 1100s, 104 of the prewar-style 1500s, 40 Aero models, and 12 of the late-production SM roadsters. But these production totals are approximate and probably include a few models built just before World War II. Some sources indicate a total of 187 cars were produced, of which 138 had the 1500 engine.

Approximately five HRGs were sold in the U.S. in 1949 and one in 1950. About 26 were imported to the U.S. in all postwar years combined. Jack Wherry, of Maquoketa, Iowa, was the importer.

Both the old- and the new-style HRGs faded away in 1956, when the company turned away from production of automobiles and into manufacturing components.

The HRG firm expired completely in 1965, after producing one more Vauxhall-powered experimental prototype a year earlier.

*HRGs gained a reputation when racers took the wheel in road and rally competitions.*

John Gunnell

# JAGUAR

Dick Langworth

# 1949-1954 XK120

**T**he world-renowned Jaguar nameplate began with William Lyons and the SS company in Britain. The Swallow Coachbuilding Company was founded in the late 1920s. It changed to SS Cars Ltd. by 1931, when the firm began making cars.

Lyons designed a rakish body for a new Standard chassis. His SS 1 was a hit at the 1931 British Motor Show and was followed by the two-seat SS 90 of 1935 and the SS100 of 1936. The early SS 100 had a 2663-cc overhead-valve six (a Standard conversion). Later, a 125-bhp, 3485-cc engine was fitted. The SS100 was fast, well mannered, and it attracted attention on both sides of the Atlantic. The 3.5-liter SS100 could hit 100 mph. SS100s were raced at Brooklands and at British hillclimbs. About 265 were built before World War II.

The Jaguar name, first used in 1935, reappeared after the war when the Coventry-based company was renamed Jaguar Cars Ltd. The SS100 was gone, but the fall 1948 Earl's Court Motor Show introduced the sensational XK120 roadster, powered by a new 3.4-liter 160-hp six.

The XK120 evolved from the experimental "100" coupe of 1938, which featured a long hood, a sloped tail and a rounded cockpit. The XK120 copied that profile, adding a narrower grille and faired-in headlights. Jaguar needed a roadster body for a Mark V chassis and the first aluminum-bodied example was built in six weeks.

Demand was strong, especially in the United States. XK120 production began in July 1949 and continued until September 1954. American deliveries began in August 1949, when car number 670005 was received by Hoffman Motors of New York. The original limited production XK120 was built to demonstrate the new dual-overhead-camshaft engine. Its immediate success called for hurry-up body tooling. The new 2,920-lb. roadster was practical, reasonably priced, beautiful, and handled well.

Faired-in sealed-beam headlamps sat alongside a narrow, oval grille flanked by slim bumpers without guards. The grille rose as a unit when the narrow, tapered hood was opened. Parking-light nacelles were chrome-plated, then changed to body-color during the production run.

After the first 1,772 cars were built, air vents were added to the front fenders. Small taillights stood alongside the long deck lid (which contained the license-plate mounting). No rear bumper was used, but some rear protection was provided by two vertical guards.

More than 200 early XK120s were built with aluminum bodies but they had steel bodies after April 1950. Leather upholstery was standard

*This photo of a 1949 Jaguar XK 120 offers an unforgettable profile of the car.*

and leather was used on the roadster's instrument panel and garnish rails. Standard equipment included a twin-blade wiper, a cigar lighter, twin blended-note horns, two batteries, a 140-mph speedometer, and a tachometer. The folding mohair top was concealed behind the seats and detachable side screens stored in a tray there.

A mono windshield was available for owners who wanted to take their XK120 racing. Fender skirts also became a popular option for models equipped with standard steel disc wheels. Wire wheels were a popular option and so were a 24-gal. gas tank and twin spare wheels. The seven-main-bearings double-overhead-camshaft 3442-cc six had an 83 x 106-mm bore and stroke. Its high-strength aluminum alloy head incorporated hemispherical combustion chambers. Camshafts were mounted at a 70-degree angle and driven by a two-stage chain system. Inclined overhead valves were used.

The standard six had an 8.0:1 compression ratio and twin S.U. sidedraft carburetors. It generated 160 hp at 5000 rpm and 195 lbs.-ft. of torque at 2500 rpm. Optional was a de-tuned version with a 7.0:1 compression ratio and 150 hp at 5000 rpm. Before long, XK120s with an optional performance package could be ordered for U.S. delivery. It included high-lift cams, a raised compression ratio, a racing clutch, a dual exhaust system, and wire wheels.

The XK120 had a 102-in. wheelbase and 173-in. length. It was 52.5 in. high and 61.5 in. wide. Tread widths were 51 in. front and 50 in. rear. Standard disc wheels carried 6.00 x 16 Dunlop tires. A four-speed manual transmission used gear ratios of 12.29:1 in first, 7.22:1 in second, 4.98:1 in third and 3.64:1 in fourth. A 3.64:1 rear axle was standard; 3.27:1, 4.0:1, or 4.3:1 ratios were available. Up front was an independent suspension with transverse wishbones, long torsion bars, and an anti-roll bar. A rigid axle with semi-elliptic leaf springs was at the rear. Hydraulic drum brakes were employed front and rear.

The XK120 had a 125 mph top speed. Zero-to-60 mph took 10.0 to 11.7 seconds. The quarter mile took 17 to 18.3 seconds to cover from a standing start. The typical XK 120 went 18-20 miles on a gallon of fuel.

Not everyone believed Jaguar's claims about the XK120, so the company held a high-speed demonstration run on the Jabbeke Highway in Belgium, where an unmodified car hit 126 mph. With its windshield removed, the XK 120 did 132 mph.

"It is typically British that Jaguars never claimed more than 120 mph for this car," said California Autonews. The *British Daily Herald* called the XK120: "...the fastest ever tourer, yet as docile in heavy traffic as the most expensive and biggest saloon."

*Country Life* noted the car: "...reaches a standard of functional beauty never before achieved by a British manufacturer." The XK was Europe's most powerful production engine.

In 1949, three XK120s entered the British Racing Driver's Club meet at Silverstone and took first and second place. XK120s won many other races.

Stirling Moss won the 1950 Tourist Trophy, while a Jaguar driven by Ian Appleyard won Alpine rallies in 1950, 1951, and 1952. Jaguars were modified for racing and the XK120C (called C-Type), with its multi-tube frame, was soon introduced. One won at the 1951 Le Mans and another with a 220-bhp engine won the 1953 LeMans.

In addition to Hoffman, Jaguar XK120 distributors included S.H. Lynch in Dallas, Texas; James Baird in Seattle, Washington; Kjell Qvale's San Francisco-based British Motor Car Distributors; Foreign Motors of Santa Barbara, California; and Roger Barlow's International Motors in Los Angeles.

Total production from 1949-1954 came to 12,078 units, including 7,631 roadsters, 2,678 fixed-head coupes, and 1,769 drophead coupes. Some 10,392 were left-hand-drive cars. About 158 Jaguars were sold in the U.S. during 1949, though not all were XK120s.

The appearance and mechanical details of the 1950 XK120 roadster were the same as 1949. All were steel bodies. Later models had air vents on the trailing ends of the front fenders. Approximately 912 Jaguars were sold in the U.S. during 1950.

At the August 1951, Geneva Motor Show, a new XK120 fixed-head coupe was announced. Its profile was very similar to the one-off 1938 SS100. More "civilized" than the roadster, the coupe was great for long-distance touring.

Its interior included walnut veneer dashboard trim and wind-up windows. The coupe looked particularly streamlined with fender skirts.

Footwell vents were added in 1951 and a heater became standard in roadsters. That model's price went to $4,039, while the new 3,050-lb. coupe retailed for $3,850. The 1952 prices were unchanged but new faired-in lights replaced the chromed sidelight housings. Approximately 3,349 Jaguars were sold in the U.S. during 1952 as XK 120 deliveries boomed.

A XK120 drophead coupe (convertible), priced at $4,250, joined the roadster and fixed-head coupe in 1953, debuting at the New York Automobile Show in the spring. The Sport Roadster's price didn't change, but the fixed-head coupe rose to $4,065.

The prices were later reduced and carried over for 1954, when all three models continued with little change.

These final prices were $3,345 for the Sport Roadster, $3,875 for the fixed-head coupe, and $3,975 for the convertible.

A special bubble-topped XK120 roadster, driven for the Belgian Royal Automobile Club by Norman Dewis, hit 172.412 mph in October 1953, with an essentially stock engine. The feat helped Jaguar maintain its standing as the "world's fastest production car."

Bob Ferguson

# 1951-1953 XK120 C-Type

**T**hree Jaguar XK120s entered the 1950 Le Mans 24-Hour race, not intending to win. Two crossed the finish line far back in the pack. This experiment revealed a special design would be needed for victory and led to the creation of the XK 120C (called the C-Type).

Added to Jaguar's sports-car lineup in 1951, the XK120 C-Type was a special high-performance model. This competition-oriented roadster had only one door. The car's entire front end flipped forward on hinges, for the improved engine access needed for racing. Initial

*Jaguar XK120 cars were marketed to people who considered themselves "consistent competitors."*

examples had large side louvers at the cowl, but the production version switched to a set of narrow side louvers.

Unlike the standard XK120, the aluminum-bodied C-Type roadster rode on a frame made up of welded steel tubes. It featured a special rear suspension that contained a transverse torsion bar and underslung trailing links. Rack-and-pinion steering was installed.

The C-Type included a special double-overhead-cam six that produced 200 hp. The cylinder head contained larger valves and ports than the regular engine. The motor also incorporated high-lift camshafts and racing pistons. Like the base engine, this one had a cast-iron block and aluminum-alloy head.

The bore and stroke and displacement were the same as for the regular XK120 engine. Also similar were the seven-main-bearing crankshaft, solid valve lifters, twin S.U. sidedraft carbs, and 12-volt Lucas ignition system. However, the C-Type motor ran a 9.0:1 compression ratio and generated 200 hp at 5800 rpm.

With a 96-in. wheelbase, the C-Type had a six-inch shorter stance than the standard XK120. Its overall length was just 157 in. A 64.5-in. width made it wider than the stock XK120. At 2,128 lbs., it weighed some 800 lbs. less than that model.

The C-Type was produced over three model years: 1951, 1952, and 1953. A total of 53 were built, including both "production" and racing versions. These cars had a 143-mph top speed and could accelerate through the quarter mile in 16.2 seconds. One of the new limited-production, high-performance XK120C roadsters with a 220-bhp engine and Dunlop disc brakes won the 1951 Le Mans race.

In 1952, the XK120 C-Type got the same changes as the regular XK120, including faired-in lights on top of the front fenders. Only a roadster was offered again.

The final year the C-Type was offered was 1953, when the high-performance roadster was priced at $5,860. *Auto Sportsman* magazine reported that the XK120C was "sold only to drivers or owners who are consistent competitors."

Dick Langworth

# 1952-1954 XK120M

**B**y the early 1950s, Jaguar was selling more sports cars than it ever expected to. The marque's popularity was based primarily on the XK120's performance and its high-profile racing victories at LeMans and in other venues. In the United States, marques like Austin, Morris, and Hillman sold in higher volume, but the dollar volume of sales of the pricier Jaguars was the highest of any imported car.

New for 1952 was the XK120M, a modified version of the production model that came with knock-off wire wheels, skirtless rear wheel openings and a 180-hp version of the twin-cam engine with dual exhausts. The XK120M was available in both the original roadster body style, as well as the new fixed-head coupe model. At $4,434, the roadster carried the lower price of the two, while the coupe (sometimes called the "hardtop") cost an additional $26.

The modified engine used in the XK120M was based on the regular 3442-cc double overhead cam in-line six with an 83 x 106-mm bore and stroke. It had the same seven-main-bearings crank, the same solid valve lifters, and a similar twin S.U. carburetor setup. However, the high-lift camshafts from the C-Type racer were fitted, along with a thicker head gasket, stiffer valve springs, and a special crankshaft damper. This increased brake horsepower to 180 at 5300 rpm.

*The Jaguar XK120 M series roadster was a faster version of the XK120.*

Also included as part of the $395 'M' package were stiffer front torsion bars and rear springs.

Road testers found the XK120M capable of 124 mph at top end, which placed it between the standard production car's 122 mph and the C-Type racer's 145 mph. Accelerating from 0-to-60 mph required some 9 sec. and quarter-mile acceleration was 17 sec. at 83 mph.

A full-fledged convertible (drophead coupe) joined the roadster and fixed-head coupe for 1953.

The drophead coupe was also available with the XK 120M's "Special Equipment" package for $4,645.

In 1953, there were no changes to speak of, except for a substantial drop in prices, which reflected a fall off in demand for Jaguars.

To move cars out the door, dealers were selling the Sport Roadster for $3,545, the fixed-head coupe for $4,075, and the drophead coupe for $4,175. Any American buyer who waited until 1954 to purchase a XK 20M was a wise man (or woman) indeed.

Bob Harrington

# 1954-1957 D-Type & XK-SS

A nother sports-racing evolution of the XK120 went into (limited) production in 1954. This became the first monocoque (uni-bodied) Jaguar. Steel-tube subframes were bolted to an aluminum/magnesium center section. However, some early models had bodies that were riveted to a square, magnesium tubular frame.

D-Type styling features included a short oval nose, a small windshield and large fin behind the headrest. Knock-off Dunlop magnesium alloy wheels were standard.

D-Types were offered only to qualified race drivers. Under the bonnet was a hopped-up version of the six-cylinder twin-cam engine with a new cylinder head, a special three-plate clutch, and a fully-synchronized four-speed gearbox.

The D-Type engine was derived from the basic 3442-cc Jaguar six with 83 x 106-mm bore and stroke dimensions, seven main bearings and solid valve lifters. The compression ratio was boosted to 9.0:1, raising output to 250 hp at 6000 rpm. Triple Weber carburetors were mounted.

A special 90-inch wheelbase chassis was used for the D-Type. That gave it a six-inch shorter stance than the earlier C-Type. The car was just 154 in. long, 38 in. high and 65.8 in. wide. It tipped the scales at 1,904 lbs. Front and rear torsion bars were featured. The rear suspension was similar to the C-Type suspension, except that it incorporated upper and lower trailing links at each side.

Tread widths were 50 in. up front and 48 in. at the rear. Size 6.50 x 16 tires were used and rack-and-pinion steering was employed.

The factory-delivery price for a D-Type was 1895 Pounds Sterling or about $10,000 in the U.S. Only 87 examples of the D-Type were produced between 1954 and 1956, including 16 that were converted for road operation beginning in 1957.

An amazing top speed of 160 mph was recorded for the Jaguar D-

*No one who raced or watched a D-type Jaguar could forget this 1950s legend.*

Type. It moved from 0-to-60 mph in just 4.7 sec. and could fly through the quarter mile in 13.7 seconds, doing 107 mph at the end.

Small quantities of the Jaguar's competition-oriented D-Type continued to emerge from the factory in Coventry, England, during 1955 and 1956. The specifications were unchanged from those of the first-year model.

Created in 1957 as a roadgoing version of the competition D-Type, the lightweight, 1,960-lb. Jaguar XK-SS was made up of leftover D-Type components. It easily qualified as the fastest street car that the automaker had ever manufactured up to this point in time.

With three Weber carburetors on the familiar 3442-cc six, 262 hp was put on tap. Each of the 16 Jaguar XK-SS models built was a right-hand-drive car, as were all D-Types. Production might have gone higher, if it wasn't for a 1957 fire that destroyed the factory tooling.

The XK-SS body was characterized by a curved windshield, small bumpers, and a rear-deck luggage rack. It lacked the high headrest of the D-Type racing car. The seats were upholstered in leather and were non-adjustable. For weather protection, a fabric top and side curtains were included. To make it a legal road car, the XK-SS came with turn signals and a muffler.

Under the XK-SS's bonnet was the same as 3442-cc DOHC six with a 9.0:1 compression ratio and triple Weber DCO3 carburetors. With these and other modifications, it generated 262 hp at 6000 rpm.

The XK-SS wheelbase was a half inch longer than that of the D-Type. It measured 168 in. from end to end. The body was 64.5 in. wide and rode on 6.50 x 16 tires. A 3.54:1 ratio rear axle was standard. Other technical features included rack-and-pinion steering.

# 1955-'57 XK140/XK140MC

**This Jaguar XK140M is a stunning addition to this rural scene.**

When Jaguar's replacement for the XK120, the restyled XK140, debuted in October 1954 (as a 1955 model), an XK140M appearance package was made available. The option included a crankshaft damper, wire wheels (either body-colored or chrome), dual exhaust, twin fog lamps, and windshield washers. The $145 package was available for all three body styles, raising the price of the Sport Roadster to $3,595, while the other models rose to $3,940.

Also offered for $295 was an XK140MC package that included the same extras, plus a C-Type cylinder head that boosted output to 210 hp at 5750 rpm and torque to 213 lbs.-ft. at 4000 rpm. Prices for Jaguar XK140MC models were $3,745 for the roadster and $4,090 for the other styles.

The XK140M models had an "A" prefix in their serial numbers. The XK140MC model could be identified by a red plaque on each camshaft cover. XK140MCs exported to the United States also has an "S" serial number prefix. In addition, engines with the C-Type cylinder head also had that letter cast into the top of the head. The XK 140 M could go from 0-to-60 mph in under 8.5 seconds.

Production of all three XK140 body styles continued with little change for 1956. As before, both the XK140M appearance package and XK140MC performance package were available. This year the Sport Roadster went up $160 in price, to $3,755, while the other body styles increased by $220 to $4,160. The XK140MC models cost $155 more than comparable XK140M models.

There was little change in 1957. The XK140M prices did increase for the series final year, but the "C" package cost $50 more. In 1957, a road test of the XK140MC model reported a 121 mph top speed and a 9.1-second 0-to-60-mph time. When the new XK150 bowed in mid-1957, the XK140s went out of production.

*The mid-1950s brought the improved XK140s to North American towns and cities.*

OCW Archive

# 1957-1961 XK150

Production of the new XK150 began in May 1957 and continued until October 1960, when it was replaced by the XKE.

Jaguar's third-generation postwar sports car wore new sheet metal and displayed a higher belt line that ran in a straight line, rather than curving down like the XK140's belt line. The front fenders were taller at the cowl. The roof line also was modified and a curved one-piece windshield replaced the former split "vee" style. The coupe's back window was also curved, wrapping around slightly.

Up front, a wider grille contained 16 thin vertical bars and had a more oval shape than its predecessor. The front bumper dipped downward at the center, ahead of the grille. A raised center section on the widened hood, which sloped toward the front of the car, was decorated with a chrome strip. A "leaping Jaguar" hood ornament was an option. The door handles were mounted higher. At the rear, the license-plate housing was relocated from the bumper to the deck lid, allowing the bumper to stretch between vertical guards and wrap around the rear fenders.

Jaguar originally offered the XK150 in only fixed-head coupe and drophead coupe models. Production of roadsters was delayed about nine months because of a fire. When it re-appeared, the roadster had wind-up windows and lacked its once traditional cut-away doors. At $4,595, the 3,108-lb. drophead coupe was now the priciest model.

The fixed-head coupe, which weighed about the same, had the lowest price of $4,475. The 42-lb. lighter roadster was introduced at midyear with a $4,520 window sticker.

Plusher and more refined than its predecessors, the XK150 was roomier inside and weighed more. The coupe and convertible no longer had burled-walnut dashboard trim and instead adopted the leather used in the roadster. Fender skirts were still available, except with wire wheels. The skirts emphasized the car's straight-across look.

Standard under the hood was the same 3442-cc 190-hp engine used in the XK140, but the 210-hp "Special Equipment" option was far more popular and used in the majority of cars manufactured. The new B-type cylinder head on the "Special Equipment" engine was painted blue, whereas the standard head was unpainted aluminum.

Testers recorded an all-out top speed of 120 mph for Jaguar's new

*Posing like a movie lead is the new Jaguar "star," the 1955 XK150.*

sports car. It reportedly took 8.5 seconds or less to move from standstill to 60 mph. For the quarter-mile acceleration test, the XK 150 required 16.9 seconds. Fuel mileage was in the 18 to 20 mpg bracket.

The XK150 continued on the 102-in. wheelbase, but overall length grew an inch to 177 in. Height was the same 55 in. as the XK 140, but when the new roadster arrived it was only 52.5 in. high. The 64.5-in. width was unchanged from that of the previous model. Tread widths changed slightly, to 51.6 in. up front and in the rear as well. Size 6.00 x 16 tires were mounted on the standard steel disc wheels.

A four-speed manual transmission was standard equipment and drove to a 3.54:1 rear axle. Overdrive cost $165 extra and the automatic transmission was a $250 option. Rack-and-pinion steering was fitted. The front geometry featured wishbones and torsion bars with an anti-roll bar. A rigid axle with semi-elliptic leaf springs was used at the rear. Dunlop four-wheel disc brakes, with servo-assist, appeared as an option, but were installed on virtually all cars.

Production of the Jaguar sports car, in the usual three body styles, continued in 1959 with little change. This year the coupe was $4,500, the roadster was $4,520, and the convertible was $4,620.

For the 1960 model year, the 3.8-liter engine (first used in the Mark IX sedan) was available under the hood of Jaguar's XK150 sports car. The engine produced 220 hp in standard form. This engine remained available through the end of XK150 production. Prices again changed to $4,520 for the roadster, $4,643 for the the 2+2 coupe, and $4,763 for the 2+2 convertible

Top speed for the base XK150 rose to 126 mph, probably with the 3.8-liter engine. Zero-to-60 mph acceleration with this engine took 8.3 seconds. The 3.8 Jag did the quarter miles in 16.7 seconds with a terminal speed of 82 mph.

The final season for the XK150 sports car was 1961. Production ceased when the completely different XKE arrived at midyear. During the early part of the run, Jaguar offered the three models, with price tags of $4,642 for the fixed-head coupe and $4,762 for the drophead.

# 1958-1961 XK150S

Jaguar's 1958 models were introduced to the U.S. market on Sept. 1, 1957, but it wasn't until the spring of 1958 that the Jaguar XK150S, with its more potent "S" engine, became available. This motor featured a straight-port head, a higher compression ratio, more radical cam timing, and three huge two-inch S.U. carburetors. Each carburetor supplied only two cylinders via separate manifolds.

All XK150S models had manual shift with overdrive and the engine's cylinder head was gold-colored. A small "S" went on the upper front corner of each door. Serial numbers for these cars started with VS1001. The engine and chassis numbers also appeared on a brass plate on the firewall.

The XK150S came in all three body styles, although only the two-passenger roadster was available in 1958 and 1959. It had a $5,120 Port-Of-Entry price and weighed 3,094 lbs. Total XK150S production (1958-61) came to 1,466 units. Of these, 924 were roadsters (36 with 3.8-liter engines), 349 were fixed-head coupes (150 with 3.8-liter engines), and 193 were drophead coupes (89 with 3.8-liter engine).

The S version of the 3442-cc, in-line six-cylinder engine had a 9.0:1 compression ratio and the triple S.U.s. This raised brake horsepower to 250 at 5500 rpm and torque to 240 lbs.-ft. at 4000 rpm. A four-speed manual transmission with overdrive was standard in the XK150S.

In 1959, the XK150S continued with little change. However, on late-1959 cars Jaguar switched to a 3781-cc six with 265 hp at 5500 rpm and 260 lbs.-ft. of torque at 4500 rpm. Like the smaller engine, this was also a dual overhead-cam in-line six with a cast-iron engine block and aluminum-alloy cylinder head. It had a 87 x 106-mm bore and stroke It used an 8.0:1 compression ratio and three S.U. carburetors.

A road test of the XK150S with the 3.8-liter engine gave the car's top speed as 135 mph or better. This car accelerated from 0-to-60 mph in about seven seconds. It could do the quarter mile, from a standing start, in 15.3 sec. and was going 87 mph at the end of the run.

For the 1960 model year, the 3.8-liter engine was available under the bonnet of both XK150 and XK150S models. The "S" version of the

*Wearing silver paint, the Jaguar XK150 fixed head coupe is stunning.*

larger six produced 265 hp and came only with manual transmission and overdrive. The 'S' engine was now available in all three body styles. The roadster remained priced at $5,120, the fixed-head 2+2 coupe was $5,075, and the drophead was $5,195.

The final season for the XK-150 sports cars was 1961 and it was dropped after the new XKE arrived at midyear. The XK 150S roadster remained available at the same price as before, while the fixed-head coupe price increased to $5,142 and the drophead coupe's price went to $5,162.

*The Jaguar XK150S is a classic beauty from every angle.*

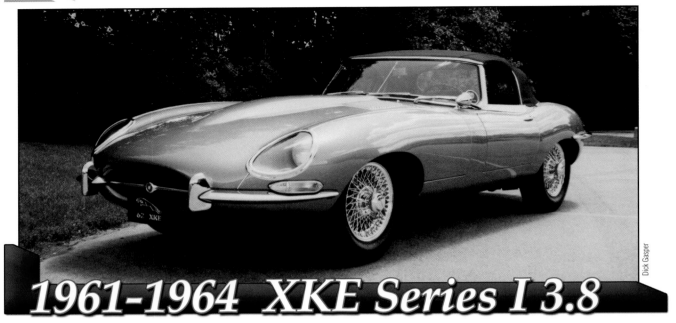

Dick Gasper

# 1961-1964 XKE Series I 3.8

The all-new and sensational-looking XKE made its debut in Geneva, Switzerland, in March of 1961. Its first United States appearance took place at the New York International Auto Show in April 1961. *Autocar* called the E-Type a "breakthrough in design of high-performance vehicles." *Car and Driver* declared its appeal to be "sensual and elemental."

Completely different in appearance from its XK120, XK140, and XK150 predecessors, the new projectile-shaped E-Type roadster and hatchback coupe debuted in March 1961 at the Geneva Motor Show. Styling was reminiscent of the D-Type racing car of the mid-1950s. The 96-in. wheelbase was six inches shorter than the XK150. The new car was more than 400 pounds lighter in weight.

The potent and previously optional 3.8-liter double overhead-cam six fitted with triple S.U. carburettors became standard in the XKE. It produced 265-hp and top speeds of nearly 150 mph. Accelerating from 0-to-60 mph took 6.5-7.0 seconds. Quarter-mile performance was 14.8 seconds and 93 mph.

Styling of the XKE was handled by Malcolm Sayer, an expert in aerodynamics. It was the first Jaguar not designed by William Lyons, who'd been knighted by this time. The company said that Lyons did provide "much input" on the design work. While the XK150 had a separate body and frame, the E-Type turned to a monocoque (unibody) body shell bolted to a multi-tube front structure. Like the front end of the D-Type racer, the whole nose tilted forward for engine acess.

The car's simple oval grille contained a single horizontal bar that matched the slim bumper. There was a small oval emblem at the center of the grille. The headlights were recessed into nacelles. At the rear was a slim, wraparound-style back bumper and narrow taillights, plus center dual exhaust pipes. Underneath was a new independent rear suspension with lower wishbones, coil springs, and a chassis-mounted differential. Four-wheel disc brakes were installed.

The XKE coupe's rear hatchback opened to the side, like a door. Painted wire wheels were standard and chrome wire wheels were optional. The early 1961-1962 models had unpainted center sections of the dashboard. The new sports car was known as the E-Type in Europe and was commonly called the XKE in the U.S.

POE price for the roadster was $5,595, while the 2,520-lb. coupe sold for an additional $300. Total production of First Series models amounted to about 7,820 roadsters and 7,670 fixed-head coupes.

*The convertible form of the Jaguar XKE is certainly sterling in silver.*

Dimensionally, the XKE had a 96-in. wheelbase and a 175.3-in. overall length. It was 48 in. high, 65.25 in. wide, and had a 50-in. front and rear tread. The standard tires were size 6.40 x 15. A four-speed manual transmission was fitted and overdrive was optional. The standard rear axle had a 3.31:1 ratio. The front suspension incorporated wishbones and torsion bars with an anti-roll bar.

A total of 3,422 Jaguars were exported to the U.S. during the year ending in July 1961 and a significant amount were XKEs. Close to 44,000 E-Type Jaguars would eventually be sold in the U.S. between 1961 and 1975, which was more than half of the 72,520 cars produced.

Production of the sleek XKE roadster and hatchback coupe, introduced in 1961, continued in 1962, 1963, and 1964 with little change. Power again came from a 3.8-liter twin-cam six with three carburetors. Even the P.O.E. prices for the roadster and the coupe were unchanged until 1964, when they were slightly reduced to $5,325 for the roadster and $5,525 for the coupe.

Tom Glatch

*Jaguar's XKE cars, like this 1963 coupe, were years ahead of competitors.*

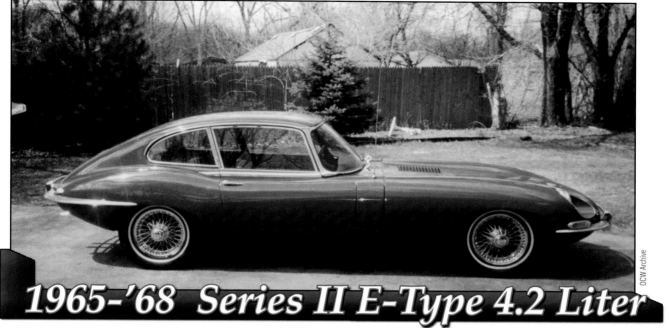

OCW Archive

# 1965-'68 Series II E-Type 4.2 Liter

A larger 4.2-liter six-cylinder engine became available for the 1965 Jaguar XKE. It had a larger bore than its predecessor. Torque got a boost to 283 lbs.-ft., but horsepower remained the same as before at 265 bhp.

Chrome lettering on the trunk lid now spelled out "E Type Jaguar 4.2." *Car and Driver* said that the 4.2-liter E-Type was "a delightful, multi-purpose two-seater which is equally at home in city traffic, on country roads, and at racing circuits," though "no faster than the 3.8."

Despite the larger engine displacement and new seats, prices for E-Type Jaguars fell. The window sticker on the 4.4-liter roadster was $5,384, while the coupe retailed for $5,580. The weights for the two models were 2,464 lbs. and 2,520 lbs. in respective order. Total E-Type production from 1965-1968 amounted to about 9,550 roadsters, 7,770 fixed-head coupes and 5,600 examples of a new 2+2 coupe that first arrived in 1966.

The seven-main-bearings engine again was, once again, an in-line six with dual overhead cams. It had new bore and stroke dimensions of 92.1 x 106-mm. The compression ratio remained at 9.0:1 and developed 283 lbs.-ft. of torque at 4000 rpm.

Fitted again were solid valve lifters and triple S.U. sidedraft carburetors. A new all-synchro four-speed gearbox was installed. The clutch, alternator, and exhaust system were also new. A removable fiberglass hardtop was optional for roadsters. A steering column with adjustable reach and height was standard equipment.

The 1965 to 1968 E-Type roadster and coupe body size did not change. Wire wheels were available. The standard instruments included a 160-mph speedometer and tachometer. With the larger-displacement engine, a new 3.54:1 final drive ratio was used. The E-Type retained rack-and-pinion steering. The front suspension again utilized wishbones and torsion bars with an anti-roll bar, while the rear layout featured lower wishbones with coil springs and an anti-roll bar

In addition to the well-established roadster and coupe, Jaguar added a 2+2 coupe to the E-Type mix in 1966. It sold for $6,070, a bit more than the carryover prices for the roadster and the coupe. It also weighed about 225 lbs. more than the two-place coupe. All three models came with the 4.2-liter engine and a four-speed manual

*Improvements were made in the Jaguar XKE Series II 4.2, like this red 2+2 coupe.*

gearbox. However, a Borg-Warner automatic transmission was available solely for the 2+2. The automatic version was priced at $6,415.

With its 105-in. wheelbase, the new 2+2 stretched 184.5 in. end to end. It also had a taller roof line. With a maximum height of 50 in., it was two inches higher than other models, although the body and track widths were the same.

The 2+2 had hinged rear quarter windows and the backs of its rear seats slid forward to enlarge the luggage area. The 2+2 had a top speed in the 136 to 140 mph bracket and it could go from 0-to-60 mph in 8.9 seconds.

No major change was evident in the Jaguar E-Type roadster, coupe or 2+2 coupe for 1966. The price of the 2+2 came down to $5,870, while prices for the other models stayed the same as before.

The XK-E 2+2 coupe with automatic transmission was priced at $6,120, almost $300 less than in the model's introductory year.

The E-Type was the only Jaguar that made it to the U.S. for the 1968 model year. The importation of Jaguar sedans was halted due to new U.S. emissions regulations. A different series of sedans would appear for the 1969 model year. Output for the export style E-Type sold here was reduced to 246 hp at 5500 rpm and 263 lbs.-ft. of torque at 3000 rpm. In home-market cars sold in England, the engine was rated for 265 hp at 5400 rpm and 283 lbs.-ft. at 4000 rpm.

Safety bumpers were new this year and the cockpit was restyled. Prices changed very slightly to $5,372 for the roadster, $5,559 for the coupe, and $5,739 for the 2+2.

The 2+2 coupe with automatic transmission was priced at $5,977. Top speed for the 1968 E-Type was reported to be 140 mph. Accelerating from 0-to-60 mph took 7.2 to 8 seconds and the E-Type covered a quarter-mile in about 15 seconds In late 1968, the second-series Jaguar E-Type debuted and British Motor Holdings and Leyland Motors merged. The British Leyland Motor Company was formed and started a brand new chapter in Jaguar history.

Tom Glatch

# 1968-'71 Series II E-Type 4.2

J aguar's new XJ sedan and the second-series E-Type debuted during 1968. The E-Type sports car now incorporated safety features formerly used only on models sold in the United States. It had larger park/signal lights and its headlights sat farther forward than before. A full-width front bumper protected a larger air-intake opening.

The taillights grew larger and were relocated below the rear bumper. New side marker lights were added. The 2+2 body had a windshield with a steeper rake angle, since its base had been moved forward. It featured a large window in the luggage hatch and hinged rear quarter windows.

Inside the new E-Types were leatherette door panels, leather-upholstered bucket seats that adjusted for reach and rake, padded visors, a grab handle, a glove compartment, and a map light. The 2+2's fully-upholstered back seat could hold two children.

Wide-spoke 15-in. wheels had center-locking quick-change hubs and wore Dunlop high-performance tires. Girling four-wheel power disc brakes were employed. The wraparound-style front and rear bumpers had overriders (guards). The roadster convertible had a large back window in its folding top.

The E-Type roadster sold for $5,534 and weighed in at 2,912 lbs. The two-passenger coupe was $5,725 and 2,912 lbs. The 2+2 carried a $5,907 price tag ($6,145 with automatic transmission) and tipped the scales at 3,024 lbs. Approximately 18,820 Series II E-Types would be produced from 1968-1970. This total included 8,630 roadsters, 4,860 fixed-head coupes and 5,330 2+2 coupes.

Used below the bonnet once again was the 4.2-liter (4235-cc) in-line, dual overhead-cam six with 92.1 x 106 mm bore-and-stroke dimensions that developed 246 hp at 5500 rpm and 263 lbs.-ft. of torque at 3000 rpm. The seven-main-bearings power plant came with

*By 1970, the XKE series, like this blue Series II roadster, were North American favorites.*

solid valve lifters and twin carburetors. Other technical specifications were virtually unchanged from 1967. Air conditioning was $482 extra and wire wheels added $132. Power steering was a $160 option.

When the engine underwent de-tuning to meet U.S. regulations, performance naturally suffered. The cars exported here had a top speed of about 120 mph, compared to 138 mph for home-market models. The 0-to-60 mph acceleration time was now 7.2-8.0 seconds while the quarter-mile numbers were 15.5-15.7 seconds and 88-89 mph.

Jaguar's 1970 models were introduced to the U.S. market on December 1, 1969. Production of the three E-Type sports-cars continued with little change in 1970, when some 6,732 Jaguars were sold in the U.S. Many of these cars now came with options such as air conditioning ($482), power steering ($160), wire wheels ($165), a hardtop for the roadster ($180), and white sidewall tires ($27).

The 1971 E-Type models were introduced to the U.S. market on Oct. 1, 1970. Prices for early-1971 six-cylinder models were raised $200. They also weighed about 50 lbs. more than early Series II cars. Power for the roadster and coupe again came from the familiar 4.2-liter twin-cam six, which produced 246 hp with twin Zenith carburetors.

A new Series III E-Type with a V-12 engine bowed in March of 1971. The V-12 had initially been meant for racing, then for a new sedan, but it was eventually introduced in the Jaguar sports cars only. At that time, only Ferrari and Lamborghini offered production-type V-12s, but the new Jaguar engine would soon became nearly as well-known as the original six.

OCW Archive

# 1971-'74 Series III E-Type V-12

Starting in March 1971, the engine beneath the bonnet of the E-Type Jaguar was a gorgeous-looking, highly-detailed, all-aluminum V-12. It was Jaguar's first all-new engine since the debut of the XK120, although the venerable twin-cam six had come in a variety of displacements over the years.

Cars carrying this power plant were called Series III models and a total of 15,290 were produced from 1971 to 1975. Of these cars, 7,990 were convertibles and 7,300 were 2+2 coupes.

Both new E-Types were basically the same as the previous six-cylinder models, although the open car was now officially called a convertible, rather than a roadster. Both featured integral steel body construction with sub-frames.

The convertible was priced at $6,950 and weighed 3,450 lbs., while the 2+2 was $375 pricier, but weighed the same. An enlarged bonnet bulge suggested the additional power that the V-12 supplied.

The wheel openings grew taller and were highlighted by marked flares and wider 6.00 x 15 tires were specified. Front and rear track also increased to 54.3 in. and 53 in., respectively. The former plain oval grille was treated to a cross-hatched insert, while the front end added a chrome molding and revised bumpers.

Both remaining body styles rode the same 105-in. wheelbase and both used the steeper-angled windshield first seen on the 2+2 coupe. The convertible was 175.3 in. long and the 2+2 was about nine inches longer. Body heights were 48 in. and 50.1 in., respectively. They were 66.1 in. wide.

"E-Type" lettering decorated the trunk lid. Models destined for the United States market wore large black bumper guards. The wheels were wider now and came in slotted steel or center-locking wire styles. The brake rotors were now of the vented type.

A detachable hardtop was a $200 option for the convertible. Also added to many of these sports cars was air conditioning for $482, power steering for $160, wire wheels for $165 or chrome disc wheels for $77, a heated rear window for the 2+2 at $44 and white sidewall tires for $36.

The new engine was a 60-degree, overhead-cam V-12 with a 90 x 70-mm bore and stroke and 5343-cc displacement. It had solid valve lifters, a 9.0:1 compression ratio and four Zenith carburetors. This engine produced 272 hp at 5850 and 304 lbs.-ft. of torque at 3600 rpm. Combustion chambers in the new engine were formed into the piston tops, which worked with flat cylinder heads.

*The Series III Jaguar XKE, like this silver convertible, used a V-12 power plant.*

Because of emissions changes in the U.S., as well as increased weight, the impact of the power boost was somewhat diminished. The V-12 in the U.S. now had a 7.8:1 compression ratio and delivered 241 hp at 5750 rpm. Torque was rated 285 lbs.-ft. at 3500 rpm. In contrast, the European V-12 had a 9.0:1 compression ratio and was rated at 265 bhp.

The 1972 Jaguars were introduced to the U.S. market on Dec. 13, 1971. Little change was evident in the E-Type cars, but prices took a rather large leap (for the time) to $7,338 for the convertible and $7,732 for the 2+2 coupe.

Jaguar had about 301 dealers in the U.S. at this time. The company was still based in Coventry, England, but its American operations were headquartered in Leonia, New Jersey.

As the '70s progressed, Jaguar—like other foreign and domestic automakers—was forced to raise prices and cut performance due to restrictive pollution laws and insurance policies in the United States. The 1973 Jaguar E-Type convertible was now an $8,475 item, while the 2+2 coupe retailed for a hefty $8,920.

Weights increased as more and more equipment was mandated for the cars and they now tipped the scale at 3,462 to 3,466 lbs. E70VR15 Dunlop tires were now standard.

For its final year in the Jaguar lineup, the 1974 E-Type convertible's engine continued in detuned form for the U.S. market, with 7.8:1 compression. No coupe was offered this year. Standard equipment included leather-faced, semi-reclining bucket seats with almond Ambla leather trimmed interior, tachometer, trip odometer, and Dunlop E70VR15 SP Sport whitewall tires on ventilated chrome disc wheels.

Body colors this year were: British Racing Green, Azure Blue, Dark Blue, Fern Grey, Greensand, Old English White, Pale Primrose, Sable, Signal Red, Silver Grey, Regency Red, and Turquoise. Prices cracked the $9,000 barrier by $200.

The final XK-E or E-Type coupes were built at the end of the 1973 model year and the last convertibles came off the line in mid-1974. Reduction to a three-day work week early in 1974 limited shipments of Jaguars to the U.S.

Jaguar

# 1976-'96 XJS GT Coupe V-12

The all-new Jaguar XJS GT coupe V-12 sports car debuted for 1976. The $19,000 car was the first Jaguar styled by an outsider, without Sir William Lyons. Features included a low-sweeping hood, smooth sides, and rounded corners.

Quad round headlights sat in oval housings at the ends of a squat, wide rectangular grille. A black rubber front bumper contained amber park/signal lights and side marker lights ahead of the front wheels.

A "flying buttress" roof line appeared at the rear of the XJS, with extensions on each side that reached all the way to the car's tail. The gas-filler lid was located on the left-hand panel. Large black moldings were placed behind each rear quarter window. Spoilers were used below the front and rear fascias. A crease line ran the full length of the car, just across the top of the modestly flared rear wheel well.

Standard equipment included a Borg-Warner Model 12 three-speed automatic transmission, air conditioning with automatic temperature control, an AM/FM stereo radio with 8-track tape player, power windows, tinted glass, fully-reclining leather-faced front seats (with adjustable headrests), and more. All instruments sat in a nacelle ahead of the driver.

Standard colors were British Racing Green, Regency Red, Silver Grey, Greensand, Signal Red, Dark Blue, Fern Grey, Old English White, Squadron Blue, Carriage Brown, and Yellow Gold. The new coupe weighed in at 3,935 lbs. About 4,020 examples were built. Sales were aided by the fact Jaguar had an unusually long 15-month model year in 1976.

The same 60-degree, overhead-cam V-12 that had powered the last of the E-Types was used. The engine was fitted with a Bosch-Lucas electronic fuel injection system rather than four Zenith carburettors. The 5343-cc engine used a slightly raised 8.0:1 compression ratio and was rated for 244-hp at 4500/5250 rpm and 269 lbs.-ft. of torque at 4500 rpm. It had slightly more horsepower with less torque than the final E-Type engine offered. Top speed of the XJS was about 150 mph.

The XJS had a 102-in. wheelbase, three inches shorter than the E-Type. Its overall length of 192.25 in. was nearly eight inches longer than the last XKE. It stood 47.8 in. high and 70.6 in. wide, with a 58.6-in. front and rear tread. Standard Dunlop 205/70VR15 Sports Super steel-belted whitewall tires rode on cast-aluminum-alloy wheels.

A three-speed automatic transmission and power-assisted rack-and-pinion steering were incorporated. The front suspension consisted of semi-trailing wishbones with coil springs and an anti-roll bar. At the rear was an independent suspension with lower wishbones, lower radius arms, coil springs, and an anti-roll bar. Four-wheel disc brakes were also provided. There was little difference

*New for 1976 was the Jaguar XJS, here in GT coupe form.*

in the 1977 XJS, when 3,861 copies of the sports model were built. The price crept up to $20,250. In 1978, the window sticker said $23,900, but there was little difference. A total of 3,217 units were produced. Ditto for 1979 (2,414 cars built) and 1980 (1,131 cars built), when the price tag climbed to $25,000 and $30,000, respectively.

By 1980, there were some revisions in the body color palette which now offered Atlantis Blue metallic, Brazilia Brown metallic, Cotswold Yellow, Damson Red, Racing Green metallic, Sebring Red, and Tudor White. Jaguar's 2+2 sports coupe wasn't officially listed for sale in the United States during 1981 when 1,252 XJS models were built.

In 1982, Jaguar's 12-cylinder coupe continued with little change, except for the adoption of a high-swirl, high-compression cylinder head—named the name H.E. (for "High Efficiency"). With a new 11.5:1 compression ratio, the 5.3-liter engine now developed 262 hp at 5000 rpm and 290 lbs.-ft. of torque at 3000 rpm. Production hit approximately 3,348 units in 1982.

A revised 1983 XJS coupe was anticipated, but did not arrive. There was a carryover model with little changed from 1982. Despite a $34,000 price, production rose to about 4,457 units. A cabriolet version of the XJS became available in Europe late in 1983, but didn't arrive in the U.S. until 1987. Except for the addition of halogen headlights and new body color choices, the Jaguar XJS coupe was a carryover from 1983. Standard features included a General Motor Turbo-Hydra-Matic 400-80 three-speed automatic transmission, power four-wheel disc brakes, power steering, full leather interior trim, a leather-bound steering wheel and more. Production rose to about 5,813 cars with a $700 price increase.

A $1,300 price increase and new Pirelli P5 tires were the only apparent 1985 changes. But the season's big news was Jaguar's second top-five ranking in the J.D. *Power's Consumer Satisfaction Index* for new cars. This represented a dramatic improvement for a company that had suffered quality problems. The 1986 XJS got new body colors and a new burl walnut style veneer treatment on the instrument board and door inserts.

A $1,300 power sun roof joined the option list. The price on the 3,980-lb. coupe remained at $36,000. Jaguar sold a total of 5,380 XJS models in the United States in 1987. A manual override was added to the climate-control system.

The 1988 XJS coupe had a new center console with wood veneer trim, heated front-seat cushions, and electrically-adjustable driver lumbar support. It sold for $41,500. A total of 4,783 XJS models were made. In 1989, there was a sizable price hike and new items included electrically-heated seats with power lumbar adjustment and a new steering wheel.

An anti-lock braking system (ABS) developed jointly by Jaguar and the Alfred Teves Company also was adopted. The familiar 5.3-liter V-12 and three-speed automatic transmission remained. Standard equipment included a tachometer, power windows and door locks, heated power mirrors, cruise control, a trip computer, tinted glass, intermittent windshield wipers, and more.

A driver's-side airbag became standard in 1990 XJS models. This change caused the telescoping steering column to disappear, but a tilt feature replaced it. A limited-production "Collection Rouge" coupe, offered only in Signal Red, cost $51,000. It included a Magnolia leather interior, elm burl veneer and diamond-polished alloy wheels. The regular coupe was $48,000.

Two new interior colors—Magnolia and Doeskin—helped Jaguar highlight its new "Classic Collection" color palette in 1991. The coupe saw a $5,000 price increase.

Revisions for 1992 included wrap-around neutral-density taillights, flared rocker panels, a new grille and new front chrome trim. An instrument panel, sport seats, steering column stalk, and computer were new interior upgrades. The coupe was now retailing for $60,500.

The 1993 XJS line added a 4.0-liter 223-hp six-cylinder engine, which was available in either body style. This increased Jaguar's sales, but also gave the V-12 the reputation for being a more collectible sports car. It was certainly rarer because of its price.

In 1994, the 4.0-liter coupe sold for $53,400, compared to $72,350 for the matching V-12.

In 1994, both engines used in XJS models were upgraded. The V-12's output was increased from 263 hp to 313 hp.

Door mirrors, grille and headlight bezels were matched to the body color on V-12 versions.

Celebrating its 20th and final year of production, the 1996 XJS became the longest running model in Jaguar history.

*Jaguar*

# 1987-'96 XJS GT Cabriolet V-12

**A**n all-new version of Jaguar's sports car debuted for 1976. The V-12-powered XJS GT coupe promoted as "a new breed of cat." It had an appearance completely different from that of the E-Type with a low-sweeping hood, four round headlights in oval housings, and a wide rectangular grille. Although the XJS V-12 would remain in production for 20 years, a convertible was not available for the first 10 years.

A Targa-roofed cabriolet version of the V-12 coupe was the first "open" model to arrive in the U.S. It showed up in the spring of 1986, as a 1987 model. This two-seat XJSC model carried a $44,850 price, compared to $39,700 for the 1987 fixed-head coupe. It had removable Targa roof panels and a manually-operated folding rear-quarter top.

The semi-open XJSC was created, in England, by making modifications to the XJS coupe. The 1987 cabriolet included a removable hardtop section with heated rear glass. This hardtop could be mounted in place of the standard folding soft top. Also featured were

*Catch a glimpse of the ruby-red Jaguar XJS convertible!*

full rear luggage-area carpeting and two locking storage bins.

In addition to the Targa-style cabriolet, Jaguar added a full-fledged 1988 XJS convertible in July 1987. Its introduction had been anticipated for some time. This 2+2 convertible was actually a conversion performed by Hess & Eisenhart, the American custom body builder from Cincinnati, Ohio. It had a power top and was available only on special order.

The 1988 XJS cabriolet had a new center console with wood veneer trim, heated front-seat cushions, and electrically-adjustable lumbar support for the driver's seat. Prices for Jaguar's open models this year were $41,500 for the 4,250-lb. Hess & Eisenhart convertible and $47,450 for the two-passenger XJSC cabriolet.

A total of 4,783 XJS models of all types were made.

The year 1989 brought a sizable hike in XJS prices. A brand new open-body model retailed for $56,000. This was not a limited-production convertible conversion. Instead, Jaguar now offered a true two-seat convertible that was built in its own plant in Coventry, England. The semi-open Targa-style cabriolet was also dropped. The new XJS convertible had a power top, a heated glass back window and a locking luggage compartment behind the seats. Other new equipment included electrically-heated seats with power lumbar adjustment, a new steering wheel and 235/60VR15 Pirelli P600 tires mounted on alloy wheels.

An anti-lock braking system (ABS), developed jointly by Jaguar and the Alfred Teves Company, was added to the equipment list in 1989. The familiar 5.3-liter V-12 and three-speed automatic transmission remained.

Other standard features included a tachometer, power windows, power door locks, heated power mirrors, cruise control, a trip computer, tinted glass, intermittent windshield wipers, an AM/FM stereo with cassette player, a power antenna, a rear defogger, fog lights and a leather-wrapped steering wheel.

A driver's-side airbag became standard in 1990 XJS convertibles. The telescoping steering column disappeared, but a tilt steering wheel replaced it. The price tag on the convertible this year was $57,000.

Magnolia and Doeskin interiors were added in 1991 and Jaguar promoted a "Classic Collection" of color and trim combinations. This year, the convertible cost $6,600 more than it had in 1990. Revisions for 1992 included new neutral-density wraparound taillights, flared rocker panels, a new grille and new front chrome trim. A redesigned instrument panel, new sport-style seats, a new steering column stalk and a new computer highlighted interior changes. The window sticker on the ragtop was up to $67,500.

For 1993, the number of XJS models doubled with the addition of a 4.0-liter 223-hp six-cylinder engine in both body styles. This helped to increase Jaguar's sales, but made the V-12 convertible Jaguar's "real" sports car.

The 4.0-liter convertible was more buyer-friendly at $61,570, but the $82,550 V-12 version was definitely the enthusiast's car. The 1993 convertible also got new front and rear cross braces and a stainless steel underfloor.

In 1994, both engines used in Jaguar XJS models were upgraded. The V-12's output was increased from 263 hp to 313 hp. On V-12 versions, the door mirrors, grille and headlight bezels were matched to the body color instead of chrome plated. The V-12 convertible now weighed 4,306 lbs.

Celebrating its 20th year of production, the XJS became the longest running model in Jaguar history in 1996.

The convertible, which had only a 10-year history, was changed to 2+2 seating. This was to be its final year of production.

# 1996-2003 XK8

One of the most elegant cars to be introduced in the 1990s was the exciting Jaguar XK8. With a brand new, state-of-the-art V-8, this sleek model was available as a 2+2 coupe for $64,900 or a 2+2 convertible for $69,900. The XK8 won the hearts of the press and of Jaguar enthusiasts.

The V-8 engine shared no parts with any previous Jaguar power plant. In addition, there was no commanality with products made by Ford—Jaguar's new parent company—except the crankshaft "woodruff" key. This car was designed to show the world that Jaguar had returned to a position of prominence in the world market.

An all-aluminum 32-valve, double-overhead-cam V-8, the new

*Introduced in 1997, the Jaguar XK8 carried Jaguar into a new century of car making.*

engine had an 86 x 86-mm bore and stroke and 3980-cc displacement. Featuring a 10.75:1 compression ratio and electronic port fuel injection, it cranked up 290 hp at 6100 rpm and 290 lbs.-ft. of torque at 4,200 rpm. The engine was capable of taking the XK8 coupe from 0-to-60 mph in 6.5 sec., while the convertible required 6.7 sec. Quarter-mile acceleration times were 15.2 seconds for the coupe and 15.5 seconds for the ragtop.

Riding a trim 101.9-in.-wheelbase platform, the XK8 stretched 187.4 in. end-to-end. Both models were 72 in. wide, but at an even 51 inches, the coupe was a tad lower than the 51.40 in. high convertible. The car had a 59.2-in. front tread and a 59-in. rear tread. Standard technical features included rack-and-pinion steering, all-wheel disc brakes and a five-speed automatic transmission.

Despite being a brand-new car for 1997, the XK8 received numerous enhancements for 1998. These included automatic headlights, an engine immobilizer system, an audio system with an integrated telephone keypad, and steering-wheel-mounted audio controls modified to accommodate an optional cell phone. Despite the improvements, the prices were unchanged.

For 1999, the 4.0-liter V-8 engine received a number of internal upgrades including dual-tipped platinum plugs, air-assist fuel injectors and a revised electronic throttle and engine management system. In addition, the XK8s offered two new color choices called Phoenix (signal red) and Alpine (light green) for the convertible only. A beige top was also offered on the convertible for the first time. This year, the coupe price rose to $65,750, while the convertible's window sticker climbed to $70,750.

As a new Millennium dawned, Jaguar put its supercharged XJR engine into the XK8 coupe and convertible to create the XKR. It was easily distinguished by its wire-mesh grille, functional louvers on the hood, a petite rear deck spoiler and 18-in. alloy wheels. The supercharged Jaguar engine made this the fastest accelerating Jaguar since the X-220, which was not marketed domestically. All XK8s received full-range traction control, rain-sensing windshield wipers and larger-diameter front brake rotors. Prices for XK8s went to $66,200 for the coupe and $71,200 for the convertible, while the corresponding XKRs went for $76,800 and $81,800.

For 2001, in an effort to increase its performance image, Jaguar offered a selection of high-performance components and to showcase the "go-fast" parts, the company introduced limited-edition "Silverstone" models of the XK8 coupe and convertible. The dual-overhead-cam 32-valve V-8 was fitted with a Rootes-type supercharger and intercooler. Although it displaced the same 3,980 cc as the standard XK 8 engine, the Silverstone edition developed 370 hp at 6150 rpm and 387 lbs.-ft. of torque at 3600 rpm.

Silverstone Edition cars were also equipped with BBS modular wheels, ultra-low profile tires and aluminum four-piston caliper Brembo brakes.

Platinum paint and unique interior appointments distinguished the Silverstone edition XK8.

From the use of stained bird's-eye maple wood on the dash to red stitching on the steering wheel, center console, door armrests, and floor mats, the Silverstone edition was the top-of-the-line Jaguar.

All 2001 XKs had de-powered front and side airbags and front seats with separate head restraints. The taillights were changed to a multi-reflector type and the front fog lights were fitted in a more flush fashion. Prices were $69,155 for the 3,726-lb. coupe and $74,155 for the 3,962-lb. convertible.

Although the 2002 XK8 was primarily a carryover model (since a major technical revision was in the wings for 2003), the sporty Jaguar was still able to make some news when the third in a series of "Austin Powers" movies debuted on July 26, 2002. Finished like the Union Jack —the flag of England—this red-white and blue promotional vehicle was featured at the New York International Automobile Show that opened on April 1 that year.

In August of 2002, at the Pebble Beach Concours d' Elegance, Jaguar introduced a new, technology-laden version of the XK8 for the 2003 model year. Although only modestly updated on the outside (Jaguar described the appearance as "a subtle variation on the theme rather than a new look"), the car boasted a more powerful 4.2-liter V-8, a state-of-the-art ZF 6-speed transmission, a standard Dynamic Stability Control system and Emergency Brake Assist feature, and an Adaptive Restraint Technology (dual-stage airbag) system. Adaptive Cruise Control was a new option.

Externally, the XK8 sported new body badging, four new exterior colors (Adriatic Blue, Jaguar Racing Green, Ebony, and Midnight), a range of trim combinations, and three new wheel designs. Xenon headlights that gave the front end a distinctive look were optional. All XJs now included the performance option specially-shaped Recaro sports seats trimmed in soft grain leather (three colors available) and the Aluminum Pack with alloy instrument bezels, door levers, pedal pads, and tread plates. Prices were set at $69,975 for the coupe model and $74,975 for the convertible.

Even lighter than the previous 200-kg. "AJ" V-8, thanks to its redesigned cylinder block and bed plate, the new 4.2-liter version employed special lightweight aluminum alloys for the block, heads and many other components. With an 86.0 x 90.3-mm bore and stroke, its capacity was increased to 4,196 cc and horsepower jumped to 300 at 6000 rpm with the torque rating going to 310 lbs.-ft. at 4100 rpm.

OCW Archive

Jaguar

# 1998-2003 XKR

**J**aguar's XK series has always been special. The underlying character of the original XK8 could be defined as: powerful, original, sensuous, and exciting. The XK8 set new sales records and became the fastest-selling sports car in Jaguar's history. In 1998, a more dramatic, supercharged XKR was unveiled. It delivered more impressive performance and added another dimension.

Supercharging had already been proven with the powerful and refined XJR6 saloon. The V-8, with its lightweight, stiff cylinder block provided the perfect platform for a forced-induction engine. It delivered a special combination of power with refinement.

The compact, light, four-cam (32-valve) V-8 had programmable variable valve phasing. The all-aluminum engine fit into Jaguar's signature reputation for high performance, smooth power, and exceptional mechanical refinement.

A Rootes-type supercharger and intercooler were fitted. The 4.0-liter (3980-cc) engine featured a 9.0:1 compression ratio and an electronic sequential port fuel-injection system. It produced 370 hp at 6150 rpm and 387 lbs.-ft. of torque at 3600 rpm.

The XKR was distinguished by its wire-mesh grille, functional hood louvers, petite rear deck spoiler and 18-in. alloy wheels. The supercharged engine made it the fastest-accelerating Jaguar since the X-220, which wasn't sold in America.

The XKR made it to the United States in 2000, the same year that all XKs received full-range traction control, rain-sensing windshield wipers, and larger-diameter front brake rotors. The coupe tipped the scales at 3,785 lbs. and sold for $66,200. The ragtop was 236 lbs. heavier and $5,000 pricier. The XKR did 0-to-60 mph in 6.9 seconds and covered the quarter mile in 13.9 seconds.

In 2000, limited-edition "Silverstone" versions of the XKR coupe and convertible celebrated Jaguar's entry into Formula 1. Platinum paint, a richer interior, BBS modular wheels, ultra-low profile tires and aluminum four-piston caliper Brembo brakes were some of the features.

All 2001 XKRs received de-powered front and side airbags and front seats with separate head restraints. Coupe prices were $80,156 for the XKR and $96,905 for the XKR S, while the ragtops were $85,155 and $96,905, respectively.

The special edition XKR 100 followed in 2001. It commemorated the birth of Jaguar founder Sir William Lyons. The XK had become an

*The Jaguar XKR showed the company was ready to continue its leadership as a fine car maker.*

icon with more than 70,000 units sold worldwide.

For 2003, Jaguar revised the beautiful XKR coupe and convertible, which changed under the skin. A larger, more powerful 4.2-litre V-8 increased the car's performance. A ZF six-speed "stepped-type" automatic transmission also ensured that drivers were able to make the most of the power. Enhanced electronic and other equipment made the new XKR even better to drive than the original.

The 400-hp XKR shared the most powerful series production engine in Jaguar's history with the latest S-TYPE R sports saloon. A package of advances over previous-generation XKs also encompassed the latest electronic driving aids.

Xenon headlights with an automatic-self-leveling function and high-performance Brembo brakes were standard on the XKR and the latest R Performance range of options including unique Recaro seats and a package of interior details. A handling package offered an improved suspension and steering systems on coupes only.

Jaguar's new AJ34 V-8 was developed at the Engineering Centre at Whitley, Coventry, England. It retained the compact, 90-degree V-8 configuration, but was structurally stiffer. With the 400-hp supercharged V-8, an XKR coupe could go from 0-to-60 mph in 5.2 seconds.

To match the increased output and the increased mechanical and thermal stresses that supercharging imposed, the XKR V-8 had pistons forged from single billets of aluminum alloy. It also featured oil jet cooling on the underside of the piston crowns, for maximum cooling and minimum distortion.

The XKR's rotor-type Eaton supercharger was belt-driven from the front of the crankshaft. It featured two industry firsts on a production car supercharger—helical rotor gears for low noise and coated rotors for increased efficiency. These innovations contributed to a supercharger speed five per cent greater than the supercharger in the 4.0-litre engine.

The state-of-the-art six-speed ZF automatic transmission provided greater mid-range punch and effortless acceleration. Jaguar's classic J-Gate shift provided automatic or manual control modes.

The XKR had the same independent front suspension used under the XK8 with double, unequal-length wishbones, coil springs and telescopic dampers. The road springs were mounted directly onto the body and the wishbones were secured to an immensely rigid, but light all-aluminum-alloy front crossbeam with hydraulic mounts between it and the engine.

The rear suspension used coil springs, independent telescopic dampers and an unequal length wishbone layout, with the drive shafts acting as upper links. Like the front suspension, the rear assembly was mounted on an isolated sub frame.

Brembo brakes were standard on the supercharged XKR. The system featured 355 x 32mm ventilated front discs and 330 x 28-mm ventilated rear discs with four-piston aluminum calipers carrying the Jaguar R Performance logo. Steel-braided brake lines completed the setup.

Three new alloy wheel designs were added to the wide choice already available.

The R Performance optional wheels were made by performance wheel specialists BBS and featured two-piece modular construction with die-cast and spun rims and titanium screws. Optional 18-in. Centaur and Hydra wheels were new for the XKR. A wide choice of other styles was available.

The XKR also featured high-intensity Xenon headlights, automatic headlight leveling and power wash as standard equipment.

*Jaguar's XKR coupe had a sleek and stunning appearance, especially from the front .*

*This concept car predicts great things are in store for Jaguar owners of the future.*

# JENSEN

Andrew Morland

# 1949-1958 Interceptor

Jensen automobiles resulted from a collaboration between two brothers, Allan and Richard Jensen. Both began their careers in the 1920s, Richard as an apprentice for Wolseley and Allan with a radiator company. In 1923, they tore apart a new Austin Chummy to turn it into a sporty two-seater and entered the modified roadster in a hillclimb. A much-impressed chief engineer from the Standard Motor Company asked the brothers to produce a similar body on a Standard chassis. This led to a production car—the Avon Standard—late in the decade.

The brothers became directors of W.J. Smith & Sons, a small coachbuilder. In 1934, they took over, adopting the name Jensen Motors Ltd. The factory was in West Bromwich, England. In addition to creating bodies for other manufacturers like Morris and Wolseley, Allan and Richard wanted to turn out their own cars. American actor Clark Gable shipped a Ford chassis overseas to be fitted with one of Jensen's low-slung bodies.

Demand for replicas of Clark's car led to the introduction of an all-out Jensen in 1935. Both 2.5- and 3.5-liter versions were produced, with a standard two-speed Columbia rear axle and hydraulic clutch. Edsel Ford authorized the supply of Ford components to the Jensens. An S-type saloon and drophead coupe soon joined the tourer.

Just before World War II came the announcement of a Jensen Type H powered by a Nash straight-eight or Lincoln V-12, but military production intervened. Civilian work resumed quickly in 1946, with the announcement of a Meadows-engined PW saloon. The car's aluminum-block straight eight had problems, but subsequent engines came from Austin's big Sheerline series and wound up in the saloon and the Interceptor cabriolet introduced in September of 1949.

Rakishly handsome, the open-bodied Jensen rode a 112.5-in.

*Admirers have enjoyed looking at this beautiful Jensen Interceptor drophead since 1954.*

wheelbase and measured 188 in. overall. It was 58 in. high and 66 in. wide. At 54.5 in., the front tread was 2.5 in. narrower than the rear tread. The price of an Interceptor was about $3,600 at the factory in England.

Only two Jensens are thought to have been sold in the U.S. during 1950, and one in 1951. In 1953, *Auto Age* magazine claimed there was only one Jensen in the entire country.

The car's appearance was similar to that of the Austin A40 Sports model, which had a Jensen-built body. With a pontoon-shaped profile, the Interceptor body was formed of aluminum panels. These were mounted on a wooden framework, atop a box-section steel chassis with a tubular center portion.

The car had full wheel openings, a one-piece windshield, inboard built-in headlights and front vent windows. Thick horizontal bars sat in a recessed grille opening that was flat on the bottom, but curved across the top and sides. Air intake vents for the brakes were added beside the grille late in 1950. A wide insignia at the front looked almost like an air scoop.

Beneath the Interceptor's bonnet was a four-main-bearings 130-hp Austin six. This engine had a 87 x 111-mm bore and stroke and displaced 3,993 cc. It had a 6.8:1 compression ratio, solid valve lifters, and a Stromberg downdraft carburetor. The factory claimed top speeds approaching 105 mph, although road testers reported closer to 95 mph. It moved from 0-to-60 mph in 12.5 sec. and could cover the quarter-mile in about 19 seconds. A low piston speed allowed quick cruising with minimal engine wear. 12-volt electricals were fitted.

Bench-type seating was advertised as being suitable for four. The convertible top's back and quarter windows were made of Perspex, which slipped into body recesses as the roof lowered. The car weighed only 2,800 lb.

The Interceptor's four-speed gearbox was synchronized on the top three gears and came with overdrive. It had gear ratios of 12.75:1 in first, 8.78:1 in second, 5.40:1 in third, 3.77:1 in fourth, 2.85:1 in overdrive and 15.4:1 in reverse.

A 3.77:1 rear axle was employed. An independent suspension with coil springs and wishbones was used up front. Semi-elliptic leaf springs supported the rear. The steering was of cam-and-roller design. Girling hydraulic drum brakes were used. The tires used were 6.00 x 16 Dunlops. There were no major changes in 1951.

An Interceptor hardtop coupe (called a saloon) joined the original cabriolet in October 1951, as a 1952 model. It had opening rear quarter windows and the standard equipment list included a Smith's heater.

Jensen's 1953 models were introduced in September 1952. Exercising a penchant for British understatement, *The Motor* magazine noted that the Interceptor's "good handling and effortless cruising are commendable features." The parking lights on the Interceptor were moved to the fender tops and a bright rub strip was added to the body sides.

A Laycock de Normanville overdrive also became available.

Both body styles were advertised as five-passenger models. Standard equipment included a tachometer, ammeter, oil pressure gauge, temperature gauge, fuel gauge, electric clock, trafficators (turn signals), leather-covered instrument panel and twin-tone horns. The price of the cabriolet, in England, was 1,700 Pounds Sterling, plus purchase tax.

For model-year 1954, the Interceptor's hood line was lowered. Gone were the chrome grille-surround molding and badge. The open Interceptor was now called a convertible. The following year, Interceptors were offered in standard and Deluxe trims. Deluxe models came with a radio, windshield washer, higher-powered headlights, passing lights, and driving lamps and two-speed windshield wipers. The Interceptor's 1955 factory price was about $4,777 in U.S. dollars.

In 1956, rectangular air vents were added to the sides of front fenders and Deluxe models added twin horizontal trim strips. Otherwise, both the saloon and convertible continued with little change. The factory price was about $4,760.

The convertible and saloon continued, with minimal change, into the 1957 model year, when the convertible was discontinued. Only the saloon (sedan) remained for 1958, which was its last year. However, the Interceptor name would be revived again in the '60s.

OCW Archive

# 1954-1957 Jensen 541

The fiberglass-bodied Jensen Type 541 appeared at the London Motor Show in October 1953. It had the same engine as the Interceptor model, but in a 500-lb. lighter coupe with a 7-1/2-in. shorter wheelbase. The body featured smoothly streamlined styling reflecting an Italian influence, although its appearance was quite similar, overall, to that of the Interceptor model.

America's Corvette and Kaiser-Darrin had bowed recently, but fiberglass body construction was uncommon on European cars, so the Type 541 was considered innovative. In fact, it was the first four-seat production car to feature a fiberglass body. Three distinct fiberglass moldings were used: one for the entire front end, a second for the roof, and a third for the rear end. The doors were made of light alloy. The body rode on a box-section tubular steel chassis.

The Type 541 had a curved one-piece windshield. Small round parking lights sat below the built-in headlights, which flanked an oval grille opening. The front-fender crease tapered to a point at the front and rear. A wraparound back window went into the fastback rear end

*The streamlined fiberglass body of the Jensen 541 made it an innovative car.*

and the wheel openings were fully rounded. Credit for the design went to Richard Jensen, who had assistance from Eric Neale. A Type 541 cost some $4,900 delivered in the United States.

The low, curvy fastback coupe body had rear quarter windows and rode an Interceptor-like chassis with coil springs in front and semi-elliptic leaf springs at the rear. The power plants were also similar, with the 2,688-lb. coupe using the same 3993-cc six-cylinder engine as the heavier Interceptor, but having three S.U. carburetors.

The car's improved power-to-weight ratio resulted in much brisker performance than that delivered by the Interceptor. The Type 541 could do the quarter mile in 18 sec. and had a top speed approaching 120 mph with a 3.54:1 rear axle According to contemporary references, the car was only slightly slower (108-mph top speed) with a higher 3.31:1 rear axle. It could move from

10 mph to 30 mph in a mere six seconds. With the optional overdrive, piston speed at 103 mph was only 2500 ft. per min., which meant reduced engine wear and better fuel economy. In fact, the Type 541 got about 24 mpg.

With its 105-in. stance, the Type 541 measured only 174 in. overall. It stood 53 in. high and was 63 in. wide. The tread width was

52 in. front and rear. The car's 5.50 x 16 Dunlop tires were mounted on steel disc wheels. A 32-ft. turn circle was measured. Buyers had a choice of 3.31:1 or 3.54:1 rear axle ratios.

Little about the 541 changed over its brief production run. In 1956, rectangular air vents and a trim strip on the sides of the front fenders were added.

Andrew Morland

# 1958-1960 Jensen 541R

In 1958, standard and DeLuxe versions of the Jensen Type 541 two-door saloon continued to be produced with few changes, but there was big news in the form of a new Type 541R model, which was introduced at the London Auto Show in October 1957.

A true high-performance car, the Type 541R could be identified by the torpedo-shaped horizontal moldings protruding along the front and rear fenders, above the wheel openings. A horizontal trim bar with a large round center emblem sat at the front of the oval grille. Four-wheel disc brakes were standard equipment.

The Type 541R engine was essentially the same 87 x 111-mm bore-and-stroke 4-liter Austin six used in other Jensens, but with a redesigned cylinder head, a longer-dwell camshaft and a stiffer crankshaft. Twin S.U. carburetors were mounted on the right side of the block on early versions instead of three on the left side (although Jensen later went back to using three carburetors in later Type 541Rs).

The solid-lifter engine had a higher compression ratio (7.6:1 compared to 7.4:1) than the regular Type 541 and produced 140 hp at 4000 rpm, although some American magazines listed horsepower ratings as high as 152.

A Laycock de Normanville overdrive unit was standard and rack-and-pinion steering replaced the cam-and-roller arrangement used in other Jensens. The factory claimed a top speed of 125 mph for the Type 541R and said it could do 0-to-60 mph in 9.3 seconds and 0-to-100 mph in 27 sec. Its quarter-mile time was 17.5 seconds.

*The covered grille gives away the identity of the 1959 Jensen 541R.*

The forward part of the Type 541R chassis was all new and featured a stiffened wall structure. The front end was hinged to tilt forward as a complete unit. The luggage compartment lid was hinged at top and the spare tire was concealed in a separate compartment below. A swiveling, driver-contolled air-intake shutter was incorporated in the performance model.

Factory body colors included Black, Ivory, Reno Red, Princess Grey, Botticelli Blue, and Deep Carriage Green. Front bucket seats and a rear bench seat with leather trim were also standard. A three-spoke steering wheel and tachometer were standard.

On the Type 541R, Armstrong piston-type shocks replaced the telescopic units used on other Jensens. Buyers also had a choice of 5.50 x 16 Dunlop tires on the standard disc wheels or 6.40 x 15 tires on optional wire wheels. The car sold for about $4,018 in England and about $6,000 in the United States.

In 1958, the standard and DeLuxe Type 541s were dropped. Jensen's focus switched to the high-performance 541R, which continued with little change, except for a price increase to $5,348 in England. Jensen made the Type 541R until the introduction of the 541S in October 1960. That year, the company also signed an agreement to produce bodies for the stylish Volvo P1800 sports car.

Andrew Morland

# 1961-1962 Jensen 541S

One final variant of the six-cylinder Type 541 appeared for a late October 1960 debut, just before Jensen turned to V-8 power plants. This car—the Type 541S—sported a restyled front end with a horizontal oval mesh-pattern grille that was slightly recessed into the opening. Dual round parking and signal lights sat below each round headlight.

An aggressive-looking air scoop stood at the front of the hood. Its edges curved outward, all the way to the grille top. The body sides displayed the same protruding moldings on front and rear fenders that were seen on the previous Type 541R model. A small air-intake opening was also located low on the cowl.

Among technical changes, an automatic transmission and a limited-slip differential became standard equipment. A four-speed manual gear box was optional at first, but was then dropped completely during the 1962 model year. The chassis side tubes were moved outward to provide additional space for passengers. For cooling purposes, an adjustable internal radiator blind replaced the former swiveling panel.

Beneath the bonnet of the Type 541S was the same 3993-cc Austin

*The 541S model was the final six-cylinder version of the Jensen.*

Princess engine as before. It had triple S.U. carburetors and carried a new 135 hp at 3700 rpm rating. However, American sources reported horsepower ratings of 152-154 at 4100 rpm.

Other new specifications included a 2.93:1 rear axle ratio and size 6.40 x 15 tires as standard equipment.

The body width increased to 67 in. and the front and rear tread widths were both increased to 55.2 in.

Standard equipment included a radio, spotlights, a first-aid kit and a fire extinguisher. This was also the first British car to come with seat belts as standard equipment. By this time, Jensen had a distributor in America—Midland Continental Corp. of New York City.

Performance-wise, the Jensen factory pegged top speed at about 110 mph and suggested that the Type 541S could do 0-to-50 mph in 9.2 sec. and accelerate through the quarter mile in 18.8 seconds.

George and Sarah Phelps

# 1963-1966 Jensen C-V8

A new Jensen with a V-8 engine under its bonnet was introduced at the Earl's Court (London) Motor Show in October of 1962. The C-V8 model was a front-engine, rear-drive car with a combination fiberglass-and-metal body on a box-section tubular steel chassis. The company built only 314 of the C-V8 models in total. Most were two-door saloons, but a very small number of convertibles was turned out. The coupes weighed about 3,300 lbs.

Styling-wise, quad headlights replaced the former single units. Each pair was mounted diagonally in nacelles that were already angled, giving the front end a distinctive look that did not catch on with the car-buying public. The split grille was much lower than those used on previous Jensens and had a crosshatch-pattern insert. There was a small air scoop on the hood. A small, winged insignia decorated the area above the grille.

As in the 541 series, the bucket seats had provision for the insertion of extra padding. The back seats were described as "virtually armchairs." Standard equipment included a transistorized twin-speaker radio, a heating-and-ventilating system, leather upholstery, front-door map pockets, diagonal front seat belts, rear armrest pockets, a map light, two-speed self-parking wipers, and a lighted electric clock.

Like 541R and 541S models, the C-V8 had protruding body side moldings. The rear moldings led into a side-by-side trio of round taillights on each side of the back panel, mounted in a sculpted opening that also contained the license plate. The trunk lid had exposed hinges at its upper end. The body was a mix of metal and fiberglass with a sheet metal floor, aluminum doors, and fiberglass roof and rear end panels. A revised tubular chassis featured central parallel tubes rather than the old peripheral-tube design.

The 5916-cc (361-cid) Chrysler hydraulic-lifter V-8 promised brisk performance. It had a 105 x 86-mm bore and stroke. With a 9.0:1 compression ratio and single Carter four-barrel carburetor, the five-main-bearings engine produced 305 hp at 4800 rpm and 395 lbs.-ft. of torque at 3000 rpm. It was attached to a TorqueFlite three-speed automatic transmission.

An optional three-speed manual gear box with overdrive could be substituted for the automatic. Standard at the rear end was a 3.54:1 axle and Powr-Lok limited-slip differential. A first for British cars was the use of an alternator, rather than a DC generator. The top speed of the C-V8 was claimed to be 132 mph. It did 0-to-60 mph in 6.3 seconds and covered a quarter mile from standstill in 16 seconds.

*The Chrysler Corporation contribution gave the name to this Jensen—the C-V8.*

The C-V8 retained a 105-in. wheelbase, but was slightly longer than previous models with a 184.5-in. overall length. It stood 55 in. high and 67 in. wide. The 55.8-in. front track was slightly narrower than the 56.1-in. rear track. The steel disc wheels carried 6.70 x 15 tires. Other chassis features included rack-and-pinion steering and Dunlop four-wheel disc brakes. The front suspension was of independent design with wishbones and coil springs. A rigid axle and semi-elliptic leaf springs were used at the rear.

For its 1963 appearance at Earl's Court, the C-V8 Mark II changed little in appearance, but had new Armstrong Selectaride shock absorbers. However, by the first of the year, the original 361-cid V-8 was replaced by a 383-cid 300-hp V-8. This engine had a 108 x 86-mm bore and stroke and 6276-cc displacement. With a 10.0:1 compression ratio, it developed 330 hp at 4600 rpm.

A higher-ratio rear axle (3.07:1) and larger 6.70 x 15 tires were supplied with the new V-8.

Jensen described the C-V8 as "among the fastest full four-seater cars in production and certainly the most individual." With the new engine, the 0-to-60 mph time was lowered to 5 sec. and the quarter mile took 14.6 to 15.5 seconds

"Driver and passengers can chat or listen to the radio comfortably at well over 100 mph," said *Autocar* magazine about the C-V8, describing it as "a car that more than fulfills great expectations."

Production of the Mark II version of the C-V8 continued with little change until it was replaced by the more powerful Mark III in July of 1965. Subtle body changes marked the Mk III edition, including a lower cowl and deeper windshield, as well as reduced brightwork around each diagonal headlamp cluster.

A heated back window also became standard, as did a dual braking system. An "FF" version which stood for "Ferguson Formula," a four-wheel-drive system (also available in a new Interceptor) was introduced late in 1966. The C-V8 FF was four inches longer in wheelbase (109 in.) and three inches longer (187.5 in.) than the standard model. Otherwise, the two were similar.

The Mark III used an improved version of the 6276-cc (383-cid) Chrysler V-8 that produced 330 hp at 4600 rpm and 425 lbs.-ft. of torque at 2800 rpm. Other specifications were essentially the same as those of the Mark II type.

Andrew Morland

# 1967-1976 Interceptor

**B**y 1967, both Jensen brothers had retired, but the company remained in the car manufacturing business for almost another decade. Financial difficulties led to a takeover by a Norwegian-born American car dealer, Kjell Qvale and the installation of Donald Healey (and his son Geoffrey) on the board.

In October of 1966, a new car that revived the Interceptor name was introduced as a 1967 model. One of the most significant changes dropped fiberglass body work. The new, all-steel fastback body had cleaner lines than the C-V8. Designed by Touring (of Italy), it was initially built by the Italian coachbuilder Vignale. The new Interceptor was longer and lower with stainless steel trim.

Largely squarish with a rectangular grille, the new car's dominant styling feature was a huge, lift-up rear window and back-angled rear quarter windows. Side-by-side quad headlights sat directly above the rectangular park/signal lights.

Standard Interceptor equipment included power windows, a heated back window, front-door map pockets, reclining front seats, twin-speaker transistorized radio, heating-and-ventilation system, tachometer, underhood lighting and more. The wood-rimmed steering wheel was mounted on an adjustable column.

Jensen produced more than 300 cars with a sophisticated four-wheel-drive system developed by Harry Ferguson. These FF ("Ferguson Formula") models were longer to accommodate the full-time, four-wheel-drive system. The two-wheel-drive version had a single near-vertical vent ahead of the cowl, the FF had two. It featured a brushed stainless top and deep hood fluting. Power rack-and-pinion steering was standard, as was Maxaret anti-skid braking. The two models were similar in appearance and mechanical details. The FF received "Car of the Year" honors from Car magazine in England.

Power for both Interceptor versions was supplied by a 6276-cc (383-cid) Chrysler V-8 with a 10.0:1 compression ratio and Carter four-barrel carburetor. It was rated for 325-330 hp at 4600 rpm and 425 lbs.-ft. of torque at 2800 rpm. Top speeds were 133 mph for the two-wheel-drive model and 130 mph for the four-wheel-drive model.

The Interceptor was 3,742 pounds or $8,520. The FF model was 5340 pounds or $12,160. Jensen built 17 Interceptors in 1966, 148 during 1967, 444 during 1968, and 529 during 1969. The FF was rarer with two made in 1966, 24 in 1967, 62 in 1968 and 115 in 1969.

*The Jensen Interceptor series of the early 1970s included the Mark III convertible.*

The base Interceptor had a 105-in. wheelbase and 188-in. length. The four-wheel-drive version had a 109-in. wheelbase and 191-in. overall length. Height and width were 53 in. and 69 in. for each model, respectively.

A TorqueFlite three-speed automatic transmission was standard with a fully-synchro four-speed manual gear box optional. The FF came only with TorqueFlite and the Ferguson Formula four-wheel-drive unit.

Rack-and-pinion steering was standard, with power-assist on the FF. The independent front suspension used wishbones and coil springs with a stabilizer bar. At the rear was Jensen's typical rigid axle with semi-elliptic leaf springs and Armstrong adjustable shock absorbers. Dunlop four-wheel disc brakes were fitted and the FF incorporated a Dunlop Maxaret anti-skid device.

The Mark II Interceptor—also referred to as the "Mk 2" or "Interceptor II" model—had modest revisions but its price grew to $13,500. The new model was introduced in October 1969. A federalized version appeared at the New York Auto Show in April 1970 and merchandising began in 1971. The four-wheel-drive FF version was updated in the same manner. A total of 526 Interceptors were produced in 1970 and 742 in 1971 along with 68 FFs in 1970 and 47 in 1971.

Subtle appearance changes were limited to the front end. Side-by-side quad headlights again flanked a rectangular, horizontal-bars grille. Parking lights were moved below the bumper.

The Interceptor's massive rear hatch provided ample luggage space. Standard power equipment included brakes, steering and windows. Offered in Britain was a special "Director" interior, which turned the grand touring car into a traveling office. As the 1970s began, Jensen was in financial trouble. A group led by Kjell Qvale, the San Francisco Jensen distributor, gained control of the firm and planned a car like the Austin Healey 3000. Donald Healey became chairman of Jensen's board. With the technical assistance of Kevin Beattie, the Jensen-Healey was created and shown at the 1972 Geneva (Switzerland) Motor Show.

Mark III and SP versions of the Interceptors were introduced in October 1971. Only the two-wheel-drive model was carried over. Appearance changes included restyled headlight surrounds. Standard Mark II equipment included many items that had formerly been optional. American market cars had air conditioning, a radio, power brakes, and power steering. Later Interceptor III models used the Interceptor SP engine.

The Interceptor SP was offered to high-performance car fans in Britain. Under its bonnet was a 7212-cc (440-cid) Chrysler V-8 with 385 hp. The "SP" designation stood for "six-pack" and it had three two-barrel carburetors.

Jensen built a total of 19 SP models in calendar-year 1971. In 1972, a total of 922 Interceptors and 121 SP models were made. Little change was evident on the 1973 Interceptor coupe, except the price increased to $15,500.

The 1973 engine carried a single four-barrel carburetor and was rated for 385 hp at 4700 rpm and 350 lbs.-ft. of torque at 2400 rpm.

Until July 1973, the high-performance Interceptor SP with the 440-cid "six pack" engine continued in production in England. Calendar-year output included 1,165 Interceptor III models and 88 SPs. The Interceptor III coupe was offered in 1974 but the SP was dropped.

The price of the 3,695-lb. car was now $16,200. Only a few minor interior changes appeared in the coupe.

Production of the Interceptor Mk III coupe and convertible continued in 1975 and 1976 without major change. Saloons destined for America had matching lambswool seat panels.

Standard equipment included air conditioning, a tachometer, power windows, four-speaker radio with automatic antenna, and more. The saloon was now up to $24,750 and 4,040 lbs.

In August 1976, the Jensen plant was closed and production ceased. Factory totals were 6,387 two-wheel-drive Interceptors produced from 1966-1976. The FF model, built from 1966-1971, had added 318 units to the count.

*The 1956 Jensen 541R promised "memorable motoring" with 110 mph speed.*

# JENSEN-HEALEY

JENSEN-HEALEY

## 1972-'76 Jensen-Healey GT

Dick Dance Collection

Financial difficulties at Jensen led to a takeover by car dealer, Kjell Qvale. Donald Healey of Austin-Healey fame became a member of the company's board of directors, along with his son Geoffrey. As a result of the Healey connection, a new car bowed at the 1972 Geneva Auto Show.

The all-new Jensen-Healey, a two-seat roadster, was powered by a Lotus-built twin-cam (16-valve) four-cylinder engine. Its all-steel unibody coachwork had a grille-less front end with recessed headlights. Large amber parking lights sat below the bumper and horizontal rectangular taillights were seen at the rear.

The car's overall profile was angular, with full wheel openings front and rear. Underneath was a mix of British components. The coil-spring front suspension, rack-and-pinion steering and the front disc brakes were borrowed from the Vauxhall Viva. The four-speed manual gearbox came from the Sunbeam.

The Jensen-Healey retailed for $4,795 or less than half the price of the Jensen Interceptor. It tipped the scales at just 2,116 lbs. The engine was a Lotus-sourced 1973-cc in-line four with dual overhead camshafts. It had 95.2 x 69.3-mm bore and stroke measurements. With twin carburetors and 8.4:1 compression, the solid-lifter motor generated 140 hp at 6500 rpm and 130 lbs.-ft. of torque at 5000 rpm. Kjell Qvale and Donald Healey originally wanted to use a Vauxhall engine to power the Jensen-Healey roadster, but it wasn't strong enough to do the job, so they turned to a the Lotus-built twin-cam derivative that was later used in Lotus cars as well.

Riding a 92-in. wheelbase, the Jensen-Healey was smaller than the Interceptor and comparable to the "Big Healey" or Austin-Healey 3000. It was 162 in. long overall, 47.75 in. high and 63.25 in. wide. The front tread was 53.25 in., the rear an inch less. It used 185/70SR13 tires. A four-speed manual transmission was fitted. The gear ratios were 11.63:1 in first, 7.42:1 in second, 4.83:1 in third, 3.73:1 in fourth and 12.37:1 in reverse. A 3.73:1 rear axle was standard.

The Jensen-Healey's front underpinnings featured double wishbones and coil springs. The rear suspension incorporated a rigid axle with four links and coil springs. Power front disc brakes were provided, with drums at the rear. The top speed was in the 120-125 mph range. Going from 0 to 60 took about 8.1 seconds. The quarter mile took 16.2 seconds.

*The Jensen-Healey was a distinctive-looking car from any angle.*

In 1973, the Jensen-Healey roadster continued into its first full model year with minor cosmetic changes. Standard equipment included a four-speed manual gearbox, power front disc brakes, a map light, twin Hi-Lo horns, two-speed wiper/washers, a locking glove box, a console, a tonneau cover, a tachometer, a heater, and diagonal seat belts.

The ventilated vinyl seats were adjustable for rake angle and had adjustable head restraints. The price was now $5,195 and a radio was $135 extra. This year, 3,846 of the cars were built.

A modest restyling of the two-seat roadster took place for 1974. It included the addition of a full-length horizontal body side style line, a curved headlight cowl and some bright trim around the front bumper (including a flashy chrome panel). Bright finishes also were added to the rear edge of the hood and to the door tops.

A matte black finish was now used on lower sills and the taillight clusters added chrome surrounds. Two body colors were added: Buttercup Yellow and Malaga Blue. A removable fiberglass roof (with heated back window) became available. There was another price increase in the $350 range, yet production increased to 4,550 units.

By 1974, three out of five Jensen-Healeys were being exported to the U.S. and Canada, though sales never reached anticipated levels. Donald Healey dropped out of the project during this time period and his name did not appear on a new model called the GT Sportwagon. A five-speed Getrag manual gearbox replaced the former four-speed in 1975, but other changes were minimal. Acceleration to 60 mph was slower than before, a result of revised rear-axle ratio. The Jensen-Healey's price had jumped considerably since the car's introduction in 1972 and was now up to $8,195. Only 1,301 copies were built.

At mid-year 1975, the roadster was replaced by a new GT Sportwagon model. A handful of Jensen-Healeys were produced during the 1976 model year, but the bulk of production was focused on the new model, a station-wagon-like GT coupe version of the roadster. Billed as "The Good Thinking Car," it was similar in construction and dimensions to the Jensen-Healey but deleted the Healey name badge. It was priced at $9,975 and weighed in at 2400 lbs.

The GT had the same wheelbase, but some other dimensions were unique to it. Overall length was 165.8 in. and the height was 48.5 in. The standard tires were size 185/70HR13. The GT's five-speed manual gear box had ratios of 11.62:1 in first, 7.45:1 in second, 5.45:1 in third, 4.28:1 in fourth, 3.45:1 in fifth and 13.80:1 in reverse. A 3.45:1 rear axle was fitted.

Unfortunately, the Lotus power plant had reliability problems that contributed to lack of buying interest in the Jensen-Healy. Sales were weak. Total Jensen-Healey production from 1972 to 1976 was 10,453. The addition of the GT Estate Wagon version didn't help. By spring 1976, receivers had taken over and the assets of the firm went under the auctioneer's hammer.

A different company was formed to handle parts and service, and, later, import cars into Britain. Actually, the Jensen Parts & Services company hung on well into the 1980s, prepared to custom-build all-new Interceptors based on the 1970s design.

*An appeal to those seeking elegance was used in this Jensen-Healey ad.*

Dick Dance Collection

*Jensen-Healeys were at home in many locales around the world.*

JENSEN IN TOKYO

JENSEN IN SYDNEY

JENSEN IN HONG KONG

JENSEN IN SAN FRANCISCO

Dick Dance Collection

# JOWETT JUPITER

Wheels on Paper, New Zealand

# 1950-1952 Sports

Jowett history reaches back to the early years of the century. In 1906, brothers Ben and Willy Jowett produced a two-cylinder, 6-hp motorcar. Jowett Motor Manufacturing Company built about 48 light cars that were similar through the beginning of World War I, in 1916.

Following the "War to End All Wars," they moved to a larger factory and operated Jowett Cars Ltd. of Idle, Bradford, Yorkshire. Jowett continued to build light and low-budget cars prior to World War II. One sporty Jowett of that period was the Short, a slant-nosed two-seater roadster. During World War II, the Jowett brothers sold their company to wealthy businessmen who, in turn, sold the company to the Lazard Brothers merchant bank. After the war, Americans became more familiar with Jowetts.

Following on the heels of the 1947 Jowett Javelin fastback saloon, Britain's first all-new postwar car, the two to three-seat Jowett Jupiter sports convertible was introduced in 1950.

Announced as "the race-bred, high-speed 3 seater," it was promoted as primarily a family car, but one with fine performance. An advertising headline for the Jowett market in the U.S. proclaimed: "Get your fast ride—in civilised comfort!"

Credit for the Jupiter's creation goes to Professor Eberan von Eberhorst, who had designed Grand Prix race cars for the Auto Union company. The impetus for a performance model came from the strong showing Jowett Javelin saloons made at two major 1949 racing events: the Monte Carlo Rally and the 24-hour Belgian Gran Prix at Spa.

"British engineering brains have built a record breaker," declared U.S. advertisements for the Jupiter in 1952. By that time, it had achieved class victories in nine major trials and races. Other ads challenged the skills of American drivers, asking: "Can you really handle a race-bred European car?" They said the Jupiter could: "...take all the good driving you can give it" while claiming it offered: "...big car comfort rare in high-speed sports cars." Jowett Jupiters also were known for their wind-up windows, all-weather folding top, and 30 miles per gallon of gas.

*Jowett proclaimed its 1952 Le Mans racing success to potential Jupiter buyers.*

The sports car sold for $2,548 and weighed 1,792 lbs. While approximately 24,000 Javelins were built from 1947-1953, the Jupiter was built only in very limited numbers—less than 900 from 1950 through 1954, according to Jowett experts. Both left- and right-hand drive versions were made available. Included Jupiters were 70 custom-built models crafted by coachbuilders. A Farina-styled custom coupe came to the U.S. and currently is being restored in California. People tended either to love or hate the Jupiter's looks. Its recessed center grille was made up of vertical bars, with the round headlights mounted alongside inboard nacelles, similar to those of the Jaguar XK 120. Below each headlight stood a side grille with horizontal bars. Trim strips led downward to the bumper and back across the top of each fender. The front-fender curve extended into the door to meet the bulging back fender. The entire front end was hinged upward for access to the engine. With its hood (convertible top) raised, the long bonnet (engine cover) and deck gave the Jupiter a rather stubby cockpit appearance.

A horizontally-opposed, overhead-valve, four-cylinder cross-flow engine was fitted with a standard oil cooler. The engine had an aluminum block with wet cast-iron cylinder liners and a cast-iron heads. With a 72.5 x 90-mm bore and stroke, it displaced 1485 ccs. Rack-and-pinion steering was used and the independent front suspension featured torsion bars and Woodhead Monroe telescopic shock absorbers. The live rear axle had additional support from a Panhard anti-tramp rod. The rear suspension used transverse torsion bars damped by the Woodhead Monroe shocks.

*Road and Track* magazine reported the Jupiter could accelerate to 60 mph in about 15 seconds and reach a top speed of more than 90 mph. It cruised at 80 mph. Accelerating from 0-to-60 mph took about 15 seconds and the Jupiter could do the standing-start quarter-mile in 20.5 seconds. Actual fuel economy was in the 24 to 28 mpg range. The four-speed manual transmission had a column-mounted gear selector with synchromesh on second, third, and fourth gears. Early ads promised a floor shift, but no Jupiters were equipped with one, according to Jowett expert Edmund Nankivell. The four-speed manual transmission had ratios of 14.62:1 in first, 8.91:1 in second, 5.63:1 in third, 4.1:1 in fourth and 14.62:1 in reverse. The standard 5.50 x 16 tires were mounted on pressed steel wheels. Originally a 4.1:1 rear axle was used on the prototype Jupiter, but production models used a 4.56:1 ratio.

The Jupiter's 93-in. wheelbase was nine inches shorter than the Javelin. It measured 56 in. high, 62 in. wide and 163 in. in overall length. It had a 52-in. front tread and 50.5-in. rear tread. Ground clearance was 7 in., versus 8.5 in. for the Javelin. Standard body colors were Metallic Copper, Turquoise Blue, British Racing Green, and Scarlet, each with beige upholstery and beige, fabric-lined folding convertible top. Jupiters had a leather-trimmed bench seat, wind-up windows, and a removable windshield. The Jupiter was first seen at the British Motor Show in New York City in April of 1950. That June, in its first racing outing, a lone Jupiter won its class at the Grand Prix d'Endurance at Le Mans, France, averaging 75.8 mph for 24 hours—a record at that time.

A Jupiter also placed first and second at the 1951 Monte Carlo Rally. A Javelin saloon finished fourth in the same event. Jowett cars also shared the Stuart trophy for best British performance. Only about five Jowetts were sold in the U.S. in 1950. American sales officially began in 1951 when eight were sent to Hoffman Motor Car Co. in New York City. All were right-hand drive. A prototype left-hand drive Jupiter was shipped to Angell Motors, Pasadena, California in 1951.

At least 113 Jupiters were imported in 1951 and 145 in 1952, according to Jowett experts. Comedian Red Skelton bought one for himself and three associates. The Skelton Jupiter survives today. Americans in service in Germany and the United Kingdom also brought Javelins home.

During 1951 and '52, three lightweight racing Jupiters, called the R-1, were built for competition using a simplified Jupiter chassis. Max Hoffman sponsored an R-1 at Watkins Glen in September 1951, driven by George Weaver. In June 1951, a stock Jupiter won its class at the SCCA Burke Mountain Hillclimb. Jupiters won at the Lake Tahoe Rally and Torrey Pines, among others.

*Connaught green was the choice for this Jowett Jupiter portrayed in its brochure.*

# 1953-1954 MI, MIA, & R-4

The Jupiter Mark IA, a variant of the earlier model, was launched at the London Motor Show in October 1952. The original Mark I Jupiter was still available in Great Britain until the end of October 1953.

The Mark IA used the basic chassis but was fitted with a longer top and a larger "tail locker." The tonneau extended behind the driver's seat, allowing a tight space for small luggage. (In the Mark I, luggage could be reached from behind the driver's seat only). Another change in the Mark IA was a painted metal instrument panel replaced the previous walnut-grained panel.

New American importers Major Seddon in New York and World Wide Import Inc. in California promoted the Mark IA.

The new model retained the bench seating and continued to offer a detachable windshield. Standard body colors were: Metallichrome Turquoise with red or beige leather upholstery and a beige top, Connaught Green with beige leather seats and a beige top, Ivory with red leather seats and a black top or scarlet with beige leather seats and a beige top.

All Jowett Jupiters now were powered by the new Series III engine with a sturdier crankshaft, new bearings and improved oil flow among the advances made in the engine. It had an aluminum block with wet cast-iron cylinder liners and a cast-iron head. With a 72.5 x 90-mm bore and stroke, it displaced 1485 ccs. The compression ratio was 8.0:1. Brake horsepower was 62.5 at 4500 rpm and torque was 94 ft.-lbs. at 3000 rpm. The three-main-bearings engine still employed hydraulic valve lifters and twin Zenith downdraft carburetors.

By 1953, the Port of Entry price for the Jupiter Mark IA sport convertible was $3,295 and it weighed 1,895 lbs. The Mark IA a 93-in. wheelbase chassis and measured 168 in. long overall.

Height was 56 in. and width was 62 in. Track widths were 52 in. up front and 52 in. at the rear. The 5.50 x 16 tires were on steel disc wheels.

The front-engined, rear-drive Jupiter had a four-speed manual transmission with synchromesh on all gears, but first. The overall gear ratios were 16.3:1 in first, 9.9:1 in second, 6.3:1 in third and 4.56:1 in fourth. A 4.56:1 rear axle was fitted. The Jupiter featured special rack-and-pinion steering and a choice of either left- or right-hand drive was offered. The independent front suspension used torsion bars with Woodhead Monroe shock absorbers. At the rear were transverse torsion bars, Woodhead Monroe shock absorbers and an anti-roll bar. Girling hydro-mechanical brakes with 10-inch drums were standard.

Competition with other, faster European sports cars was intense. Just 11 Jupiter Mark IA cars were shipped to the United States in 1953 and only one more in 1954, according to Jowett expert Edmund Nankivell.

With the demise of the conventional Javelin in 1953 and Jupiter in 1954, Jowett made one more stab at the marketplace with the R-4 competition model. Wearing a streamlined, laminated plastic body, it rode a shorter 84-in. wheelbase, weighed 450 lbs. less than Jupiters and had semi-elliptic leaf springs instead of torsion bars at the rear.

Its engine was rated at 64 hp and, with overdrive, it delivered a top speed of just over 100 mph. The R4 wasn't enough to save the faltering Jowett company. Only three were built. When International Harvester made Jowett an offer, the factory was sold and attention was turned to supplying spare parts for postwar cars and aircraft parts for the aerospace industry. Current owners find the Jowett Jupiter both eye-catching and a pleasant car to drive. Jupiters have a high survival rate—better than 50 percent worldwide according to sources.

# LEA-FRANCIS

BASIC PRICE
£1240

Dick Dance Collection

## 1948-1954 Sports Roadster

The Lea-Francis company is remembered in America for its small two-seater sports car of the late 1940s. Never a major producer, the firm's Coventry-built chassis went beneath a number of different body styles. Before disappearing in the early 1950s, Lea-Francis turned out more than 3,400 postwar vehicles.

In 1895, Richard Lea and Graham Francis built bicycles and soon formed Lea & Francis Ltd. in Coventry, England. They made two-wheelers and turned to motorcycles a few years before the First World War. They expanded to automobiles in 1903, creating a separate company.

Designed by Alexander Craig, the 3.5-liter three-cylinder tourer was both expensive and unusual. After selling only two, Lea-Francis sold the rights to Singer. After the First World War, Lea and Francis turned again to four-wheeled transport. Their four-cylinder model had about two liters displacement. Less than two dozen found buyers, but the partners forged ahead. By the mid-1920s, the firm was selling 750 or more cars annually.

In 1924, they made an initial stab at the sport arena with a 10-hp four-cylinder tourer that performed very well at the Royal Automobile Club's Six-Day Trial. During the next few years came several sport-touring models with overhead-valve engines. In 1927, a Lea-Francis appeared with a low-pressure Cozette supercharger (Rootes-type). Soon after that came a Hyper-Sports supercharged Lea-Francis, with a rakish radiator design, fabric body, 28-in. wire wheels and four-speed "crash box." A similar car won the Ulster (Northern Ireland) Tourist Trophy race.

The success of the Meadows-engined vehicles, coupled with some significant competitive victories, was followed by the introduction of the model LFS 14/40. Its 1.7-liter twin-cam Vulcan-built engine suffered severe reliability problems, harming Lea-Francis' reputation and sales.

**The 2-1/2-litre brochure cover proclaims the Lea-Francis as "fascinating to handle."**

By 1931, the company was in receivership. The original partners dropped out but production continued in small numbers. In 1936, the company's assets were sold.

Riding to the rescue of Lea-Francis were George Leek and Hugh Rose, who had a car to build and formed Lea-Francis Engineering Ltd. in 1937. About 100 Lea-Francis Twelve and Fourteen models were built by the time World War II broke out.

Wartime profits allowed the company to resume production of the Fourteen passenger-car early in 1946, with bodies by A.P. Aircraft Ltd. A two-seat sports car on a 99-in. wheelbase debuted in 1948. The new two-seat Sports Tourer's look was accented by cut-down doors (with a graceful curved front edge), notched rear fender skirts and built-in headlights. The 2,200-lb. "roadster" came with either the 1.5-liter (Twelve) or 1.8-liter (Fourteen) engine. A total of 551 Lea-Francis models were sold in 1948, two in the United States.

The engine used in the Twelve was an in-line, overhead-valve four-cylinder with a 69 x 100-mm bore and stroke and 64 hp at 5300 rpm. The Fourteen engine had a 75 x 100-mm bore and stroke and 1767-cc displacement. The Fourteen Sports model used an 8.0:1 compression ratio that boosted output to 87 hp at 5200 rpm. Both engines had three main bearings, solid valve lifters, and twin S.U. carburetors.

The Sports Tourers were 165 in. long, 63 in. wide and shared the same 51.5-in. front and 52.4-in. rear track measurements as other Lea-Francis models. The standard steel disc wheels carried 5.25 x 17 tires. The four-speed manual gearbox drove to a 4.55:1 rear axle on the 14 Sports and to a 4.87:1 rear axle on the 12 Sports.

Burman worm-and-nut steering was used. Both Sports models

had semi-elliptic leaf springs up front and a rigid rear axle supported by semi-elliptic leaf springs. The 14 Sports model had a top speed of 85 mph.

In 1949, the Fourteen was the only Sports Tourer available. The Twelve series was dropped. Changes were minimal. About 500 Lea-Francis models of all types were produced during 1949. Two were sold in the U.S. that year.

Fourteen Saloons and Wagons were offered in 1950, but the Sports Roadster model was available only in a new Eighteen series. The Roadster's appearance was similar to that of the earlier Sports Tourer, with separate fenders and cut-down doors. It also had a fold-flat windshield and all-weather equipment. The rear fender skirts had a cut out (curved) lower edge. Bucket seats held two up front, while two youngsters could squeeze into the tiny rear compartment. Built-in headlights were mounted low on the front fenders.

For identity, it adopted the narrow, vertical-bars grille of the new Eighteen Saloon. A slanted windshield met triangular vent panes. Almost 700 Lea-Francis models of all types were produced during 1950, with merely three selling in the U.S.

Under the new model's bonnet was a familiar type engine with a larger 85-mm bore, but the same 100-mm stroke used in the Twelve and Fourteen.

This 2.5-liter (2496-cc) four used a 7.0:1 compression ratio and produced 100 hp at 4000 rpm. It could power the roadster to speeds of 95 mph or even 100 mph. Most technical specifications were the same as those for earlier Sports models, although a new, higher-geared 3.50:1 rear axle was used. In 1951 and 1952, the $3,895 and 2,576-lb. Sports Roadster continued to be sold with few changes. And few Roadsters were counted among the 600 cars made in 1951 and the 170 built in 1952 Lea-Francis exhibited its wares at the London Show for the last time in October of 1952.

Little changed during the final two model years in 1953 and 1954, although the price went up to $3,985. Sport Roadster body colors were black, maroon, green, cream, Metallic Light Blue, and Metallic Grey.

Lea-Francis still officially existed as an auto manufacturer after 1952. Car production was discontinued after 1954.

At the 1960 London Motor Show, a modernized Ford Zephyr-powered Lea-Francis (known as the Lynx) appeared. It had a bizarre round grille and drew little attention before it disappeared.

By 1962, company assets were sold to a separate organization that later offered parts and service. Another prototype, a V-8 model known as the Francesca, emerged in 1963 Years later, in 1980, yet another prototype for a sports car attempted to revamp the old badge, but serious production never occurred.

*A Two/Four Seater Body with Winding, Windows*

**OVERSEAS FEATURE**

The above illustration shows the left-hand driving position with instrument panel layout. Instruments are calibrated in English or Metric standards, as specified. In this view the winding door-windows are shown in the raised position where they provide an ideal windshield when driving with the hood down. Below, is an illustration of an Export Model showing the clean appearance when in use as an open two-seater.

The illustration on the left is of a model for the Home Market which shows the attractive lines of the car with the tonneau cover fastened over three seats. The tonneau cover is designed to completely cover the seating compartments.

Developed on modern lines this cut-away two/four-seater body terminates in a flowing tail with the spare wheel under a circular cover. The rear wings are fitted with detachable valances. Wide doors give access to a workmanlike driving compartment with separate and adjustable bucket seats. The body is practical and comfortable, the steering light and direct.

**LEA-FRANCIS CARS LIMITED, COVENTRY, ENGLAND**

Printed in England

Dick Dance Collection

*Look closely to see both right- and left-hand drive versions of the Lea-Francis.*

# LOTUS

Bob Harrington

# 1957-1971 Seven

Years before Lotus, Colin Chapman developed racing cars using highly-tuned Ford and Austin Seven engines. Chapman's first Austin Special was finished in his garage early in 1948. By 1949, his Mark 2 racer, powered by a Ford Ten engine, was performing well in hill climbs and speed trials. Chapman was in the Royal Air Force, but continued to develop racing vehicles. His dual role continued after his discharge, as he became an engineer for the British Aluminum Company. Not until 1955, would Chapman assume a full-time role at Lotus.

In the early years, each Lotus had a specific number, starting with Mark 1 and progressing one digit at a time. The numbers weren't always used in descriptions of Lotus cars after the Mark 11 (or "Eleven") and the "Mark" prefix often was omitted. Series numbers were sometimes given with Roman numerals (I, II, etc.), but more often as Arabic numbers like S1.

An Austin Seven engine went into the 1951 Mark 3, which had independent front suspension and a lightweight aluminum body. Two Mark 3s were offered, followed by a Mark 4—the first to use a space-frame chassis. In 1952, Chapman formed Lotus Engineering Company with Michael Allen and produced the Mark 6. Riding a multi-tube frame with stressed aluminum panels, it carried Ford running gear and a de-stroked Ford Consul engine.

Frank Costin joined the company in 1953. By 1954, the Mark 8 had space-frame construction and a choice of engines (either a 1497-cc MG four or the 1098-cc FWA Coventry-Climax engine). Chassis features included a De Dion rear end and inboard brakes. As the Mark 8 turned into the Mark 9, the De Dion version took the Le Mans name, while a lower-priced Club model included a Ford gearbox and drum brakes.

Comforts and conveniences weren't among the features of the Seven. It was sold in kit form, partly to sidestep the British purchase tax. Later examples came as a kit or assembled. Many considered the Spartan Seven a supreme example of the "pure," no-frills sports car. The car provided precise handling and cornering, making it perfect for low-budget racing, as well as occasional sport motoring on the road.

Chapman designed the 1,655-lb. body, which had cycle fenders, free-standing headlights, a tiny cockpit and an upright windshield that folded flat. Most bodies were fashioned of light alloy and mounted on a multi-tubular space frame. The basic power train was an 1172-cc Ford

*Three Lotus Sevens emphasize the unique look of this British racing machine.*

100E L-head four hooked to a three-speed manual gearbox. A modified Aquaplane cylinder head was optional, as were dual S.U. carburetors. Burman worm-and-nut steering was used on the first few dozen examples, then rack-and-pinion steering became standard.

A wide selection of engines (mostly British Ford) eventually became available: old-fashioned L-heads, newer overhead-valve types and even twin-cams. Displacements ranged from about 1000- to 1588-cc and horsepower ratings spanned 40 to 125. Austerity also extended to the standard equipment list, as side curtains and a soft top were optional. The Series 1 Lotus Seven debuted in 1957 and remained in production until August 1960. Other versions included the Super Seven (with a Coventry Climax engine) and the Seven America, made for export.

The British Ford 100E in-line engine, a side-valve four, was considered "base" equipment for early Lotus Sevens. With a 63.5 x 92.5-mm bore and stroke, it had 1172 ccs of displacement. An 8.5:1 compression ratio helped it generate 36/40 hp at 4500 rpm. The three-main-bearings engine used solid valve lifters and a Zenith or Solex carburetor. The car had a top speed of 81-90 mph. It could go from 0-to-60 in 17.8 seconds and from standing still through a quarter mile in just 20.8 seconds.

The Seven had an 88.0-in. wheelbase and measured 123.0 in. overall. It stood only 28 in. high and 53 in. wide. Standard equipment included a set of narrow, but tall, 4.50 x 15 or 5.20 x 15 tires. A three-speed manual transmission was fitted. Lower wishbones with coil springs, shocks, and an anti-roll bar made up the front suspension, while the rear suspension consisted of a rigid axle with coil springs, a Panhard rod and trailing arms. Drum brakes were fitted all around.

Production of the original cycle-fendered Seven continued in the 1958-1959 period with minimal change, but it was joined by the Super Seven and Seven America models. The Super Seven carried an 1098-cc Coventry Climax FWA engine, a four-speed gearbox, a tachometer and knock-on wire wheels. It had a top speed of about 105 mph. Zero-to-60 mph took 8.3 seconds and the quarter mile was a 16.1-second run.

The "America" model had long sweeping front fenders, rather

than cycle-style units. This design later became standard on all models. It also came with a 948-cc BMC A-type engine and gearbox. Export versions included options like a spare wheel, hubcaps, a windshield wiper, a tachometer, side curtains, and a top.

The second-series Seven S2 debuted in October 1960 and lasted until mid-1968. The power plants used in this car included the Ford 1172-cc L-head four, as well as BMC 948- and 1098-cc engines. The revised chassis weighed less than its predecessor and used fewer tubes.

The body panels and fenders were of fiberglass and the nose was modified. Full-length front fenders were available. Standard equipment now included windshield wipers and a spare wheel, with side curtains and a heater optional. Left-hand drive now was available. Wire wheels were no longer offered.

By 1961, two additional engines were offered: a 997-cc Ford Anglia 105E and Ford's classic 109E (available in the Super Seven Cosworth). The "America" designation was dropped after 1960 and replaced by "Seven A." An all-synchro four-speed gearbox was standard with the 105E engine, which came with S.U. or Weber carburetors. The 109E version had much larger displacement than its British-Ford counterpart and used a Cosworth-modified head, camshaft, and exhaust manifold. For U.S. racers, higher compression ratios were available. Performance of the Cosworth version included 7.6 sec. for 0-to-60 mph and about 15.8 sec. for the quarter mile.

From 1962-1968, production of the second-series Lotus Seven, now with full-length fenders, continued with minimal change. A 1498-cc British Ford 116E Cortina four and a Cosworth version of this engine also became available in the Super Seven 1500. The Cosworth-modified Cortina 116E engine carried two Weber carburetors and produced 95 hp at 6000 rpm and 95 ft.-lbs. of torque. at 4500 rpm on 9.5:1 compression. The Lotus Seven A now carried a $2,995 price tag, while the more powerful Super Seven sold for $3,445. This model was eight inches longer than the regular Lotus Seven and weighed 950 lbs. more.

The 1969 Series 3 Lotus Seven debuted in 1968 and continued production into 1970. The exhaust-system mountings were modified and extended the full car length. Rear-track grew to 52.5 in. and required wider rear fenders. Either air-intake louvers or a scoop were installed on the S3 hoods. Rocker switches were installed on the instrument panel. An external filler cap was used for replenishing the gas tank.

There was a new crop of engines with the Ford Escort 1300 cc, the Ford 1600 cc, and the Lotus-Ford 1558-cc Twin-Cam four. The most potent Sevens of this generation (dubbed S or SS models) were Holbay-tuned versions of the 1558-cc engine that produced 125 hp. The Series 4 Lotus Seven debuted in 1970 and continued into 1973 when production was taken over by the Caterham organization. These cars used fiberglass bodies and were mounted on a tube/ladder chassis with integral steel panels. The hood was hinged at the front, and fixed side windows contained sliding panels.

The front suspension was similar to the Europa, with a twin-wishbone anti-roll bar. At the rear was an Escort-type axle with leading and trailing arms. Front disc, rear drum brakes were installed. Powertrains were the same as Series 3, except that no Twin-Cam engines were installed in this final series. The weight of the cars rose to the 1,300-lb. range.

Beginning in spring 1973, Caterham Car Sales (at Caterham, Surrey) took over production of the Lotus Seven sports-racer,

continuing the Super Seven S3 version into the '80s. These cars carried "Caterham 7" (not Lotus) identification. Twin-Cam, 1600 GT and Holbay Sprint 1700 engines were installed.

Approximately 242 Series 1 Lotus Sevens were produced from 1957-1960. As many as 1,370 of the Series 2 Lotus Sevens were produced from 1960-1968. After that, 350 Series 3 and 1,000 Series 4 models were produced through 1973, along with more than 850 cars with a Caterham engine.

**Lotus Seven engines:**

Base Four: Inline, overhead-valve four-cylinder. British Ford 100E. Cast-iron block and head. Displacement: 1172-cc. Bore & stroke: 63.5 x 92.5 mm. Compression Ratio: 7.0:1 (8.5:1 for export). Brake Horsepower: 36/40 at 4500 rpm (45 at 4500 rpm for export). Torque: 52 lbs.-ft. at 2500 rpm. Three main bearings. Solid valve lifters. One Solex or Zenith carburetor except two S.U. carburetors on export models.

**Super Seven Base Four:** Inline, overhead-cam four-cylinder. Coventry Climax. Displacement: 1098-cc. Bore & stroke: 72 x 67 mm. Compression ratio: 9.8:1. Brake horsepower: 75 at 6250 rpm. Torque: 65 lbs.-ft. at 4000 rpm. Solid valve lifters. Two S.U. carburetors.

**America Base Four:** Inline, overhead-valve four-cylinder. BMC A-type. Displacement: 948-cc. Bore & Stroke: 62.9 x 76.2 mm. Compression ratio: 8.9:1. Brake horsepower: 37 at 4800 rpm. Torque: 50 lbs.-ft. at 2500 rpm. Solid valve lifters. S.U. carburetor.

**Seven A Base Four (1961):** Inline, overhead-valve four-cylinder (British Ford Anglia 105E). Cast-iron block and head. Displacement: 997-cc. Bore & stroke: 81 x 48.4 mm. Compression ratio: 8.9:1. Brake horsepower: 39 at 5000 rpm. Torque: 52 lbs.-ft. at 2700 rpm. Three main bearings. Solid valve lifters. Two SU carburetors.

**Cosworth 109E (1961):** Inline, overhead-valve four-cylinder (Cosworth-modified British Ford 109E). Displacement: 81.7 cid. (1340-cc). Bore & stroke: 3.19 x 2.56 in. (81 x 65 mm). Compression Ratio: 9.5:1. Brake horsepower: 80 at 5800 rpm. Torque: 80 ft.-lbs. at 4000 rpm. Solid valve lifters. Two Weber 40DCOE carburetors.

**1300 Base Four:** Inline, overhead-valve four-cylinder (British Ford Escort). Cast-iron block and head. Displacement: 79.2 cid. (1298-cc). Bore & stroke: 3.19 x 2.48 in. (81 x 63 mm). Five main bearings. Solid valve lifters.

**1600 Base Four:** Inline, overhead-valve four-cylinder (British Ford 225E). Cast-iron block and head. Displacement: 1599-cc. Bore & stroke: 81 x 77.6 mm. Compression ratio: 9.0:1. Brake horsepower: 84 at 5500 rpm. Five main bearings. Solid valve lifters. Weber downdraft carburetor.

**Twin Cam Base Four:** Inline, overhead-valve four-cylinder. British Ford 225E. Cast-iron block and head. Displacement: 1599-cc. Bore & stroke: 81 x 77.6 mm. Compression ratio: 9.0:1. Brake horsepower: 115/118 at 5500 rpm (125/130 SAE at 6250 rpm). Torque: 112 ft.-lbs. at 4600 rpm. Solid valve lifters. Weber downdraft carburetor.

Bob Harrington

# 1957 Eleven

Lotus displayed its wares at the London Motor Show for the first time in 1955. A Mark 11 (Eleven) replaced the Mark 9 in 1956, a year that was also notable for the debut of the first single-seat Lotus race car. In the next year, the Mark 11 adopted a wishbone-type front suspension.

The Eleven was actually an evolution of the earlier Mark 1 through Mark 9 racing cars. Four distinct versions of the open two-seater were available in 1957. They were called the Sports, the Club, the LeMans 75 and the Le Mans 100.

The Club and Sports models had fixed windshields. The Sports sold for $2,880 and weighed just 868 lbs. The Club had a price of $3,665 and was lightened to 812 lbs. to make it go faster. The two Le Mans models included a wraparound windshield and a head fairing. The 100 was priciest at $4,550. Both weighed 854 lbs.

The engine used in the Eleven Sports model was the same British Ford 100 E engine that was standard in Lotus Sevens. This in-line, side-valve four had a 63.5 x 92.5-mm bore and stroke and displaced 1172-cc. It ran an 8.5:1 compression ratio and developed 36/40 hp at 4500 rpm. The solid-lifter engine had three main bearings and a Zenith or Solex carburetor.

Buyers of Lotus Eleven Le Mans 75 and Club models got an in-line, overhead-cam four with 72 x 67-mm bore and stroke dimensions and 1097 ccs. With its relatively high 9.8:1. compression ratio it generated

*Aerodynamics were important to the designers of the streamlined Lotus Eleven.*

75 hp at 6350 rpm and 68 lbs.-ft. of torque at 5000 rpm. A Stage II version was good for 83 at 6800 rpm.

Base four in the Eleven Le Mans 100 was an overhead-cam engine with 76 x 80-mm bore and stroke and 1462 ccs of displacement. It had an 8.6:1 compression ratio and churned out 100 hp at 6200 rpm and 92 lbs.-ft. of torque at 4400 rpm.

At 85 in., the Eleven's wheelbase was three inches shorter than that of the already-small Lotus Seven. The Club version was 47 in. high. Maximum tread width was also 47 in. A four-speed manual was fitted. The front suspension combined lower wishbones with coil springs, shocks and an anti-roll bar. At the rear, was a rigid axle with coil springs, a Panhard rod, and trailing arms. The Club had disc brakes and the other Elevens had drum brakes.

Top speeds varied by model: 105 mph for the Eleven Sports, 120 mph for the Eleven Club, 145 mph for the Eleven Le Mans 75 and 165 mph for the Eleven Le Mans 100. Like other Lotus cars, the Elevens were built by Lotus Engineering Co. Ltd., Hornsey, London, England, and were distributed in the United States by Jay Chamberlain Lotus Cars, of Burbank, California.

Andrew Morland

# 1958-1963 Elite

The prototype Lotus made for street driving débuted at the Earls Court Motor Show in October of 1957. Production began in May 1958, though time passed before examples went on sale. Approximately 988 first-generation Elites were produced between 1959 and 1963 before the name faded away, temporarily.

The Elite had uni-body construction — in fiberglass rather than steel. Beneath its bonnet lurked a 1216-cc Coventry Climax engine and a BMC gearbox.

While fiberglass auto body construction was not unknown, the Elite's all-fiberglass monocoque (integral) body and chassis were unique in the industry. The two-seat coupe used virtually no steel body reinforcement, relying wholly on glass-reinforced epoxide and polyester resin for its structural rigidity. Lotus literature claimed the fiberglass would give "exceptional strength, very good impact resistance, first class sound damping and good thermal insulation." It was also remarkably light weight.

The car's center tunnel and body sills were used as box-section structural members. Tubular steel reinforcing materials, built into the cowl, extended upward to form the windshield posts. Two light steel reinforcements connected the engine and suspension mounting points and a transverse tube connected the upper-front strut mountings.

Elite styling features included a hood that sloped downward between the headlights, a low-mounted oval-shaped air intake, a windshield with a mildly-curved "wraparound" design, a curved back window, front vent wings, hinged quarter windows, a separate luggage compartment, and a "cut-off" tail section.

The door glass was fixed and proved to be an impractical feature that later was changed. Prior to this revision, the windows had to be either removed completely or kept in place. The doors also lacked exterior handles.

The Series 1 Elite was offered in "several attractive standard colour schemes." Typically, it sold in kit form with a factory price of about $3,640. Early versions sold in the United States for about $4,780,

*The red body color and wire wheels highlight the appealing 1961 Lotus Elite.*

but the Port of Entry price dropped to about $4,108 for 1960 and 1961 models. Standard equipment included a four-inch, 8,000-rpm tachometer and a matching 140-mph speedometer.

Beneath the sloped bonnet was an all-aluminum 1216-cc overhead-cam, Coventry Climax four-cylinder engine. This was an in-line, overhead-cam FEW type with an aluminum block and an aluminum head. It had a 76.2 x 66.6-mm bore and stroke and an 8.5:1 compression ratio. In standard tune it developed 75 hp at 6100 rpm and 82 lbs.-ft. of torque at 4900 rpm. Optional tunes helped the Elite climb as high as 105 hp. A BMC (B-type) four-speed manual gearbox was installed, with a short gearshift lever directly above the selector forks. No remote gearshift linkage was provided. A built-in ventilation system used vents above the rear window. The Elite's top speed was about 118 mph.

The little coupe had an 88.2-in. wheelbase and measured 148 inches long overall. It was 46 in. high, 58 in. wide, and weighed just 1,208 lbs. The chassis contained an all-independent suspension and all-disc brakes (inboard at the rear). The front and rear track widths were the same 47 in.

Coil springs were used in front, with an anti-roll bar. The Series 1 Elite had a MacPherson-style rear suspension, which Lotus liked to call a "Chapman strut." The factory said it came with a "double-articulated drive shaft giving lateral location." Knock-off wire wheels with 4.80 x 15 or 4.90 x 15 tires were standard.

Starting at mid-year 1959, the interior protrusion of rear coil springs was capped rather than faired. The Series 2 model (introduced in 1960) turned to modified lower wishbones at the rear and substituted a ZF four-speed gearbox for the original BMC transmission. Late in 1960, Special Equipment models became available. These late-in-the-game "Super 95" and "Super 105" versions had more power than the original Elites.

The Elite coupe was advertised as the "Brilliant new offspring of the mighty Lotus racers." Literature advised that an Elite kit "is assembled in just 24 hours with normal hand tools — simply bolt it together!" Major options available for the cars included a heater, demister, seat belts, a quick-release fuel filler cap, and full-race tuning.

Production of the Series 2 Elite two-seat coupe continued from 1963 to 1966 without major change. The price rose to about $4,780 in 1963 and was at $4,995 by 1966. The 1216-cc overhead-cam four

with 80 hp was the standard engine. It had a 10.0:1 compression ratio and twin S.U. carburetors. Higher ratings of 83 hp, 95 hp and 105 bhp were available. Bolt-on steel disc wheels replaced knock-offs as standard equipment, although the wires were an option. Other standard features included 4.80 x 15 tires and a 4.55:1 rear axle. Another extra was a ZF four-speed synchronized gearbox (Elite).

"Lotus cars are built for drivers who work at it," declared a 1963 U.S. ad for the Elite. *Car and Driver* considered the Elite to be "noisy as the boiler room of a tramp steamer" and gave higher ratings to the new Elan.

John Gunnell

# 1962-1973 Elan

In 1962, Lotus Cars Ltd., of Cheshunt, Herts, England, brought out its next road car, the Elan two-seat roadster. It was powered by a twin-cam conversion of the Ford Classic 116E engine. The first-series Elan — or Lotus Mark 26 in factory nomenclature — was introduced as a two-seat roadster (actually a roll-up-windows convertible) in 1962.

A fixed-head coupe was added to the line in September 1965. Four series were produced between 1962 and 1973. Elan Plus 2 and Plus 2S models followed. In 1971, the Elan +2S 130 came out. It featured a speedy 126-hp engine.

The Elan was the first Lotus to use a folded-steel "backbone" chassis under a fiberglass body. From 1962-1965, only a convertible was offered, but a removable hardtop was an early option. Styling features included pop-up headlights, a curved windshield, roll-up side windows, and slim bumpers. Like other Lotuses, the Elan came in both kit and fully-assembled form. For a short time in the Elan's lifespan, special black-and-gold finish was available.

Elan's Series 2 (Lotus Mk 36) came out late in 1964. Series 2 Elans added chrome gauge bezels, a full-width dashboard with locking glove box, a quick-release gas cap, a 3.07:1 final-drive ratio, and new oval-shaped taillights. The battery moved to the trunk and center-lock wheels became optional.

The Series 3 fixed-head coupe (Lotus Mk 45) arrived late in 1965. Series 3 Elans came with power windows and window frames as standard equipment. They had a new trunk lid. A 3.55:1 axle ratio was optional. The Series 3 convertible (Lotus 45) was available in dealerships by mid-1966. Early convertibles were fully open, but fixed window frames were added in 1966. A Special Equipment Elan also became available in early 1966.

The twin-cam Lotus-Ford engine was a 1558-cc in-line four that produced 105 hp at 5500 rpm and 108 lbs.-ft. of torque using two twin-choke 40DCOE Weber side draft carburetors. It ran a 9.5:1 compression ratio. The engine consisted of a British Ford block with

***The Lotus Elan roadster had clean lines, enhanced by concealed headlights.***

a Lotus-designed twin-cam aluminum head that was also used in the Lotus Cortina. This engine was employed into 1967. However, a small number of early Elans (about 22) came with a 1498-cc 100-hp engine. There was also a 115-hp Special Equipment engine.

A four-speed manual transmission was standard, but a close-ratio gearbox was optional. A fully-independent suspension was used with unequal-length A-arms, coil springs, an anti-roll bar up front and Chapman struts with lower A-arms and coil springs at the rear. The wheelbase was 84 inches and the Elan measured 145 in. overall. Rack-and-pinion steering was installed, along with all-disc brakes. A 3.99:1 rear axle was fitted and buyers got a choice of 5.20 x 13 or 145 x 13 tires.

As many as 12,224 Elans could have been produced from 1962 to 1973, but some sources report a lower total of 9,659 units for this same period. In 1964, the convertible was priced at $4,194 and the coupe sold for $4,206. An American road test listed Elan weights as 1420 lbs. dry and gave a curb weight of 1485 lbs. The early Elans (through 1966) had a top speed of about 112 to 120 mph. They accelerated from 0-60 mph in the 7.1 to 9.0 second bracket (7.54 sec. for the S2). The standard Elan could do the quarter mile in 15.7 seconds at 87 mph. The figures for the Elan S2 were 15.9 seconds and 87.5 mph.

The Elan first appeared in October 1962 and was available in 1963. Cox & Pulver Inc. of New York City and Dutchess Auto Co. of New York City were distributors. *Car and Driver* advised readers that the "Elan's well-bred manners come from an ultra-soft, all-independent suspension with lots of wheel travel," adding that it qualified as "a boulevardier's car." They ranked it far different from the Elite, which was considered as "noisy as the boiler room of a tramp steamer."

Lotus gained a certain measure of publicity when actress Diana

Rigg drove an Elan in her role as Mrs. Peel on "The Avengers" TV series.

Production of the Elan convertible and coupe continued into 1971, in S3 and S4 series, before giving way to the "Big-Valve" Sprint edition.

Series 4 Elans debuted in early spring 1968, wearing slightly-flared wheel openings and 155 x 13 tires. They also had new taillights and a power bulge atop the hood. European Elans eventually switched from twin-choke Weber carburetors to Dell'orto units. "Federalized" U.S. versions, starting in the late 1960s, came with twin Zenith-Stromberg carburetors.

A longer-wheelbase Elan +2 (also known as Plus Two, or Plus 2) emerged in 1967. It used the 115- to 118-hp "Special Equipment" engine. As the name suggested, this was ostensibly a 2+2 coupe, rather than a two-seater. It rode a 96-in. wheelbase. The space for two extra passengers was minimal, but the +2 carried better trim and more equipment than its two-seat counterpart. Unlike the two-seat Elan, the +2 was never sold in kit form.

By 1968, prices had gone up to $4,545 for the convertible and $4,605 for the coupe. The two-passenger models still weighed around 1,500 lbs., while the +2 was more than 550 lbs. heavier. Approximately 4,798 Elan +2s may have produced from 1967-1974. Some sources have put the total as low as 3,330, while others show figures as high as 5,200).

"Sophistication is the word for this car," declared the *Car and Driver '67 Yearbook* of the Elan S2, branding it "a purist's dream." At this time, Colin Chapman acquired a larger factory at Hethel (near Norwich).

A +2S Elan coupe debuted in March 1969, when an alternator replaced the former DC generator. The new model carried a $5,995 window sticker. Otherwise, production continued with minimal change. Lotus/East of Salisbury, Connecticut was now handling distribution of Lotus cars..

Production of the original Elan continued into 1971 in the S4 series and the coupe cost $4,895 by this time. Then, from 1971-1973, the Elan evolved into the Elan Sprint. A more potent "Big Valve" version of the 1558-cc twin-cam engine, producing 126 hp, powered the Sprint coupe and convertible. Under the hood of the new $6,800 Elan +2S 130 coupe was the same higher-powered engine used in the new Elan Sprint. In the fall of 1972 a five-speed manual gearbox became available. The handful of Elans with this transmission were given the designation +2S 130/5. The Elan name disappeared for awhile after 1973, but it was destined to be revived in 1990.

Dr. David Koski

# *1967-1975 Europa*

**L**otus turned to a mid-engine layout with the mid-engined Europa (Type 46), which was introduced late in 1966 and went on sale early the following year. All Series 1 Europas were initially sold outside of England, as Lotus had agreed to limit sales to continental Europe for the first two years of the car's life. Europas appeared officially in the U.S. market late in 1969. Like most early Lotus models, Europas came either fully assembled or in kit form.

The Europa's fiberglass body was permanently bonded to the frame. The front-end styling was similar to that of the Elite, with a low nose, a small oval air intake and exposed headlights set into recessed scoops. The new car — which retailed for about $3,795 in 1968 — had tall, wide sail panels that gave the early models a rather bizarre profile at the rear-quarter section of the body.

The tall rear quarters made the coupe look almost like

*There was nothing quite like the look of the Lotus Europa.*

a small van; hence the nickname "bread van." The strange appearance was accentuated by the squat rear window, which appeared to be little more than a horizontal slit. Later version of the Europa would wear lower sail panels, but still vaguely resembled a tiny pickup truck (though with much-improved visibility). The door windows were fixed (non-movable) and the seats were non-adjustable. A removable flat cover sat above the engine.

The Europa weighed in at just 1,350 lbs. Its drive train came from the front-wheel-drive Renault 16, but the aluminum-alloy engine rotated 180 degrees to allow mounting it behind the two-seat cockpit. The wheelbase of the rectangular steel "backbone" chassis was 91 in.

and the coupe measured about 157.5 in. long overall. It was 42.5 in. high and 64.5 in. wide. The 53.5-in. front tread width was a half inch wider than the rear tread. Size 155 x 13 tires were fitted.

The overhead-valve Renault four had a 76 x 81-mm bore and stroke and 1470-cc displacement. It developed 78-82 hp at 6,000 rpm and 76 ft.-lbs. of torque at 4,000 rpm. It had a 10.25:1 compression ratio, solid valve lifters and a two-barrel Solex carburetor.

A Renault four-speed gearbox was used in the rear transaxle. Standard Europa gear ratios: were 3.61:1 in first, 2.25:1 in second, 1.48:1 in third and 1.03:1 in fourth. A 3.56:1 rear axle was standard equipment. The brake system used discs in front and drums at the rear. The rack-and-pinion steering system included a telescoping steering column. The front suspension had unequal-length A-arms with coil springs and an anti-roll bar. At the rear were lower A-arms with upper lateral links (formed by the driveshaft), upper and lower trailing arms, coil springs, and an anti-roll bar.

Lotus/East, located in Salisbury, Connecticut, distributed Lotus models including the Europa. A total of 9,230 Europas were produced between 1967 and 1972. While praising the Europa's technical details, *Car Life* magazine noted that "homeliest car in the world" would be a fitting title for it and said that it wore "just about as ugly an ill-finished body as could possibly be imagined."

The Series 2 Europa was announced in 1968 and available by July 1969 and Europas were certified for official sale in the U.S. in late 1969. U.S.-market versions of the car were built with a larger 1565-cc Renault engine and rated at 87.5 hp. The fiberglass body was bolted into position, rather than bonded. Electrically-operated windows replaced the former fixed units.

The engine cover added a hinge and the space for luggage was expanded. The Series 2 coupe listed for $4,296 (in 1970) and weighed 1,350 lbs (1,250 lbs. in the U.S.). The same engines were used

Production of the Series 2, with the 1565-cc four-cylinder engine, continued as late as 1972. The new Series 3 (more often called the Europa Twin-Cam) debuted in 1971. It carried the Elan-type 105-hp twin-cam Lotus engine. The sail panels were lowered a bit, lessening the car's bizarre profile. Top speed also got a boost to about 120 mph.

New cast alloy wheels were installed. Twin-Cam Europas also had a new front spoiler. The tailpipe now exited separately, rather than protruding from the car's rear panel.

The more powerful, and more expensive, Europa Special emerged late in 1972. It carried a 126-hp version of the Lotus twin-cam 1558-cc engine – the same engine used in the Lotus Elan Sprint.

The S2 coupe carried a list price in the $4,520 range and the Europa Special sold for $7,292 in 1974. A five-speed gearbox was optional at first and standard in later cars. The Europa Special had a top speed over 125 mph.

# 1976-1975 Eclat

I n 1976, the new Lotus Eclat arrived. This was a front-engined, front-wheel-drive slope-back model that would later evolve into the Excel. It was constructed with a fiberglass body on a steel backbone frame.

The 1978 Eclat Type 520 had a Port of Entry price of $15,350 and a curb weight of 2,390 lbs. Other American prices included $16,698 for the Type 521, $17,688 for the Type 522, $18,250 for the Type 523, and $18,755 for the Type 524.

Power came from the same engine used as the Elite, but with slightly more horsepower in the Eclat. The base Sprint 520 model came with a four-speed gearbox. Other versions of the car — the Type 521, Type 522, Type 523, and Type 524 variants — used a five-speed manual transmission or a three-speed automatic. The Type 522 also included halogen headlights, air conditioning, and tinted glass. The Type 523 added power steering.

The Eclat's Lotus 907 inline four-cylinder engine featured dual-overhead-cams (16-valves) and an aluminum block and head. With a 95.2 x 69-mm bore and stroke it displaced 1973 cc. It had five main bearings, solid valve lifters, and a 9.5:1 compression ratio. Two Zenith CD2SE (or Dell'orto) carburetors fed the motor. Horsepower ratings up to 160 at 6200 rpm were available and torque was 140 ft.-lbs. at 4900 rpm.

*The mid-70s Lotus Eclat used a fiberglass body and stiletto styling.*

The Eclat rode a 97.8-in. wheelbase and was 175.5 in. long, 47.25 in. high and 71.5 in. wide. It had a 58.5-in. front tread and 59-in. rear tread. Size 185/70HR13 tires were standard equipment, but size 205/60VR14 was used on the Type 521.

The steering was rack-and-pinion. Upper A-arms, lower lateral links, coil springs, and lower longitudinal links serving as anti-roll bars made up the front suspension. The independent rear suspension featured upper and lower lateral links, angled trailing arms and coil springs. Four-wheel disc brakes were fitted.

A total of 931 Lotus cars were produced in 1976, followed by 1,074 in 1977, 1,200 in 1978, and 1,031 in 1979. Lotus East Inc., of Millerton, New York, handled distribution.

Throughout the late 1970s and into the '80s, Lotus was only a sporadic entrant into the U.S. market. Not until the advent of the Series 3 in 1983 would it again become a regular player in the American sports-car arena. The big-screen "James Bond" did Lotus no harm by driving a Turbo Esprit in the 1977 film "The Spy Who Loved Me."

Tom Collins

# 1976-1979 Elite

With the Lotus Elan and Lotus Europa out of the model lineup and Lotus Seven production assigned to the Caterham organization, Lotus brought out a completely new series of models by 1976. The first of the trio was the front-engined, front-wheel-drive Elite. This model could be identified by its square tail. It carried the same name as the first road going Lotus released back in the late 1950s.

There were four variations on the same 2+2 coupe theme. The Type 501 was the base model. It listed for $15,548 and weighed 2,413 lbs. The Type 502 added halogen headlamps, tinted glass, air conditioning and carried a $16,417 sticker price. The Type 503, with power steering, sold for $19,090 while the Type 504, with automatic transmission, was $525 more expensive yet. A 1973-cc all-alloy Lotus Type 907 twin-cam four provided the power for all three new models.

The Elite's Lotus inline four-cylinder engine featured 16 valves, with dual overhead cams, an aluminum block, and an aluminum cylinder head. A 95.2 x 69-mm bore and stroke gave it a displacement

*The Lotus Elite combined dramatic styling and hatchback practicality.*

of 1973 cc. It had five main bearings, solid valve lifters, and a 9.5:1 compression ratio. Two Zenith CD2SE (or Dell'orto) carburetors fed the motor. In the Elite, this engine was rated at 155 hp at 6500 rpm and 135 ft.-lbs. of torque at 4900 rpm.

The Elite could move from 0 to 60 mph in 8.5 seconds.

The Elite had a 97.6-in. wheelbase and was 175.5 in. long, 47.6 in. high, and 71.5 in. wide. It had 58.5 in. front and rear tread widths. Size 205/ 60VR14 tires were standard equipment. The steering was rack-and-pinion. Upper A-arms, lower lateral links, coil springs, and lower longitudinal links serving as anti-roll bars made up the front suspension. The independent rear suspension featured upper and lower lateral links, angled trailing arms and coil springs.

Tom Collins

OCW Archive

# 1976-2003 Esprit

The best known and longest-lived of three Lotus models introduced in 1976 is the low, angular, mid-engined Esprit. It initially appeared, in prototype form, at the 1972 Turin (Italy) auto show. The Esprit began as an Ital Design styling exercise under the direction of Giorgetto Giugiaro (who also named the car). Few changes were evident when it finally left the assembly line, some time after the production version was first displayed at a motor show in the autumn of 1974. Customer deliveries didn't start until mid-1976.

The first Esprit rode the same platform as the Lotus Europa. With a design that was much more angular and sharp-edged than prior models, the Esprit displayed a distinct wedge profile with a low, slim, squared-off nose and a short, sloped tail end. The driver faced a large, steeply-raked windshield, while the back window resided in a lift-up hatch. The futuristic design looked good and was aerodynamic. It was durable too, with body colors impregnated directly into the fiberglass rather than painted on.

Mounted in the middle of the car, behind the cockpit, was a 1973-cc Lotus-designed, twin-cam, four-cylinder engine that produced as much as 160 hp. The same engine was used in the new Elite and Eclat as well as the Maserati Merak and Citroen SM. Esprit engine output dropped to 140 hp at 6500 rpm in 1977-1978, then rose to 156 at 7000 rpm in 1979. The U.S.-market version of the car, with 8.4:1 compression, was rated for 140 hp at 6500 rpm and used two Zenith-Stromberg carburetors.

All-disc brakes were installed, along with rack-and-pinion steering and a five-speed manual gearbox. The wheelbase of the Esprit's steel backbone chassis was 96 in. and the two-seater measured almost 168 inches long overall. Tread dimension was six inches wider than the Europa. In European trim, an early Esprit could hit 135 mph, though 120 mph was about the limit of U.S. versions, which carried a lower-powered (140-hp) engine. The cars became available here in 1977.

While Lotus traditionally offered its cars in both kit and assembled form, the Esprit came only ready-to-roll. In 1979, Series 2 versions with wider wheels and a front lip spoiler became available.

In 1976, the Series 1 model had a $15,990 price. A few years later, in 1979, the Series 2 version carried a $27,000 window sticker. Total series production was 1,060 units for the S1 and 88 for the S2. The Turbo Esprit that appeared in the 1977 James Bond film "The Spy Who Loved Me" renewed worldwide interest in the marque.

A larger 2174-cc twin-cam engine went into the 1980-1989 Series 2.2 Lotus Esprit, although horsepower did not increase. This engine produced 160 hp at 6500 rpm. For extra potency customers could choose a turbocharged version—using the same engine with a Garrett AiResearch T3 turbocharger. It had a 7.5:1 compression ratio: 7.5:1 and developed 210 hp at 6000 rpm and 200 ft.-lbs. of torque. at 4000 rpm.

The Esprit Turbo rode a more rigid chassis and carried a modified rear suspension with 15-in. wheels. Styling modifications included a deep front air dam and aero rocker-panel extensions, which were enough to boost top speed close to the 150-mph mark. Standard tires used for the Turbo were 195/60VR15 in front and 235/60VR15 at the

*The Lotus Esprit—like the 1989 Turbo in this ad—encouraged people not to follow the crowd.*

rear. This compared to 205/60VR14 front/205/70VR14 rear for non-Turbo models.

By 1983, the normally-aspirated S3 Esprit adopted all the changes that had formerly gone into the Turbo, along with wider optional wheels and tires. In 1986, the turbocharged engine was converted from carburetors to a Bosch fuel-injection system. General Motors bought Lotus in 1986 and promised not to interfere with its workings.

In recent years, Lotus also has turned to consultancy duties for other manufacturers in such areas as engine design, suspension systems, and techniques for molding fiberglass. In December 1988, Group Lotus established Lotus Cars USA Inc. as its American distributor. Secret agent James Bond again drove a Lotus Esprit in the 1981 film "For Your Eyes Only."

As the 1990s began, the Esprit Turbo — now called the Turbo SE — remained in the Lotus lineup and the American marketplace. This version (the "SE" stood for "special Equipment") had an airbag system and was powered by an updated 2.2-liter aluminum alloy engine. In this latest incarnation, the four-cylinder power plant produced 264 hp, enough to send an Esprit from a standing start to 60 mph in 4.7 seconds — and to 100 mph in 11.9 seconds. Its top speed ran close to 165 mph.

SE equipment included a leather interior, a polished burr-elm instrument panel, air conditioning, power windows, power door locks, a power fuel flap, heated power mirrors, a three-phase ice warning system, a removable roof panel (with deflector), tinted glass, and a 100-watt Sony XR7100 AM/ FM radio with cassette player. The two-passenger coupe sold for $40,975 per seat or $14.53 per pound, since it weighed 2,820 lbs.

The Lotus Esprit Turbo SE played a role in two popular 1990 American movies. The first was "Pretty Woman" starring Richard Gere and Julia Roberts. Gere's character remarked the car "... corners like it's on rails." The second Lotus was seen in "Taking Care of Business," which starred Charles Grodin and Jim Belushi. At that time, Lotus sold about 300 Esprit Turbo SE models per year in the U.S. market.

In 1992, the back of the Esprit Turbo SE received a taller spoiler, a re-worked rear fascia and a glass-less rear hatch. Twenty yellow-and-green Jim Clark editions of the car were offered with an asking price of $95,995.

In 1994, power steering became standard, the rear wing and lower sills were revised, and the alloy wheels were changed to 17-in. models. In 1995 larger brakes were the only significant change.

The biggest transformation in the Esprit's history would have to be the 1997 changeover to a Lotus designed V-8. With twin turbo chargers, the horsepower rating increased from 300 to 350. This engine was a double-overhead-cam (32-valve) V-8 with an aluminum block and aluminum heads, twin turbochargers, and an intercooler. Its 83 x 81-mm bore and stroke brought displacement to 3506 cc. Its torque output was 295 ft.-lbs. at 4250 rpm.

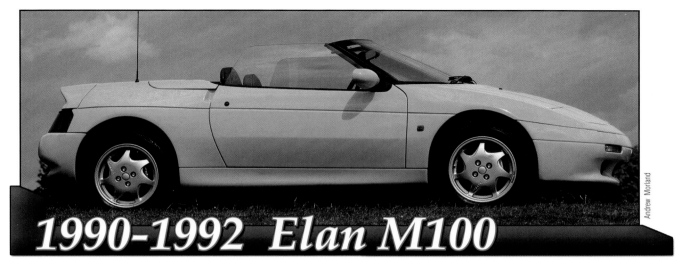

Andrew Morland

# 1990-1992 Elan M100

s the 1990s began, Lotus Cars Ltd., of Hethel, Norwich, England, took a cue from its roots, issuing a modern version of the old Elan. The new Elan M100 roadster was introduced in 1989 and first appeared in the United States at the Detroit and Los Angeles auto shows in January 1991.

This model was imported to the U.S. only during 1991, when 528 cars were sold here. Of these, 312 were red, 102 were white, 52 were yellow, 37 were green, 19 were silver, and six were black.

The M100 was the first all-new Lotus model since 1975. The car had front-wheel drive and carried a 1.6-liter twin-cam turbocharged engine with an air-to-air intercooler. Lotus and Isuzu collaborated on the engine and Isuzu built it. A five-speed gearbox was standard, along with power rack-and-pinion steering and front and rear disc brakes.

The GRP (glass-reinforced-plastic) body shell bolted rigidly to the multi-piece bonded, riveted and bolted-together steel backbone chassis that incorporated suspension-mounting points.

Standard equipment for the $33,900 open-bodied model included a leather-rimmed steering wheel, central power door locking, electric power windows, electronically-adjustable and heated door-mounted power rearview mirrors, leather upholstery, bronze-tinted glass, a driver's side airbag, an AM/FM cassette radio with power antenna, air conditioning and alloy wheels. It weighed in at 2,249 lbs. Only about 324 Lotus cars were sold in the U.S. during 1990 and the relatively high sticker price kept total sales on the low side as well.

The in-line four-cylinder engine featured dual overhead camshafts and 16 valves. It had an 80 x 79-mm bore and stroke and displaced 1588 cc. With an 8.2:1 compression ratio it developed 165 hp at 6600 rpm and 148 lbs.-ft. of torque at 4200 rpm. It relied on a multi-point fuel injection system for fuel delivery.

Purists were shocked by the Elan M100's front-wheel-drive arrangement. Reviewers moaned that it lacked the "tail-wagging" handling of real sports cars, but the Isuzu-built turbo four made a reasonable 162 hp.

## The Lotus Elan SE of the 1990s was an attractive convertible.

It was said to be designed to "allow 100 percent of owners to use 90 percent of its performance 90 percent of the time." With only 2,870 lbs. to move, the two-seater could zoom from 0 to 60 mph in 6.6 seconds. The factory claimed a top speed of 135 mph, and it could cover the standing-start quarter mile in 15.1 seconds, according to *Motor Trend*.

Built on an 88.6-in. chassis, the M100 roadster had an overall length of 152.4 in. It stood just 48.4 in. high and was 68.3 in. wide. The car was low to the ground, with a 5.1-in. road clearance and had a 62/38 percent front-to-rear weight distribution. The front and rear tread measurements were both the same at 58.5 in. The standard tires for the M100 were size 205/50ZR15 radials. The later Elan S2 added "experimental" 16-in. Goodyear tires mounted on 16-in. alloy wheels.

Other features included a five-speed manual transmission, rack-and-pinion steering, and four-wheel solid disc brakes (10-in. diameter front and 9.3-in. diameter rear). The front sub-frame was bolted to the backbone chassis and incorporated mounting points for the front suspension, which featured "interactive" unequal-length wishbones, coil springs, dampers, and an anti-roll bar. The independent rear suspension system was comprised of upper links, lower wishbones, co-axial coil springs, dampers, and an anti-roll bar.

General Motors owned Lotus by the time the Elan M100 made the scene, and "The General" lost money on every car built. As the M100's price tag rose to $40,989, sales slowed even further and production was halted in the summer of 1992. By that time, only 3,000 cars had been sold worldwide.

Two years later, Lotus revived the car as the Elan S2, of which 800 were made to use up the inventory of Isuzu-built engines. A Kia version of the car was also available in the Far East until the summer of 1999.

Dr. David Koski

# 1995-2003 Elise

The "spiritual successor" to the much-loved Lotus Elan of the 1960s would have to be the four-cylinder Lotus Elise introduced in 1995. This lightweight two-seat roadster has never been sold in the United States, but some enthusiasts have been able to bring this fabulously fun car into the country for "display" or track-only purposes.

Lotus fortunes ebbed in the 1980s, after the premature death of Colin Chapman. The 54-year-old British sports car legend died on Dec. 16, 1982, when he suffered a heart attack. Lacking Chapman's talent at pulling the company up from the depths, the factory racing team ran into trouble building winning cars and lining up sponsors. At the end of 1994, it withdrew from Formula 1 competition.

On the sales/production front, the pricey, front-drive Elan M100 and the ever-present Esprit were not hitting sales goals and General Motors went looking for a buyer for its British property. Romano Artioli, of Bugatti Industries, grabbed the opportunity. The Elise—named after his granddaughter—became his pet project. The no-frills $35,000 sports car was designed along classic Lotus lines with high-tech handling and performance.

Powered by a front-mounted 1796-cc all-aluminum in-line four-cylinder engine sourced from Rover, the Elise incorporated dual overhead cams and 16 valves. The 1,520-lb. two-seater had 118 hp at 5500 rpm to motivate it, as well as 122 lbs.-ft. of torque at 3000 rpm. It could move from 0-to-60 mph in 5.5 seconds. A Sport 190 version was even hotter, developing 190 hp at 7500 rpm, and 140 lbs.-ft. of torque at 5500 rpm. It was good for a 4.4-second 0-to-60 mph time and could do 0-to-100 mph in 13.2 seconds.

The Elise showcased traditional Lotus styling with curvaceous body feature lines, a low nose, high fenders, and a silhouette seen earlier in the Elite 11 and 19. Minimum overhang permitted the longest possible wheelbase for a small car. It had a 2300-mm wheelbase and 3785-mm overall length. The body was made of two handmade fiberglass "shells" bolted to the chassis and two resin-injection-molded side panels containing the door openings. The flat aluminum underbody reduced lift and drag.

The ultra-lightweight aluminum monocoque tub chassis weighed only 150 lbs. The aluminum panels were bonded together with an epoxy reinforced with Ejot self-threading fasteners. Twin cross-sectional "tubes" on each side of the car were joined transversely, at the front and rear, with torque boxes and a flat under panel. The engine/transaxle unit sat in a steel sub-frame bolted to the rear of the chassis. A front crash structure and rear "crumple zone" also added to driver safety. A

***The unique stance of the Lotus Elise seems to appeal to drivers of all ages.***

massive roll bar protected passengers in the event of a roll over.

The Elise suspension featured double wishbones, single coil springs, mono-tube dampers, and an anti-roll bar at both ends. The suspension uprights were formed of extruded aluminum, as were the control pedals. The suspension was completely adjustable. To stop the Elise, 11-in. diameter aluminum-silicon matrix composite brakes were employed. These were light in weight and conducted heat away from the discs.

The Elise was unveiled at the 1995 Frankfurt Motor Show in Germany and promoted as "the star of the show." The first dealer deliveries took place in late 1996. Various versions of the car were sold outside the United States over the years.

The Series One was a 1.8-liter 118-hp machine with five-spoke wheels on early models and 12-spoke wheels on later editions. A hardtop "Sport" model appeared next, followed by the Sport 190, which had a 188-hp VHPD engine, faired-in headlights and a roll cage. The Elise 49, which had the appearance of the 26R model and came in the racing team's Grand Prix colors, was released in February 1998.

In November 1998, the 135-hp Sport 135 incorporated a racing gearbox, improved cast iron brakes, a better exhaust system and different wheels and tires. Announced in February 1999, the Sprint model had a VVC (Variable Valve Control) engine, but no windshield. Next came the 111S, which used the original 1.8-liter K-series engine block, but with a VVC head that helped it generate 143 hp.

The 340R version of the Elise was more like the old Lotus Seven. An improved version of Sport 135, the Sport 160, put out 160 hp due to its revised engine-management software and cylinder head changes. The Exige version of the Elise was a 190-hp competition hardtop incorporating a close-ratio gearbox, a modified suspension, modified wheels, and other racing hardware.

The current "production" version of the Elise is the Series 2 (Elise MY 2001), which was released at the British International Motor Show in October 2000. It had all-new wider and lower body panels designed by Steve Crijns, plus an almost-all-new technical makeup combining a cleaner-running high-performance engine with better steering and road-handling characteristics. Its Euro 3 emissions-compliant K-series power plant produced 120 hp and a top speed of 125 mph. Going from 0-to-60 mph took just 5.6 seconds.

# MARAUDER

John Wheater

# 1950-1952 Marauder

The Marauder was created by a team of people who had formerly worked on the production of a single-seat racing car. This marque was originally the product of Wilks, Mackie & Co. Ltd. of Dorridge, Warwickshire, England, which evolved into the Marauder Car Co. Ltd., of Kenilworth, Warwickshire. Two models known as the "A" and the "100" were offered. The information given below applies to the "A," except where noted.

In 1950, *Motor Trend* described the $2,600 Marauder A as a "fast touring car." It was based on the chassis of the Rover 75, a four-door sedan with a 75-hp six-cylinder engine. The Marauder had a shorter, lighter version of the Rover's box-section frame and modified 80-hp version of its 2103-cc engine with inclined overhead valves, stiffer valve springs and a 7.6:1 compression ratio. It was powerful enough to hit 90 mph and could go from a standing start to 50 mph in 13 seconds—not bad for a rather large, 2,622-lb. sports car.

Some of the Marauder sport roadster's body panels came from Rover, too, but the body itself was constructed by Richard Mead, who produced bodies for Alvis and Bentley. A small grille was made up of four thick horizontal bars and a vertical center divider bar. The car had a short hood panel and a long nosepiece. Small round parking lights stood below the headlights. Rear-hinged "suicide" style doors and wheel openings with flares at the front characterized the body.

Bright rocker panel moldings ran between the wheel openings on each side. The front fenders incorporated flush-fitting trafficators that flipped out to indicate when the driver was turning a corner. Fixed-head coupe bodies differed somewhat from the roadster. They had a

*One of the rarest of the British-made sports cars is the Marauder.*

narrow vertical-style grille and a smaller windshield.

Provision was made for fresh-air heating/ventilation and for the installation of a radio. Standard features included a combination fuel and oil-level indicator, a reserve fuel switch, a map light, a cigar lighter and a choke warning light. Sliding "Perspex" side curtains set in metal frames could be attached to the doors with threaded dowels.

Perched on a 102-in. wheelbase and having an overall length of 166 in., the Marauder was 52 in. high and 66 in. wide. The 51.6-in. front tread was slightly narrower than the 50.8-in. rear tread. The ventilated disc wheels held tall and narrow 6.00 x 15 tires.

The Marauder employed a four-speed manual transmission with gear ratios of 14.5:1 in first, 8.77:1 in second, 5.92:1 in third, 4.3:1 in fourth and 13.17:1 in reverse, except in the case of some early models that had an overall ratio of 8.24:1 in second gear and 5.82:1 in third. With an optional overdrive, the gear ratios changed to 10.07:1 in first, 6.09:1 in second, 4.11:1 in third and 3.0:1 in fourth.

A 4.3:1 rear axle was standard in Marauders. Burman recirculating-ball steering was fitted. An independent coil spring suspension was used up front, while a rigid axle with variable-rate semi-elliptic leaf springs was seen at the rear. Girling hydro-mechanical drum brakes were fitted all around.

The second model—the Marauder 100—-was a larger car with a more powerful 2392-cc 105-hp six-cylinder engine running triple S.U.

carburetors (as opposed to the A model's twin S.U.s). Production of this model started in 1951. Marauder 100s were built only on special order and are extremely rare. They were capable of reaching at least 100 mph.

Marauders were intended for both competition use and road use. The cars were not officially exported to the United States. In fact, only a few Marauders were ever built. Most of them were roadsters, but a fixed-head coupe was also offered in England.

*A gathering of the surviving Marauders known to exist makes this a memorable photo.*

# MARCOS

Bob Harrington

# 1962-1981 Marcos GT

Co-founders, Jem Marsh and Frank Costin dreamed up this small, sporty British car and combined the first three letters from each of their last names to identify it. Marsh had previously worked in the technical department at Firestone, while Costin was an aircraft designer and engineer who'd contributed ideas to the Lotus company. Legend has it they met at a Hitchin, Hertfordshire, England, pub and decided to build a car to compete with the Lotus 7.

In 1959, Marsh founded Speedex Casting & Accessories Ltd. for the purpose of supplying parts and fiberglass body shells to other firms. The company name changed to Monocoque Chassis & Body Co. Ltd. in 1961 and to Marcos Cars Ltd. in 1962. The company was taken over by D & H Fibreglass Techniques Ltd. in 1975. Starting in 1981, yet another company, Jem Marsh Performance Cars, continued production.

The first Marcos vehicle was designed by Frank Costin. It was a two-seat roadster with a different kind of uni-body construction. The body was crafted out of marine plywood and fiberglass atop a composite chassis. It was called the Xylon, the Greek word for "wood." The first car had gull-wing doors, cycle fenders, Triumph Herald steering, a Herald front suspension, and a Nash Metropolitan (or Standard) rear end. This model had a 1.0-liter British Ford engine that was powerful enough for a top speed of about 120 mph.

After a period of being involved in racing, Marsh and Costin turned to a production version with full fenders. They formed Marcos Cars Ltd. in 1962. Kit cars—rather than fully-assembled vehicles—became their major product.

The Marcos GT was introduced in 1964. Long and low in appearance, the Marcos coupe had a steeply raked windshield and door windows, a pointed nose, and full wheel openings. A straight fastback roofline led past a severely curved rear window and trunk lid, to a chopped-off tail.

The headlights were recessed in nacelles and sat behind clear curved windows. The entire nose section hinged forward and it was held in

*The Marcos GT still competes on road courses around the world.*

place by side latches.

By 1971, standard equipment included a leather-rimmed steering wheel, front disc brakes, carpeting, a tachometer, a cigarette lighter, two-speed windshield wipers and washers, non-adjustable bucket seats, adjustable pedals, a console, a sunroof, power windows, and dual air horns. The option list included air conditioning and leather seats.

This kit car utilized a Volvo 1800 engine and was again plywood-based. It was followed by the 1600GT, which had a 1.6-liter Ford four-cylinder engine beneath its bonnet. Subsequent examples took their power from Ford V-4s and V-6s, as well as the Volvo in-line six. Another model was the four-seat Mantis, a Triumph-powered coupe capable of 140 mph.

By 1970, Marcos coupes were available in the United States, but stateside sales didn't last long, since the cars couldn't meet America's tightening federal vehicle regulations.

Financial troubles hit the company hard by 1972 and production came to a halt, except for production of the low-cost fiberglass-bodied Mini-Marcos, which had been introduced in 1965 and was based on a Morris Mini van modified by former British test pilot Dizzy Addicot. That car had the distinction of accepting a selection of BMC Mini components. A new company name and ownership came in 1975 and allowed production of the Mini-Marcos to continue as late as 1981. That model was joined by a Midas 2+2 coupe.

Another name change (to Midas Cars) came in 1981, furthering production of the Midas in kit and assembled form. Meanwhile, co-founder Jem Marsh started yet another company to reintroduce the old GT. By the 1980s, however, awareness of the Marcos had long since evaporated among most American enthusiasts.

*The 1964 Marcos 1800 IRS even had aerodynamic headlight covers.*

*The 1995 Marcos Mantera V-8 400 coupe had American admirers, but was not imported to the U. S.*

# MCLAREN F1

## 1999-2000 Sportscar

**P**riced at $1,131,120, the McLaren F1 is a car that was never officially imported into the United States. Only about 100 examples were built and just a handful made it into the hands of American enthusiasts. Nevertheless, it certainly qualifies as one of the most historically-significant British sports cars of the 1990s and the New Millennium. It was produced by McLaren Cars Limited, of Woking, England.

Flushed with the successes of their dominance of F1 racing, McLaren set out to build the world's fastest car. Designer Gordon Murray had sketched his idea of a three-seater with a center driving position decades before the F1 became a reality. Extensive use of exotic materials—such as carbon fiber, titanium and gold—helped to make the car a remarkably light 2,840 lbs.

A custom built BMW V-12 engine displaced 6.0-liters and made a spine-tingling 627 hp. Thanks to a cleverly-designed undercarriage, the McLaren was capable of attaining speeds over 230 mph, despite the absence of spoilers and wings. A venturi was sculpted into the bottom and used the air rushing under the car to help glue it to the road.

The dual overhead-cam four-cylinder engine had 48 valves. With an 86 x 87-mm bore and stroke is displaced 6064 cc. McLaren used a 10.5:1 to squeeze out 627 hp at 7400 rpm and 479 lbs.-ft. of torque at 4000 rpm. An electronic sequential-port fuel-injection system fed the high-tech power plant. The engine drove through a six-speed manual gearbox.

The F1 could speed from 0-to-60 mph in 3.2 seconds and did the quarter mile in 11.1 seconds at 138 mph. Its top speed was approximately 220 mph.

This super sports car was constructed on a 107-in. wheelbase and was 168.8 in. long. It stood 44.9 in. high and was 71.7 in. wide. With a 61.7-in. front tread and 58.0-in. rear tread, it was a stable ride at high speeds. Rack-and-pinion steering was fitted along with four-wheel disc brakes.

*The McLaren F 1 is considered one of the elite—the "super cars" in the world.*

*The McLaren F 1 is about as far from a "grocery getter" as a driver can get!*

# MG

OCW Archive

# 1945-1949 MG TC

Few British sports cars have enjoyed the popularity of the MG two-seat roadster or had such a strong influence on American drivers and amateur racers. More than any other single make, MG was responsible for introducing the joys (and quirks) of traditional-styled sports cars to America.

The two letters simply stand for "Morris Garages." Through its long life, the marque was identified by an octagonal symbol that contained those two letters. MG itself became known for the motto, "Safety Fast." The M.G. Car Company Ltd. (part of Nuffield Exports Ltd.), was based in Cowley, Oxford, England. Its plant was located at Abingdon-on-Thames, Berkshire.

MG actually descended from surprisingly large vehicles beginning with the Bullnose Morris of 1923. The first MG 14/40 of the 1920s carried a 1.8-liter engine. Later Mk I/II/III series were powered by 2.5-liter Morris overhead-cam sixes. In 1928, the sporty M-type Midget appeared, based on the Morris Minor of that era and powered by 746-cc and 847-cc engines. It was followed by a series of similar models, dubbed C, D, J, PA, and PB.

In the 1930s, MGs won the Brooklands 500, Double-Twelve and Grand Prix events. Tazio Nuvolari drove a supercharged K3 Magnette to win the 1933 Ulster Tourist Trophy. Over a five-year period, MGs won 37 major international events. MG also created the first 750-cc car to reach 120 mph and the first 1100-cc car to top 200 mph.

The MG J-Types—produced from 1932 to 1934—were rough riders with 847-cc engines capable of nearly 80 mph. They were the first MG Midget cars with a four-speed gearbox in every model.

The PA was the first Midget with running boards. Its successor, the PB, came in roadster and tourer form and a handful of streamlined PB Airline coupes were also built. The P-series MGs were the last to carry overhead-cam engines.

The most familiar prewar MG predecessors arrived in the mid-1930s. TA and TB Midget sports roadsters were powered by 1292-cc (then 1250-cc) four-cylinder engines. By 1936, the earlier overhead-cam engines had given way to a pushrod (overhead valve) design.

*The MG TC two-seater was all about fun and "safety fast" driving.*

Cecil Kimber of the Morris Garages is credited with production of the first MG sports car and with the T-series of the late 1930s. Production of the TA started in 1936, one year after Lord Nuffield sold his firm to the Nuffield Organisation, which had evolved from the original Morris Motors.

The TA used a long-stroke four-cylinder engine. The production models had a slab-shaped gas tank at the rear. Longer in wheelbase (94 in.) than the P-series, the TA also had a wider tread, and wore the 19-in. wire wheels. Lockheed hydraulic brakes provided the stopping power.

Initial TAs had a "crash box" transmission, but before long it was altered. With the windshield folded, a TA could come close to 80 mph in a tad over 23 seconds.

The TB Midget turned to a shorter-stroke overhead-valve engine, known as the XPAG. While bore/stroke dimensions of the TA had been 63.5 x 102 mm, the TB had a 66.5-mm bore and 90-mm stroke. It developed 54.4 hp at 5200 rpm. Only 3,003 TA and 379 TB models were built.

The TC, announced in late 1945 at the London Motor Show, was only slightly modified from the 1939 prewar TB design. The body was four inches wider and the running boards were narrower. Only a modest number of prewar MGs ever reached America. The TC changed all that. It helped to ignite a near-fanatical fondness for sports cars in the 1950s. American servicemen returning from England took a powerful fancy to the traditional-styled roadster and brought back quite a few when they returned.

By 1947, MG had an expanded distribution network in the U.S. MG TCs began trickling into the United States not too long after English production commenced in late 1945. Nothing remotely like the TC was offered by Detroit. Fans were able to overlook drawbacks like a harsh ride, a cramped cockpit, and sluggish performance.

All TCs had right-hand drive. Nothing else offered such a pure look and so much automotive character for a fairly modest price. The TC was economical to drive and easy to maintain.

The early British roadsters tended to demand regular maintenance and repair. The TC's flaws and idiosyncrasies were easily offset by its many charms.

A ladder-type chassis with channel-section side members differed little from prewar designs. Wood framing held the car's steel body panels, in a construction style closer to that of American cars of the 1920s.

Sweeping, separate fenders with freestanding headlights led into short running boards. The body was itself four inches wider than the prewar TB, but overall width remained the same. Adding to the rakish lines were rear-hinged cut-away doors. Ahead of the long hood stood a traditional vertical-bar grille. The low windshield could be folded for "wind-in-the-face" motoring.

A soft top fit over a rather complex metal frame, assisted by snap-inside curtains. Putting up the top and curtains was daunting and tedious. Bumpers were not included.

The TC's 1250-cc engine, hooked to a four-speed gearbox (nonsynchronized in first gear), which emitted a lovely sound out the exhaust that served as part of the car's charm. The XPAG engine differed little from the 1939 version used in the TB.

Twin S.U. carburettors, three main bearings, solid valve lifters, and a 7.25:1 compression ratio were among the sturdy engine's factory specifications. A 12-volt electrical system was used at a time when most U.S.-built cars had 6-volt systems.

American road testers reported a top speed of 80-82 mph for the TC, while a more realistic 74 to 78 mph figure was promoted in Great Britain. Zero-to-60-mph acceleration was in the 19.5 to 22.7 second range. Running the quarter mile took 21.8 seconds.

The four-speed gearbox had gear ratios of 17.32:1 in first, 10.0:1 in second, 6.93:1 in third and 5.125:1 in fourth. A low 5.125:1 ratio rear axle was standard. Cam-and-lever steering was employed. The front suspension consisted of a rigid axle with semi-elliptic leaf springs.

Because of the hard springs, the TC's ride was bouncy over even modest bumps. The car could get shaky going around quick corners, too. The speedometer sat ahead of the passenger. All TCs had right-hand drive. The brakes were Lockheed hydraulics, with front and rear drums.

Out of total TC production of 10,000 units, 3,408 were sold in Britain and 2,001 were officially exported to the United States. Many cars were simply brought to the U.S. by individuals. An estimated 682 MGs were officially sold here during 1948 and 857 in 1949.

The MG company called the TC "the sports car America loved first." MG engines were capable of tight tuning for race purposes, but the car's poor aerodynamics cut back on its racing performance. Its short wheelbase and quick steering made it a popular choice for the rallies and gymkhanas that began to flourish in the 1950s.

John Gunnell

# 1949-1953 MG TD

**C**reated by Cecil Cousins, who'd been with MG since the 1920s, the TD Series "MG Midget Car" entered production in November 1949 to replace the classic TC. Syd Enever and Alec Hounslow built the mock-up for the new series during a two-week period in 1949. They cut up an MG YA chassis and fit a cobbled up TC body to it. The engine was the same XPAG type used in the TC, but was attached to a new gearbox.

The Nuffield Organisation, owners of the M.G. Car Company Ltd., demanded an affordable, basic new sports car that could move quickly from the drawing board to the assembly line. The TC body was used to retain its trademark looks and combine them with technical improvements like front coil springs, rack-and-pinion steering, a hypoid rear axle and optional left-hand drive. The first TD-TD0251- was completed in November 1949.

*The MG TD offered internal improvements and updated styling, but kept all the fun.*

The "251" in the serial number represented the digits in the factory's telephone numer, a rather odd tradition that was maintained until MG became part of the British Motor Corporation or BMC.

The TD was designed with American buyers in mind. A total of 29,664 TDs were produced from 1949-1953, of which 23,488 of them were sold in the United States.

Smoother, more modern lines replaced the TC's vertical look. The TD's dramatically lower stance resulted from using 15-inch tires, rather than the original 19-inch style. Sales literature said that its "very lines suggest action. Hollywood stars acclaim the Midget as the greatest little sports car in the world."

The TD platform was a revised version of the box-section chassis used on the Y-series saloon (sedan). A "kickup" above the rear wheels allowed the use of softer springs and increased wheel travel.

Wire wheels were no longer standard equipment and not on the options list, although many TDs were later fitted with a wire wheel kit. Early TDs actually came with solid steel disc wheels, although steel disc wheels with round ventilation holes were used on most cars produced. Since the first batch of TDs made were also prone to scuttle (cowl) shake, a roll-bar-type scuttle support was added starting with chassis no. 0351 in December 1949.

Quickly created by modifying a TC body, the new TD coachwork looked very fresh and more modern. It was notably wider and less angular than its predecessor. The TD was slightly longer than the TC. Measurements included a 94-in. wheelbase, a 145-in. overall length, a 53-in. top-of-the-windshield height, a 58.6-in. maximum width, a 47.4-in. front tread and a 50 in. rear tread. The 4.00 x 15 five-stud steel disc wheels originally held 5.50 x 15 Dunlop tires.

The upright grille continued to use vertical slats. In standard factory trim, the grille slats were painted to match the color of the seats, although there were exceptions to this rule. A large octagonal MG emblem decorated a trim piece on the upper center of the raditor with its octagonal cap.

The headlights were mounted on down-curved bars running between the radiator and the "clam shell" style fenders, which were lower than TC fenders. The fenders carried chrome-plated "King of the Road" wing lamps. Chrome headlight buckets were available from 1949 to early 1951. Late 1951 to 1953 TDs had them done in body color. From some point in 1952 until 1953, the painted headlamps did not have "King of the Road" emblems. Twin horns and an oil-bath air cleaner mounted atop a separate air cleaner manifold were standard equipment.

The length of the telescoping steering column could be manually adjusted by a nut. The new plastic steering wheel had a tan-grey marbelized finish and the MG octagon within the spring-spoke steering wheel's hub. The flat windshield could folded forward for bug-in-the-face driving, rallying, or racing.

A tan folding canvas top was standard, but two designs were seen. Early TDs used a two-bow style, while later editions had a top with three bows. Matching side curtains fastened to the doors and rear quarters. Directional lights were not standard on TDs until November 1952.

Drivetrain changes between the TC and TD were slight. While some sources mentioned an 80-mph top speed, Tom McCahill reported a more believable 72 mph as the fastest he achieved.

The TD engine was a sturdy little in-line four-cylinder with overhead valves, solid valve lifters and three main bearings. It had a cast iron block and head. A 66.5 x 90-mm bore and stroke gave it 1250-cc. Displacement. It rand a 7.25:1 compression ratio and dual S.U. carburetors. The engine produced 54.4 hp at 5200 rpm and 64 ft.-lbs. of torque at 2600 rpm.

A 12- volt electrical system was used. Early cars had a cylinder head that used short-reach spark plugs and a smooth oil pan. Later TDs required long-reach plugs and had a finned oil pan. Cars with the later 8-in. clutch assembly were produced from August 1951 on. These are known as TD2 models, but should not be confused with the TD MKII, a model built or retrofitted with a racing kit. The engine used in TD1 models, built from November 1949 to August 1951, aren't interchangeable with the later TD2 engine because of the clutch differences..

The TD's four-speed manual transmission had a non-scynchronized first gear. Overall gear ratios were 17.938:1 in first, 10.609:1 in second, 7.098:1 in third and 5.125:1 in fourth. The standard 5.125:1 rear axle ratio meant the car was turning about 4,000 rpms in fourth at 50 to 55 mph. The low gearing came in handy on hills. Many enthusiasts have their axles modified to maintain highway speeds.

MG's basic TD roadster changed little in 1953. Standard body colors were now black or ivory with red or green leather upholstery, MG Red with red upholstery, Silver Streak Grey with red upholstery, and Woodland Green with green upholstery. British Racing Green wasn't an option. Rectangular taillights were used until October 1952, then replaced with round ones. The 1953 price tag was up to $1,945 (later $2,115) and weight increased to 2,065 lbs.

At the Earl's Court Motor Show in London in October 1952, MGs were advertised for $1,460 in America. Sales brochures called MG "the one you've always wanted to drive." The roadster "Goes like a flash . . . grips the road like a limpet."

By 1953, the Nuffield Organization had become part of the British Motor Corporation (BMC). Some of the company's American distributors, such as S.H. "Wacky" Arnolt in Chicago, created special MG models with Italian-designed aluminum coupe bodies. Inskip Motors, of New York, also offered a four-seat TD, but the company built no more than four examples.

*The MG TD often comes to mind when North Americans bring up the subject of British cars.*

# 1951-1953 TD MKII

**S**tarting in 1950, a limited-production Mark II competition version of the MG TD was a possibility. Priced at about $200 more than the standard TD ($2,145 in 1951) and weighing about 50 lbs. more, the Mark II factory tuning kit had sales of at least 1,710 over four model years.

American dealers began to sell MK II conversion kits as early as 1950 and the performance edition became known in the United States as the TDC or TD Competition model. Owners of ordinary TDs could upgrade their cars to MK II tune, making some MK IIs hard to spot.

Some cars have small enameled "TD Mark II" plaques towards the front of the hood. Some also have chrome grilles and chrome headlamp buckets. Other special features include Andrex friction-type shock absorbers mounted in addition to the standard shocks, dual electric fuel pumps (instead of a single electric pump) and two larger 1.5-in. S.U. carburetors. Starting with car no. TD/C/22613, a larger intake manifold was used and a bulge was added to the right hood side to accommodate it.

Though retaining the TD's 1250-cc. XPAG engine, MK IIs with Stage 1 tuning had a higher 8.6:1 compression ratio and 60 hp, versus the standard 54. Four additional stages of tune were possible.

The MK II upgrading was a reflection of the TD's struggle to keep up with more powerful sports cars offered by other manufacturers in Great Britain and other countries, as well as new American products that were introduced like the Corvette, Thunderbird and Kaiser-Darrin. To keep up with such competition, American distributors turned out several modified Mugs that appeared at the International Motor Show in New York.

Other features used on some TD MK IIs starting with car TD/C/22613 include black-and-white wheel medallions, an enameled rear bumper emblem, a black-on-white radiator medallion, a dashboard assist handle and a larger spare tire medallion. Some MK IIs also feature a Lucas high-performance ignition coil and a higher (numerically lower) rear axle ratio.

The competition-oriented Mark II was advertised as "for the enthusiast - the fellow who wants just that little bit extra." That rare Mark II (TDC) edition could also get suspension and other modifications out of Mug's Factory Tuning Manual. In fact, the manual listed a variety of engine tuning kits (Stage II, Stage III, etc.) that could be used with any TD model.

*The MG TD MKII had a chrome radiator and a "Mark II" plate on its hood.*

In August 1951, a stock Mark II version set 23 Class F records at the Bonneville (Utah) Salt Flats with a 12-hour run averaging 75.34 mph. Despite such efforts, MG faced serious competition in the marketplace from the Triumph TR2, a low-priced English "cousin" that had a much more powerful engine, a 105-mph top speed and some more modern amenities.

In 1954, John Bentley explained the TD MK It's low sales in his booklet All the World's 1954 Cars. "The 1950 TD model . . . a radical departure from the TC and earned the displeasure of sports car purists . . . actually gained sales over its competitor, though hopelessly outclassed in the 1-1/2-liter racing category," Bentley noted. "Racing enthusiasts account for a very small percentage of MG buyers, and because of this the later Mark II (with a soaped-up engine and a higher axle ratio) was not a signal success."

*Two fuel pumps were used, both SU type L, in the MG TD MKII.*

Dick Dance Collection

# 1953-1955 TF 1250

The new MG TF, introduced in October 1953, was mainly a facelifted TD that did not radically change the character or appearance of the "MG Midget" from previous years. John Thornley and Syd Enever, of the MG Car Co. Ltd., had tried to talk Leonard Lord into financing an all-new MG. He refused, so the two men put the first TF together in two weeks. The model survived only until April 1955.

TFs built between September 17 1953 and December 31, 1953 are considered 1953 models. Those built from Jan. 4 to Dec. 30, 1954, are 1954 models, and the cars made in the Jan. 4, 1955 to April 4, 1955 period are 1955 models.

The TF's mechanical underpinnings were initially unchanged from those of the TD, except for revisions to the carburetors, fuel pump springs, and valves and a higher rear axle ratio. A larger-displacement XPEG engine was gradually introduced, between July 1954 and November 1954, for a new TF 1500 model. During its lifespan, the TF was widely criticized and this inspired MG to find the funding necessary to bring out the new MGA as a 1956 model.

A slanted-back chrome grille with a curvier shell and fewer vertical slats, along with swoopier swept-back front fender lines, helped make the TF look much longer. Actually, it was a mere two inches longer than the TD.

The front profile had a smooth-flowing, blunt "V" shape. A dummy radiator cap sat on top of the grille, but the radiator filler was actually hidden behind it. The headlights were blended into the fenders with large fairings. The single round lenses protruded a bit and were circled by wide chrome rings. The front and rear bumpers and overriders (bumper guards) were unchanged from the TD type.

Behind the bottom portion of the grille was a lower, more sharply sloped hood line. The louvers on the hood side panels were much shorter than those on the TD and the hood sides were fixed in place, no longer folding upwards.

The hood's top panels were center-hinged and could be opened by pressing push-buttons on either side. The lower hood could not accommodate the TD-type oil-bath air cleaner and air cleaner manifold, so the TF's larger S.U. carburetors had separate Vokes air cleaners on each carburetor body.

TD-style ventilated disc wheels were standard on the TF, but center-locking wire wheels were optional and common on U.S.-market models. The 1953 and 1954 wire wheels are different. White sidewall tires were also seen on many TFs, especially in America. The gas tank and outside spare tire also sat at a more rakish angle and a much larger MG octagon emblem, similar to the raditor badge, decorated the spare wheel.

TF buyers who ordered a factory accessory luggage rack found it

*A facelift and other changes gave MG buyers a new choice in 1954—the TF series.*

was a different style than those used on the TD. The TF's rack had long, straight rear braces.

The dashboard was set back a few inches to give occupants more interior room, and it was padded around the rim with leather-covered foam rubber for extra safety. The instrument panel was redesigned and had three MG-logo-style octagonal-shaped gauges in its center. Open glove boxes were placed at each end of the dashboard. Separate leather-trimmed bucket-style seats with curved backrests were found inside, each independently adjustable.

The cowl line was also taller than before. A new windshield had dual wipers mounted at its base, which improved the view of the road ahead. Round taillights, like those of the 1953 TD, were continued.

MG body construction was the same as before, with steel body panels and a sheet metal frame over a structural wooden skeleton frame. The scuttle bar provided support below the cowl. A 4.875: 1 rear axle was now standard equipment and promoted smoother, higher-speed highway driving. Standard TF body colors were grey with grey upholstery, green with green or biscuit upholstery, maroon with maroon or biscuit upholstery, and black with maroon, biscuit, or green upholstery. As mentioned previously, all TFs had chrome-plated grille slats. Turn signal lights, which became standard in 1953, were supplied with all TFs sold here.

The XPAG engine had the same basic specs as the TD engine, but incorporated some modifications made for the earlier Mark II version, including larger carburetors, larger engine valves, and the side-mounted air cleaners.

The compression ratio was boosted to 8.0:1, which was .8 higher than the standard TD, but .6 lower than the MK II TD. Engine output was 57.5 hp at 5500 rpm. The torque rating was 65 lbs.-ft. at 3000 rpm. With its improvements, the initial TF was faster than the standard TD.

The factory claimed a top speed of 80-82 mph, but the World-wide *Automotive Yearbook of 1954* simply said "top speed has been boosted by at least eight miles per hour." Magazines reported 0-to-60-mph times in the 18.9 to 22.2 second range and that the TF could do the quarter-mile in 22.6 seconds at 61 mph. Fuel economy was about 23 mpg;.

The TF had the same 94-in. wheelbase and 47.4 /50-in. tread widths as the TD, but all other measurements varied slightly. The length was 147 in., the height to the top of the windshield was 52.5 in. and the maximum width was 59 in. Dunlop 5.50 x 15 tires were again standard fare. Gear ratios on the four-speed manual gearbox were also revised to 17.06:1 in first, 10.09:1 in second, 6.725:1 in third and 4.875:1 in fourth. Suspension and brake specifications were the same as for the TD.

A total of 6,200 TF models were produced in 1953 and '54 and by 1954, it was reported that about 20,000 MG roadsters had been sold in America since the TC was introduced here. Hambro Automotive Corp., in New York City, was the main distributor of TFs in the United States.

The TF was scorned for being old-fashioned when it was new, but seems to bring the highest asking prices for T-Series MGs today. Although many enthusiasts still prefer the starker lines of the TC and TD, the TF is a more driver-friendly machine with styling changes that seem to have more appeal today. However much improved, the TF was still mainly a facelifted TD that really couldn't compete in the mid-'50s with the Triumph TR2's performance or power.

The automotive press was not kind to the final T-Series, said to be due to MG's reluctance to provide cars for writer reviews.

Bob Mendelsohn

# 1954-1955 TF 1500

T he TF 1500 represented a final effort to keep the venerable T-Series "MG Midget" alive in the face of competition from more powerful and speedier cars fielded by other sports car makers, as well as the more luxurious "sporty" cars that were coming out in America.

Prior to the release of this model, the TD, TD MK II and TF 1250 had all fallen 250 cc short of the 1-1/2-liter Class F sports-car engine displacement limit. As *Road & Track* noted, MG fanciers had been "agitating" for a "full 1500 engine" and they now nearly had it (the actual figure was 1466 cc).

"There's a new (bee) in its bonnet. Drive it and you'll agree that it outperforms all its famous predecessors," said an advertisement placed by Hambro Trading of America, the New York based importer of MGs.

The new engine—indicated by the letters "XPEG" on the brass engine tag, as well as on a firewall tag—was changed only by a bore increase from 66.5 mm to 72 mm. Yet, to achieve this, MG had to cast a new cylinder block with siamesed cylinders. This was done to insure that a wall thickness of .20-.25-inches would be maintained between the "holes."

According to *Road & Track*, the extra cc's added five miles per hour to the TF's top speed and reduced the 0-to-60-mph acceleration time by three seconds. The quarter mile took two less seconds and the terminal speed at the end of the quarter mile was two miles per hour faster.

***The prized MG TF 1500 included an upgraded engine but minor changes on its exterior.***

*Road & Track* also noted that a carburetion fault — a "flat spot" below 2500 rpm — that it had discovered in testing the TF 1250, did not occur while testing the TF 1500. "The larger engine now seems to have offset the over carburetion (two 1-1/2-inch S.U.s), which was so noticeable last year," stated the December 1954 road test and technical description.

The actual bore and stroke dimensions were 72 mm x 90 mm which, combined with an 8.0:1 compression ratio and twin carburetors with individual air cleaners, produced 65 hp at 5500 rpm and 76 lbs.-ft. of torque at 3000 rpm. This was enough power to cruise comfortably at 75-80 mph and top speed in road test situations was around 86 mph. Testers put the 0-to-60-mph time at 16.2 seconds and the fastest quarter mile run took 20.5 seconds. According to *Road & Track*, the transmission gear ratios were 17.1:1 in first, 10.1:1 in second, 6.75:1 in third, and 4.85:1 in fourth.

Externally the TF 1500 was the same as the previous TF 1250, apart from having bright "TF 1500" plaques added to the sides of its bonnet and a couple of different color combinations.

This model was available in black with red, green or biscuit upholstery, red with red or biscuit upholstery, green with green or biscuit upholstery and ivory with red or green upholstery. Initially, it was not a replacement for the 1250, since the two versions of the TF were built in alternating batches and available at the same time from July 1954 until April 1955.

In the beginning, the XPEG engine was made available only in North America. With a $1,995 Port-of-Entry price ($2,130 with wire wheels) the TF 1500 was a good bargain here. In fact, the 65-hp, wire-wheeled 1955 model sold for $100 less than the 1954 TF 1250 without wire wheels! The car outsold the TD MK II, but even at that, only about 3,400 TF 1500s were produced in 1954 and 1955. *Road & Track* originally wondered if the displacement boost was "too little, too late," but rated the TF 1500 "America's Best Sports Car Buy."

Despite being the last of a long line of T-Series MGs—and a model that wasn't well received as a new car—the TF 1500 is highly prized today, with recent asking prices for restored examples running as high as $47,000.

John Gunnell

Dick Dance Collection

# 1956-1959 MGA 1500

**M**G fielded a pair of aluminum-bodied cars called EX182s at the 1955 Le Mans 24-hour race in France. They were prototypes of an all-new MG body design and finished fifth and sixth in their class. Like the production MGA that followed in 1956, the prototypes had swept-out frame side members that permitted lower seating. An earlier prototype, seen in 1952, had simply used MG TD running gear, but since the British Motorcar Corporation had taken over operation of MG by 1955, the new MGA adopted a BMC engine. This power plant was identical in displacement to the one used in the MG Magnette sedan and produced 68 hp in the roadster.

Manufacturing of MGAs started in September 1955. When the production version of the car appeared at the London Motor Show in October 1955, *Motor Trend* opined that MG had "At long last abandoned its old-but-handsome lines for new and handsomer ones. . . considerably slicker than its Le Mans prototype suggested."

While not everyone was pleased by the change, MG's roadster was totally restyled. It had a modern, rounded look to replace the traditional squarish profile. Except for the front suspension and emblem, just about everything was at least partly new.

The familiar MG octagon emblem was mounted at the upper center of the new rectangular grille, which contained side-by-side blocks of vertical ribs. The MGA's one-piece "alligator-style" hood was hinged at the rear, as was common with American cars. A revised chassis had deep box-section steel side members that swept outward, placing the occupants between the frame rails instead of above them. Six tubular crossmembers added rigidity to the structure. The front suspension used twin A-arms with coil springs, while the rear featured semi-elliptic leaf springs.

The doors were hinged at the front and had no outside handles. The streamlined body included an enclosed trunk and a slightly-curved windshield. The instruments were round and the 4-inch-diameter white-on-black tachometer and speedometer were positioned on either side of the steering column. Two Lucas 6-volt batteries were mounted behind the adjustable bucket-type seats, which had leather-covered

*The MG "A" series introduced a totally new style of sports cars in North America.*

cushions and backs. Each door contained a storage pocket.

Standard MGA equipment included tools, a center-mounted mirror, a quick-release gas cap, and a spring-spoke steering wheel. The detachable side curtains contained a spring-loaded flap that could be opened when needed at toll-booths and the like. Standard color schemes were black with red or green upholstery (with an Ice Blue or black top); Orient Red or Old English White with red or black upholstery (with a black top), and Tyrolite Green or Glacier Blue with grey or black upholstery (and an Ice Blue top).

Change was less drastic beneath the MGA's bonnet, which now held a modified 1489-cc BMC B-series overhead-valve four-cylinder engine with 73.025 x 88.9 mm bore-and-stroke dimensions. The three-main bearing engine had an 8.3:1 compression ratio and twin S.U. carburetors. It was rated for 68 hp at 5500 rpm and 77 lbs.-ft. of torque at 3500 rpm. Top speed for the MGA was pegged at 90 to 98 mph. Runs from 0-to-60 mph varied in time from 14.5 to 15.9 seconds. The quarter mile could be covered in 19.6 to 20.4 seconds.

A new four-speed transmission was derived from that used in the Magnette, reverse gear was positioned to the left (alongside second). Overall gear ratios were 15.652:1 in first, 9.52:1 in second, 5.908:1 in third, 4.3:1 in fourth, and 20.468:1 in reverse. A 4.3:1 ratio rear axle was fitted. Steering was rack and pinion. The independent front suspension used twin wishbones and coil springs. At the rear was a rigid axle with semi-elliptic leaf springs. Hydraulic drum brakes sat at each corner. A 12-gal. fuel tank was fitted.

*Motor Trend* praised the new MG's handling qualities, noting that "there just don't seem to be many ways you can get into trouble." The magazine added that the MGA "certainly puts the fun back into driving." The magazine's road tester managed to achieve quicker acceleration times than those of the final TF roadster.

A total of 58,750 MGAs were built from 1955 through May 1959 and more than 13,000 were sold in 1956 alone. Of these, about 6,044 were delivered by U.S. dealers.

Hambro Automotive Corp., of New York City and Gough Industries Inc., of Los Angeles, California, handled U.S. distribution. The base model had a Port-of-Entry price of $2,195. The roadster cost $2,330 when equipped with wire wheels.

Pre-production testing of MGAs included high-speed runs at the MIRA track in Montlhery, France' and on the Nurburgring in Germany, plus extensive testing in the Alps.

A factory-sponsored trio won the team award at the 1956 Sebring (Florida) 12-hour race.

A fixed-head coupe with roll-up glass windows and small vent wings was introduced at the October 1956 London Motor Show. It joined the original MGA roadster in 1957.

The BMC engine used in both cars gained four horsepower and had stronger new bearings. Better streamlining gave the coupe a top speed of 102 mph, compared to the open model's 93 mph.

The new coupe had a wraparound windshield and back window, vertical inside door handles, and outside-mounted door handles.

Its trunk opened from inside the car, via a handle behind the driver's seat.

A removable hardtop also became available for the roadster. The price on the original MGA climbed to $2,269, while the coupe listed for $2,620 P.O.E.

In 1958, the prices rose to $2,462 for the MGA roadster and $2,695 for the coupe.

Approximately 13,496 MGs were sold in the U.S. that year.

Production of the standard roadster and coupe continued for most of the 1959 model year, with the same 1489-cc engine and little change otherwise.

Prices for the 1,904-lb. roadster and 2,004-lb. coupe were the same as in 1958.

Late in the season, a 1600 series with larger Twin-Cam engine was introduced.

Bob Harrington

# 1959-1960 1600 Twin-Cam

The Twin-Cam MGA was announced in April 1958. Enthusiasts took careful note of the announcement of the new model, which promised a sharp gain in performance. The new 1588-cc dual-overhead-cam four-cylinder engine had a larger displacement than the standard four, and it delivered a whopping 108 hp--50 percent more than the regular power plant. A potent machine, the Twin-Cam used larger 1.75-in. model H6 S.U. carburetors, 80-degree inclined valves, hemispherical combustion chambers, and inverted bucket-style tappets. It also required high-octane fuel. At announcement time, the hopped-up MG, with its cross-flow aluminum-alloy cylinder head, sounded tempting to many fans.

The engine had chain-driven overhead cams and a 9.9:1 compression ratio. The MG factory initially announced a rating of 107 hp at 6500 rpm, but this was changed to 108 hp at 6700 rpm. It developed 104 lbs.-ft. of torque at 4500 rpm. Later, a 100-hp version of the Twin-Cam was substituted to help combat reliability problems experienced with the original, higher-compression-ratio engine.

Eventually, the Twin-Cam engine developed a reputation for reliability problems, including premature detonation and piston burning. The engine's drawbacks were noticed especially when the cars were run at higher rpms. The Twin-Cam model also became known as an oil burner. By the time the factory made modifications, including a drop in compression ratio from the initial 9.9:1, the damage had been done. Sales were negatively impacted and the Twin-Cam model was doomed to extinction.

*One might think of the Twin Cam version of the MGA as the "hot blooded" version.*

The Twin-Cam had a wider (47.9-in.) front track, compared to the 1500's 47.5 in. track and, instead of the standard MGA's 5.60 x 15 Dunlop tires, it used Dunlop 5.90 x 15 "Road Speed" tires. Four-wheel Dunlop disc brakes were standard. Top speeds were in the 115 to 120-mph range. Acceleration, from a standing start to 100 mph, was claimed to take only about 30 seconds. The factory advised that engineering changes made for the Twin-Cam were so extensive conversions of existing models would be impractical. For instance, the stock MGA steering mechanism had to be altered to allow engine clearance. Center-lock, vented disc wheels were standard. Wire wheels were not available.

Except for an oval air vent on each side of the hood, the appearance of the Twin-Cam was virtually identical to that of other MGA models. Twin-Cam roadsters came in black with red or green upholstery (with blue or black tops), Orient Red or Old English White with red or black upholstery (and a black top) and Ash Green or Glacier Blue with grey or black upholstery (with a blue top). Coupe colors were: black with red or green upholstery, Orient Red or Old English White with red or black upholstery, and Ash Green or Mineral Blue with grey or black upholstery.

The Twin-Cam roadster listed for $3,320 in 1959 and tipped the scale at 2,185 lbs. The coupe version was priced $320 higher and carried 60 additional pounds of weight. Approximately 2,210 Twin-Cam MGAs were built between 1958 and 1961.

Production of both models continued into early 1960, with little change. Due to declining demand, prices dropped to $3,069 for the roadster and $3,263 for the coupe. Production of Twin-Cams continued until April 1960, but slowed to a trickle in the final months.

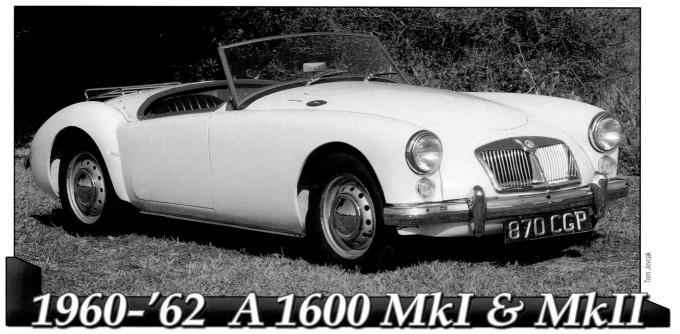

Tom Jevcak

# 1960-'62 A 1600 MkI & MkII

The MGA 1600 Mark I debuted in May of 1959, and was sold along with the Twin-Cam model (which was marketed between May 1959 and April 1960). Its bigger engine was the major change for both the roadster and coupe models. In essence, it was a pushrod-operated, overhead-valve version of the Twin-Cam power plant with much lower compression.

In terms of appearance, the 1600 was similar to earlier MGA models, but had amber front turn-signal lenses. Standard colors for the 1960 roadster were black with red or beige upholstery and a grey top; Chariot Red with red or beige upholstery and a beige top; Chariot Red with red or beige upholstery with a grey top; Iris Blue with black upholstery and a blue top; Alamo Beige with red upholstery and a beige top; Dove Grey with red upholstery and a grey top; or Old English White with red or black upholstery and a grey top.

Coupe colors were: black with red or beige upholstery; Chariot Red with red, beige or black upholstery; Iris Blue with black upholstery; Alamo Beige or Dove Grey with red upholstery and Old English White with red or black upholstery.

The 1600 MK I roadster retailed for $2,444 and weighed 1,904 lbs. The coupe was $2,667 and 2,004 lbs. A total of 31,501 MGA 1600 MK I models were built between 1959 and 1961. Approximately 13,069 MGs were sold in the U.S. during 1960, and 8,806 in 1961. The chassis and technical specifications for both years were virtually identical to those of the MGA 1500, with only minor variations.

The 1600's in-line, overhead-valve four-cylinder engine had a cast-iron block and head. With a bore and stroke of 75.4 x 88.9-mm, it displaced 1588 cc. It had solid valve lifters, an 8.3:1 compression ratio and twin S.U. carburetors. The output was 79.5 hp at 5600 rpm and 87 lbs.-ft. of torque at 3800 rpm. With a top speed of 100 mph, the MGA 1600 handled 0-to-60-mph acceleration in 13.3 seconds and the quarter mile in 19.0 seconds. Fuel mileage was about 28 mpg.

A revised Mark II edition of the 1600 series made the scene in 1962. It carried a larger engine that produced 90 hp. The MK II's overall appearance was similar to that of the earlier MGA 1600, except the vertical grille bars now were recessed at the base of the grille and the center divider bar jutted forward.

*Ways to spot the MGA 1600 Mk II are its inset grille and its horizontal taillights.*

A single horizontal lens characterized a new taillight design. This car was produced for only one year before it was replaced by the all-new MGB. The roadster sold for $2,449 and weighed 1,960 lbs. The coupe had a $2,685 sticker price and weighed 2,060 lbs.

A total of 8,719 MGA 1600 Mk II models were built from June 1961 to June 1962.

The MK II engine was similar in its overall design to the old one, but it had a 76.2 x 88.9 mm bore and stroke and 1622 cc of displacement. These changes produced 90 hp at 5500 rpm and 97 lbs.-ft. of torque at 4000 rpm. MK IIs built for the U.S. market also had oil coolers. Top speed was in the 103-105 mph bracket. The MK II could move from 0-to-60 mph in 12.8 to 14.2 seconds and did the quarter-mile in 18.7 to 19 seconds at about 73 mph. Fuel economy was 21 to 30 mpg.

The standard four-speed manual transmission had gear ratios of 3.64:1 in first, 2.214:1 in second, 1.374:1 in third, 1.00:1 in fourth and 4.76:1 in reverse. Also available was a close-ratio gearbox with respective ratios of 2.44:1, 1.62:1, 1.27:1, 1.00:1 and 3.20:1 in reverse. For the first time since the

A series debuted, the rear axle ratio was changed (to 4.10:1). Otherwise, everything was pretty much the same as on other MGAs.

Stretching 94 inches between the front and rear wheels, the MGA had an overall length of 156 in. It was 50 in. high and 57.3 in. wide.

Tread widths were 47.5 in. up front and 48.8 in. at the rear. The standard Dunlop 5.60 x 15 tires were mounted on 4J x 15 four-stud steel disc wheels.

"More power to your safety" was the theme of the more potent MGA 1600 MK II. "Power to overtake with safety. Power to surmount difficulties" promised the most-favored British automaker.

Production of the MGA ceased in June 1962, after just one year of manufacturing the Mk II 1600 version. Production of the MGB then started in October.

Jonathan Stein

# 1961-'62 1600 MkII De Luxe

Starting late in 1961, after production of the Twin-Cam version of the MGA ceased, a small number of specially-equipped and decorated MGA 1600 MK II De Luxe roadsters and coupes were built. These hybrid cars were not mentioned in regular factory sales literature or technical manuals. They combined the 1622-cc MK II engine with the Twin-Cam' model's chassis and four-wheel disc brakes.

Under the bonnet was the four-cylinder, in-line, monobloc four-cylinder power plant, which was water-cooled and had push-rod-operated overhead valves. It used a 76.2 x 88.9-mm bore and stroke, giving it a capacity of 1,622 cc. The engine was attached to a four-speed or close-ratio four-speed manual transmission and hypoid bevel rear axle.

MG experts have determined the De Luxe models were probably marketed to use up the remaining inventory of Twin-Cam parts after a decision was made to drop the Mark II and go to the all-new MGB.

The author has seen one of these cars, a blue roadster, at Road America, in Elkhart Lake, Wisconsin. It had a "De Luxe" badge on the rear, although there is obviously no documentation that this was original or that all of the De Luxe models turned out had this type of

*MGA Deluxe cars were not publicized in sales brochures, but drivers found out about them.*

trim. It is known that just over 40 percent of the approximately 2,000 De Luxe models built were made in the last 2-1/2 months of MGA production.

The Dunlop four-wheel disc brakes employed on De Luxe models were the same as those used on E-Type Jaguars. This was a $250 option on the MGA. One De Luxe roadster was road tested in the May 1962 issue of *Sports Car Graphic* magazine. However, it was described as a MK II with disc brakes, rather than a De Luxe.

One of these cars—a 1961 coupe bearing registration number 151 ABL—was an MG-works-sponsored competition car that gained some notoriety. Driven by the Morley brothers, it took a first in class at the 1962 Monte Carlo Rally and was second overall, in the GT class, to a factory-backed Austin-Healey 3000.

Rauno Aaltonen piloted this same car in the 1962 Tulip Rally and beat Porsche, Mercedes-Benz, Jaguar, and Austin-Healey competitors up the Co. l de Turini.

Dick Dance Collection

# 1963-'66 MGB & GT MkI

The MGB was introduced at the London Motor Show in October 1962, four months after the final MGA had been produced. The new roadster had been in development for four years. A prototype by Frua (of Italy) had been rejected, so the final design was done by MG itself, under the direction of Syd Enever. Both a roadster and a grand touring coupe were planned, but only the roadster was available in the first three years of production.

Slightly smaller than its predecessor, the new slab-sided roadster rode a 91-in. wheelbase and was 153 in. long. Its profile was more rectangular than the MGA's, with a horizontal upper line, full-length body side trim moldings, and flattened rear wheel openings.

Its low, full-width horizontal-style grille contained a pattern of tightly-spaced vertical ribs. The headlights sat back a bit from the grille, above rectangular parking lights. The windshield had a greater wraparound curve. At the rear were vertical-style taillights. The pancake-type hood was hinged at the rear.

The MGB would go through four main versions with the earliest ones known as MKIs. The 1963 roadster listed for a $2,658 New York Port-of-Entry price ($100 more with wire wheels) and weighed 1,920 lbs. The "B" would prove to be the best-selling MG model of all time and is immensely popular today.

More than half a million MGBs (387,675 roadsters and 125,597 GT models) would be manufactured between 1962 and 1980. During that period, a total of 300,274 roadsters was exported to the U.S., where Hambro Automotive Corp., of New York City, handled distribution.

Inside the new car were two individual, leather-upholstered, adjustable bucket seats. Though commonly referred to as a "roadster," the open-bodied MGB actually had wind-up door windows like a true convertible. Unlike the MGA roadster, it featured outside door handles and hinged vent windows.

Behind the seats was an open luggage area, where the removable soft top could be stored. A tonneau was provided to cover the area when the top was not in place. The traditional "fly-off" hand brake was gone, replaced by an ordinary design and the glove box was on the passenger side of the instrument panel. Full instrumentation was provided on the dashboard. Although the new car was shorter, overall, than the MGA, it was roomy inside.

Structurally, there was a big change, as the MGB used unibody construction (with double-box-section sills below the doors) rather than the former separate body and frame. This made the car lighter, but stronger, than earlier models. Suspension was similar to the MGA, with control arms and coil springs up front and semi-elliptic leaf springs at

**The MGB MKI series was an all new sports car offering in 1963.**

the rear (but with one less leaf than before). Lever-type shock absorbers remained standard.

Beneath the hood of the MGB was a 1798-cc version of the BMC B-series four with an 80.26 x 88.9 mm bore and stroke. Horsepower —94 at 5500 rpm—was only modestly boosted from that of the MGA, but torque got a sizable increase to 107 lbs.-ft. at 3500 rpm. An 8.75:1 compression ratio was specified and twin S.U. carburetors were fitted. The MGB had a top speed of 103 to 105 mph. It could do 0-to-60 mph in 11 to 12.5 seconds and the quarter-mile in 18.1 to 18.5 sec. at about 75 mph.

Dimensionally, the MGB sat on a 91-in. wheelbase and had an overall length of 153.25 in. At 49.4 in. high, it was actually slightly lower than an MG Midget, but at 60 in., it was much wider than its companion model. The front tread was 49 in. wide and the rear tread was a quarter-inch wider. Steel disc wheels and Dunlop 5.60 x 14 tires were standard. Wire wheels were optional.

A diaphragm clutch connected the engine and transmission. The early B's four-speed manual transmission had overall ratios of 3.63:1 in first, 2.21:1 in second, 1.37:1 in third, and 1.00:1 in fourth. The standard final drive ratio was 3.91:1. The front suspension featured wishbones and coil springs with lever shock absorbers. At the rear was a rigid axle and semi-elliptic leaf springs with lever shock absorbers. Disc brakes were used up front, with drums in the rear. A 12-gallon fuel tank was fitted.

Little updating was evident in the 1964 MGB. In fact, even the price was unchanged. A Laycock de Normanville overdrive unit became available. It operated on third and fourth gears via a toggle switch. This option took longer to arrive on examples destined for the U.S.

Inside the 1965 MGB's four-cylinder engine was a new five-bearing crankshaft to replace the former three-main configuration; plus a new oil cooler and a revised rear oil seal. For competition purposes, at least, the three-main crank had suffered too much "whipping." On the MGB dashboard was a new electric tachometer. The price dropped to $2,607 as production took off and MG began to realize some volume production efficiencies.

The 1798-cc engine retained the same bore and stroke, but the compression ratio rose to 8.8:1 and output inched up to 98 hp at 5400 rpm. Torque was rated 110 lbs.-ft. at 3000 rpm. Solid valve lifters and twin S.U. semi-downdraft carburetors were retained. The slight boost in power raised the top speed to 105-110 mph. Acceleration figures were 11 seconds for 0-to-60 mph and 18 seconds for the quarter-mile. The '65 MGB was good for 22 to 28 mpg.

In 1965, a closed version of the MGB arrived. This MGB GT sported a hatchback body styled by Italian car designer Pinin Farina. The front end treatment, as well as the rear fenders, were about the same as those used on the roadster, but the windshield was higher to raise the roof line. The roof line curved over the doors and slanted towards the rear end panel. A hinged tailgate with a large rear window provided access to the cargo area.

A small rear seat was added behind the front bucket seats, but was really suitable only for children. Luckily, this seat could be folded flat to

form a large luggage compartment. Merchandised as a 1966 model, the MGB GT was targeted mainly to American buyers. It sold for $3,095 and weighed in at 2,190 lbs. Although heavier than the roadster, the GT's aerodynamics aided its road performance.

It was slower-accelerating than the open car. Nevertheless, the GT became very popular with "Walter Mittys" who liked the idea of owning a sports car, but just couldn't tolerate a roadster.

The 1966 MK I roadster was a carryover model. The 1,920-lb. car continued to sell for $2,607—or $2,705 with wire wheels. Approximately 21,709 MGs of all types were sold in the U.S. during 1966. BMC/Hambro Automotive Corp.—which handled the U.S. distribution of MGs—relocated to Ridgefield, New Jersey, in 1965.

Bob Houillon

# 1967-'71 MGB & GT MkII

**B**y the late 1960s, the MGB was being promoted as "America's largest-selling imported sports car . . . the obvious choice for the man who wants to be different." The MGB GT coupe was described as an "authentic GT with continental flair and American spirit . . . for men wanting power and comfort in equal measure." The "B" was the darling of the automotive press with its 100-mph-plus go power, performance handling, roominess, reliability, and excellent build quality.

Late in model-year 1967, MK II versions of the MGB roadster and MGB GT hatchback coupe became available. In the past, the MKII designation often indicated a larger engine or more powerful engine, but this time the size of the power plant remained the same at 1,798 cc and output was unchanged. As in 1965 and 1966 MGB models, the horsepower rating remained 98 at 5400 rpm, with 110 lbs.-ft. of torque at 3000 rpm on tap.

The biggest change was MG installed a new transmission with synchromesh on all four gears in the MGB MK II. This gear box also featured a better set of ratios. The improved transmission necessitated the widening of the transmission tunnel, which also allowed MG to soon offer the option of automatic transmission.

Pricewise, the MGB MK II roadster edged up to $2,615, although the weight of the car remained unchanged from MK I roadster specifications. The MGB GT coupe's price remained the same as it was in 1966. Almost all other major technical specifications were also the same as before

A model called the MGB GT Special was also marketed during 1967. This dressed-up car was primarily the result of a marketing effort designed to pump up American interest in the GT body style. A targeted advertising campaign was launched to promote what was

*The MGB MkII is one of the most memorable late-1960s British sports cars in North America.*

officially described as the "First Anniversary MGB GT Special." This version of the closed MGB included an assortment of special equipment at no extra cost.

MG factory dealers received the special equipment as a kit that could be added to any MGB GT they had in inventory. That makes it impossible to say how many cars had the package and it is more difficult to authenticate that any particular car left the factory in Abingdon with the special equipment.

The kits included special name plaques, a wood-rimmed Moto-Lita steering wheel, a wooden shift knob and a streamlined, racing-style outside rearview mirror on the left front fender. Wire wheels and white sidewall tires were also included.

In 1968 and 1969, the production MK II version of the MGB roadster and GT hatchback continued with little change. There was a drop in advertised horsepower to 92 at 5400 rpm, even though the compression ratio remained at 8.8:1. The torque rating remained at 110 lbs.-ft.. at 3000 rpm. The rated horsepower drop was due to a new emission control system. An automatic transmission was also available, but only about 5,000 of these gear boxes were installed in MGBs before the option was cancelled in 1973.

In 1968, the roadster sold for $2,670, while the GT carried a $3,160 price tag. Despite its lower-powered engine, the 1969 model had a price increase to $2,817 and the GT's window sticker increased to $3,202. Approximately 17,834 MGs of all types were sold in the U.S. in 1968 and 22,114 in 1969. Most were MGBs and MGB GTs.

More than 20 styling changes were announced for MGB models for the 1970 model year. Most of them were less noticeable than the switch to a recessed black-out-style grille, with a center emblem that was set inside a thin, bright surround molding. Amber rectangular parking lights again stood below the recessed headlights. Models destined for the U.S. had side marker lights ahead of the front fenders. Port-of- Entry prices were $2,875 for the 1,920-lb. roadster and $3,260 for the 2,190-lb. coupe. Rostyle mag-type wheels were standard with 155 x 14 radial tires (165 x 14 for the MGB GT coupe). Inside, vinyl replaced leather on the adjustable bucket seats and a leather-covered steering wheel was standard for both models.

Standard equipment included reclining ambia bucket seats with adjustable head restraints, padded sunvisors, three-point seat belts, a heater and defroster, front and rear side marker lights, a cigarette lighter and ashtray, map pockets, fitted carpeting, rubber floor mats, and door sill kick plates.

As before, the MGB GT coupe had an "occasional" rear seat that folded flat for extra luggage storage. Both models had roll-up windows and hinged vent wings. Standard body colors were: Flame Red, Bronze Yellow, British Racing Green, Blue Royale, Pale Primrose and Glacier White.

By 1971, U.S. market models added rubber-tipped overriders (bumper guards). Also in 1971, the MGB and MGB GT had a new, redesigned black-out-style grille. A steering-column lock also became standard equipment.

Prices took a substantial leap in 1971 and went up to $3,075 for the open car and $3,435 for the GT. Weights also rose to 2,303 and 2,401 lbs., respectively.

The 1970 and 1971 models continued to use the 1798-cc overhead-valve four with 92 hp at 5400 rpm. Dimensions and technical specifications were virtually unchanged.

The four-speed manual gear box with overdrive had overall ratios of 13.45:1 in first, 8.47:1 in second, 5.40:1 in third, 4.43:1 in third overdrive, 3.91:1 in fourth and 3.20:1 in fourth overdrive.

Available options included a removable hardtop, Dunlop 60-spoke center-lock wire wheels (painted or chromed), a heater, an electrically-heated rear window (for the GT), overdrive, a solid-state AM radio or AM/FM radio, a center console with an electric clock, a center armrest, a wood-rim steering wheel, a wood gearshift knob, rubber floor mats, white sidewall tires, and a selection of SCCA (Sports Car Club of America) approved competition parts.

The "smogged" MGB had a top speed of 105 mph-plus. Its 0-to-60-mph acceleration was 11.8 seconds and it did the quarter-mile in 18.45 seconds at 77 mph.

Tom Hahn

# 1972-'74 MGB, GT & V-8

**M**ark III versions of the MGB and MGB GT were introduced in October 1971 as 1972 models. Changes were modest, except for a new center console and armrests. A restyled instrument panel incorporated a locking glove box. The seats in the GT coupe had leather inserts. Three new body colors were added: Gold, Aqua, and Dark Green. Prices continued to rise to $3,320 for the roadster and $3,615 for the GT coupe.

Under the bonnet, the 1798-cc four-cylinder engine was modified for use with low-lead or regular fuel. It now carried ratings of 78.5 hp at 5500 rpm and 94 lbs.-ft. of torque at 3000 rpm. As in the past few years, twin S.U. HIF carburetors—another effort to improve exhaust emissions—were used.

For 1973—the final year of the Mark III—the grille was revised again. The MG emblem returned to the upper grille molding. Thick new bumper guards were required and added to the car's overall length. Prices also took a sharp jump. In the summer of 1973, a V-8 version of the MGB debuted in England.

*The MGB MkIII was a popular-selling British sports car among North American buyers.*

Production of the MGB V-8 lasted longer than production of the earlier six-cylinder MGC, a car that looked basically like a "B," but carried a "C" designation. However, the number of V-8-powered cars built was smaller than the MGC production total. The seldom-seen MGB V-8 was identified by V-8 badges in the grille and ahead of the doors.

Some historians say that the concept of putting a V-8 engine into the MGB started with Ken Costello, the British proprietor of an engine tuning shop. Others point out that the factory in Abingdon had built a V-8 prototype as early as 1970, at least a year before Costello did his first V-8 conversion.

Costello produced a few dozen MGBs with V-8 engines between 1971 and 1973. Although MG probably had the idea first, Costello was able to create his MGB V-8s quicker because he did not have to deal with the same corporate politics, as well as the various regulations that were making it harder for manufacturers to certify new cars.

By late 1973, Abingdon announced its new V-8 model. A Rover-built 3532-cc aluminum-block V-8 was used. This engine had actually evolved from a Buick design of the 1960s. It weighed less than BMC's cast-iron four-cylinder. Only slight modifications were required to squeeze the V-8 into the "B." The bulkhead had to be slightly re-shaped and a low-rise exhaust manifold was required to get the engine under the stock MG bonnet.

The front and rear suspensions did not have to be drastically changed, but the V-8 did ride an inch higher than regular MGBs. It was attached to an MGC gear box with slightly modified gear ratios.

These production engine installations were performed at the MG factory and resulted in an MGB with an 88.9 x 71.1-mm bore and

stroke for 3528 cc displacement. The engine ran an 8.25:1 compression ratio and twin, horizontal S.U. carburetors. It produced 137 hp at 5000 rpm and 193 lbs-ft. of torque at 2900 rpm—enough to send a V-8 model to 60 mph in close to seven seconds. The V-8 had a top speed of 121.8 mph. Fewer than 2,600 MGB V-8s were produced between 1973 and 1976.

While retaining a 91-in. wheelbase, the new "B," with its rubber-coated overriders, was slightly longer at 159.2 in. Both the front and rear treads were now uniform at 49.5 in. The Rostyle sculpted steel wheels carried 155SR14 radial tires on four-cylinder roadsters, larger 165SR14 radials on four-cylinder GTs, and still larger 175HR14 radials on V-8s. Overall transmission ratios also varied according to engine. Standard rear axle ratios were 3.91:1 for the standard car, 3.07:1 for the V-8 model, and 3.307:1 for the V-8 with overdrive.

OCW Archive

# 1975-1980 MGB MkIV

The MK IV MGB appeared at the London Motor Show in October 1974, but didn't arrive in the U.S. market until late in the 1975 model year. It would remain in production until 1980. The MK IV series' most noticeable change was a large, matte-black, polyurethane nose and matching tail section.

To the chagrin of many enthusiasts, chrome bumpers and grilles would not be seen again on an MGB. The GT coupe body style was also dropped for 1975. The V-8 model survived one more year. The price for the base four-cylinder roadster rose to an eye-popping $4,350 and would continue to ascend from there.

Beneath the MGB's bonnet, the carburetion setup was switched from twin S.U.s to a single Zenith-Stromberg 175CD5T model. Plenty of horsepower was lost in this transition. The in-line, overhead-valve four-cylinder power plant stayed at 1798 cc but now had a lower 8.0:1 compression ratio. It produced just 62.5 hp at 5500 rpm and 86 lbs.-ft. of torque at 2500 rpm. The transmission gear ratios were changed as well, to give better gas mileage. The new bumper design reduced length very slightly at 158.3 in.

MG fans didn't react well to either the appearance changes or the performance downgrades that were enacted at the start and were retained throughout this final series. For many years, collectors would shy away from the "rubber bumper" cars. These MGBs are growing somewhat more popular today, since the last-series cars are a quarter-century old—like the MGB GT Jubilee Edition, produced during 1975. It was finished in British Racing Green with gold V-8-type wheels.

Production of the V-8 MG continued into 1976, but the bulk of sales still went to the MGB four-banger, which endured a hefty price hike to $4,795. Wire wheels added $135 and overdrive was $225 extra. In 1977, the roadster added a zip-in rear window. Standard 1977

*One easy way to spot the MGB MkIV series is its black polyurethane nose and tail.*

colors were the same as the Midget. Production of the larger open MG continued into 1980 with minimal change. Engine cooling was handled by twin electric fans, but horsepower remained low compared to earlier models. Prices jumped sharply for each of the MGB's final model years. Standard equipment included a tonneau cover, power front disc brakes, four-spoke steering wheel with padded rim, 165SR14 tires, and a zip-out rear window.

By 1978, the MGB was a $5,649 car that weighed 2,338 lbs. The following year, the price rose to $6,550. In 1980, the final year of production, you got only $50 change after handing your MG dealer $8,000!

A total of 17,271 MGBs were sold in the U.S. during 1978 and 16,860 in 1979. Production of "Bs" halted in October 1980. The last version to enter the U.S. was the 1980 "Limited Edition." These cars were painted all black with gunmetal-gray stripes along the body side at the bottom and a spoiler below the polyurethane nose. The final 1,000 "Limited" models were produced for the home market. Of these, 420 were bronze-colored roadsters and 580 were pewter-colored GT coupes.

In all, more than half a million MGBs (approximately 387,675 roadsters and 125,597 GT models) were built from 1962-1980. A total of 300,274 roadsters were exported to the U.S. Many industry observers, during the late 1970s, had hoped that MG would boost its horsepower to earlier levels and return the roadster to its former glory, but this never happened.

Tom Jevcak

# 1967-1969 MGC

**B**ritish-Leyland knew four-cylinder MG roadsters had been the best-selling British sports cars for over 20 years. The Austin-Healey 3000 was getting to be an "old" car and ready for retirement. So British-Leyland decided a modernized six-cylinder sports car with an MG badge might sell even better than an updated Healey. The six-cylinder MGC was based on the MGB and MGB GT. Starting in November 1966, a total of 13 pre-production MGC versions were assembled. The production version was announced for 1967.

Both the MGB roadster and MGB GT coupe body shells were used, with minor modifications, to make MGCs. Pilot production began in October 1967. Regular-production roadsters began leaving the factory in November. Car no. 138 was the first production unit. The first GT was built in December. Regular assemblies would continue until August of 1969, with the greatest number of cars being built in 1968.

The new MG was powered by an overhead-valve in-line six with pushrod-operated valves, solid valve lifters, and seven main bearings. The 2912-cc engine had an 83.36 x 78.90-mm bore and stroke. With a 9.0:1 compression ratio and twin S.U. HS6 carburettors it developed 150 hp at 5250 rpm and 174 lbs.-ft. of torque at 3500 rpm. In addition to a top speed in the 120 to 122 mph range, the MGC could go from 0-to-60 mph in 10 seconds

Automotive writers criticized the "C," in spite of its 121-mph tested top speed. *Autocar Road Test Number 2159*, published in November 1967, said the new model lacked low-speed torque and claimed the six-cylinder engine was "reluctant to rev." The test car had a noisy fan, "odd" transmission gear ratios, light brakes, low-geared steering, and poor fuel economy (19 mpg). The magazine noted an automatic transmission—made by Borg-Warner—was available for the first time in an MG. About the engine, *Autocar* said, "it is smooth and flexible, but completely lacking in sporty characteristics."

Theoretically, the MGC should have been one of the hottest-selling British sports cars to come down the pike. With prices of $3,350 for the 2,445-lb. roadster and $3,715 for the 2,595-lb. GT, it was very affordable for a six-cylinder machine. The MGB body was already handsome and roomy and a hood blister required to accommodate the C's six-cylinder engine made it look more powerful. Unfortunately, the car had some technical issues that, combined with the poor press it received, held back its sales.

By 1967, Abingdon no longer had full control of all engineering considerations that went into MGs, particularly engines. The MGC's six-cylinder power plant was a corporate engine that was much too heavy for the MGB body and helped make the C about 350 lb. heavier overall. This added bulk made the car less of a "balanced" package than its four-cylinder mates, and its handling suffered.

## The MGC used an inline six-cylinder engine during its short production life.

Squeezing the C-series engine into the MGB body surfaced other issues. MG was unable to position the power plant far enough to the rear to maintain desirable weight distribution characteristics. Shoe horning the larger automatic transmission in—mainly for American buyers—was another issue. Having the engine too far forward made the MGC very nose-heavy. According to *Autocar*, the front end weight increased from 52.6 percent to 55.7 percent, requiring a 4-psi increase in recommended tire pressures. To handle the changes, a lowered steering gear ratio was used and the wheel castor angle was reduced.

To help accommodate the larger engine and radiator, the hood bulge was added to the MGB body and 15-in. road wheels were fitted. The front cross-member was removed to clear the bottom of the engine, leading to the use of a torsion-bar front suspension. The rear suspension was like that of the MGB, but with a beefier rear axle. Front and rear spring rates were also increased.

Despite such changes, the steering in the car felt "heavy." Three and a half turns of the 16.5-in. diameter steering wheel were required for a turn that took just 2.9 cranks previously. The car exhibited very noticeable understeer, making the front end slow to respond to the driver's wishes.

Corporate politics played a role in MGC history. MG had become part of the British-Leyland group, where Triumph products were the "Favorite Son." Since the MGC would have hurt sales of the Triumph TR6, it was treated with "back burner" importance by upper management and its sales suffered even more.

The poor reception the press gave the MGC undoubtedly shortened its production life. Its introduction was soon followed by the formation of the British Leyland Group. The MGC and the Triumph TR6 wound up competing for the same sector of the sports-car market. There was considerable feeling against anything emanating from the old BMC part of the group at the time, and it took only a month or so for the board to make a decision on the future of the six-cylinder MG model. The MGC was dropped from the range in 1969, while the TR6 continued until 1976.

Just over 9,000 MGCs were made over four calendar years, of which 4,544 were roadsters and 4,458 were GTs. The 1966 pre-production units included nine open cars and four closed ones. In 1967, only 182 roadsters and 38 GTs were produced. The next year the totals jumped to 2,596 and 2,491, respectively.

Production tapered off in the last year, 1969, to 1,757 roadsters and 1,925 GTs.

Dick Dance Collection

# 1962-1964 Midget MkI

***The new 1962 MG Midget proclaimed its sporty heritage.***

In 1962, the new MG Midget — Model GAN1 — joined the MGA. Factory sales brochures promoted the little roadster's "sporting appeal from a sporting heritage" and said that the Midget "starts ahead with love at first sight." Officially introduced in June of 1961, as a 1962 model, the modern Midget helped MG become the best-selling British sports car for nearly two decades. A total of 16,080 were built between June 1961 and October 1962.

The new MK I Midget was built at the same MG factory in Abingdon where the Austin-Healey Sprite was produced. Cynics called it a "badge-engineered" version of the Sprite MK II, which had been introduced earlier in 1961. This view was accurate, as the diminutive new MG roadster differed from its "cousin" in little more than grille and trim details. It was priced at $1,939 (which was $71 higher than the Sprite's window sticker), but had a 1,316-lb. shipping weight, compared to the Sprite's shipping weight of 1400 lb.

A wide, vertical-bar grille characterized the front of the MG version. Rectangular parking lights were positioned below the built-in circular headlights. The Midget had squared-off wheel arches, small vent windows, a conventional trunk and long, horizontal body side trim strips just above the front wheel openings.

Though truly a two-seater, the Midget sported a tiny carpeted area behind the bucket seats that could (barely) hold small children. A tachometer was standard, along with a windshield washer, bumper overriders, and stowage bags for the top and sliding side curtains. Standard colors included Tartan Red with a Red or Black interior and Red top, Clipper Blue with a Dark Blue interior and top, Farina Grey or Old English White or black with a red interior and grey top and Old English White with a black interior and grey top.

The Midget had a 62.9 x 76.2-mm bore and stroke 948-cc overhead-valve four-cylinder engine like that used in the Morris Minor. It had three main bearings, solid valve lifters, an 8.3:1 compression ratio and twin S.U. HS2 semi-downdraft carburetors. The engine produced 46.4 hp at 5500 rpm. It was linked to a close-ratio four-speed gearbox.

Within a few months of the roadster's debut, a 9.0:1 high-compression head became available. It raised output to 50 hp at 5500 rpm and produced 52.5 ft.-lbs. of torque at 4000 rpm. In performance testing, the Midget registered an 85-89-mph top speed, a 20.2-second 0-to-60-mph time and a 21.9-second quarter mile.

Poised on an 80-in. wheelbase, the unibodied Midget was only 136 in. long overall. It stood 49.5 in. high to the top of its windshield and measured 53 in. wide. The front tread, at 45.75 in., was one inch wider than the rear tread. The Midget came with 5.20 x 13 Dunlop Gold Seal tubeless Nylon tires mounted on four-stud ventilated disc wheels.

Like its MGB big brother, the Midget had a four-speed manual gear box with a floor-mounted shifter, but it had different overall gear ratios which were 3.20:1 in first, 1.916:1 in second, 1.357:1 in third, 1.00:1 in fourth and 4.114:1 in reverse. The Midget could also be purchased with optional first-gear ratios of 3.63:1 or 2.93:1. A 4.22:1 rear axle was standard.

Other technical features included rack-and-pinion steering, four-wheel drum brakes and a 7.2-gal. fuel tank. The independent front suspension incorporated wishbones, coil springs with lever shock absorbers and an anti-roll bar. At the rear were trailing arms and quarter-elliptic leaf springs with lever shock absorbers.

Disc brakes were added to the front of the 1963 MG Midget which — although labeled Model GAN2 — was still considered a MK I edition. It got a larger 1098-cc four-cylinder engine. The diameter of the clutch was also enlarged to enable it to handle the increased power of the higher-compression engine. The early Midgets continued to employ an ignition system with a key switch and remote pull-cable starter. They also lacked outside door handles or a glove box. The little roadster's price rose by $6 and its weight increased by 140 lb.

The new engine was again an in-line, overhead-valve four-cylinder with a cast-iron block and head. It had a 64.58 x 83.72-mm bore and stroke and an 8.9:1 compression ratio. Brake horsepower was 55 at 5500 rpm and it developed 61 ft.-lbs. of torque at 2500 rpm. With the larger power plant, the Midget's top speed increased to nearly 92 mph. It could now do the quarter mile in 20.1 seconds. Fuel economy was in the 32 mpg range.

Options available for the 1963 MG Midget included a radio, a heater, Ace Mercury wheel discs, a removable hardtop, white sidewall tires, heavy-duty tires, twin horns, a luggage carrier, a rear compartment cushion, a lighter, fender mirrors, a tonneau cover, a rail and stowage bag and a locking gas cap.

For the early part of the 1964 model year, the MK I version of the MG Midget continued without alteration. The Port of Entry price climbed by another $6, but the weight remained unchanged. It was then replaced by the Mark II. In all, a total of 9,601 MG Midget Mk I (GAN2) roadsters were built.

Daniel Donahue Jr.

# 1964-1966 Midget MkII

I n the 1964-1966 period, the MG Midget continued to provide sports car buffs with an affordable alternative to big roadsters or what we would today call an "entry-level" machine. Its squarish body design dated back to 1961, when the vehicle now known as the "Spridget" (Sprite/Midget) replaced the classic "Bug-Eye" Sprite in the Austin-Healey lineup. The following year, what was essentially the same car was also made available with MG badges.

A MK II version of the MG Midget was introduced in mid-1964. Roll-up windows and vent wings were the major change for the new $1,945 (GAN3) model. In addition, the windshield was taller and more curved. locking outside door handles were installed, a combined ignition/starter switch replaced the former cable-operated starter, self-canceling turn signals became standard, the late '64 A-series engine added a few more horsepower and Dunlop center-lock wire wheels were made available as an option. These were found on most Midgets imported to the United States.

## The MG Midget MkII was promoted as an affordable sports car.

At chassis level, semi-elliptic rear springs replaced the former quarter-elliptic units, but MG stuck with its traditional lever-type shock absorbers. The 1098-cc eingine remained below the bonnet, but it now had 8.9:1 compression.

Brake horsepower was 59 at 5750 rpm and torque was 62 ft.-lbs. at 3250 rpm. Top speed inched up to 93 mph. Dimensions and tire sizes were unchanged, along with transmission and chassis specifications.

There were no siginicant updates or upgrade for 1965 or 1966, but the P.O.E. price rose to $2,055. The Midget also gained about 120 lbs.

A total of 26,601 Midget MK II roadsters were built between 1964 and October 1966.

Daniel Donahue Jr.

# 1967-1974 Midget MkIII

The MG Midget MK III roadster was introduced at the London motor show in October 1966, as a 1967 model. It featured a larger version of the BMC A-series four-banger. An air-injection system was added to the emissions control system and an oil cooler was optional equipment.

The in-line, overhead-valve four-cylinder engine had a cast-iron block and cast iron cylinder head. With a 70.6 x 81.3-mm bore and stroke the new engine displaced 1275 cc. With an 8.8:1 compression ratio, it developed 65 hp at 6000 rpm and 72 ft.-lbs. of torque at 3000 rpm. Other specifications included three main bearings, solid valve lifters and twin S.U. semi-downdraft carburetors. This engine was a de-tuned version of the power plant used in the Mini Cooper 'S.' In its de-tuned state, it significantly reduced the Midget's 0-to-60 mph time to 14.7 sec. Tested top speed was now 94-96 mph. The MK III could run the quarter-mile in 19.9 seconcds. Fuel mileage was in the 24 to -32 mpg range.

Except for the new engine and a slightly longer 137.6-in. overall length (thanks to new bumper guards), the early MK III had essentially the same specifications as the MK II. Its modified folding top no longer required manual installation of the top bows and ribs. The East Coast Port of Entry price (in New York city) for the 1,512-lb. 1967 Midget was $2,174. West Coast, Great Lakes or Gulf Port deliveries added additional charges. To get a car delivered on the West Coast at the time cost only about $85 additional.

Little change was made to the Mark III version of the Midget in 1968 and 1969. It continued using the 1275-cc four-cylinder engine, but lost a few horses. The power output was down to 62 hp at 6000 rpm and the torque rating was 72 ft.-lbs. at 3000 rpm. The East Coast Port of Entry price rose slightly each of these years, moving to $2,215 in 1968 and $2,252 in 1969. MG Midget prices in the U.S. did include wire wheels.

Little significant change was evident for the 1970 model year, when the East Coast P.O.E. price climbed to $2,279. As before, the Mark III — billed as the "lowest-priced true sports car made" — carried a 1275-cc engine. Its four-speed gearbox was synchronized on the upper three gears.

*MG's Midget MkIII carried a larger BMC four-cylinder engine beneath its "bonnet."*

Standard 1970 Midget equipment included twin windtone horns, two-speed windshield wipers and washers, back-up lights, a heater and defroster, reclining washable ambia bucket seats with adjustable head restraints, three-point seat belts, a cigarette lighter, a gearshift gaiter, fitted carpeting, rubber floor mats, padded sun visors and front/rear lighted side markers. Roll-up windows and hinged vent wings were standard.

"The Midget's got a price tag to match its name," said the 1970 MG sales brochure, "and the kind of track performance that puts some so called 'sports cars' to shame." A Midget, they claimed, was the "choice of the guy who makes the young way his way." That young-thinking owner could get his Midget in any of the standard BMC colors, such as Flame Red, Bronze Yellow, British Racing Green, Blue Royale, Pale Primrose and Glacier White.

Austin-Healey's Sprite, which differed little from the MG Midget except for trim and emblem, was dropped from production in 1971. Thereafter, the only alternative was the MG version of the same basic car, which was available until 1979.

The English magazine *Autocar* tested a 1275-cc MG Midget MK III in its February 1971 issue, making note of its appeal to female enthusiasts, as well as its insurance advantages. The publication called it, "the best car of the type."

In 1971, a 3.9:1 rear axle was substututed as standard equipment instead of the previous 4.22:1 axle. The body sills were also now finished in black, with the word "MIDGET" spelled out in heavy chrome-plated block letters. In the Autocar "Autotest" the Midget hit 93 mph. Zero-to-60 mph took 14.1 seconds and 19.6 seconds were required to cover the quarter mile. The car provided 29.6 mpg overall fuel economy.

The gearing was described as "well-chosen" and steering was "light, very accurate (and) highly responsive." With manual front disc brakes and rear drums, the car gave "stopping power on a dry track

with the rear wheels just locking."

Between 1972 and 1973, production of the small two-seaters continued with little evident change, other than more rounded rear wheel openings. Engine compression was modified in response to emissions regulations. The Midget's mag-style wheels held radial tires and a restyled dashboard contained a new locking glove box.

The price tag was up to $2,520 in 1972 and rose to $2,795 the following year. The 1275-cc engine had an 8.0:1 compression ratio and was rated for 54.5 hp at 5500 rpm and 67 ft.-lbs. of torque at 3250 rpm It had tree main bearings, solid valve lifters and two semi-downdraft S.U. carburetors. New 145 x 13 size bias-ply tires were standard. Radial tires were optional.

Little change was evident in the smallest MG for its final season in Mark III in 1974, except for the addition of huge, padded bumper guards made from soft black rubber. Midgets also had a collapsible steering column. The constantly-rising price was now just a five-dollar bill away from $3,000. In addition, with all the added safety and pollution equipment, the Midget weighed in at 1,698 lbs. Speedy it wasn't!

As many as 99,896 Midget MK III roadsters were made between 1967 and 1974. Today, the best preserved are catching the attention of MG collectors.

# 1975-1979 Midget MkIV

**The 1978 MG Midget MkIV featured a black bumper and a simpler grille shape.**

The MG Midget Mk IV or "1500" – the final version of the Midget - was introduced in October 1974. Production of this series continued into the summer of 1979. With a massive "rubber" nose (actually made of soft black polyurethane plastic) replacing the previous chromed grille, the Mark IV was easy enough to spot. Actually, no grille was evident at all. It had only a low, wide opening with a tiny "MG" octagon emblem at its center. A similar black "rubber" bumper went at the rear this year.

The protuberances were MG's far-from-elegant response to the United States' persistently stricter vehicle-safety regulations.

Appearancewise, the $3,549 Midget's rear wheel openings, which had been rounded for a few years, reverted again to a flat-toppedshape.

The British magazine *Autocar* road tested a 1500 Midget in its June 1975 issue. This home-market edition was able to do 102 mph.

Zero-to-60-mph acceleration took 12.3 sec. It could do the standing-start quarter mile in 27.9 sec. However, the de-tuned American versions of the car were slower.

*Autocar* described the MK IV as follows:

"Smallest British Leyland sports car given much more punch by bigger engine. Quick, accurate steering, but handling throttle-sensitive and inclined to oversteer. Harsh ride, excessive wind noise with hood (convertible top) up. Undergeared. Limited range."

For 1976, the Midget price rose to $3,949 and a third windshield wiper was added to meet visibility standards.

In 1977, the East Coast Port of Entry price rose again to $4,150. Standard body colors that year were Brooklands Green, Chartreuse, Damask Red, Flamenco, Glacier White, Sandglow and Tahiti Blue. Interior color options were Autumn Leaf or Black.

Under the MK IV Midget's bonnet was a bigger 1493-cc Triumph Spitfire engine with a 73.7 x 87.5-mm bore and stroke.

Use of this engine was the result of MG's merger into British Leyland in the late 1960s. With a single Zenith CD4 carburetor (rather than the more traditional twin S.U. units), the overhead-valve in-line four produced 55 hp in U.S. tune.

It had a 9.1:1 compression ratio. Brake horsepower was 55.5 at 5000 rpmand it produced 67.1 ft.-lbs. of torque at 2500 rpm.

The MK IV Midget tipped the sale at 3,549 lb. in 1975. It retained the previous 80-in. wh eelbase and was now 141 in. long. It stood 48.3 in. high and 54 in. wide. Tread widths were 46.3 in. up front and 44.8 in. at the rear. The standard 145 x 13 radial tires were mounted on 4.5Jx13 wheels.

Its little MG's four-speed gearbox was now fully synchronized, while a taller suspension raised its headlight level. Midget gear ratios were 3.412:1 in first, 2.112:1 in second, 1.433:1 in third and 1.00:1 in fourth. The standard final drive ratio was 3.90:1. Steering was by rack and pinion. The front suspension had wishbones, coil springs and lever shock absorbers as standard features, while an anti-roll bar was optional. At the rear was a rigid axle with semi-elliptic leaf springs and lever-type shock absorbers. Production of the final Midget version

continued into 1978 and the summer of 1979 with little change, except for substantial price hikes. The 1,826-lb. roadster sold for $4,495 in its next-to-last year and $5,200 the final one. Standard equipment included an anti-roll bar, bucket seats with knit-back expanded vinyl upholstery, a locking glove box, a three-spoke steering wheel with a padded rim, a tachometer, a tripmeter, 145SR13 radial tires on mag-style 13-in. wheels, opening vent wings, two-speed windshield wiper/washer system, a cegarette lighter and a trunk light. Basic engine specs were unchanged, but output ratings were 50 hp at 5000 rpm and 67 ft.-lb. at 2500 rpm.

Andrew Morland

# 1994-2003 MGR (Rover V-8)

R umors of a revived MG persisted over the years. The appearance of an EX-E experimental prototype in the mid-1980s sparked excitement. As the 1990s began, further speculation about a modern MG continued.

Early in 1994, Britain's Rover Group was taken over by Germany's BMW. On March 16, 2000, "fundamental reorganization plans" resulted in the sale of key parts of the group. The new parent firm was MG Rover Holdings Limited, an independent, medium-sized British company based in Longbridge.

Under the new ownership, MG Rover Group Limited started life with a debt-free balance sheet and a strong revenue stream that included car, parts and accessory sales and vehicle financing. Today, MG Rover Group Limited, a subsidiary company of MG Rover Holdings Limited, is directly responsible for the design and manufacture of cars under the MG and Rover brands. A car called the MGF became Britain's top-selling roadster.

In 2001, MG Rover Group introduced a new range of MG sports saloons — the MG ZR, MG ZS, MG ZT — as well as the MG ZT-T sports wagon. All of these cars are produced on a fully-integrated, single manufacturing site at Longbridge. Gasoline engines and gear boxes are supplied by Powertrain Limited, another MG Rover Holdings company. Internationally, MG Rover Group sells cars in more than 65 markets.

The modern MG range of vehicles wears the sporting octagon that dates back to 1924. Models include the MGTF two-door sports convertible, the three- and five-door MGZR hatchbacks, the MGZS four-door saloon and five-door hatchback, the MGZT executive saloon and the high-performance MG ZT 260 and MG ZT 385 derivatives of the Executive ZTX80 coupe, which is due for limited production in 2003. These models are powered by a variety of engines that include 1.4-, 1.6- and 1.8-liter jobs, a 1.8-liter Turbo and 2.0- and 2.5-liter V-6s. Gas or diesel versions are offered, plus a choice of a five-speed speed manual or electronic Steptronic transmission.

*A new generation of MGs is symbolized by the late 1990s MGR V-8 roadster.*

A wide range of configurations and options are available with these vehicles to allow buyers to customize their car. Choices are further increased with an additional range of "Monogram" paints, trims and options.

On a different note, the British Motor Heritage Ltd. (a subsidiary of the Rover Group), began to produce complete body shells for the 1962 to 1980 MGB, to replace those unibodied structures that had deteriorated beyond repair.

The first such reproduction body shell was assembled in February 1988 and was supposed to be made available to restorers in both Britain and the U.S. Late in 1989, company representatives toured the U.S. in a rebodied MGB, appearing at automotive shows and trade events to publicize the availability of the all-metal bodies, which were created using some of the original tooling.

Lowell W. Smith

*This MGR is one of just 2,000 that were made.*

# MORGAN

Andrew Morland

# 1945-1950 4/4 Series I

**M**organ cars made their first public appearance at the 1910 Olympia Motor Show, where a pair of single-seat, chain-drive 3-wheelers drew a few orders for delivery in 1911. After changing to the manufacture of two-seat cars with three wheels, sales took off a bit. With a low retail price of 85 guineas and 69.4-mpg fuel economy, Morgans were well-suited for low-cost transportation and sold fairly well. W.G. McMinnies, the editor of *Cyclecar* magazine, gave Morgan a great deal of publicity and made the cars popular with motor sports enthusiasts.

Morgan's first four-wheeler, the 4/4, was announced at the end of 1935 and came out in 1937. This was a timely decision, since three-wheelers were no longer selling very strongly. An 1122-cc Coventry-Climax four-cylinder engine powered the 4/4 and competition versions performed well at races like Le Mans. Shortly before World War II, this engine was replaced with a 1267-cc Standard four. A total of 824 examples of the Morgan 4/4 sports roadster were built before WWII. A 4/4 drophead coupe was added to the offerings in November 1938 and 61 were built before hostilities erupted.

The Morgan Motor Co. Ltd. resumed production at Malvern Link, Worcestershire, England, after WWII. Manufacturing of the postwar 4/4 Series I resumed late in 1945. When the British government began allocating steel in relation to the number of export customers a company had, there was extra pressure on Morgan to exports its products. The company set up distributors in the United States, Canada, South America, Australia, South Africa and Europe and the bulk of output went to the U.S. and the other export markets. Ken Hill, author of *The Morgan: 75 Years on the Road,* said that a "Worth Waiting For" ad appeared early in 1948, to indicate that Morgan would

*The post-World War II Morgan 4/4 came as an open roadster or drophead coupe.*

be ready with home-market cars for the Earl's Court Motor Show, in London, in October of that year.

Though not as quick or agile as the MG TC and MG TD, the Morgan 4/4 was similar in character to those popular cars. It generally appealed to the same sort of drivers—those willing to exchange a comfortable ride and luxuries for superior handling and outright enjoyment.

Like the three-wheelers that first brought Morgan fame, the 4/4 championed traditional design and engineering and would keep many of those details for years—indeed decades—to come. Trademark features included Morgan's sliding-pillar front suspension and Z-section frame side members. The wood-framed steel body was mounted on a steel chassis.

Upright in profile and traditionally styled in the manner of 1930s sports cars, the postwar 4/4 came as an open roadster or drophead coupe with a full top. Separately mounted headlights and fenders were used. The wood-framed body was produced at the Morgan facility. A three-spoke steering wheel was added during 1947.

The early postwar cars used four-cylinder power plants sourced from the Standard Motor Company and known as the "Standard Special." This in-line, overhead-valve four-cylinder engine featured a cast-iron block with replaceable cylinder liners. It had a 63.5 x 100-mm bore and stroke and displaced 1267 cc. The engine, like many British power plants, had three main bearings and solid valve lifters. With a 7.1:1 compression ratio and a Solex carburetor, it generated 40 hp at

4300 rpm. The 4/4 had a top speed of 70 mph.

The Morgan 4/4 rode on a 92-in. wheelbase. The roadster measured 136 in. overall and the convertible was 139.5 in. long. Both body styles were 55 in. wide. Tread widths, front and rear, for both models, were 45 in. Buyers got a choice of 4.50 x 17 or 5.00 x 16 tires as standard equipment. The cars averaged about 1,568 lbs.

With a front-engine, rear-drive layout, the Morgan was a conventional car. It had a four-speed manual transmission and a 4.72:1 final drive ratio. In addition to the sliding pillars with coil springs up front, the 4/4 had a rigid axle with semi-elliptic leaf springs at the rear.

Hydraulically activated drum brakes were fitted front and rear.

Approximately 578 Morgan 4/4s were produced from 1946-1950. Less than half a dozen Morgans are known to have been sold in the U.S. during 1948-1949. During 1947, the company announced that it was changing to a just-one-engine program and said that, as a result of this, the 1267-cc engine would be discontinued after 1949. This policy amounted to the discontinuation of the 4/4 model.

It was replaced, in 1950, with the Plus 4, a model that looked much like the 4/4, but used a 1.8-liter Vanguard engine. The 4/4 model name would be revived in 1955, but for a completely different car.

Andrew Morland

# 1950-1968 Plus 4

H.F.S. Morgan came from a line of clergymen, studied engineering and apprenticed at the Great Western Railway. He opened a garage in 1906 at Malvern Link in Worcestershire. By 1909, he'd built a three-wheeled car with a vee-twin engine. H.F.S. set up Morgan Motor Co. Ltd. in 1910. Harrods, the London department store, was the first agent for Morgan. By World War I, Morgan was making nearly 1,000 three-wheelers annually.

Morgan's first four-wheeler—the 4/4—arrived in 1935. The Plus 4 model, introduced in 1950, didn't look much different than the 4/4, but carried a more powerful Standard Vanguard engine. The Plus 4 was billed as "a small car with a larger engine and wonderful all round performance." Morgan's 1952 London Show brochure described the Plus 4 as a "comfortable long distance touring car and one that will give…economical and trouble free motoring." The Plus 4's chassis frame was more rigid than the 4/4 with larger tires and improved open-car weather protection.

A 1954 Plus 4 two-seater ad read: "Going Places—the sporty Morgan Plus 4 gets you there quicker!" Its "sloping radiator shell, faired headlamps, restyled wings and streamlined tail and petrol tank unit, give a new look to the 1954 Morgan 2-seater."

The Plus 4 continued using steel body panels over a wooden framework on a ladder-type steel chassis with "Z-section" side members. The bodies were crafted at the Morgan facility, but most other components came from outside suppliers. The new roadster rode a 96-in. wheelbase and carried a 2088-cc 68-hp overhead-valve four-

*There were both two- and four-seater versions of the Plus Four Morgans.*

cylinder engine. It was attached to a Moss four-speed manual gearbox. Versions of the Standard-Triumph engine were used through the 1950s and '60s. Later, the Plus 4 adopted engines from each new Triumph sports car: TR2, TR3, then TR4.

The Plus 4's appearance included separate fenders and headlights, a two-piece center-hinged hood, rear-hinged doors, a hidden gas tank, and minimal running boards. Removable side curtains gave rudimentary weather protection. Some examples included leather hood straps.

The Morgan front end went through a three-stage evolutionary process with the 1950 models retaining the flat vertical-bar grille used on early 4/4s. A few were built with an intermediate semi-cowled grille. In 1954, that interim unit was replaced by the famed "fencer's mask" design.

A center-mounted fog light enjoyed a rebirth. Later models also had a smoother tail, a more sloping nose and semi-faired-in headlights. The "butterfly-hinged" hood had side louvers. Later models added a 6000-rpm tachometer. Aluminum bodies could be special-ordered.

Morgan's model lineup consisted of the two-seater roadster, a 2+2 roadster, a two-seat drophead coupe and—for a brief period starting in 1951—a 2+2 convertible. The extra 2+2-style seats were suited only for "occasional" use. The convertible tops could be positioned half-open.

The suspension featured sliding pillars with coil springs up front and a rigid rear axle with underslung semi-elliptic leaf springs. Standard 1952 body colors were black, British Racing Green, Nile Blue, and Carnation Red.

The drophead coupe came with detachable side curtains. The two-seater Sports model still had twin spare tires mounted on the back. In 1954, the 1,680-lb. two-passenger roadster was $2,450 while the drophead coupe sold for $200 more. A Plus 4 four-seater coupe was announced at the 1954 London Motor Show and produced sporadically over the next 2-1/2 years. Only 51 were built, all with the Vanguard engine. The base engine used through 1962 was the in-line, overhead-valve four from the Triumph TR2. This 1991-cc power plant had an 83 x 92-mm bore and stroke. With an 8.5:1 compression ratio and twin S.U. carburetors, it made 90 hp at 4800 rpm and 117 lbs.-ft. of torque at 3000 rpm.

"Four Magnificent Models to choose from," promised the Morgan catalog issued at the London show in October 1955. An ad for the Plus 4 four-seat sports drophead coupe promised it was "ideally suited for the 'family' man." The TR2-engined version was advertised as the "New Super Morgan." The Plus 4 was advertised in the U.S. as the "last of the real classics." American ads also touted the Morgan's race victories.

Seats in the 1955 Morgan two-seater tourer had their own pneumatic cushion with a single back squab. The dashboard held a speedometer and tachometer. The four-seater tourer had a smaller gas tank under the rear seats and came with either a TR2 or Vanguard engine.

The two-seater coupe had the same engines and removable sliding windows. In 1955, the 1,848-lb. two-passenger roadster carried a $2,595 price tag, and the 2+2 version was about 56 lbs. heavier and $50 pricier. The drophead was $2,695.

Standard 1955 Plus 4 equipment included a "Brooklands" race-type steering wheel, a badge bar, a tachometer, a fog lamp, bumpers with overriders, and leather (or leatherette) upholstery. Standard 1955 colors were Larch Green, Kingfisher Blue, ivory, Carnation Red, Ming Blue, and black. Ads in the U.S. during 1955 noted the use of larger (16-in.) "Indianapolis" type wheels.

Morgan's 1956 sales catalog listed options including a tonneau cover (for either two- or four-seaters), fog lamps, a Smith's heater, Horvell wheel trims, leather upholstery, a Brooklands steering wheel, and flashing turn indicators. Models offered for 1956 were the two-seater tourer, two-seater coupe, and four-seater tourer.

Standard 1956 colors were Larch Green, Wembley Blue, and Carnation Red. The upholstery was black. Special body or upholstery colors cost 10 pounds extra (in Britain). Three bodies were offered: the two-seat drophead coupe, open two-seater, and open four-seater.

For 1958, the two-seater tourer, four-seater tourer, and two-seater coupe were offered. The two-seater (and later the four-seater) grew by four inches and the two-seater's fuel tank was moved farther down in the chassis. Options were similar to 1956, but a windshield washer and knock-on wire wheels were added. The 1959 Morgan catalog listed the TR engine, but not the Vanguard.

Peter Morgan became managing director following the death of H.F.S. Morgan in 1959. By 1962, Morgan adopted the 2138-cc 105-hp TR4 engine. The standard Plus 4 had a top speed in the 96 to105 mph range. A Morgan could do the quarter mile in 17.1 to 18.5 seconds withl economy up to 35 mpg claimed.

Most 1960s Morgan coupes had center-lock wire wheels and delivered a rough ride that roadster drivers loved or hated. Morgan produced only 26 coupes through 1966. Standard Plus 4 colors in the 1960s were Westminster Green, Kingfisher Blue, crimson and white. Prices for 1963 models were $2,962 for the 1,764-lb. two-passenger roadster, $3,048 for the 2+2 roadster, and $3,352 for the drophead coupe.

Plus 4 production continued with periodic mechanical improvements through the 1968 model year. By the late-1960s, its styling was old-fashioned and the four-cylinder Triumph engine was becoming obsolete.

Morgan switched to a V-8. As many as 4,754 Plus 4s were produced between 1950 and 1968, including some 893 with the 2088-cc Vanguard engine.

Andrew Morland

*The four-seat version of the Morgan Plus 4 was considered the family sports car.*

David Gooley

# 1961-'68 Plus 4 Super Sports

**M**organ first used the term "Super Sports" on a 1933 three-wheeled model that had an extra-powerful (10-hp) Ford engine. The company continued making three-wheeled cars until 1951, when the final shipment of 10 MX4 three-wheeled Super Sports was made and sent to Australia. These vehicles were actually made from leftover parts. Although the Morgan three-wheeler was gone, the Super Sports name would be revived, in the early 1960s, for a high-performance version of a car with four wheels—the famous Morgan Plus 4.

Morgan started manufacturing a sports car called the 4/4 in 1935. This model was powered by a Coventry Climax engine and became known as the Series I. It was made until 1950. By that time, a 1267-cc Standard engine was beating below its bonnet. When Standard stopped manufacturing this engine, Morgan went looking for a replacement. Company founder H.F.S. Morgan did not want to use an engine with a displacement larger than 1500 ccs but his son Peter convinced him to use a 2,088-cc Vanguard engine in a larger chassis with a Moss four-speed gearbox. Peter took his father for a ride in the prototype car. H.F.S. was so impressed that he agreed to build the car, which was dubbed the "Plus 4."

The 1961 Morgan Super Sports model was a two-door roadster version of the Plus 4 with a hopped-up engine. The power plant was specially tuned by an organization run by Chris Lawrence. In addition to getting more power, the Plus 4 Super Sports carried a lightweight alloy body and wore 5.60 x 15 tires. An oil cooler was also positioned behind the Super Sports' grille.

The hopped-up engine was a 2138-cc (86 x 92-mm bore and stroke) in-line, overhead-valve Triumph four banger with a cast-iron block and head. It produced 115 hp at 5500 rpm and 128 lbs.-ft. of torque at 3400 rpm.

The engine was sent to Westerham Motors, in Acton, England, for modifications including an increased (9.0:1) compression ratio, polishing of the cylinder head, installation of a high-lift camshaft, component balancing, the mounting of a square-section four-branch exhaust manifold, and installation of Weber 42 or 45 DCOE carburetors.

Like the regular Plus 4 two-passenger roadster, the Super Sports was built on a 96-in.-wheelbase chassis. It measured the same 144 in. long, 52 in. high, and 56 in. wide as the basic Plus 4. With its fatter tires, the Super Sports' front and rear tread widths were a tad wider than the standard 47 in. Four-stud pressed steel disc wheels with

*A powerful engine and light alloy body made the Morgan Plus Four Super Sports very special.*

chromed caps were standard and wire wheels were optional.

A four-speed manual gearbox was fitted in the Super Sports model. Cam-gear steering was used. The front suspension system incorporated sliding pillars with coil springs. At the rear was a rigid axle with semi-elliptic leaf springs. Girling hydraulic brakes (front disc/rear drum) were fitted. As a result of the performance and handling changes, the 1961 Plus 4 Super Sports could do 115 mph at top end. A 0-to-60-mph run took just 7.8 seconds.

Starting in 1962, Morgan's regular Plus 4 was powered by the same basic 2138-cc Triumph engine used in Super Sports models. However, this was a milder 100-105-hp version with twin Stromberg carburetors. The more potent 115-120-hp Weber-carbed engine, tuned by the Chris Lawrence organization, remained the core of the $3,893 Super Sports roadster.

During 1962, Chris Lawrence and Richard Shepherd-Baron drove TOK258—a Morgan Plus 4 Super Sports—to a class victory in the 2-liter class at Le Mans. The car covered 2,565 miles and averaged almost 94 mph for 24 hours. This achievement became Morgan's greatest racing result. The next year a Le Mans Super Sports model was made available, for $3,961, to commemorate the victory.

In 1966, Morgan's two-seat models, including the Super Sports, got a new, lower body. Although few other major changes were made, the later Morgan Plus 4 Super Sports tested out as a modestly faster machine. Its recorded top speed was 120 mph and it could do the standing-start quarter mile in 15.4 seconds.

Production of the Plus Four series with 2138-cc engine ceased by early 1969, when the Morgan fell victim to tightening federal regulations in the United States. That status would persist into the 1970s and early '80s, with certification remaining elusive. No Morgans were officially exported to the U.S. between 1972 and 1985. In October 1985, the Plus 4 was produced again. This time it was powered by a 2-liter Twin-Cam Fiat engine that delivered 122 hp. Still later, a Rover engine was used.

While the Plus 4 was made on and off for a half century, the Super Sports version was made fewer years and in much smaller numbers. A total of just 101 Super Sports roadsters with the high-performance Lawrence-tuned engine were ever produced.

Andrew Morland

# 1963-1966 Plus 4 Plus

I n its long history, Morgan made only one swing away from the traditional (prewar) look. Peter Morgan decided it was time to step into the future and designed a modern car conceived to carry his company there. The decidedly different Plus Four Plus coupe was announced at the 1963 Earl's Court Motor Show and was an unexpected addition to the Morgan range. Peter Morgan's daughter, Lady Jane Colwyn, posed with the Plus Four Plus when it was introduced.

Production began by 1964. This model was very successful in rallies, but enthusiasts felt it was not in the Morgan image and production was discontinued within two years. Only 26 of the cars were ever built. However, the Plus Four Plus demonstrated that it was feasible to produce a modern coupe on the traditional Morgan chassis.

"The enthusiast," Morgan claimed about the Plus Four Plus, "will find this the ideal sports car for tireless long-distance traveling." The car's handling was said to have been as good as that of other Morgans. However, the public wasn't enamored of the styling, even though advertising promised "new smooth sweeping lines." Other ads encouraged customers to "Make friends with a Morgan Plus Four Plus" and to "Drive well and influence people with your new Morgan Plus Four Plus."

The slim "bubbletop" two-seater coupe body rode a strengthened Plus Four chassis with the 2138-cc Triumph TR4 engine under its bonnet. This power plant developed 105 hp at 4750 rpm. A skinny-looking top gave the coupe a weird, if not distinctive, upper profile that some called "bell-shaped." This design was not universally loved, but otherwise the Plus-Four-Plus looked fine. The new car had basically slab-sided—though rounded—body contours with straight fender lines. There was a vertical look to it at the front and rear ends. Full-rounded wheel openings were seen. "This model was way ahead of its time and added unexpected style to the Morgan line," says John H. Shealy II, in his book *The Rare Ones: Peter Morgan and the Plus Four Plus*. Shealy, who owned two of the cars and restored four for other owners, added, "I always admired Peter for bringing out the Plus Four Plus, as it really added to the legend of the Morgan Marque."

## *The Morgan Plus Four Plus never caught on with avid Morgan traditionalists.*

Instead of Morgan's traditional steel-over-wood construction, the Plus Four Plus coupe wore a fiberglass body. Up front were Morgan's familiar small, vertical-bar grille and bumper. The headlights were fully built into the fenders, with rounded rectangular parking lights below. Air intake openings stood low, alongside the grille, and were decorated with horizontal bars.

The coupe's curved windshield was yet another "first" for Morgan, as were its wind-down semicircular glass windows (which didn't wind down quite all the way).

Other styling features of the Plus Four Plus coupe included two round taillights on each side in a vertical panel, a separate trunk with external hinges, and a gas filler just ahead of the trunk lid. Overall, there was little to remind the observer of the usual Morgans with their cut-down doors and old-fashioned appearance.

Most of the coupes had center-lock wire wheels and delivered the same sort of rough ride that roadster drivers had learned to love (or hate). Morgan planned to build only 50 coupes, but barely reached half that total by 1966. The Plus Four Plus could hit about 110 mph and reach 60 mph in about 12.5 seconds. Standard colors were Westminster Green, Kingfisher Blue, Crimson, and White. According to Shealy's book *Morgan — Pride of the British*, most of the 26 examples produced over its four-year official life were exported, and 10 of them were sold in the U.S.

The price of the 1,820-lb. Plus Four Plus coupe in England was 1,250 pounds, including tax. The coupe used the same 96-in. wheelbase as roadsters. It was 152 in. long overall, 51 in. high, and 61 in. wide. Front and rear track widths were 49 in. The standard 5.60 x 15 tires rode on steel disc wheels. Wire wheels were an option. A 3.78:1 rear axle was used. Other technical specifications and layouts were the same as those for Morgan Plus Four roadsters.

Norbert Bries/ Northshore Imports

# 1968-2003 4/4 1600/1800

Morgan Motor Co. Ltd., of Malvern Link, in Worcestershire, England, was in trouble by the late 1960s. Morgans were disappearing from lists of U.S. import car lists, the victims of tightening federal regulations. Morgan stayed alive, but the U.S. market remained closed in the 1970s and '80s. It was impossible to get Morgans certified in the U.S., where the bulk of sales had been realized.

Despite this, another engine went into the Morgan 4/4 during 1968—the 1599-cc four-cylinder Ford "Crossflow" or "Kent" power plant, also used in English Ford Capris and Cortinas, and in early Ford Pintos.

It was the first of several four-cylinder engines of about 1600-cc capacity that would be used beneath the 4/4's bonnet. The Ford Kent was used from 1968-1982, and these were the first to be known as 4/4 1600 models.

The in-line, overhead-valve engine had a cast-iron block and head. With an 81 x 77.6-mm bore and stroke it actually displaced 1599 cc. It had five main bearings, solid valve lifters and a 9.0:1 compression ratio. With a single Weber carburetor, its rated output was 74 hp at 4750 rpm and 98 lbs.-ft. of torque at 2500 rpm. A competition version also was available, rated 88-96 hp at 4750-5500 rpm.

The 4/4 1600 two-passenger roadster weighed 1,455 lbs. By this time, a four-seat 2+2 roadster was also available. The chassis serial number for 4/4 1600 models, starting with B1600, was stamped on the frame cross member beneath the front seats. The new engine gave the 4/4 a top speed in the 100-mph neighborhood. Its 0-to-60-mph acceleration was about 9.8 seconds. This engine was linked to a four-speed manual gearbox.

The 4/4 remained on a 96-in. wheelbase, with an overall length of 144 in. It stood 51 in. high and had a 56-in. body width. The track, front and rear, was 47 in. Size 165 x 15 radial tires were new for the 4/4 1600 model. Chassis features were common to other Morgans.

Ads for the 1970 4/4 1600 called it "The Birthday Car," noting the 60th anniversary of Morgan's founding. "Disc brakes, vivid acceleration, positive control, a little comfort and a lot of fun," was the promise for purchasers, who could get their Morgans in standard, mildly tuned or four-seater versions. More than 600 Morgans (including 100 three-wheelers) showed up for a 60th anniversary celebration at Prescott, England, organized by Morgan clubs in Great Britain.

Production of the 1.6-liter Morgan 4/4 continued after 1970 still

*The Morgan 4/4 1600 and 1800 series cars made great-looking racing vehicles.*

using the 1600 Ford Kent engine. Morgans weren't officially exported to the U.S. from 1972 to 1975. Starting in 1976, cars became available through Isis Imports of San Francisco, Calif.

To meet U.S. regulations, these cars had to be retrofitted with roll bars, door bracing, and safety bumpers. Other revisions included the addition of sun visors, back-up lights, side marker lights and repositioning the taillights.

From 1981-1985, Fiat's 1600 Twin Cam four also was used in the Morgan 4/4 1600. It also had a cast-iron block and light alloy head. The Fiat engine used an 84 x 71.5-mm bore and stroke and displaced 1585 cc. With a 9.5:1b compression ratio, it was good for 97/98 hp at 6000 rpm and 94 lbs.-ft. of torque at 3800-4000 rpm. It carried either a Weber or Solex two-barrel carburetor.

In 1982, a five-speed transmission replaced the four-speed unit. Supplies of the Ford Crossflow four dried up and were replaced with a British Ford "CVH" engine (related to the engine used in the Ford Escort). The in-line Ford CVH used an overhead-cam four-cylinder (Ford XR3 "CVH") engine with a cast-iron block and light alloy head. It had an 80 x 79.5-mm bore and stroke and displaced 1597 cc. With a 9.5:1 compression ratio and a single two-barrel Weber carburetor, it developed 96 hp at 6000 rpm. Torque was rated 98 lbs.-ft. at 4000 rpm.

British advertisements in 1982 promoted the Morgan as the "first of the real sports cars." When the Morgan's use of the Rover V-8 engine was finally certified as U.S. emissions-legal, it was thought their model lineup might have a clear field ahead of it.

Emissions were only part of the problem. Bumper and side-impact regulations had to be met, which wasn't easy for a company with such limited production. The only Morgans officially available for sale in the U.S. during the 1980s were those converted to propane power.

The CVH engine was replaced with Ford's 1600 EFI (electronic fuel-injected) four in 1991, with this power plant continuing to be used as late as 1993. By this time, the top speed for the 4/4 1600 had climbed as high as 115 mph. In 1992, the 1798-cc Ford "Zeta" (Zetec) engine was used for the 4/4, which technically turned it into the 4/4 1800.

The Morgan Motor Company still is officially owned and run by the Morgan family, as it has been since its inception in 1909. Peter

Morgan was Chairman and Joint Managing Director, until his death in the fall of 2003. The other Joint Managing Director is Mr. Charles Morgan, Peter's son.

The 4/4 still is available in two models—the two-passenger or four-passenger roadster. The cars still are built around an ash-frame and a steel chassis.

The waiting list for any Morgan in the UK is around 12 months, which is the best delivery time Morgan has achieved since the 1970s. Prices aren't quoted since they would be obsolete by delivery.

"…the traditional shaped cars with the full range of engines and other options will continue to be available for the foreseeable future," says Morgan. Recent advertisements suggest they may not be available in the U.S. forever.

The two-passenger roadster is 153 in. long, 59 in. wide and 52 in. high. The four-passenger model is five inches longer, an inch wider and weighs 1300 kg (2,860 lbs.). Both feature a separate Z-shaped section chassis with five tubular or box-section cross members. Both models are available in Royal Ivory, Corsa Red, Indigo Blue, black, and Connaught Green. Buyers can select any single or two-tone colour combination from the ICI Autocolour range. Painted center-lock wire wheels are standard.

Technical features include rack-and-pinion steering, a five-speed transmission, independent sliding-pillar front suspension with coil springs and gas-filled telescopic shocks, semi-elliptic rear springs with similar shocks, stainless steel exhaust, and Lockheed front disc/rear drum brakes. The DOCH 16-valve 1796-cc engine runs a 10.0:1 compression ratio and develops 114 hp at 5800 rpm and 118 lbs.-ft. of torque at 4500 rpm. The two-passenger has a 131 power-to-weight ratio and the four-passenger ratio is 117.

# 1955-1968 4/4 Series II, III, & IV

Morgan's first post World War II model was a revived version of the 4/4, which had originally been introduced in 1937. The postwar 4/4 was the only four-wheel Morgan automobile sold from 1945-1949.

When the new Plus 4 arrived in 1950, it looked similar to the 4/4, but used a larger engine. By 1955, Morgan discovered it needed a less-expensive model and dusted off the 4/4 name for it. The revived 4/4 two-door roadster carried a Port of Entry price of $1,995 and weighed 1430 lbs.

The new 4/4 was viewed as the earlier car's replacement. Morgan's other model, the Plus Four, had become a powerful and pricey machine by the mid-1950s. Morgan wanted to complement it with a lower-powered, more affordable model and the 4/4 filled the bill.

It was nearly identical to the Plus Four, with the same cowled vertical-bar radiator grille, sloped tail and semi-faired-in headlights. In 1957, *Motor Trend* called the 4/4 Series II the "lowest priced sports car in America."

Engines were the only big difference. The Plus Four relied on a Standard-Triumph power plant and 4/4's engine came from the English Ford family. This Ford F100E (a.k.a. "Ford Ten") was an in-line, L-head, four-cylinder engine with a cast-iron block and head. It had a 63.5 x 92.5-mm bore and stroke and 1172-cc displacement. With a single Solex downdraft carburetor, the motor produced 36-39 hp at 4400 rpm and 52 lbs.-ft. of torque at 2500 rpm.

A competition version of the Ford engine was made available with an aluminum head, twin carburetors, and a modified camshaft. The hotter version was rated 40 hp at 5100 rpm and used an 8.0:1 compression ratio. The base 4/4 had a top speed of 75-78 mph and could accelerate from 0-to-60 mph in 26.9-29 seconds. Fuel mileage was around 20 to 22 mpg.

A three-speed manual transmission formed a unit with the engine. The overall transmission gear ratios were 15.07:1 in first, 8.25:1 in second, 4.4:1 in third, and 19.71:1 in reverse. The standard final drive ratio was 4.4:1. Vital statistics for the new 4/4 included a 96-in. wheelbase, a 144-in. overall length, a 50-in. height, a 56-in. width and 47-in. front and rear track widths. Steel disc wheels with 5.00 x 16 tires were standard. Series III and Series IV versions changed to 5.20 x 15 tires.

Only a two-passenger roadster (called the Two Seater Tourer in Britain) was offered initially. Chassis construction used a front suspension that consisted of sliding pillars with coil springs and a rigid axle with semi-elliptic rear leaf springs. Four-wheel drum brakes were used until 1960, when front discs and rear drums were installed.

Morgan's 1958 sales catalog listed a 4/4 Series II competition model with a specially tuned engine, which made its debut prior to the 1957 Motor Show. The car's specifications were similar to those of other 4/4s, but the competition model sported a carefully assembled engine with an aquaplane aluminum head, improved intake and exhaust manifolds, twin S.U. carburetors, and an 8.0:1 compression ratio.

Peter Morgan brought more youthful thinking to the product line. Starting in 1960, the 4/4 Series III was made available and was nicknamed Morgan's "Anniversary Model." The Series III used an over-square overhead-valve "Kent" 997-cc four with an 81 x 48.4 mm bore and stroke. The same engine was used in the British Ford 105E Anglia series. It was rated for 39 hp at 5000 rpm and had one Solex downdraft carburetor. The initial price for the Series III roadster was $2,240. It again tipped the scales at 1,430 lbs.

In the Series III, a four-speed gearbox replaced the three-speed unit. The side-curtain fasteners were moved to the outside of the doors and the taillights were restyled. The Series III also featured toggle switches on a new dashboard. The Morgan 4/4 Series III qualifies as the rarest version of a famous line, according to *More Morgan*.

In 1961, the Morgan 4/4 Series IV arrived using a 1340-cc Ford Consul Classic engine (81 x 65.1-mm bore and stroke) with an 8.5:1 compression ratio. This motor produced 54 hp at 5000 rpm. It reduced the car's 0-to-60-mph acceleration time to as little as 10.5 seconds while boosting the top speed to 92 mph.

With the introduction of the Morgan 4/4 Series V in 1963, the engine grew to 1498 cc. In basic trim, this engine produced 65 hp, but more potent editions developed for competition use were also marketed. A four-speed manual gearbox was the only transmission choice. Front disc/rear drum brakes remained standard. The 1,456-lb. roadster's P.O.E. price was now up to $2,394.

"Small car, Big performance" was the claim for the competition version of the Morgan 4//4 Series V, which sold for $270 more than a Series IV model. The compression ratio was boosted from 8.3:1 to 9.0:1 and the engine switched from a Zenith 33N carburetor to a Weber model DCD22 two-barrel.

A closer-ratio gearbox was also installed, and this helped to cut the car's 0-to-60-mph acceleration time down to 11.9 seconds. The top speed climbed to 95-100 mph. Wire wheels were made available at extra cost.

"There's something about a Morgan," said one British ad for the Morgan 4/4 Series V. "Each car is assembled by craftsmen, each is road tested before collection, each carries the unmistakable stamp of the individualist." Production of the Series V halted in 1968, when it was replaced by the 4/4 1600.

Factory records show a total of 387 Morgan 4/4 Series II models were made, followed by 59 Series IIIs and 206 Series IVs. The 4/4 Series V proved to be the most popular of the early postwar versions. The 4/4 1600 arrived next and began the modern era of the 4/4. model.

Norbert Bries/Northshore Imports

# 1968-2003 Plus 8

**W**ith the demise of the Plus Four in 1968, Morgan made a major move into V-8 power for its traditional-style roadster. While Triumph had dropped its V-8, Rover was just beginning to install a V-8 engine in its sedans and made it available to Morgan.

The all-aluminum V-8 was a Buick design, used in early 1960s Buick Specials, Oldsmobile F-85s and Pontiac Tempests. Except for the installation of S.U. carburetors, the Rover V-8 varied little from the original GM power plant and it weighed no more than the Triumph four that it replaced.

Most early Plus 8s wore a steel body over the customary wooden framework, though some had aluminum bodies. Inside, rocker switches replaced toggles and matte-black instrument panels replaced chrome units.

According to *The Morgan: 75 Years on the Road*, a steel floor replaced the former wood section from the pedal board to the seat mounting area. Bucket seats and a triple-wiper setup also was added. The Plus 8's cut-away doors and separate fenders differed little from the earlier Morgans.

"For 1968 a brand new Morgan, the +8," promised British ads. "Leap to the legal limit in a staggering 7.5 seconds." The original Plus 8 came only as a two-passenger roadster with a 98-in. wheelbase and a 152-in. overall length. The car stood 49 in. high and 57 in. wide.

To make space for the new V-8, Plus 4 chassis side-members had to be moved apart. Fenders were widened to accept bigger wheels and tires. Cast alloy wheels replaced center-lock wire wheels. Standard equipment also included 185 x 15 tires.

The aluminum Rover engine was a 90-degree, overhead-valve V-8 with an 88.9 x 71.1-mm bore and stroke. This five-main-bearings-unit had hydraulic valve lifters, a 10.5:1 compression ratio, and was fitted with twin S.U. carburetors. Its official output was 184 hp at 5200 rpm and 226 lbs.-ft. of torque at 3600 rpm. Some U.S. sources listed output

*Morgan literature described the Plus 8 as the "drive of your lifetime."*

as low as 143 hp at 5000 rpm and 202 lbs.-ft. at 2700 rpm. The car had a 3.58:1 final drive ratio.

Performance was considerably swifter with a top speed in the 125 mph range. The first Plus 8 did 0-to-60-mph in as little as 6.5 seconds and covered the quarter mile in 16.8 seconds. The Plus 8 remained quite similar to the original concept over the next four decades.

Production of the eight-cylinder Morgan continued after 1970, even though Americans weren't entitled to an officially certified version. The fender widths and tread dimensions were widened several times to accommodate fatter tires. In May 1972, an all-synchromesh Rover four-speed manual transmission replaced the former Moss gearbox. The engine output was changed to 151 hp at 5000 rpm and 210 lbs.-ft. of torque at 2700 rpm.

Early in 1977, a five-speed gear box was introduced and the V-8 engine was revised. It went to 155 hp at 5250 rpm and 199 lbs.-ft. of torque at 2500 rpm, a format that lasted until 1985. Starting in the late 1970s, a handful of Plus 8s converted to run on propane trickled into the U.S. via California—the only Morgans available in the U.S. Enthusiasts were still waiting for the Rover engine to earn EPA emissions-certification.

In the mid-1980s, Morgan adopted a fuel-injected version of the Rover V-8, as well as rack-and-pinion steering. It produced 190 hp at 5200 rpm and 220 lbs.-ft. of torque at 4000 rpm. Top speed had risen to 130 mph. Acceleration from a standing start to 60 mph took just 5.6 to 6.5 seconds. About 14.5 seconds were required to make the quarter mile.

By this time, tread widths were up to 52 in. front and 53 in. rear, and overall width grew to 62 in. Larger 205 x 15 tires were required to carry the extra bulk. By the late 1980s, Morgan reported that a total of 484 Plus 8 models had been built with the early Moss gearbox. More than 2,600 Plus 8 Morgans were produced. Several 1982 British ads promoted Morgan as "first of the real sports cars." When the Rover V-8 was finally certified for U.S. sales, Morgans still faced strict bumper and side-impact standards.

The early 1990s brought a rapid series of engine changes to four-cylinder Morgans. A BBC television program also brought in hundreds of orders for the cars. Industrialist Sir John Harvey's "Trouble Shooter" studied the automaker, creating conflicts with the Morgan family, but also generating a long waiting list for sales.

Charles Morgan and car dealer Bill Wykeham raced a specifically designed aluminum chassis Plus 8 in seven rounds of the international 1996 BPR race series (later the FIA GT series). This car proved Morgan racing potential but revealed limitations due to old-fashioned aerodynamics. The 1997 production models received aluminum "superform" wings, longer doors, and a new fascia to accommodate airbags. A 4.6-liter V-8 was introduced and Morgan began using water-based paints. With production of 11 cars per week beginning in February 1999, the yearly factory output was greater than it had been since before World War II.

In November 2000, Peter Morgan celebrated his 81st birthday. Morgan announced the Plus 8's existing 3.9 and 4.6 Rover V-8 engines would be replaced by a new 4.0-liter Rover V-8. When a standard European Whole Vehicle Approval System took effect, Morgan decided to comply with the rules instead of using a low-volume exclusion.

This guaranteed its cars would be certified in export markets, where about half of all Morgans were sold. Combined with racing and the development of the +8 for the federal market in the U.S., the move set the stage for the all-new Aero 8 introduction in 2000.

The 2003 Plus 8 used the 4.0-liter 16-valve V-8, with a 94 x 71.1-cc bore and stroke and 3946 cc of displacement. It developed 190 hp at 4800 rpm and 225 lbs.-ft. of torque at 3500 rpm. The two-passenger roadster was 13 ft. long, 63 in. wide (66 in. with optional wheels), and 45 in. high.

Current Morgans come in Royal Ivory, Corsa Red, Indigo Blue, black, and Connaught Green. Any single or two-tone combination from the ICI Autocolour range is an available option. Five-stud bolt-on 6.5 x 15-in. alloy wheels with 205/60/15 tyres are standard equipment. Options include 6.5 x 16-in. center-lock wire wheels with 205/55/16 tyres. A five-speed transmission is used. The front suspension still employs independent sliding pillars combined with coil springs and gas filled telescopic shock absorbers. The rear is fitted with semi-elliptic leaf springs with gas telescopic shock absorbers. Up front are Lockheed disc brakes, with drum brakes at the rear.

Norbert Bries/Northshore Imports

*Coming right at you, the Morgan Plus 8.*

David Gooley

# 1985-2000 Plus 4

The Morgan Plus 4 was reintroduced in October of 1985. Though looking much the same as before on the outside, the revived Plus 4 now had a 1995-cc Fiat Twin-Cam engine. This power plant was used in the Plus 4 through 1988.

Charles Morgan, grandson of the founder, joined the company full time in 1985. He followed a company tradition by becoming one of the many third-generation Morgan employees. The company and its dealers stepped up the involvement in motor sports. Rick Bourne came second overall in the Pirelli Marathon in a Morgan Plus Four Supersports, echoing the success of the Plus Four in the International rallies of the 1950's.

In May of 1988, a 1994-cc Rover M16 four-cylinder engine replaced the Fiat power plant. The Morgan Sports Car Championships also began in 1988. This event turned into an annual competition designed to give marque enthusiasts the chance to race their cars in a one-make series. Before long, over 300 cars were taking part.

The success of the Morgan Sports Car Championships prompted a Hillclimb Championship exclusively for Morgans and encouraged the German Morgan Owners Club to start a race series in Europe called the Continental Morgan Championship.

*Morgan used both Rover and Fiat engines to power the Plus 4 series from 1985 to 2000.*

The early 1990s saw a rapid series of engine changes. During 1992, the M16 Rover engine in the Plus 4 was updated to T16 specifications, but engine displacement remained at 1994 ccs.

In 1997 the production models were extensively overhauled, with the standardization of the new aluminum "superform" wings for all but 4/4 models. Morgans also got longer doors and a new fascia to allow for airbags. Production improvements included a new water-based paint system. By 1999, Morgan was building an average of 11 cars per week, a level that hadn't been seen since before World War II.

In 1999, Morgan started to build a prototype of the new Aero 8 model. This was probably the most radical Morgan ever made, at least right up there with the Plus Four Plus. The new car had a racing car suspension and a BMW 4.4-liter V-8. The gearbox was a six-speed Getrag unit. A new production plant was built. Morgan stopped making the Plus 4 roadster in 2000, which was the model's 55th anniversary.

David Gooley

# 2000-2003 Aero 8

**T**he new Morgan Aero 8 marks the culmination of the largest development program ever undertaken by Morgan in more than 90 years of sports car manufacture," Charles Morgan said in his 2000 paper titled *The Birth of a Morgan*.

"In a four-year project, I encouraged a small but dedicated in-house team at Morgan's Malvern factory to create a completely new car from the ground up." Charles explained that the name of the car came from the Morgan Aero, a sporty three-wheeler built between 1919 and 1936 that featured aero screens, instead of a conventional windshield, to give it better aerodynamics.

The launch of the Morgan Aero 8 came in February 2000 at the Geneva Motor Show. The new, all-aluminum roadster was Morgan's first all-new car in 64 years and definitely stole the spotlight. "Initial overall public opinion was excellent and orders begin to flood into the factory," the British automaker reported later the same year.

The Aero 8 was a street car largely based on the design of the Morgan Works' GT2 racing car that competed in the 1997 FIA GT Championship. Many production model features were conceived and proven in racing events. Highlighting the new model was a 1Astra CAD-designed aluminum alloy monocoque body tub specially treated and bonded with Gurrit Essex cement and riveted with Bulhof rivets. Aluminum also was used in the suspension and other areas, helping to achieve a vehicle weight of just 1,000 kg (2,204 lbs.).

In 1998, Morgan built the first Aero 8 prototype. "The objective of the development program was to recreate the position we held in 1968 when we launched the Plus 8," explained Charles Morgan. "At that time it was the car with just about the most flexible performance you could buy due to the combination of its light weight and large capacity engine." With the Aero 8, the idea was to achieve the same goal by making an ultra-light, aluminum-intensive vehicle.

The roadster stretched 13 ft. 2 in. overall, was 52-in. high, and 59-in. wide. Its provocative, curved body was designed in-house at

***One could consider the Aero 8 the ultimate Morgan available to the public.***

the Morgan Works using CATIA CAD software and extensive wind tunnel testing. The body had a drag coefficient of 0.39, a 40 percent improvement over the Plus 8 model. The Aero 8 body panels were made from aluminum and mounted on a wooden frame—kiln-dried Belgian ash as earlier Morgans used.

A partnership with BMW culminated in development of the Aero 8 power train. Morgan's in-house team—headed by Charles Morgan and technical director Chris Lawrence—tapped resources and engineers from BMW and Robert Bosch Motorsport to help create a new engine management system.

The 4.4-liter BMW-built 32-valve V-8 featured VANOS variable inlet valve timing, cruise control, on-board diagnostics, an immobiliser and drive-by-wire technology. It had an 82.7 x 92-mm bore and stroke and a 4398-cc capacity. It produced 286 hp at 5400 rpm and 324 lbs.-ft. of torque at 3600 rpm. Other features included a 10.0:1 compression ratio, a Robert Bosch fuel-injection setup and a stainless steel exhaust system.

The engine was mounted in a cradle constructed from aluminum extrusions. The design offered necessary strength and durability for crash safety. Aluminum was also used to manufacture some braking and suspension units.

The engine was mated to a six-speed Getrag gearbox, the first manual gearbox with a self-adjusting clutch.

The Aero 8's rear transaxle was a BTR hydradrive with a limited-slip differential and a 3.08:1 final drive ratio. The front suspension featured long transverse Eibach coil springs over Koni shocks. Rear-mounted independent long transverse wishbones were used with cantilever-mounted, fully floating Eibach coil springs over Koni shocks. The four-wheel disc brake system was fabricated by AP Racing to Morgan specifications. The wheels were five-spoke, 18-in. OZ magnesium alloys.

In March 2000, Morgan appointed Steve Morris to be its new manufacturing manager, charged with integrating the Aero 8 into Morgan production. Part of the agreement between Morgan and BMW included all Morgan dealers receiving full BMW training on the new engine, drivetrain, and engine management system.

In April, the Aero 8 National and International dealer road show began in Kent at Brands Hatch Morgans. Analysis of weekly quality audits proved the Aero 8 was Morgan's best ever. Before long the trim shop was expanded and the repair shop was modernized in efforts to speed up Aero 8 assemblies. A July 2000 announcement proclaimed Morgan production was the highest in nearly 80 years.

In August 2000, Morgan won the BENevolent award. BEN—the Motor and Allied Trades Benevolent Fund—presented Morgan with a BENchmark certificate for its excellent support to the motor industry.

Two months later, the Aero 8 debuted at the British International Motor Show 2000 in Birmingham. The Morgan Motor Company achieved the worldwide registration of the shape of its cars, including the waterfall grille, something no other car manufacturer has achieved.

Morgan Motor Company also won the *Autocar* Award for Specialist Manufacturer of the Year 2000: "Morgan has transformed not only its product but, in the process, its business too," said the press.

November 2000 brought the official press launch of the Aero 8. During a three-day event, Morgan invited journalists and photographers to test drive and photograph the new model. The next month the Aero 8 dealer road show ended in Luxembourg at Garage Aloyse Zimmer. Aero 8 orders reached 551 by the end of the first model's first year.

The BMW engine propelled the Aero 8 to 60 mph in less than five seconds. The car had a top speed of 160 mph. Its aerodynamic profile was such that the drag coefficient was similar whether the roof is up or down. A flat underbody and discreet Venturi tunnel at the rear contributed to the high-speed stability of the car.

The first orders for Aero 8s were signed as early as September 1999. The car was scheduled to enter regular production by the end of July 2000 with a production target of approximately 200 cars per year. Morgan allowed customers already on the waiting list for other models to jump to the "head of the line" for an Aero 8. American customers were told they'd have to wait about a year for the car to be certified.

The introductory price of the Aero 8 in the United Kingdom (including VAT) was 49,950 pounds. Standard equipment included heated electric windows, five-spoke alloy wheels, a mohair hood (soft top), and the six-speed gearbox. Numerous options were available. Morgan said Aero buyers had a choice of 30,000 body colors with 40 color options available for the leather interior.

*The Morgan Aero 8 featured a BMW engine and could reach speeds of up to 160 mph.*

Norbert Bries/Northshire Imports

# NASH-HEALEY

OCW Archive

# 1951-1954 Nash-Healey

W hile most new cars are developed after lengthy deliberations, the impetus for the Nash-Healey stemmed from a chance encounter. Late in 1949, George Mason, president of Nash-Kelvinator, and British sports car guru Donald Healey were sailing from Europe on the *Queen Elizabeth*.

Mason sought an image boost for Nash, which was considered a bit stodgy. Healey sought an engine source for his sports car. He favored Cadillac's new V-8 and Nash had only a six back then. They agreed on a British-American hybrid sports car with Nash mechanical components.

A prototype appeared at 1950 auto shows in London and Paris, and production began late that year. Assembled by Healey at Warwick, England, the cars were sold by Nash dealers in the United States. Early examples also were sold in Britain, Europe, and Canada, but the U.S. soon became the sole outlet. Nash said 1951 production and sales would to be "limited, until after the American market was thoroughly explored."

The Nash-Healey debuted at the Chicago Auto Show on Feb. 16, 1951, with a $4,063 price tag. An early press release called it the "first American sports car introduced by an established automobile manufacturer since the mid-20's." It added that prices would be "substantially higher" than for other Nash models. The optimistic Nash estimate for top speed was 125 mph.

The car was scheduled to undergo "exhaustive" engineering tests at Daytona, Salt Lake Flats and Indianapolis Speedway. Tom McCahill of *Mechanix Illustrated* wrote he'd never "driven a sports car that handled better or gave the driver so much control." "The Nash-Healey rides far better than the average sports car without…ill effect upon handling qualities," advised *Motor Trend*.

The two-seat Nash-Healey roadster used an aluminum body and other structural parts. Panelcraft produced the body, which sat on an ordinary Healey chassis with a trailing-link front suspension. It had a 102-in. wheelbase and a 170-in. overall length. The car was just 55.5 in. high and measured 66 in. wide. Front and rear tread widths were a uniform 53 in.

*The Nash-Healey was a successful blend of American and British technology.*

A small airscoop was at the center of the broad, low hood. The slab-sided body wore a grille, headlights, and other body items pirated from the Ambassador Airflyte sedan. The grille had outward-curved vertical chrome bars within a heavy chrome molding. Model designations were evident on the front fenders.

Inside was a leather-finished instrument panel. The adjustable single seat was upholstered in English leather over latex foam cushions. The spare tire and luggage compartment were reached through a nearly horizontal deck. Standard equipment included an adjustable steering wheel, turn signals, and chrome wheel covers.

Under the hood was a modified Nash Ambassador in-line, overhead-valve six-cylinder engine. The "Dual Jet Fire" engine combined a cast-iron block and an aluminum cylinder head. With an 86 x 111-mm bore and stroke, 3847 cc is displaced. An 8.1:1 high-compression head was used along with a hotter-than-standard camshaft. The seven-main-bearings motor featured solid valve lifters and twin horizontal S.U. carburettors.

It produced 125 hp at 4000 rpm and 210 lbs.-ft. of torque at 1600 rpm. Premium fuel was required. The car's true top speed was about 102 to 104 mph.

Coil springs were installed at all four wheels, with the Healey trailing link suspension up front. Each front wheel was mounted on a swinging arm pivoted ahead of the wheel center line. Rear-mounted coil springs worked with direct-acting shock absorbers. Duo servo drum brakes were installed, along with a 3.54:1 axle and 6.40 x 15 whitewall tires. The three-speed transmission came with standard overdrive. Nash torque-tube drive fed the power to the back wheels.

Nash-Healeys quickly took up racing. The first car, wearing a special monoposto body, placed ninth in the 1950 Mille Miglia and fourth at the 24 Hours of Le Mans averaging 87.6 mph in the 2,100-mile race.

The same car, with a new coupe body, was third in its class (sixth overall) at Le Mans the next year. At the 1952 Le Mans event, an open version ranked third overall, taking second in the Index of Performance. Nash-Healey was also fourth in its class (seventh overall) at the '52 Mille Miglia. In 1953, a Nash-Healey convertible finished 11th overall at Le Mans.

Since Italian designer Pinin Farina restyled the 1952 Nash sedans, a roadster revision seemed logical. The second Nash-Healey had a lower windshield, bulging back fenders, and small fins to minimize the slab-sided look. Headlights sat within a grille with two horizontal bars and a round insignia in the center. Small round parking lights stood at the fender tips.

A tiny center scoop topped the hood. A steel body replaced the aluminum. Nash again supplied engine and mechanical components to Healey. After completing the chassis, Healey sent it to Farina for body installation.

The price of the 2,750-lb. car climbed to $5,868.

A larger 4140-cc engine with Carter carburetors became available during the year. This LeMans Dual Jetfire engine had an 88.9 x 111-mm bore and stroke and an 8.0:1 compression ratio. It produced 140 hp at 4000 rpm and 230 lbs.-ft. of torque at 2000 rpm. In 1953, a Le Mans coupe on a longer wheelbase (with rear quarter windows) joined the open model, now called a convertible. For its final year, only the Le Mans version remained, wearing a three-piece wraparound rear window. Over its four-year life, 506 Nash-Healeys were produced.

In 1953, the two-seat convertible ($5,909) was joined by a Pinin Farina-styled, 108-in. wheelbase Le Mans hardtop coupe ($6,399) with a steel top and rear quarter windows. The coupe was shown for the first time at the Chicago Auto Show in March 1953. Its low hood and high fender contour extended to the rear deck, without interruption.

Trailing rear-fender fins accented the flowing front-to-rear lines. The rear fenders rose slightly above the rear deck, forming a "molded" part of the body. Smoothly-rounded front fenders extended forward of the grille line

Standard equipment included leather upholstery, whitewall tires, a tachometer, wheel covers, a cigarette lighter, and an ashtray.

The list price of the Nash-Healey convertible dropped to $5,555 in 1954, while the Le Mans coupe sold for only $5,128. Prices as low as $4,721 were published in U.S. directories for final models. A total of 104 Nash-Healeys were turned out in 1951, and an additional 150 cars were produced in 1952.

A total of 162 Nash-Healeys were produced in 1953 and just 90 were in 1954. Total production for all four years was just 506 units.

*The Nash-Healey roadster featured a body designed by Pinin Farina of Italy.*

# PANTHER

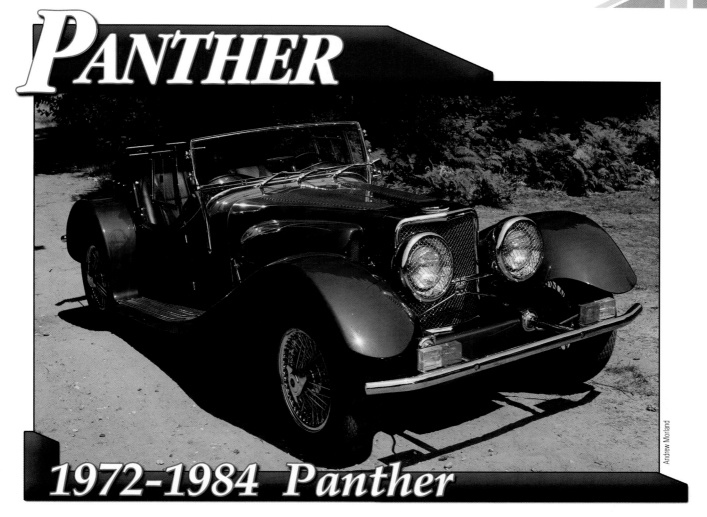

Andrew Morland

# 1972-1984 Panther

In the 1960s, motor-racing fan Robert Jankel started producing about one specialty car per year in Great Britain. Manufacturing cars was a far cry from Jankel's "day" job in the fashion industry, but in 1971, Jankel abandoned fashion and founded Panther Westwinds Ltd. at Surrey, England. His first car was the $35,000 J-72 roadster. The second was the $92,000 DeVille, styled like an early Bugatti.

The interesting-looking J-72 roadster resembled the Jaguar SS100 roadster of the late 1930s. The aluminum-bodied J-72 was powered by a Jaguar 4.2-litre six-cylinder engine and was hooked to a Jaguar four-speed manual transmission with overdrive. It weighed just 2,576 lbs. Side scoops on the louvered hood created space for the XK-derived engine, which was wider than the classic SS100 power plant.

The in-line, dual-overhead-cam six had a 92 x 106-mm bore and stroke and 4235 ccs of piston displacement. The cast-iron block carried an aluminum alloy head. It had an 8.0:1 compression ratio. Output was 190 hp at 5000 rpm and 200 lbs.-ft. of torque at 2000 rpm. Twin S.U. carburetors were fitted, and J-72 buyers could choose a Borg-Warner 65 automatic transmission.

Briefly in the early 1970s, the Panther DeVille V-12 engine also was available in the roadster. This engine, Jaguar's 60-degree, overhead-cam 5343-cc V-12, had a 90 x 70-mm bore and stroke and a 9.0:1 compression ratio. The solid-lifter V-12 used a Lucas-Bosch fuel injection system. It developed 244 hp at 5250 rpm.

The J-72's ladder-type frame was welded from square steel tubing and sat on a 111-in. wheel base. Jaguar components formed the front suspension, while coil springs and a limited-slip differential brought up the rear. The knock-off wire wheels held 225/

**The Panther J-72 reminded many of the classic 1930s Jaguar SS100 roadster.**

70VR15 tires, which required wider fenders than the original SS100. Modern Lucas P-100 sealed-beam headlights were used, though the housings were similar in size to the originals. The sliding side windows were made of acrylic plastic with leather seats and a gauge-filled dashboard inside.

Panther J-72s were known for high-quality components and carefully finished coachwork. Previously, Panther had supplied custom interiors for Rolls-Royces. With a top speed of 128 mph, the J-72 moved from 0-to-60 mph in under 10 seconds. The standing-start quarter mile took 17 seconds at about 90 mph.

Panther Westwinds Ltd. created additional models throughout the 1970s, though most were produced in extremely limited numbers and some never reached the production stage. Starting in 1976, the smaller Panther Lima roadster became available. The $9,300 sports car used a fiberglass body atop a Vauxhall chassis.

The Lima initially used a Vauxhall in-line, overhead-valve four-cylinder with a cast-iron block and head. It had 97.5 x 76.2-mm bore and stroke dimensions and a 2279-cc displacement capacity with an 8.5:1 compression ratio. This engine produced 108 hp at 5000 rpm and 138 lbs.-ft. of torque at 3000 rpm. It used a Zenith-Stromberg one-barrel carburetor Limas were also available with a Holley-Weber carburetor and an AiResearch turbocharger. Later Limas could even have a 200-cid 110-hp V-6. Transmission options included a four-speed manual gearbox or a three-speed automatic.

The Lima had a short 97-in. wheelbase and

measured just 142.2 in. end-to-end. It was 48 in. high and 63.4 in. wide with tread widths of 52.3 in. up front and 52 in. in the rear. Rack-and-pinion steering was fitted. The front suspension incorporated A-arms, coil springs, and an anti-roll bar. The rear suspension featured a rigid axle with coil springs and anti-roll bar. Four-wheel disc brakes were standard.

Panther displayed a Ferrari-based replica, following the pattern of the early 125S, at the Geneva auto show in 1974. Around the same time, Panther also produced an aluminum-bodied version of the Triumph Dolomite, named the Rio. With a 2.0-liter four that developed 127 hp, the Rio was claimed to accelerate to 60 mph in 8.7 seconds and hit 115 mph.

Late in 1980, the Panther firm was acquired by a South Korean businessman named Young Chull Kim. By 1981, each of the existing models was abandoned and the company focused on conversions of other makes.

Panthers, including the Lima's replacement, the Kallista, were assembled in England using South Korean-manufactured aluminum bodies and chassis. By the mid-1980s, the Kallista roadster (which evolved from the Lima by 1982) was offered in the U.S. market. This roadster actually came with either Ford four-cylinder or V-6 engines.

Two roadster models were available and differed mainly by their engines—either a 1.6-liter four or a 2.8-liter V-6. Prices in 1982 were 6,945 pounds and 7,485 pounds, respectively. The Kallista with the

fuel-injected V-6 was 8,985 pounds.

The smaller engine was an overhead-cam four-cylinder with an 80 x 79.5-mm bore and stroke and 1597 cc. This five-main-bearing power plant had a Weber-Venturi carburetor and a 9.5:1 compression ratio. It generated 96 hp at 6000 rpm and 98 lbs.-ft. of torque at 4000 rpm. The four-main-bearing V-6, fitted with a Solex-Venturi carburetor and using a slightly lower 9.2:1 compression ratio, was good for 135 hp at 5200 rpm and 162 lbs.-ft. of torque at 3000 rpm. When fitted with Bosch K-Jetronic fuel-injection, the 2.8-liter V-6 was rated 150 hp at 5700 rpm and 159 lbs.-ft. of torque at 4000 rpm. The carbureted V-6 was good for 110 mph and the fuel-injected V-6 was 13 mph faster.

The Kallista had a 100.4-in. wheelbase and an overall length of 153.7 in. It was 49 in. high and 67.3 in. wide with a front tread of 57.5 in. and a rear tread width of 54.3 in. Five-speed manual or three-speed automatic transmissions were available. The Kallista had rack-and-pinion steering like the Lima The front suspension used A-arms with coil springs. At the rear was a rigid axle with trailing arms, a Panhard rod, and coil springs. Front disc/rear drum brakes were used.

By 1985 the Kallista had entered the U.S. market. Cars certified here were powered by a Mustang 2.3-liter four-cylinder engine. In 1989, the Kallista was still listed for $24,000 and could be ordered with a five-speed manual gearbox or a four-speed automatic transmission.

Andrew Morland

*The unique Panther Lima roadster began production in 1976.*

# PEERLESS

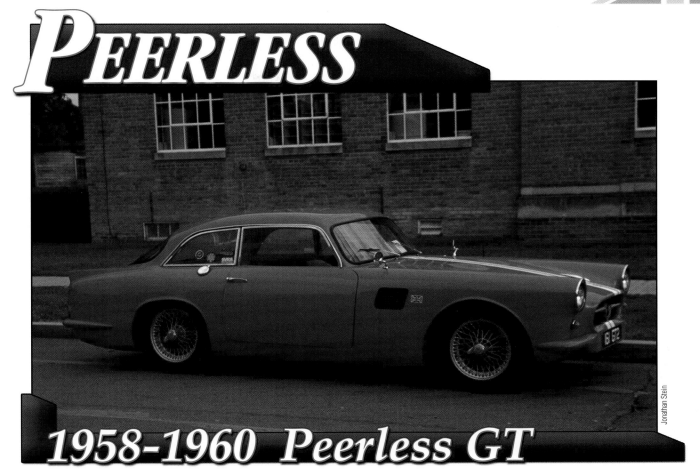

Jonathan Stein

# 1958-1960 Peerless GT

E ven when a specialty motorcar doesn't quite succeed, it often leads to something better—or at least to something else. So went the short-lived Peerless, a British-built four-seat sports coupe of the late 1950s. Produced by a company that had been formed by Bernard Rodger, the prototype coupe was announced in August 1957 and appeared at the Paris Salon that fall.

The car was called the Warwick and displayed a "W" in the center of its grille. The "Warwick" prototype was announced in August 1957, but wasn't sold in England as a Peerless until after the Earl's Court (London) Auto Show of October 1958. The Peerless name stemmed from the fact that production took place in a garage that, after World War I, was a sales site for reconditioned American-made Peerless trucks.

Wearing a 16-gauge aluminum body (with fiberglass molded floor, bulkhead, trunk area, etc.), the prototype Gran Turismo coupe rode an electrically-welded tubular space frame. Performance wasn't its only "plus" factor.

"The Peerless GT," said a Paris show brochure, "is, for the first time in a small car, a real 4-seater for full-sized adults," with "over 7 cubic feet of usable space" for luggage. The brochure also promised European motorists 30-mpg economy.

Ads for the Peerless GT Two-Litre announced a "fine English Gran Tourismo four-seater coupe with competition performance and a moderate price. In addition to abundant luggage space, the Peerless "…combines exhilarating performance, extraordinary road-holding characteristics, and four-seat passenger comfort to make it a highly desirable car for all-around driving."

Servicing problems were kept to a minimum using Triumph mechanical pieces, including the TR3 engine and gearbox. Twin wishbones and coil springs were used for the independent front suspension with a De Dion tube on semi-elliptic leaf springs at the rear, with a Salisbury differential and Layrub propeller shaft. Sankey

***The Peerless used a Triumph engine and running gear under its body shell.***

15-in. 4J steel disc wheels held 5.50 x 15 Avon Turbo-Speed tires. Dunlop center-lock wire wheels with 4J rims were optional. Two side-mounted gas tanks held seven gallons each. Either left or right hand steering was available. Air slats provided ventilation. Options included a Laycock de Normanville overdrive on the upper three gears of the four-speed box.

By mid-1958, Peerless bodies were being made from fiberglass, rather than aluminum, by James Whitson and Co. Ltd. The aero-styled profile was made of polyester resin reinforced with fiberglass. The four-seat coupe's clean, upright profile featured long rear quarter windows and rounded wheel openings.

A simple oval front opening held crossbar-style grille bars and a round insignia with the letter "P" in its center. Tiny round parking lights stood below the headlamps. Slim wraparound bumpers were installed. Standard body colors were red, white, blue, grey, and British Racing Green.

The interior featured genuine foam-padded leather seats, carpeting, an adjustable wood-rim steering wheel, a fresh air heater/defroster, electric wipers, and a recessed instrument panel. The luggage compartment held eight cubic feet of cargo. In Britain, the standard Peerless model sold for 998 pounds or just under $4,000.

American automotive journalists praised the Peerless as being more civilized than a TR3. *Road & Track* proclaimed the coupe was worth its U.S. asking price. It hit 110 mph with fuel economy in the 32-mpg neighborhood.

"There is a certain pleasure in driving a 'fooler,'" the testers said. "It is a great deal more satisfying to have a car which invites comments from fellow enthusiasts. The Peerless assures both fun and comments".

Compared to the Triumph TR3, *Road & Track* noted Peerless "... has the same engine noises and exhaust notes, but . . . is a distinctive and quite different automobile with its own 'feel.'" During testing, they found the Peerless to be "nearly as good to 70 mph, slightly better over the standing quarter-mile and definitely faster to 90," adding "...once the Peerless gets over 70 mph its streamlining is enough to offset the disadvantage of its 3.7 axle and it will equal the performance of the TR3 with the 4.10 axle ratio."

The 1959 Phase 2 Peerless brought a few improvements, notably in body finish, recessed headlights moldings, a mesh grille pattern, and the addition of sharp-edged tailfins. There were no chassis modifications. The seats, floor tray, wheel arches, and more were made of the same fiberglass-reinforced polyester resin material as the body. The black padded Vynide fascia board had a typewriter finish on the recessed instrument panel. A carpet-lined glove box was used.

The wraparound rear bumpers went within a few inches of the back wheels, stopping inside the vertical taillights. The battery was moved inside to the left front fender. A quick-release gas cap stood on the left side, below the swing-out rear quarter window.

Unfortunately, the Peerless blend of styling, sportiness, luxury and performance failed to capture a sufficient number of American customers.

Predicted production levels of 25 cars per week never materialized and the cars were criticized for poor assembly and finish, as well as noise problems. Bernard Rodger filed for bankruptcy in January 1960.

About 325 Peerless coupes were built, including some 250 in a one-year period.

The end of the car wasn't the end of the story. After the bankruptcy, Bernard Rodger served as technical director of the Warwick firm. He planned to build an improved Peerless.

The Warwick GT was made from 1960-1962. It also used a 100-bhp Triumph TR3 engine and transmission with bodies from the James Whitson firm.

Similar in appearance to the Peerless, the Warwick GT had a recessed oval grille with crosshatch pattern and vertical center divider, tiny round parking lights below the headlights, and a sloping hood. Large rear quarter windows were used.

The price was 1,620 pounds with overdrive as standard equipment. Dunlop wire wheels were the only option.

Expectations of building five cars per week never materialized. and the company ran out of cash quickly. No more than 59 Warwicks were produced—and some sources suggest half that number.

Bernard Rodger bought the company in December 1960, but it didn't last much longer. Rodger and Rowland Ham (managing director, later chairman) then experimented with a Warwick powered by a 3.5-liter Buick aluminum V-8.

Aimed at American buyers, the car entered production in the summer of 1961. It was built through 1964, two years longer than the Triumph-engined version. This concept later evolved into the Gordon-Keeble.

*The short-lived Peerless GT was an innovative car but was not popular in America.*

# RELIANT

Thomas Touw

# 1962-1963 Sabre SEI

Early in 1935, designer Tom L. Williams founded the firm Reliant Engineering Co. Ltd., in Tomworth, England. Williams created a prototype of a three-wheeler with a one-cylinder engine and chain drive. Williams was no stranger to powered three-wheelers, having designed the Safety Seven a few years earlier at the Raleigh Cycle Company. When Raleigh discontinued this three-wheel van, Williams obtained the rights and began to arrange for production on his own.

In mid-1935, the first such van was ready for delivery. A two-cylinder version with shaft drive arrived in the following year. Reliant was building its own bodies by 1936. A four-cylinder model (using an Austin Seven engine) came out in 1938. By the time World War II erupted, Reliant was turning out its own engine, which was similar to the Austin design. Van production resumed early in 1946, months after the war ended.

Passenger-car production began in 1952 with the Regal, an open four-seater with a three-wheel layout. The lightweight design could be registered as a motorcycle in Britain. Within a year, examples of the compact three-wheeler began to arrive on the West Coast of the U.S. A switch from the original metal bodies to fiberglass construction came in 1956.

Unlike most automakers of that day, Reliant didn't stick close to home, but helped initiate operations in developing nations. Starting in 1958, a Sussita station wagon that was based on a Reliant design went into production in Israel. That was followed by the Sabra sports car, which was constructed on a ladder frame chassis designed by Lesley Ballamy of Reliant.

Autocars Company Ltd., an Israeli company, bought the rights to Ballamay's design and one of Ashley's fiberglass bodies. Reliant also re-engineered a 1703-cc Ford Consul engine for the project. These components were turned into the Sabra, which was produced in Haifa, Israel, between 1959 and 1964.

Reliant supplied Autocars with 200 "kits," but it is not known exactly how many Sabras were assembled.

The Reliant Sabre was based on the Sabra. The chassis no. 1 roadster-convertible was actually built as a prototype in 1960 and this powder blue car still survives. The production model SE1 arrived in 1961. The British version of the two-seat roadster had the same styling and a removable hard top.

The curvaceous fiberglass-body had a low, protruding nose that carried a tilted grille. A front-hinged nose gave full access to the engine for servicing. The front fenders bulged above hood level. On

*The Reliant Sabre and the Israeli Sabra had nearly identical styling.*

the hood was a large air scoop in front of a curved windshield. Massive twin vertical bumpers were mounted alongside the oval grille opening, which contained two vertical center ribs. The headlights had bright rims and stood far back from the nose. Round parking lights were mounted farther forward, alongside the bumpers. The front wheel openings were rounded and the rear wheel openings were squared-off.

At the rear of the car was a molded-in, wraparound-style bumper with vertical taillights. The back-up lights were mounted at the base, with round lamps alongside. A recessed gas filler cap was seen on the left side, while a lid at the rear gave access to a small luggage area. Luggage access was limited, however, as the lid could not open fully.

Both an open two-seater with folding soft top and, later, a closed Gran Turismo (GT) coupe were available. On both models the bodies were molded in reinforced fiberglass. Inside, the cockpit was said to be spacious enough to permit "straight arm" driving if desired. Hooded instruments in the glare-free, aircraft-type fascia included a speedometer, tachometer, water temperature and oil pressure gauges and clock. Aero-style seats gave maximum support for fast cornering. Standard equipment included a wood-rimmed steering wheel, carpeting, a heater and simulated knock-off wheel covers.

The Ford Consul engine was an in-line, overhead-valve four-cylinder with cast iron block and head. It had an 82.6 x 79.5-mm bore and stroke. With a 7.8:1 compression ratio and single Zenith carburetor, the solid-lifter four produced 57 hp at 4400 rpm. The four-cylinder engine was also available in a "high-tune" with an 8.9:1 compression ratio and twin S.U. carburetors, in which format it produced up to 73 hp. A hydraulically-operated clutch hooked up with the ZF four-speed synchromesh gearbox. The four-cylinder model had a top speed of 90 to 93 mph and accelerated through the quarter mile in about 20 seconds.

For the 1962 model year, a six-cylinder version of the Sabre became available. This SE2 model used a 2553-cc Ford Zodiac engine. This motor had an 82.6 x 79.5-mm bore and stroke., solid valve lifters, an 8.3:1 compression ratio, and one Zenith carburettor. It was rated for 109 hp at 4800 rpm. The six-cylinder engine was linked to a Ford gearbox. The six could hit 111 mph and did the quarter mile in 17.6 seconds. Unfortunately, it cost about the same as an Austin-Healey 3000, which made it hard to sell.

The appearance of the six-cylinder model was modified from the four-cylinder version. It adopted a more conventional GT/sports coupe look with clean, uncluttered lines and 2 + 2 seating capacity. Full rounded wheel openings surrounding wire wheels and modestly finned rear fenders helped give the fastback coupe an attractive stance.

Both cars used a 90-in. wheelbase, but the 165-in. long four-cylinder model was 5-1/2 in. longer than the six-cylinder version. Both models were 61 in. wide, but the six had 50-in. front and rear tread widths, two inches wider than the four. Coil springs were used all around on all models, along with front disc/rear drum brakes. The final drive ratio was 3.55:1 or 3.58:1. Standard tires were size 155 x 15 on the four and 165 x 15 on the six.

Thomas Touw

# 1964-1985 *Scimitar*

Reliant introduced a four-seat, four-wheeled mini-sedan called the Rebel in 1964 and also gained considerable publicity among sports car and GT car fans with a car that was seldom seen in the United States. This 2+2 coupe was called the Scimitar GT (a.k.a. Scimitar coupe or SE4).

Like other Reliants, the new grand touring coupe wore a fiberglass body styled by David Ogle Associates. This industrial design firm was founded in 1960 by David Ogle in Letchworth, north of London.

The two-door, fibreglass body was hand moulded at Reliant's old factory in Tamworth, England. The complete shell was bonded together. The SE4 had quad headlights in recessed housings. An insignia stood just ahead of the horizontal hood lid. The doors held vent windows. A body side trim crease followed the line of the front wheel opening, extending to the rear of the car.

In England, the base price for the 2,200-lb. Scimitar coupe was 1,068 pounds. Very few Scimitars were ever brought to the United States—though Reliant experts say 1,005 coupes were produced.

The Scimitar sports car was initially powered by a specially tuned Ford Zephyr in-line, overhead-valve six with a cast-iron block and head. This four-main-bearing, solid-lifter engine had an 82.6 x 79.5-mm bore and stroke and displaced 2553 cc. With an 8.3:1 compression ratio and three S.U. HS4 carburetors it produced 120 hp at 5000 rpm and 140 lbs.-ft.. of torque at 2600 rpm.

Overdrive was optional for the Scimitar's full-synchromesh four-speed manual transmission. The overdrive provided direct drive in top gear, controlled by a dashboard switch. The car's top speed was 117 to 121 mph and accelerated through the quarter mile in 18 seconds. It could go from 0-to-50 in 8.5 seconds with about 19 mpg fuel economy.

The Scimitar coupe had a 92-in. wheelbase, was 167 in. long, 51.5 in. high, and 64 in. wide. Both the front and rear treads measured 50

*The Reliant Scimitar was a 2+2 built with a fiberglass body.*

in. The center-lock wire wheels held 165 x 15 tires. The standard final drive ratio was 3.88:1. Rack-and-pinion steering was fitted. The front suspension consisted of wishbones and coil springs with a rigid axle, and coil springs and a modified Watt linkage at the rear. Front disc/rear drum brakes were standard, as was a 24-gallon gas tank.

A 2994-cc (3-liter) V-6 engine replaced the in-line six in 1967. This cast-iron, overhead-valve power plant came with a 93.7 x 72.4-mm bore and stroke. It had four main bearings, an 8.9:1 compression ratio, and a Weber two-barrel carburetor. It was good for 144 hp at 4750 rpm and 192 lbs.-ft. of torque at 3000 rpm.

Later, it was followed by an optional 2495-cc (2.5-liter) V-6 with 9.1:1 compression and a Zenith carburettor that produced 119 hp at 4750 rpm and 146 lbs.-ft. of torque at 3000 rpm. Other 1967 Scimitar GT specifications remained similar to those of the 1966 model.

A new Grand Touring Estate (GTE) station wagon was introduced in 1968. According to the sales brochure, it combined the features of a grand touring coupe with those of an estate car. The GTE came with the larger V-6, rode a longer 99.5-in. wheelbase, and was 171 in. long. Steel disc wheels and 185 x 14 tires were used. Quite quick for a station wagon, even with automatic transmission, the GTE went from 0-to-60 mph in less than 10 seconds.

Quad round headlights stood in slightly recessed housings alongside a small rectangular grille with thin horizontal bars. "Scimitar" block letters sat above the grille. Sword emblems were on the hood and the cowl.

Body colors included Nevada Yellow, Wessex Green, Shetland Blue, Highland Purple, Everest White, Beaujolais Red, Capricorn Blue and Ivory Beige. Interiors came in black or tan. Standard features

included a 140-mph speedometer, a 7,000-rpm tachometer, reclining aero-type front seats (upholstered in leathercloth), fold-down rear seats, a clock, a lighter, front and rear wiper/washers, and a two-speaker Radiomobile radio. Overdrive was standard and a Borg-Warner three-speed automatic transmission was optional.

Resdesigned in 1975, the GTE became the SE6. It was longer, wider, and higher, and rode on a longer 104-in. wheelbase. Appearance was similar to earlier models, but the inner headlights were smaller and had rectangular inner housings. They were connected with the blacked-out rectangular grille. Its rear seats folded indvidually.

Standard SE6 equipment included a 140-mph speedometer, a 7000-rpm tachometer, a heated rear window, two-speed intermittent wipers, a tinted windshield, a gas-strut-supported rear window opening, and reclining front seats.

Twelve body colors were available with interiors in black, dark blue, chocolate or tan. Factory literature promised "...high maximum speed approaching 120 mph, vivid acceleration and economical fuel consumption." An overdrive four-speed manual transmission was standard and a three-speed automatic transmission was optional.

GTE Estate production continued into 1985, with later versions employing a 2.8-liter V-6. Reliant claimed the GTE was "...accepted throughout the motoring world as the original high-performance estate." Sales literature described it as "reminiscent of traditional sports cars in its performance and feel, [providing] the modern inter-city executive with effortless motorway travel."

The Reliant GTE was a favorite car of stars and many were owned by well-known British personalities during the 1970s. Included were members of the Royal family. Princess Anne had seven GTEs and reportedly still owns one. She was even caught speeding in her GTE. A convertible version of Reliant's sports car arrived in 1980, joining the GTE Estate. Reliant said it was a "...stylish and sophisticated high performance 4 seater . . . a reminder of your earlier sports car days or the realization of a dream." The rear seats folded individually and the GTS convertible was promoted as a car that offered the "exhilaration of an open car . . . for the whole family." Its appearance and specifications were similar to the GTE, with a slim targa bar evident when the top was folded.

A galvanized chassis and the efficient Ford engines gave the Reliant great longevity according to Reliant experts.

In 1984, Reliant announced a new and completely different replacement for the Scimitar, called the SS1 or Small Sports. It was powered by either a 1.3-liter or 1.6-liter Ford engine and was designed by Michelotti.

Billed as the "affordable small sports car," this open two-seater was remarkably quick, especially when it was teamed with an optional 1.8-liter turbocharged engine.

Reliant three-wheelers also remained in production throughout this period. Reliant bought out the Bond company (another producer of three-wheeled vehicles) in 1969 and soon was producing about three-fourths of all British three-wheelers.

*The Reliant Sabre Six looked like an MGB-GT or Triumph GT-6 but was not marketed in North America.*

# RILEY

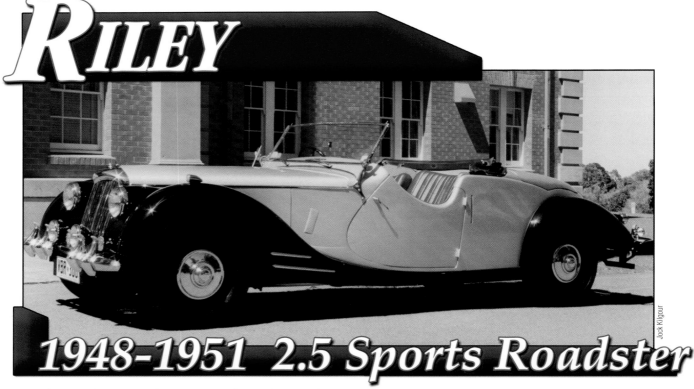

Jock Kilgour

# 1948-1951 2.5 Sports Roadster

L ike several other British motor car makers, Riley traced its origins to fabric making and to the manufacture of woven materials and the machines to create them. In 1890, the weaving business was fading fast and William Riley added a bicycle plant. By 1898, Percy Riley, one of William's five sons, created a two-seat motorized vehicle with a single-cylinder engine noted for its use of mechanically actuated intake valves. Just before the turn of the century, the Riley Cycle Company sold three- and four-wheel powered cycles.

After relying on engines from outside sources, three of the younger Rileys set up a separate firm to produce their own power plants using Percy's valve configuration. By 1907, with their vehicles using steering wheels and other automotive details, they turned toward making a full-fledged car.

Powered by a 12/18-hp 90-degree V-twin engine, it wore the world's first detachable wire wheels. Riley soon became best known for producing the wire wheels—and founded a separate company to concentrate on producing two- or four-cylinder automobiles.

Through the early 1920s, Riley turned out a new open four-seater with 2.5-liter four-cylinder engine and four-speed gearbox. While not a true two-seat sports car, the Redwinger, in particular, still earned a fair number of racing trophies.

By 1926, the famed Riley Nine carried an engine design that would be used for the next three decades. Pushrods from twin camshafts high on each side of the cylinder block actuated the inclined overhead valves, while pistons reached toward hemispherical combustion chambers. More than 10,000 Nines were built through 1938, including at least 100 low-slung Brookland editions and about 75 short-wheelbase Imps.

Fluid flywheels and Wilson preselector gearboxes became available on Rileys by 1934. A year later came the 1496-cc four-cylinder engine. It was destined to power 1.5-liter Rileys for two decades. Among the notable bodies to carry the 1.5-liter four were the Kestrel and the limited-production Sprite two-seater, introduced in 1936.

A handful of six-cylinder and V-8 Rileys also appeared during the 1930s, including the rare 1934-'35 MPH two-seater, but four-cylinder engines remained the company's forte. Financial woes led to receivership in 1938, followed by acquisition by Lord Nuffield and

*The stately 1949 2.5 Riley sports roadster is owned by Jock Kilgour of Belair, South Australia.*

subsequent takeover by Morris Motors.

Postwar production began before the end of 1945 with an all-new 1.5-liter Twelve four-door saloon. It wore a fresh body, but had Riley's traditional look and succeeded the pre-war saloon of 1939-1940. Its redesigned chassis used torsion-bar front suspension and updated exterior styling. Late in 1946, a similar-looking 2.5-liter model joined the smaller Riley. It was also offered only in four-door saloon form, but on a longer wheelbase. In 1948, Riley production moved from its traditional Coventry site to the MG plant at Abingdon. Drophead coupe and roadster models arrived that year.

The 2.5-liter roadster was Riley's version of a sports car. Its grille was slightly slanted, with adjacent faired-in headlights and tiny parking lights atop the front fenders. Auxiliary lights were mounted on the front bumper. Both the front and rear end held split bumpers.

Riley's "torsionic front suspension," said a sales brochure, "keeps you on a level keel--all the time." The torsion bars ran parallel to the frame side rails. A rigid axle with semi-elliptic leaf springs brought up the rear. Standard equipment included a Bluemel three-spoke steering wheel on an adjustable column with English leather upholstery and walnut wood trim.

Riley's 149-cid (2443-cc) engine had twin camshafts, short pushrods and rockers, valves set at 90 degrees, and hemispherical combustion chambers. It had three main bearings, solid valve lifters, 12-volt electricals, a 6.8:1 compression ratio and twin S.U. H4 carburettors. The engine delivered 100 hp at 4500 rpm and 134 lbs.-ft. of torque at 3000 rpm. Riley claimed a top speed of 100 mph, although road testers didn't reach that speed.

The roadster—and its companion drophead coupe—never delivered expected sales success, largely because of their relatively high price and low power output. The price at the factory in England was approximately $2,682 for the 2.5-liter Sport Roadster. A total of 507 roadsters (and 502 drophead coupes) were produced, from 1948 to 1951.

In America, Riley's three-seater roadster was priced at $3,500 and featured a fold-down flat windshield, rakish cutdown rear-hinged doors with gracefully curved leading edges like the saloon, and drophead and specially designed bumper overriders.

Riley literature claimed the roadster's trunk would "...carry easily four suitcases, two attaché cases and a bag of golf clubs." The sporty drophead coupe (which carried a $3,600 P.O.E. price) was described as a "...sleek, open-to-the-air, high performer for those days when the sun makes you feel it's good to be alive."

The Sports Roadster first appeared in the spring of 1948 and the drophead coupe arrived late that same year. For 1949, Riley's convertible tops were released from the dashboard, rather than from outside. The 1949 instruments were grouped on a mahogany center facia panel with a round clock on one side and matching speedometer on the other.

Production of the drophead coupe ceased in 1950 and the roadster was dropped in 1951.

Corporate literature for all three models promised the thrill of sports car performance adding: "Its proverbial high speed, exceptional road holding, and safe braking make it a thrill to drive. Its fine styling makes it a thrill to own."

Ads in 1953 by J.S. Inskip Inc. in New York City promised "the touring car with sports car performance," quoting a price of $3,700. The 2.5-litre was "For the man who wants an automobile that performs like a racer yet has the refinements of a luxury, all-purpose car...[with] "...remarkable successes in the most competitive events all over the world, including Monte Carlo Rallies and Alpine Trials."

In 1952, British Motor Corp. (BMC) was formed by the merger of Austin and Morris (including Riley). As a final irony (some might say insult), the distinguished diamond-shaped Riley badge was soon seen on 1960s BMC clones like the Mini-based Elf and 1100-level Kestrel. The last new Rileys were produced in 1969. "Real" examples had left the market long before that year and the last "sports cars" departed even earlier.

Rod Richards/Riley Club of So. Australia

# SINGER

OCW Archive

# 1946-1954 Nine Roadster

**S**inger is an old-line British motor car firm, founded by George Singer at Coventry in 1905. Singer started with bicycles and turned out "Xtraordinary" two-wheelers—as well as tricycles—at his plant beginning in 1876. In 1901, Singer obtained rights to the Perks and Birch motor wheel and began producing motorized bicycles and tricycles. Power was applied to the front wheel. These evolved into three-wheeled vehicles with steering wheels.

Two cars entered the picture in 1905, manufactured under license from Lea-Francis. They had horizontal engines and 30-in. long connecting rods. Additional models arrived the following year powered by two-, three-, and four-cylinder engines. The four was of more conventional construction. Singer soon adopted front-mounted vertical power plants.

Financial woes forced Singer into receivership in 1908 and George Singer died the next year. After faltering, Singer and Co. Ltd. was revived and re-formed. Most engines, during the next few years, were supplied by White and Poppe, though some were produced by Singer. The company was known for small-engined cars throughout its history, but the biggest Singer came early: a 4.1 liter model available prior to the outbreak of World War I. And the little 1.1-liter Ten debuted in 1912 and remained in the lineup after the Armistice. Motorcycle production ended in 1915.

After the war, Singer introduced a sports edition of the Ten that was capable of 60 mph. A 2.0-liter L-head six-cylinder engine emerged in 1922. Four-wheel brakes became available in 1924. The 1926

*The Singer Nine of the late 1940s and early 1950s was advertised as "the perfect light roadster."*

lineup included the four-seat Junior with an 848-cc overhead-cam engine. Juniors turned out to be quite popular, selling at least 25,000 copies over a four-year period. Singer's success made it England's number three car producer by 1928. The basic Singer engine design continued through 1956.

Singer's Ten, with a 1.3-liter engine, became the Senior by 1927. Cone clutches departed in 1928 and the Junior adopted four-wheel brakes. In 1932, the Singer Nine two-seater replaced the Junior. By that time, Singers were available with left-hand drive for export. A total of eight models were available in 1932. In 1933, Singer looked to early success with the sports car market and redesigned the Nine to create the 972-cc Nine Sports, followed by the Nine Le Mans. The Nines performed well in reliability trials, but three of four Singer entries in the 1935 Tourist Trophy Race suffered severe steering failures.

Some Singers adopted no-clutch gearshifting in 1934 and independent front suspension was installed on the new Eleven, with its overhead-cam engine. The aerodynamic Eleven Airstream was said to have been inspired by the Czechoslovakian Tatra. Customers didn't care for its unconventional look. Singer introduced a Bantam model in 1936. Depression-era plant closures and financial ills led to a reshuffling and a 1937 name change to Singer Motors Ltd. Over the next decade and a half, Singer engines wound up beneath the bonnets of the limited-production HRG sports car.

Shortly before World War II, Singer introduced a Nine roadster which returned after the war. Singer re-entered the postwar market with the Nine roadster, plus the Ten and Twelve sedans. Postwar Singers were produced in Birmingham. Marketing to the U.S. began and sales literature was distributed by Fergus Motors of New York City. One sales catalog said the Nine had "new post-war improvements" that made it "the perfect light roadster of today." A Nine: "…combines excellent performance with smart lines and ample body-space…the ideal car for every driver…"

The four-passenger Nine roadster had an East Coast Port of Entry price of $2,195. It included adjustable front bucket seats with leather upholstery. The headlights were mounted between the fenders and radiator with tiny parking lights that sat on the fenders. The chrome radiator grille, with wide vertical slats, sat ahead of the four-panel hood. The Nine also had a sloping rear deck. Knurled nuts permitted one-piece windshield adjustment.

The 1074-cc overhead cam four developed 37 hp at 5000 rpm. It had three main bearings, solid valve lifters, a 6.9:1 compression ratio and an S.U. downdraft carburetor. A British road tester put its top speed at 65 mph. It required 37.6 seconds to go 0-to-60 mph and 24.7 seconds to do the standing-start quarter mile. The engine joined a three-speed gearbox. The "Easy Clean" wheels held 5.00 x 16 tires. The frame was underslung at the rear. Riding a 91-in. wheelbase, the Nine measured 149.75 in. overall, including the front and rear bumpers.

The 1,736-lb. roadster's cut-down doors were hinged at the front. Side curtains with rigid glass and chrome-plated bumpers were included. Improvements over the prewar model included moving the engine three inches forward. That allowed additional space between

the front and rear seats and to improve the car's ride. Standard colors available on early postwar Nine roadsters included maroon with fawn or burgundy upholstery, black with brown, fawn or Signal Red upholstery and Signal Red with matching Signal Red upholstery.

In 1950, Nine roadster modifications gave it a 4A designation and slashed the U.S. market price. Singer sales literature advised the revised model had some "really worth-while improvements," including a four-speed gearbox, which would deliver "a new thrill, as well as an entirely fresh conception of light car performance." Greater seating capacity and refined trim made it the "perfect light Roadster of today."

Nines now were upholstered in Vynide imitation leather with real leather now optional. Glass windows also were optional. Standard colors included maroon with burgundy upholstery, black or Signal Red with Signal Red upholstery, grey with red upholstery, and green with brown upholstery.

A 1951 ad showed Lucille Ball sitting in her Singer Nine roadster. "For economy minded America," the ad read, "the perfect light roadster of today is the four passenger Singer … the easiest handling car you've ever owned."

The Singer 4A was followed by the 4AB, 4AC, and 4AD models which were introduced about the same time. The 4AB carried over the 4A's 1074-cc engine and introduced independent front suspension to Singers. The 4AD, also known as the SM 1500 Roadster, was the export version of the 4AB and was powered by a larger 1497-cc engine. An interim 4AC Singer was considered but not put into production according to Singer expert Peter McKercher of Ottawa, Ontario.

The Singer 4AD (the SM 1500) was a popular Singer offering and was sold by Vaughan Motors of New York City and Vaughan-Singer Motors of Hollywood, California. Vaughan even modified some of the Singers with louvered bonnets plus different cams and ignition timing.

OCW Archive

# 1950-1956 SM 1500/SMX Roadster

**S**inger Motors, Ltd., of Birmingham, England, made scaled-down versions of large passenger cars since the early days of the automotive industry. In 1949, Singer introduced its best known car in America: the SM 1500. Singer made 428 sedans in that series in its first year—a figure that jumped to 6,358 by 1952. Enthusiasts enjoyed the SM 1500 roadster, of which 3,450

*Singer portrayed the SM 1520/ SMS in this official 1952 publicity shot.*

were built over the full model run.

The Singer roadster made inroads into the tremendous popularity enjoyed by the MG TD roadster by 1953, although prewar-styled sports cars soon dropped off in sales, beginning around 1954, as the modern Jaguar XK120 and Austin-Healey 100 gained recognition.

The 1949 SM 1500 sedan had an all-new notchback profile and up to six passengers. It had a steering-column-mounted gearshift lever. Flush fenders contained built-in headlights and the grille was made up of horizontal bars that were longer at the base which formed a curve at the left and right. Small round parking lights sat directly below the headlights on a nearly flat front panel. Standard body colors were Geneva Blue, Cotswold Beige, Warwick Green, and black, each with beige upholstery. The instrument panel contained a speedometer, electric clock, and gauges ahead of the driver.

Production of the modern-styled sedan continued with little change in 1950, but the big news was the debut of a new SM roadster. According to the company's sale brochure, the roadster was created exclusively for export. It was displayed at the Paris auto show in 1951. The new roadster was often referred to as simply the SM or SM Sports model. It weighed 1,848 lbs. and carried an East Coast P.O.E. price of $1,995. A 1952 advertisement focused on California, advising the Singer SM Sports Roadster was "…your answer to California's challenge of the open road."

The three-main-bearings engine used in the SM 1500 was an important part of its growing threat to MG sales. While the earlier Nine roadster was viewed as under-powered, the later roadster used the same 1497-cc inline, overhead-cam four-cylinder employed in the SM 1500 sedan. It had a cast-iron block and head with a 73 x 89.4-mm bore and stroke and a 7.0:1 compression ratio. A single Solex F.A.I. downdraft carburetor was used. Output was rated 48/50 hp at 4500 rpm. The SM 1500 roadster's top speed was in the 73 to 77 mph range. It moved from 0-to-60 mph in 18.9 seconds according to one road tester, but another said it took 24.3 seconds. The quarter-mile acceleration time was about 20.9 seconds.

The 1954 Singer offered even more performance twin Solex downdraft carburettors and a 7.47:1 compression ratio. It developed 58 hp at 4600 rpm. The 0-to-60-mph time was reduced to 14 seconds and maximum speed increased to 84 mph.

The SM 1500 roadster shared the 91-in. wheelbase of the Singer Nine roadster and was only about an inch longer with a 152-in. bumper-to-bumper measurement. It was slightly higher at 58.5 in. and slightly wider at 58 in. The front tread was 46.75 in. Size 5.50 x 16 tires were standard fare.

A four-speed manual transmission was used with overall gear ratios of 14.5:1 in first, 9.45:1 in second, 6.12:1 in third and 4.87:1 in fourth. The standard final drive ratio was 4.87:1. Worm-and-ball steering was used and the front suspension featured wishbones with coil springs and an anti-roll device. At the rear was a rigid axle with semi-elliptic leaf springs. Drum brakes were used all around.

Singer made automotive history at the 1954 London Auto Show by becoming the first British carmaker to offer a completely fiberglass-bodied car—called the SMX roadster. Only four examples were ever built. Singer grew reluctant about the SMX when it became apparent the production of high quality fiberglass body panels was beyond the company's capabilities. Singer commissioned the tooling required to make steel-bodied versions of the SMX, but retooling costs for the new design were prohibitively expensive. The SMX was killed after the four fiberglass-bodied cars were built.

The SMX styling significantly updated the SM with its single round headlights built into the front fenders. A sloping rear end incorporated a non-opening deck and the old-fashioned "open body tub" that hid under a tonneau cover. The fiberglass body was said to be stronger than Singer's regular Duraluminum body and five times stronger than a steel body. A full four-seat roadster, the SMX had front bucket seats and a rear bench seat. A forward-tilting rear panel provided access to the rear luggage compartment.

The fiberglass SMX body consisted of five separate panels. The hood and front fenders were molded as a single section that could be lifted to expose the engine. The doors were separate sections. A fourth section was the cowling over the firewall, which supported the chrome-framed windshield. The last section was the rear deck and rear fenders.

The lightweight SMX roadster was equipped with the the 58-hp engine featuring the higher compression ratio and twin Solex carburetors. Its standard gear ratios were 14.53:1 in low, 9.45:1 in second, 6.12:1 in third, and 4.88:1 in high. With a 1,820-lb. car weight, the plastic-bodied SMX was said to have a 90-mph top speed. Like other Singers, it rode a 91-in. wheelbase and was about 151.5 in. long. It carried a larger 10-gal. petrol tank and 5.50 x 15 tires. The smaller-diameter, larger cross-sectional tires were fitted to deliver a better quality ride.

Late in 1955, Singer was acquired by Rootes, controlled by William Rootes. This led to the Gazelle, essentially a Hillman Minx with Singer's overhead-cam engine. The Singer name appeared on cars as late as 1970, but after 1958 they were little more than badge-engineered Rootes models. The era of Singer as a separate entity was gone.

*This 1936 Singer was called the Le Mans Speed Special.*

# SUNBEAM

Andrew Morland

# 1953-1955 Alpine

John Marston's late 19th-century business in Great Britain was metal lacquering, but his avocation was cycling. In 1887 he formed the Sunbeamland Cycle Factory at Wolverhampton. It evolved into John Marston Ltd. In 1899, the company's first prototype automobile came out of the shop. A two-cylinder vehicle followed in 1901. Those cars led to the first production model—the Sunbeam Mabley Voiturette.

By 1909, Sunbeam offered a selection of chain-driven models with L-head four-cylinder engines. The T-head 14/18-hp model followed with either chain or shaft drive. Sunbeam became involved in racing during these early years, which helped their bottom line as did production of ambulances, aircraft, and marine engines during World War I.,

Sunbeam joined with Talbot and Darracq in 1920 to form STD Motors Ltd. Some of Sunbeam's 1920s sports-touring models carried Talbot overhead-cam engines. By 1927, Sunbeams set the world land speed record on five separate occasions. Sunbeam offered a straight-eight engine in 1926, then eliminated their four-cylinder models after 1927.

After 1935, Sunbeam ceased to exist as an independent. The STD (Sunbeam-Talbot-Darracq) combination failed, went into receivership and Rootes purchased what was left. By 1938, several variants of Rootes' Hillman Minx and Humber Super Snipe were on the market, under the Sunbeam-Talbot nameplate. A new company was formed: Sunbeam-Talbot Ltd. A 2-litre model also debuted, then reappeared—along with

*The Sunbeam Alpine was considered "the new queen of sports cars" in 1953.*

the Ten—after World War II. Those two were produced into 1948, followed by Sunbeam-Talbot 80 and 90 saloons and drophead coupes.

The type 80 lasted only until 1950, but the 90's engine grew from 1944 to 2267 cc. The 90 formed the basis for the Alpine sports car. Early postwar cars were marketed as Sunbeams in France (to avoid confusion with Talbot-Lago). The Talbot name was dropped on the sports car first and later on other cars. Sunbeam-Talbot Ltd. remained the corporate name until 1970. The cars were built at Ryton-on-Dunsmore, in Warwickshire. The Alpines originated from a Sunbeam-Talbot 90 specially built by George Hartwell, who sold and modified Rootes products in Bournemouth, England.

The two-seat Sunbeam Alpine sport roadster joined the Sunbeam-Talbot sedan and drophead coupe in 1953 with a $2,899 East Coast P.O.E. price tag. Designated a MK I, it weighed 2,848 lbs. and had styling features like a louvered hood and a sizable trunk with exposed hinges on its lid. The Alpine had vertical grille bars, auxiliary side grilles, and tiny parking lights at the outboard tips of the fenders.

A 1953 American ad referred to the Alpine Sports roadster as the "new queen among sports cars" and said it was "bred in the Alps." Another ad advised readers to "Drive a Sunbeam ... and leave others in the shade." *Motor Trend* called the Alpine more of a "touring car."

Inside were contour-correct individual bucket seats, with

the cockpit surround finished in padded leather. Detachable side windows included sliding panes. The doors lacked outside handles. A full range of options included plastic racing windshields and "Plus Performance Kits" for competition, plus a heater, radio, cockpit cover, tachometer, badge bar, outside mirror and windshield washer. Body colors were: Alpine Mist or ivory with bright red upholstery; or Coronation Red or Sapphire Blue with Light Fawn upholstery. The wheels were finished in body color, except for the ivory body, which came with bright red wheels.

The 2267-cc overhead-valve four-cylinder engine had an 81 x 110-mm bore and stroke. It featured a special 7.42:1 high-compression cylinder, and enlarged and polished intake ports. Initial output was 77 hp at 4200 rpm. The engine had three main bearings, solid valve lifters and a single Stromberg downdraft carburetor. Production versions of the Alpine had a top speed of about 90 mph and accelerated through the quarter mile in 21.1 seconds.

The Sunbeam incorporated a hand-controlled automatic ignition override. A close-ratio four-speed manual transmission with column-mounted gearshift lever was called "synchromatic fingertip gear changing."

Overall gear ratios were 11.04:1 in first, 8.54:1 in second, 5.19:1 in third, 3.90:1 in fourth, and 13.96:1 in reverse. The standard final drive ratio was 3.90:1, with a 4.22:1 axle available in the Alpine. Burman variable-ratio steering was fitted. The front suspension featured coil springs with a torsion bar and a rigid axle with semi-elliptic leaf springs and a transverse stabilizer was at the rear. Hydraulically actuated drum brakes were used all around.

The Alpine rode a 97.5-in. wheelbase and was 168.25 in. long, 59 in. high, and 62.5 in. wide. The front tread was 47.5 in., with a slightly wider rear tread of 50.5 in. The perforated disc wheels held 5.50 x 16 tires.

Sterling Moss hit 120 mph in a specially prepared Sunbeam Alpine at Jabbeke, Belgium on March 3, 1953. The Rootes Group entered six new Alpines for the 1953 Alpine Rally and their success was repeated in the 1954 Alpine Rally when they recorded perfect scores.

With its affordable price, roominess, lively performance, and excellent quality, the Sunbeam Alpine was a hit in America. In his 1954 book *All The World's 1954 Cars*, John Bentley stated, "Over 1,000 Sunbeam-Talbots have now found U.S. buyers."

The 1954 model was called the Mk III, though Sunbeam Alpine expert Bob Hamilton of Canada says no Mk II or Mk IIA was produced. Available in a tuned version with overdrive, it had a special engine performance kit that cost $300 extra. This boosted output to 80 hp at 4200 rpm and gave a 17-second 0-to-60-mph performance with a top speed of about 95 mph.

The Alpine also took first place in class in the 1953 Great American Mountain Rally, a 1,000-mile trek through the Green Mountains of New England.

Alpine roadster production continued through 1955 with the same 80-hp engine. The 1955 edition carried a P.O.E. price of $2,699, which suggests Rootes Motors Inc. was having some difficulty selling the cars, despite having distributors in New York City, Long Island City, Beverly Hills, and San Francisco.

H. Wieand Bowman addressed this problem in his *World-Wide Automotive Yearbook of 1954*. "The Alpine...is not in a particularly favorable price position, selling as it does for $2,900 (Port of Entry U.S.). It is pitted against formidable sales competition from the Austin-Healey 100 and is priced well above the new Triumph TR2."

# 1960-1967 Alpine

The he original Sunbeam Alpine lasted only into 1955, but the model name was revived for a completely different sports car introduced during 1959. "Sleek—Swift—Spectacular" was Sunbeam's description of the new 1960 Alpine in its U.S. sales literature. The new little roadster was created as a rival to the MGB and Triumph TR3. It was said to be named for the mountain passes where prototypes had been tested, although there was surely a link to the company's early-1950s sports touring car.

Unibody construction made the new car different from its namesake. Like the early 1950s Sunbeam Alpine Sport, this version borrowed a number of elements from its counterpart Rootes Group sedan, which in this case was the Hillman Minx-based Rapier. Beneath its handsome surface lurked a Hillman Husky station wagon chassis

**The 1960s Sunbeam Alpine combined Sunbeam Rapier and Hillman Husky components.**

and Sunbeam Rapier mechanical components.

The engineering and initial assembly work was not performed by Rootes (Sunbeam-Talbot), but instead by the Armstrong-Siddeley firm. The styling was wholly contemporary in the American mode. Up front was a curved windshield and a squat grille with a curved upper molding and slim horizontal bars. Round parking lights sat below the slightly hooded headlights. The Alpine had long, pointed, but still rounded tail fins that contained the taillights. Roll-up windows and a tachometer were standard equipment.

Extra-cost options for the new Alpine included a clock, an ammeter, and a cigarette lighter. A padded center armrest included a locking storage compartment. A removable hardtop was available to turn the roadster into a closed coupe. Standard body colors were Thistle Grey or Moonstone with Scarlet upholstery, or Carnival Red, Glen Green, Embassy Black, or Moonstone with Black upholstery. Both soft and hard tops were black.

Perched on an 86-in. wheelbase, the Alpine measured 155.2 in. long, 51.5 in. high, and 60.5 in. wide. The 51-in. front tread was wider than the 48.5-in. rear tread. Perforated steel disc wheels held 5.60 x 13 tires. The four-speed manual had overall gear ratios of 13.013:1 in first, 8.324:1 in second, 5.413:1 in third, 3.89:1 in fourth, and 16.483:1 in reverse. A choice of 3.89:1 or 4.55:1 rear axle ratios was offered. Burman recirculating ball steering was used. The front suspension incorporated coil springs with swinging links. At the rear was a rigid axle with semi-elliptic leaf springs. Girling front disc were installed in conjunction with rear drums.

Under the bonnet of early editions—called Alpine I's—was an engine pirated from the Rapier III. This overhead-valve in-line four-cylinder had solid valve lifters and a crankshaft supported by three main bearings. With a 79 x 76.2-mm bore and stroke, it displaced 1494 cc. Using a 9.2:1 compression ratio and twin Zenith downdraft carburetors, it produced 83.5 hp at 5300 rpm and 89.5 lbs.-ft. of torque at 3600 rpm.

A claimed top speed of 100 mph was put forth for the Alpine I. It could do 0-to-60 mph in 18.8 seconds or less and accelerated through the quarter-mile in 19.5 seconds at 73 mph. The base model without extras listed for $2,595 and tipped the scales at 2,082 lbs. A total of 11,904 cars were built in this early series.

The Alpine II, which debuted in October 1960, was priced at $2,595 and weighed 2,082 lbs. It switched to a 1592-cc version of the four-cylinder Rapier engine bored out to 81.5 mm. With a 9.1:1 compression ratio, it developed 86 hp at 5000 rpm and 94 lbs.-ft.

of torque at 3800 rpm. The bigger engine helped sales, which grew to 19,956 units.

The Alpine III, introduced in March 1963, was also priced at $2,595, but weighed a bit more at 2,180 lbs. It also used the 1.6-liter 86-hp engine, but a slightly de-tuned version of that power plant was used in a new GT model.

This $2,749 sports car came with a removable hardtop, but had no folding soft top. The top added 50 lbs. to the car's weight. A Laycock de Normanville overdrive unit was optional by this time, as was a close-ratio gearbox. Only 5,863 Alpine IIIs were built.

A seldom-seen Le Mans edition of the Alpine was available in 1962 and 1963. This fastback coupe, created by Harrington coachbuilders, lopped off the tailfins and added a fiberglass roof. It sold for $3,995 and weighed 2,112 lbs. Only 250 were made. Stage 2 and Stage 3 tuning of the engine resulted in ratings of 88, 93 or 100-hp.

Another evolution of the Alpine roadster arrived in early 1964. The Alpine IV retained the former 1592-cc engine with a base 90-hp rating. This version retained the original $2,595 window sticker and weighed 2,180 lbs.

It was relatively popular and 12,406 were produced. The production total included the GT edition, which listed for $2,749 and weighed 2,230 lbs. with its hardtop. An all-synchro gearbox was introduced in September 1964.

Introduced late in 1965, the Alpine V switched to a 1725-cc engine. This in-line, overhead-valve four had an 81.5 x 82.55-mm bore and stroke, a 9.2:1 compression ratio, and two Stromberg carburetors. It cranked out 99 hp at 5500 rpm and 103 lbs.-ft. of torque at 3700 rpm.

The Alpine V carried a lower $2,567 price tag and a lower 2,091-lb. weight, which suggests some "de-contenting," as they describe it in the auto industry today. Sales were strong, with 19,112 units produced. The Alpine V had a 118-mph top speed. It did 0-to-60 mph in 11.5 seconds. The Sunbeam Alpine remained in production through 1967.

John Gunnell

# 1964-1967 Tiger

The Sunbeam Tiger, introduced in 1964, was essentially a V-8 version of the four-cylinder Alpine, introduced in 1959. The 1960 Alpine, while highly regarded as a comfortable sports-touring car, with superior braking and good acceleration, was also successfully raced. In 1961, an Alpine, with a fastback body crafted by Harrington, won the Thermal Efficiency Index at Le Mans. Unfortunately, the Alpines just weren't as fast as MGs and Triumphs in most sports car competitions and this was thought to be holding back sales in the United States.

Former racecar driver Carroll Shelby, a Texan best known for developing the Shelby-Cobra, actually handled preliminary engineering

*The Sunbeam Tiger packed a Ford V-8 engine into the lithe Alpine roadster body.*

work on the Tiger as well. Familiar with the Cobra's racing reputation, Rootes' West Coast manager Ian Garrad arranged a meeting with Shelby and John Panks, the American director of Rootes Group.

Shelby envisioned an Alpine with a small-block Ford V-8 under its bonnet and agreed to work out the transplant for $10,000, plus a per-car commission on production units. He had Shelby American engineer Phil Remington squeeze a 260-cid V-8 into one car linking it to a T-10 gearbox. The firewall was reworked, rack-and-pinion steering added, the cooling system was upgraded and modifications were done to the rear end and exhaust system.

Garrad loved the resulting machine and had the prototype shipped to England, where it got an initially cool reception from Rootes engineers. Then Lord Rootes himself slid behind the wheel and brought the car to a meeting of corporate executives. The tone immediately changed to acceptance and Rootes ordered 3,000 V-8 engines from Ford Motor Company.

Later Tiger development was done the Sunbeam-Talbot arm of the Rootes Group. Quite a bit of re-engineering was required to stuff a V-8 into the little roadster. Sunbeam Tiger expert Steve Laifman says Rootes built the first 10 models, then early production was given to Thrupp and Marberly. Full production later was subcontracted to Jensen with body panels crafted by the Standard Pressed Steel Company. This allowed Sunbeam to continue building the high-volume four-cylinder Alpine without interrupting the production lines.

Though not the first example of a British roadster stuffed with a V-8, the Tiger ranks as one of the most memorable attempts. Shelby had set the trend by turning the British AC sports car into the Cobra. Although Rootes was then partially linked to America's Chrysler Corporation, the small-block V-8 engines were supplied by Ford Motor Company. A 260-cid 164-hp V-8 was used first, and a 289-cid V-8 later powered the Tiger MK II.

Tigers differed only slightly in appearance from the Alpine. A slim, full-length body side trim strip was added. Tiger IIs got egg crate-pattern grille inserts and dual rocker panel stripes. The Ford-powered Tiger debuted at the New York Auto Show in April 1964. The Tiger model name was derived from the V-12-powered Sunbeam Special that set the land-speed record in 1926.

The new Tiger was also fast, with a top speed of up to 124 mph with the smaller V-8. This version could zip from a standing start to 60 mph in about 8.4 seconds, compared to 11.5 seconds for the Alpine V. In fact, 7.8-second 0-to-60 runs were reported. The standing-start quarter mile could be done in around 16.5 seconds at 89 mph!

The 260-cid (4261-cc) V-8 was a cast-iron, push-rod engine with five main bearings. It had a 3.80 x 2.87-in. (96.5 x 73-mm) bore and stroke. With an 8.8:1 compression ratio and a Ford two-barrel carburetor, it generated 164 hp at 4400 rpm and 258 lbs.-ft. of torque at 2200 rpm. Tiger MK II models also had a Ford overhead-valve V-8, the 289 cid which featured a larger bore plus different heads and valves. Along the way, the compression ratio was raised to 9.3:1. This boosted output to 200 hp at 4400 rpm and 282 lbs-ft. at 2400 rpm.

A four-speed gearbox was installed, but it was one of Ford's design, rather than the usual Rootes unit. Rack-and-pinion steering was used and helped Sunbeam cope with space problems. The Tiger was identical to the four-cylinder Alpine, but it had smaller 5.90 x 13 tires. The Tiger's higher weight meant several chassis modifications were required including stiffened springs, a sturdier rear axle, and the addition of a Panhard rod. No change was made to the front-disc/rear-drum braking system.

The Tiger I two-passenger Sports Roadster was priced at $3,425 and tipped the scales at 2,407 lbs. A total of 3,756 examples were produced. This was followed by the MK IA model, which had a production run of 2,694 units. Both of these versions used the smaller V-8. The 289-cid-powered Tiger MK II was the rarest version with just 633 assembled.

In July of 1964, Tigers with special Lister Coupe bodies ran over 160 mph at Le Mans. Other cars were rally winners in Europe, including a first in class at the 1964 Geneva Rally, the 1965 Monte Carlo Rally, and the 1965 International Scottish Rally.

Another Tiger came in first overall in the International Police Rally. In 1965, Gordon Chittenden set the American Hot Rod Association national drag racing record with a 12.95-second, 108 mph run down the quarter mile in the Larry Reed Sportscars Tiger.

Also in 1965, Stan Peterson won the National Hot Rod Association Class C World Championship in a Tiger. A team sponsored by Los Angeles' famous Hollywood Sportscars dealership swept many West Coast road racing events.

*A race-prepared Sunbeam Tiger Le Mans coupe still is very much at home on road courses.*

# TRIUMPH

Ken Ayer

# 1948-1949 1800/2000

**T**riumph was originally known for making bicycles, starting in 1887. Those led to motorcycles and then, in 1903, to a three-wheeled motorcar. Triumph turned to making four-wheel vehicles in 1923. The first was powered by a 1.4-liter four-cylinder engine with four-speed gearbox. A 1.9-liter model followed in 1925 and a 2.2-liter two years later. None of these quite took the public by storm. Triumph's first real success came with the 1928 Super Seven, which carried a much smaller 747-cc engine. It was soon enlarged to 832-cc in the Super Eight. A supercharged sports edition was offered briefly, too, along with a line of family-style sedans.

A name change in 1930 transformed the Triumph Cycle Co. Ltd. into Triumph Motor Co. Ltd. Six-cylinder power arrived in 1931 with the Scorpion, while a Coventry-Climax engine went into the Super Nine a year later. Saloons of that era featured pillarless door construction. Triumph Glorias of the mid-1930s were the sporty members of the lineup, with 1.1- to 1.5-liter four-cylinder engines and 1.5- or 2.0-liter sixes. Overhead-valve Triumph-built engines replaced the Coventry-Climax units. A Dolomite series replaced the Gloria line in the late 1930s and was offered with a 1.8-liter four or 2.0-liter six. Dolomite roadsters were particularly handsome.

Triumph became a subsidiary of the Standard Motor Co. after World War II, the result of a receivership that took place just before the war. The name Standard-Triumph Motor Co. appeared on sales literature, although the Triumph Motor Co. designation hung on into the 1960s and '70s. Because of the ownership change, postwar Triumphs retained little connection to the Triumphs of the prewar era, but were based instead on Standard components.

In the spring of 1946, Triumph unleashed the dramatic, low-slung 1800 Roadster. This "sports car" included a three-passenger front bench with a folding center armrest, plus the last "dickey" seat

*The Triumph 1800/2000 series was a bridge from 1930s styles to 1950s sports cars.*

(England's answer to the rumble seat) installed on a regular production automobile. Triumph described the setup as two occasional seats that folded forward into a recess behind the front seats, with access from the rear of the car. The car's soft top folded down completely behind the front seat. Rumble-seat passengers had their own fold-up windshield, yet climbing in and out of the outside back seat wasn't easy.

In 1949, *Motor Trend* explained the folding seats were normally in stowed position. When swung backward, the forward section of the "turtleback" lifted forward to create a "windbreaker" for the two lucky or unlucky passengers.

Styling of the rear end was the work of Arthur Ballard, while Frank Callaby earned credit for the 1800's front end design. Roll-up windows were installed for the front passengers. Twin outside horns sat below the headlights, to the rear of the front bumper. Standard colors were black with beige upholstery and a black or fawn top, dark metallic grey with blue upholstery and a black or grey top, or maroon with red upholstery and a black or fawn top.

Under the 1800's bonnet was a push rod, four-cylinder in-line engine with a sturdy chromium iron block, solid valve lifters, and three main bearings to support the crankshaft. It had a 73 x 106-mm bore and stroke or 1776 cc. With a 6.7:1 compression ratio (initially announced as 7.5:1) and a single Solex carburetor, the sports model produced 65 hp at 4500 rpm and 92 lbs.-ft. of torque at 2000 rpm. A 12-volt electrical system was incorporated.

The 1800 roadster supposedly had a top speed of 84 mph. Going from 0-to-60 mph took about 34.4 seconds, while a 0-to-50-mph time of 15 seconds was claimed.

The roadster rode on a 100-in. wheelbase and measured 168.5-in. front to rear. It was 56 in. high and 65 in. wide. Triumph used a 49.75-in. front tread and 54.75-in. rear tread. The 5.75 x 16 tires were on steel disc wheels.

The four-speed transmission had overall gear ratios of 18.04:1 in first (and reverse), 11.1:1 in second, 6.64:1 in third, and 4.57:1 in fourth. The standard final drive ratio was 4.57:1. Marles cam-and-twin-roller steering was employed.

The independent front suspension was by transverse leaf springs, with a rigid axle and semi-elliptic leaf springs at the rear. The brakes were hydraulically activated drum types all around.

The roadster had a separate body, with light alloy panels over ash wood framework, mounted on a ladder-type tubular steel frame.

Triumph's 1800 series evolved into the 2000 series in 1949 and a sports roadster was included. A larger new Standard Vanguard engine displaced 2088 cc and developed 68 hp at 4200 rpm.

The roadster was the first model to get the larger engine, which was later used in closed cars.

Instead of a four-speed gearbox, the 2000 used a fully synchronized three-speed transmission, again with column-mounted gearshift.

The front suspension got a big change to wishbones with coil springs and an anti-roll bar. The 2000 roadster sold for $2,950 P.O.E. in the United States and weighed in at 2,352 lbs.

A total of 2,501 Triumph 1800 roadsters were produced from 1946 to 1948 and about 750 of them were intended for export. Only about 31 Triumphs were sold in the U.S. during 1948. A total of 2,000 Triumph 2000 roadsters were produced in 1948-1949.

# 1954-1955 TR2

Bob Harington

**The classic inset grilled belonged only to the Triumph TR2 series, like this 1955 racer.**

**T**he name Triumph had been associated with sporty cars for a long time. As early as the late 1920s, a Triumph model with the unusual name Gnat found acceptance among sports car enthusiasts in Great Britain.

During the 1934 Monte Carlo Rally, Donald Healey himself had won the light-car class in a Triumph Gloria, one of seven Triumphs to finish that particular reliability run. In the 1930s, the supercharged Triumph Super Seven had set the pace again. In 1945, Triumph Motor Car Company, Ltd. was acquired by the Standard Motor Company and Triumph became a subsidiary of that firm.

In the early postwar years, the Triumph badge was seen on some conservative-looking, fancy versions of the Standard saloon. The head of Standard Motor Company, Sir John Black, decided he needed a sports car and at first tried to purchase Morgan. Failing in this attempt, he created his own sports car and exhibited it at the 1952 London Motor Show. This car—known as both the 20TS and the TR1—was underpowered, softly-suspended, and somewhat gawky looking.

There was obvious interest in such a model and, by 1953, Triumph was ready to launch its first postwar sports car, the TR2 roadster.

Leading off a series of TR models that would last until the end of the Triumph nameplate in 1981, was a distinctive car with sharply cut-down doors and a deeply-inset grille opening called the TR2. The styling of this steel-bodied two-seater, designed by Walter Belgrove, often generated a love-it-or-hate-it response, although it is clearly considered "classical" today.

Under the bonnet of the new sports car was a sleeved-down 2.0-liter, 90-hp version of the Vanguard engine which could propel the TR2 to 100 mph. The roadster proved itself a capable contender in sports-car-racing competitions, as well as a popular sports-touring machine. It sold particularly well in the United States and other nations outside Britain.

The TR designation obviously meant "Triumph," but was presented different ways throughout the history of the series. Early sales literature generally used periods in the Triumph sports car's designation, calling it the "T.R.2." Many U.S. publications placed a hyphen within the model name, presenting it as the "TR-2." Later Triumph promotional material omitted both the periods and the hyphen and it became the "TR2."

Early TR2 advertising promised "more performance per dollar than any other car in the world" and claimed 0-to-50-mph acceleration in 7.5 seconds. "You're as young as you feel at the wheel of a T.R.2," the ads continued, "the car that lets you drive, and doesn't drive you!"

In his *World-Wide Automotive Year Book*, published by *Motor Trend* in 1954, H. Wieand Bowman reported, "The performance, durable construction and eye appeal of the TR2 are all exceptionally fine. Its fabric top has a low sweeping profile with more eye appeal than several of its more expensive competitors for the sports car market. Public reception of the Triumph sports car, to date, indicates the company's re-entrance into the sports car market should pay off for them."

Few sports cars—or cars of any sort for that matter—were as easy to identify as the TR2 roadster. Its flowing fender lines extended across the dip-down doors. The headlights had a semi-built-in "bug-eye" look and the wide front and rear wheel openings were fully rounded.

A roomy trunk was part of Triumph's rather pleasant package. Inside the cockpit, two large dials faced the driver. Other supplementary instruments were located in the center of the dashboard. The Triumph TR2 roadster carried an East Coast Port-of-Entry price of $2,448 and weighed just 1,960 lbs.

Under the bonnet of the TR2 was a 1991-cc four-cylinder pushrod engine with an 83 x 92-mm bore and stroke. The three-main-bearings solid-lifter power plant used a cast iron block and had an 8.5:1 compression ratio. With twin S.U. carburetors it developed 90 hp at 4800 rpm and 117 lbs.-ft. of torque at 3000 rpm. The power flowed rearwards, through a Vanguard four-speed gearbox, to a 3.7:1 rear axle.

The TR2 delivered a top speed of 103 to 104 mph. It could go from 0-to-60 mph in 11.9 to13.7 seconds and flash through the standing-start quarter-mile in 19.6 seconds at 70 mph. Fitted with an optional overdrive and a belly pan (or "undershield" in British terminology), one Triumph hit 124.095 mph on the world-famous Jabbeke Highway in Belgium.

Advertisements promoted this performance as being timed by the Royal Auto Club of Belgium using a car "in speed trim." Test driver Ken Richardson was behind the wheel of that particular TR2. A speed of 108.499 mph was recorded for the TR2 in "touring trim," which was essentially the same equipment without the Laycock de Normanville overdrive. A TR2 also won the British Royal Automobile Club rally in March 1954.

The TR2 had an 88-in. wheelbase with a 148-in. overall length. It was 50 in. high with the top up, 55.5 in. wide, and had a 44.8-in. front tread and 45.5-in. rear tread. Ground clearance was a mere six inches. The independent front suspension, pirated from the Triumph Mayflower, consisted of coil springs up front. Semi-elliptic leaf springs were employed at the rear. The standard 5.50 x 15 tires were mounted on disc wheels. Lockheed hydraulic brakes were used front and rear.

Late in the model run, center-lock wire wheels became optional equipment, as did a seldom-seen lift-off hardtop and an overdrive transmission. The doors also were shortened up a bit, in response to complaints of difficulty exiting when the car was parked next to a low curb. An optional suitcase fit precisely into the luggage compartment, which was quite small. Inside was a grab bar for the passenger and the cowl had holes drilled for small racing shields. Top speeds of 103 mph or more were reported from stock cars with regular factory hardware.

Production of the TR2 ran from August 1953 to October 1955. Standard-Triumph Motor Co., a new U.S. company, was founded by Sir John Black, the head of Triumph.

Fergus Motors in New York City and Standard-Triumph Motor Co. in New York and Los Angeles distributed the cars in the U.S. early on. Approximately 8,636 Triumph TR2s were produced over the full model run and 5,521 of them were exported to the "Colonies."

*Motor Trend* magazine tried out the first TR2 to reach the West Coast. It was a white roadster with Rose upholstery, a red top, and red side curtains.

The view from the driver's seat reminded them of the Crosley Hotshot.

Mike McClelland

# 1956-1957 TR3/TR3A/TR3B

"New from the word 'Go' —the exciting story of the new Triumph TR3," said an advertisement from June 1956. "New styling, new engineering, a new idea in fun-plus-convenience… the sports car buy of the year."

The ad highlighted horsepower, speed, acceleration, and fuel economy, and invited people to "Zest-drive a Triumph soon."

The TR3 was introduced at the 1955 London Motor Show. Production began in October 1955 and continued until September 1956. Front disc brakes were installed for the remainder of the production run, up to October 1957. Some sources cited this as the first use of disc brakes in a regular production car, although the credit actually belongs to Chrysler Corporation, which introduced Ausco-Lambert "self-energizing" disc brakes on its 1950 Imperial.

"How to drive a fast bargain" was the American advertisement theme for the TR3 that ran in 1956. The car originally sold for $2,595

*One of the most popular British sports cars in North America was the Triumph TR3.*

East Coast Port-of-Entry, although a June 1956 advertisement showed a $2,599 price. By 1957 it cost $2,625. The hardtop version, promoted as a separate model, was priced at $2,790 in 1957.

The TR3's grille opening had a similar shape to that used for the TR2 but its front-end appearance changed considerably. It had a non-recessed grille with larger openings mounted over the old one. The grille pattern consisted of six vertical ahead of seven horizontal bars. Stainless steel fender beading was another new item. A broad bonnet provided good access to the four-cylinder engine. Headlights sat almost "bug-eye" style, above the front fenders.

One change was made in reaction to customer complaints about the TR2's doors hitting the curb when they were opened. The doors were lower than the floor level of the car. On the TR3, the floor was extended to create a body sill and the doors were redesigned to be four inches higher at the bottom.

TR3 body colors were: Pearl White, Signal Red, black, Salvador Blue, British Racing Green, Sunset Red, and beige. Wire wheels also were optional, as was a detachable hardtop.

The TR2 was strictly a two-seater, but the TR3 offered a children's seat as an optional fitting. Up front there were two comfortable individually adjustable bucket seats. An "occasional" rear seat, that provided enough space for kids to squeeze into, could be added. One optimistic advertisement depicted a woman driving, a man in the passenger seat, and two teens in back. The dashboard had grouped instruments with a larger circular tach and speedometer on the left and engine instruments on the right. The back of the passenger seat folded forward for access to a rear storage space. A selection of nine different colored leather interiors was offered. Soft tops came in black or fawn and the side curtains came in black, fawn, or white.

The TR3's push-rod-operated in-line four was basically the same cast-iron engine used in the TR2 with an 83 x 92-mm bore and stroke and 1991 cc displacement. The compression ratio remained at 8.5:1. Modified intake ports and larger-choke S.U. carburetors boosted horsepower to 95 at 4800 rpm. The torque rating was 117 lbs.-ft. at 3000 rpm. The TR3's added weight meant performance and economy suffered slightly.

Early engines used a "Le Mans" cylinder head, which was changed during the production to a "high-port" design that added power. The later cars generated 100 hp at 5000 rpm.

"The TR3 does not drag its feet," wrote Karl Ludvigson in the March 1956 issue of *Sports Car Illustrated*. "The engine winds fast in a smooth and purposeful manner. The sharp exhaust note of the TRs has gone, but the car still belts away from a standing start with a real kick-in-the-back."

Top speed for the TR3 was about 105 mph (110 mph for the later 100-hp version). The car went from 0-to-60 mph in 12.5 to 13.2 seconds. A 0-to-60 run of 9.2 seconds was reported in one road test, perhaps for the 100-hp job. The quarter mile could be covered in 18.9 seconds at 74 mph. One test reported 16.9 seconds and 81.9 mph. Fuel mileage of 26 to 35 mpg was claimed.

John Bolster, of *Autosport* magazine, found the TR3 "a fast and economical sports car," but also noted, "…this TR3 was fractionally slower than 'my' original TR2." He guessed that most other TR3s "… should have more speed."

The TR3 retained the TR2's 88-in. wheelbase and 151-in. overall length. Also unchanged were the height, width, and track measurements, as well as tire size. Michelin 'X' steel-belted radial tires were available as optional extras. The TR3 had one of the longest optional equipment lists of any British car of this era.

The four-speed manual gearbox, with synchronizers on all but first gear, had the same ratios: 3.38:1 in first, 2.00:1 in second, 1.325:1 in third and 1.00:1 in fourth. Overdrive was available. The standard final drive ratio remained at 3.7:1.

Cam-and-lever steering was used. The independent front suspension was constructed of unequal-length A-arms with coil springs. At the rear was a conventional rigid axle with semi-elliptic leaf springs. Hydraulic drum brakes were used all around, but starting in October 1956, Girling front disc brakes were installed.

A TR3 ad said it combined "sports car performance with family convenience." In France, a TR3 could be purchased by Americans for just $1,925.

In North America, the Triumph sports car was available at Standard Triumph Motor Company, Inc. in New York City, Cal Sales in Gardena, California, South Eastern Motors in Hollywood, Florida, and The Standard Motor Company, Ltd. (Canada) in Toronto, Ontario. As many as 16,847 Triumph TR3s were produced over the full model run, from 1955 to 1957, and 15,561 were sent to export markets.

Jeff Bruggink

# 1961-1967 TR4/TR4A

**T**riumph introduced the restyled TR4 in 1961, as a 1962 model. It had a new 2.1-liter engine and rack-and-pinion steering. "The TR4: It Won Its First Medal Standing Still" said an April 1962 advertisement that heralded Triumph's first place and a gold medal for coachwork at the Earls Court Show, in London, six days after the car's release.

Totally restyled, with the assistance of Italian designer Giovanni Michelotti, the TR4 represented Triumph's "next-generation" full-size sports car. Two models were available. The 2,072 lb. roadster had an East Coast Port-of-Entry price of $2,849. The coupe—which had a POE price of $2,999—-was not a roadster with a detachable hardtop.

*The restyled Triumph TR4 was introduced as a longer, lower 1962 roadster.*

It had a removable steel roof panel, but a fixed-in-position rear light (rear window) and frame. Owners who feared getting caught in the rain after leaving the steel roof home could order an optional fabric top to cover the opening between the fixed windshield and fixed rear window. Production of the TR4 started in August 1961 and lasted until January 1965, even though American Triumph dealers lacked sufficient faith in the new car.

The TR4 persisted for four model years and, following that run, a similar TR4A model arrived and remained available until August 1967. Approximately 40,253 Triumph TR4s were produced over the full model run, from 1961-1964. About 28,465 TR4As were produced between 1965 and 1967.

The TR4 front end retained some of the TR3's styling trademarks like a lattice-work grille and "frog-eye" headlights. These were presented in totally new ways. The wide grille had fewer vertical blades, which gave it a more horizontal look. The grille was slightly recessed under the lip of the bonnet and incorporated headlights below humps that formed small eyelids.

The wraparound style front bumper had large overriders inboard of the headlight position. The flat TR3 windshield gave way to a larger, slightly curved windshield. The left side of the hood had a "power blister" that provided clearance for the inclined carburetors.

The new sports car's body had a much different look. It was longer, lower, wider, more square and more contemporary, with straight-through fender lines and a wider stance. The doors were no longer cut down and had only a modest recess along the window sill. The rear end look was totally different from any previous TR. The taper-tail was gone and the new trunk lid was on level with the hood, curving gently down at the rear. The fenders "slab sided" appearance ended with a hint of tail fins. The rear lamps looked like "gel caps" mounted vertically in the fender ends.

A major convenience advance was wind-up side windows, a first for Triumph roadsters. The TR4's new face-level ventilation system featured the same type of air ducts with butterfly valves and wheel adjuster many cars use today. Standard TR4 exterior body colors were: Spa White, Signal Red, black, Powder Blue, or British Racing Green.

Triumph listed the TR4 as a two-passenger model. Individually adjustable front bucket seats were provided. A padded backrest was behind the seats and seat cushions were optional. The seats, door panels, and backrest were trimmed in pleated imitation leather with piping in a contrasting color. Genuine leather was optional. Upholstery could be black, red, or blue and was color-keyed to the body color. Convertible tops came only in black or white.

Instrumentation was split into two groups. A large circular speedometer and a match tachometer sat directly in front of the driver. A trapezoid-shaped panel in the center held the ammeter, oil pressure gauge, thermo gauge, and fuel gauge. Below this was a horizontal panel housing the choke, wiper, lights, ignition, and windscreen washer controls. There was a locking glove box on the passenger side. The three-spoke steering wheel was of an attractive "banjo" design.

Chassis details weren't much different than the TR3A, except for rack-and-pinion steering. The TR4 retained an 88-in. wheelbase with an overall length of 156 in., a bit more than the TR3. Its top-of-the-windshield height was 50 in. It was much wider than earlier TRs at 57.5 in. The front tread was 49 in., the rear tread was an inch narrower. The steel disc wheels held 5.90 x 15 tires and wire wheels were optional as usual.

Under the hood was a 2138-cc engine with an 86 x 92-mm bore and stroke, the same used in late TR3Bs. The use of twin S.U. carburettors and a 9.0:1 compression ratio was carried over. In England, this engine was rated 100 hp at 4600 rpm, but the U.S. rating was 105 hp at 4750 rpm. Torque was 128 lbs.-ft. at 3350 rpm.

The smaller 1991-cc engine remained available for use in 2.0-liter class racing. It was rated 100 hp at 5000 rpm and 117 lbs.-ft. of torque at 3000 rpm. The TR4's top speed was in excess of 110 mph and it was tested at 11.5 seconds for 0-to-60 mph and 18.2 seconds for the quarter mile.

Introduced along with the new Spitfire MKII at the Geneva International Auto Show in the spring of 1965, the Triumph TR4A had "deep" changes including a modified grille, revised badges and emblems, more luxurious interior furnishings, a fancier hood (convertible top), and a re-worked rear chassis with an independent suspension incorporating semi-trailing arms and coil springs. Modest modifications were made to the TR4's engine, which resulted in a four percent power increase. It now produced 104 hp at 4700 rpm (105 hp at 4150 rpm in the U.S.) and 132 lbs.-ft. of torque at 3350 rpm.

The 1965-1966 TR4A roadster had a $2,840 window sticker in dealerships on America's East Coast. It tipped the scales at 2,072 lbs. The same vintage coupe cost $147 more. In 1967, the TR4A's last season, the prices increased by $59 and the weight actually dropped by about 70 lbs.

An interesting Triumph owner survey published in the April 1969 *Road & Track* showed 67 percent of TR4 owners and 72 percent of TR4A owners would buy another Triumph. They overwhelmingly picked handling as the car's best feature, followed by fuel economy, reliability, performance, and comfort. Brakes were praised and oil leaks were criticized. The worst features were a hard ride, noisiness, and the top. Quality control, vibration, heater operation, and the seats were labeled the cars' worst features.

Jeff Bruggink

Center-lock wire wheels: painted ($110).
Smith's heater ($65).
Radio ($57.50).
White sidewall tires ($35).
Tonneau cover ($35).
Windshield washers ($20).
Overdrive ($160).
Competition anti-sway bar ($19.50).
Dunlop high-speed tyres ($35).
Skid plate ($17).
Aluminum sump ($26.25).
Competition springs ($4).
Competition shock absorbers ($4).

Johnathan Stein

# 1967-1968 TR5

The newest member of Triumph's full-size sports car line entered production in September 1967. The TR5 was much like the TR4 at first impression, but there was a big difference under the bonnet where a six-cylinder fuel-injected engine lurked. On the outside, the TR5 looked much the same. The body was slightly reworked and interior was upgraded a bit. Nevertheless, the TR5 saw limited deliveries and survived just a short time before it was replaced by the 1968 TR6. While the TR5 actually sold fairly well, in spite of its "interim" status, for the 15 months it was offered, its too-short lifespan kept sales down to a mere 2,947 units. Of these, 1,161 cars were made for the home market and 1,786 were exported.

The real impetus for the TR5 was the fact that the TR4 had been restyled, but not re-engineered. The power train dated back to the 1950s. This put Triumph behind the curve in performance, a problem that needed to be addressed if Triumph hoped to keep apace with MG and Austin-Healey in sales. Transplanting the basic engine from the Triumph 2000 saloon into the sports car was the answer.

This power plant was given a longer stroke, to bring it to 2.5-liters, and fitted with Lucas' mechanical Petrol Injection (PI) system. The TR5 became the first mass-produced British car to use fuel injection. The system allowed the use of a high-performance, large-overlap camshaft and a 9.5:1 compression ratio. This resulted in an engine that developed 142 to 150 hp at 5500 rpm and 164 lbs.-ft. of torque at 3000 rpm.

Britain's *Motor* magazine, in its May 4, 1968 issue, described the TR5 as "invigorating injection." The publication said the TR5 offered "tremendous performance from fuel injection, good handling and brakes with firm ride; (and) comfortable spacious accommodation for two." It recorded a 0-to-60-mph time of 8.1 seconds and a 16.5-second standing-start quarter mile run. Its top speed, as reported by John Bolster in *Autosport's* May 31, 1968 issue was 120 mph.

Triumph made a few changes between the TR4 and the TR5. The grille was slightly revised, the Triumph name disappeared from the hood, and the name badge moved from centered above the hood to the left-hand side, which was said to make the car look wider. The chrome trim on the front fender and door was widened and the rear fenders got new side-marker lights. In addition, a chrome rocker panel molding was added and back-up lights were put on the standard equipment list.

Like the TR4, the TR5 was easy to get into and roomy inside. A wood grained dash inlay was new and made the instrument layout look a little simpler, although it was basically unchanged from before.

In the name of safety (a big movement in 1967) the shiny banjo-string steering wheel gave way to one with three thick spokes and a cushioned center button. Standard equipment included 12-

### The Triumph TR5 series used a fuel-injected six-cylinder engine.

volt starting and lighting with an alternator, a speedometer, a rev counter (tachometer), an ammeter, an oil pressure indicator, a water temperature gauge, a fuel gauge, a heater and demister, two-speed windscreen wipers and washers, and back-up lights.

Several changes were made inside, mostly to add safety equipment. These included a "dipping" (day/night) rearview mirror, the elimination of the passenger grab handle and a padded dashboard cover.

The hood (convertible top) was improved so that it could be raised and lowered in a few seconds and had only two fixings (fasteners) that clipped into sockets in the top of the windscreen surround (windshield frame). A cover was provided to protect the top when not in use.

The push-rod-operated overhead-valve in-line six had a 74.7 x 95-mm bore and stroke and 2,498-cc displacement. It featured a Lucas electric fuel pump, an AC full-flow oil filter, a Lucas coil, and a Lucas distributor. A single dry plate diaphragm-spring clutch was fitted ahead of the four-speed manual gearbox with center-mounted remote control lever (floor shifter). The transmission had overall gear ratios of 1.0, 1.33, 2.01, and 3.14. A 3.45:1 rear axle was used.

The TR5's steel body rode on a steel chassis. The front independent suspension incorporated wishbones, helical springs and telescopic dampers, while the independent rear suspension used semi-trailing arms, helical springs, and telescopic shocks. Girling four-wheel disc brakes with vacuum servo action were installed.

The steering was rack-and-pinion type. Size 165-15 radial-ply tires were mounted on the bolt-on pressed-steel wheels. Wires were an option again. The stock wheel covers, which were designed to look like cast-alloy rims, drew a little criticism.

Road tester John Bolster gave the TR5 a good appraisal in *Autosport*. "Without any doubt, this is the best Triumph yet!" he declared. "It is a car of exciting appearance with sporting lines, but it has the luxury and mechanical refinement usually associated with large and expensive saloons. Fuel injection adds interest to the specification but above all improves the performance and flexibility. Very soon, a prestige car without fuel injection will be unthinkable."

In the real world, the Lucas fuel-injection system experienced some teething problems, largely due to high temperatures under the bonnet and a whining noise made by the high-pressure fuel pump. In a few cases, under hood fires erupted. But the system gave a clear boost in performance and this is what makes the rare TR5 a desirable car today. The fact that the TR5 was not offered in America also kept production low.

bob Harrington

# 1968 TR250

Adding more power to the TR roadster was accomplished by adding two more cylinders to the engine. European buyers were treated to a TR5 PI model…the "PI" stood for port fuel injection. Lucas designed this fuel-injection system, which helped the new six crank put out 150 hp. Instead of the TR5 PI, American customers got the less-potent TR 250, which had under its bonnet a 111-hp carbureted version of the same 2.5-liter engine.

The appearance of both cars was similar to that of the TR4A, except for a new grille. But needless to say, performance differed wildly between the two. As Bob Brown put it in *Car and Driver*, "The TR250 we tested moseyed through the quarter mile in 18.8 seconds. At 74 mph – that's 2 mph and 1.7 seconds slower than a TR4A."

Of course, the United States Government was largely to blame for the fact that the new six-cylinder Triumph sold here was slower than the previous four-cylinder model. To make the car comply to U.S. pollution laws, the fuel-injection hardware had to be swapped for a pair of standard carburetors tuned to run on the lean side of the scale.

Said *Car and Driver*, "Lean mixtures, which are not conducive to maximum power, are essential for minimum smog emission and, if the TR250's jets were much smaller, they'd be blanks. Normally, with the throttle fully closed, vacuum zooms up on overrun and sucks raw gas out of the idle jets, enriching the mixture and polluting the air. So Triumph doesn't let the TR250's throttle butterflies loose completely. When you get off the accelerator, the carbs are still propped open slightly. This means the engine loses revs very slowly, like a John Deere tractor motor with a 100-lb. flywheel."

Externally, the grille used on the TR250 and TR5 varied from the TR4 grille by losing the small, vertical, center bar. This left only a pattern of full-width horizontal bars to fill the opening. The TR250s destined for American buyers had reflective racing stripes across the hood and front fenders ahead of the front wheel wells. The standard steel disc wheels came with covers that were designed to resemble "mag" wheels and even had dummy lug nuts. But many of the TR250 convertibles wore optional center-lock wire wheels instead. Radial tires now were standard. A new magnetic gas cap was introduced.

Inside the cars, the TR4 style interior was redone to make it comply with new federal safety regulations. *Car and Driver* stated, "The seats are better, but the cramped upright Victorian driving position —combined with the miserable ride—leaves you aching, literally, for major improvements in these areas."

The steering wheel got a leather-and-sponge-rubber rim and now

***The TR250 was sold in North America with racing stripes, mag-type wheels and radial tires.***

had padded spokes. The gearshift lever was also padded. The old toggle switches protruding from the dash were replaced with safer rocker-style switches. A reflective material was sewn into the folding hood (convertible top) to make it more visible at night.

The TR250 engine was an in-line, overhead-valve six-cylinder with a cast-iron block and head. It had a 74.7 x 76-mm bore and stroke and 2498-cc displacement. Four main bearings supported the crank in the solid-lifter power plant. It had two Zenith-Stromberg horizontal carburettors and an 8.5:1 compression ratio. This added up to 111 hp at 4500 rpm and 152 lbs.-ft. of torque at 3000 rpm. Road testers estimated top speed at about 107 mph and 10.6 seconds was required to get from 0-to-60 mph.

"To pay extra for a nearly-identical-but-slower car doesn't make much sense, but the TR250 does have some definite advantages," *Car and Driver* admitted. "A Six is inherently smoother than a Four and the TR4A's Four was so rough as to justify the price increase on that basis alone. The Six is also a lot more tractable than the Four, and can pull away without bucking from lower rpm, which means less shifting."

Both the TR5 and the TR250 had the 88-in. wheelbase and an overall length of 153.6 in. They were 50 in. high to the top of the windshield and 58 in. wide. The front tread width was 49.25 in. and the rear tread width was a slightly narrower 48.75 in. The standard disc wheels carried 185/HR15 radial tires.

A four-speed manual transmission was standard and overdrive was available. The final drive ratio was lowered to 3.45:1 for the six-cylinder drive train, because it produced more torque than the four. Rack-and-pinion steering was employed and was significantly redesigned to reduce rear movement of the column in a collision impact. The front suspension relied on unequal-length A-arms with coil springs. The rear independent suspension featured semi-trailing arms and coil springs. A rigid rear axle option for American TR250 models was dropped. For brakes, Triumph used Girling discs up front and Girling drums at the rear.

The TR250 was marketed in two models. The convertible had an East Coast Port-of-Entry price of $3,175 and the coupe version was priced the same. The convertible weighed 2,165 lbs. and the coupe (actually a hardtop with a detachable roof panel) weighed 2,268 lbs.

The TR5 came in the same models and was not sold on this side of the pond. Production of the two models lasted less than two years, ceasing before the end of 1968.

About 8,484 of the TR250s were made, with this figure reflecting a fall-off in American interest in the TR series for the first time in seven years. The TR250's reputation for having less power combined with the negative write-ups in car magazines, had soured the market here.

This helped sales of the fuel-injected TR5 in the home market, since it freed up production capacity at the Triumph factory in Coventry. In other words, for every TR250 not built, Triumph could make another TR5. Unfortunately, the extra output for Great Britain and Europe wasn't enough to fully compensate for the U.S. sales decline, as only 2,947 TR5s were made.

David LaComb

# 1969-1971 TR6

The TR250 and the European TR5 PI had served as interim models for Triumph enthusiasts awaiting the debut of the next "real" Triumph open sports car — the TR6. That debut came late in September of 1968, when the first Triumph TR6s were seen. Introduced as a 1969 model, the TR6 had actually been under development at the time the TR5 was introduced. It bowed just 15 months later.

The TR5 and the TR6 were based on the same body shell, but the TR6 was restyled by Karmann of Osnabruk, the German designer best known for his Volkswagen-based sports car. The new car had a more masculine character. Styling was similar to the TR5, but the appearances of the front and rear ends changed considerably.

Styling updates included a long hood with no power bulge, additional front body overhang, a wider blacked-out grille with a single horizontal bar and center insignia, and the repositioning of headlights out on the fenders. Stylists tacked on a Kammback-type chopped-off tail that resembled the GT6 and Stag. Horizontal taillights wrapped around the body corners. There was more trunk space.

The basic TR was an open-bodied sports car. In 1969, it carried an East Coast Port-of-Entry price of $3,275 and came in at 2,156 lbs. A detachable, one-piece steel hardtop was again an extra. By 1970, Triumph listed the TR6 convertible at $3,375 and the hardtop at $3,520. Prices went up to $3,595 and $3,818, respectively, in 1971. In 1972, the convertible carried a $3,723 price tag. By 1976, Triumph was getting $6,050 for the open version.

The TR6 interior had plenty of legroom with creature comforts including cut-pile floor carpeting and plusher-looking bucket seats. Cut-pile carpeting was also used to trim the trunk floor. An uncluttered dashboard featured full instrumentation. Interior trim colors included No. 11 Black (all years), No. 12 Matador Red (1969-1971), No. 13 Light Tan (1969), No. 27 Shadow Blue (1969-1975), No. 33 New Tan (1970-1974), No. 63 Chestnut (1973-1975), and No. 74 Beige (1975-1976).

***The Triumph TR6 featured a body styled by Karmann of Osnabruk, Germany.***

Except for the addition of a front anti-roll bar, little was new beneath the surface. Two engine setups were used in TR6s, but which one you got depended upon where you lived. As in the case of the TR250 versus TR5 PI, the 2.5-liter six came with different types of induction systems here and overseas. Americans got a carbureted engine that was smog-legal, but had considerably less horsepower than the fuel-injected version, which was offered to European buyers only.

Both engines were essentially the same in-line, overhead-valve six with four main bearings, a cast-iron block and a cast-iron cylinder head. It had a 74.7 x 76-mm bore and stroke, bringing displacement to 2498 cc. The U.S.-spec version of the engine carried twin Zenith-Stromberg carburetors and had an 8.6:1 compression ratio. It developed 104 hp at 4500 rpm and 142 lbs.-ft. of torque at 3000 rpm. The TR6 PI, available in Europe, had a Lucas fuel-injection system that was good for 150 hp at 5500 rpm and 164 lbs.-ft. of torque at 3500 rpm. (In January 1973, this engine was de-tuned and rated for 124 hp at 5500 rpm and 143 lbs.-ft. of torque at 3500 rpm).

Not all differences between Export and Home Market versions of the TR6 were limited to those seen under the bonnet. U.S.-spec cars also had built-in headrests and the headrests on some early cars folded forward, so a flat tonneau cover could be fitted.

Later, headrests were fixed in position and required a tonneau cover with "pockets" for the headrests. European buyers could order different optional headrests. A black-finished windshield frame arrived in 1970, prior to the introduction of black-finished windshield wiper arms. U.S.-spec cars also had a special fuel filler that wouldn't leak in a rollover. Later North American TR6s came with a Union Jack flag badge on the rear fenders.

With its 88-in. wheelbase, the TR6 was 155 in. long, 50 in.

high, and 58 in. wide. Front and rear tread widths were 50.25 in. and 49.75 in., respectively. The usual Triumph all-synchromesh four-speed manual transmission was base equipment and overdrive was available at extra cost. Rack-and-pinion steering was supplied.

The front had unequal-length A-arms with coil springs. A front anti-roll bar was added to improve the ride quality. A rigid axle with semi-trailing arms and coil springs was fitted at the rear. Front disc/rear drum brakes were provided. Wider 5-1/2-in. wide wheels were another change.

Only a few significant changes were made to the TR6 during the early 1970s. The transmission ratios were altered in mid-1971. In 1973, a lip-style front spoiler was added, some bright metal trim was redesigned and new fire-resistant seating materials were used. The 1974 model got black bumper overriders designed to meet U.S. safety standards.

The engine used in 1972-1973 models had a lower 7.75:1 compression ratio and produced 106 hp at 4900 rpm and 133 lbs.-ft. at 3000 rpm. In Europe, the fuel-injected version got a different camshaft with only 36 degrees of overlap.

The TR6 sold better than any other TR-series car in Triumph's history and 90 percent of those sales went to customers in the U.S. Production continued into mid-1976, even after the debut of the TR7 and new TR6s were still being sold in 1977.

Approximately 250,000 TRs were made since the early 1950s and 94,619 of those cars were 1969-1976 TR6s. About 78,000 of these were sold in the United States over eight calendar years.

Like other Triumphs with independent rear suspension, the TR6 wasn't raced as much when new as it was later on. In the 1980s and 1990s, sports car buffs developed parts and setups to make them competitive in Sports Car Club of America venues. One of the better known TR6 race cars was Bob Tullius' Group 44 TR6.

### Triumph TR6 colors

A total of 22 different factory paint colors were offered for TR6s over the years. They included No. 17 Damson (1969-1972), No. 19 White (all years), No. 23 Sienna (1970-1973), No. 25 Conifer Green (1969-1970), No. 32 Signal Red (1969-1971), No. 34 Jasmine (1969-1972), No. 54 Saffron (1971-1972), No. 55 Laurel Green (1969-1971), No. 56 Royal Blue (1969-1971), No. 64 Mimosa Yellow (1973-mid-1976), 65 Emerald Green (1972-1974), 72 Pimento Red (1972-1976), No. 75 British Racing Green (1975-1976), No. 82 Carmine Red (1973-1976), No. 83 Maple (1974-1976), No. 84 Topaz (1975-1976), No. 85 Java (1975-1976), No. 92 Magenta (1973-1974), No. 93 Russet Brown (mid-1976), No. 94 Inca Yellow (mid-1976), No. 96 Sapphire Blue, No. 106 Mallard Blue-Green (1973-1974), No. 126 French Blue (1973-mid-1976), No. 136 Delft Blue (1975-mid-1976), and Tahiti Blue (1976).

OCW Archive

# 1970-1977 Stag

The Stag was a sporting-type car for the 1970s and beyond. The concept behind the new model dated back to the GT6 era and had historical links to an experimental styling model called the "Zebu," seen as early as 1958.

Triumph designer Les Moore styled the first Zebu version, later revised by Giovanni Michelotti, who helped design all Triumph body styles produced between 1957 and 1970.

In the mid-'60s, Michelotti's studio designed a large, five-seat saloon with the long nose/short deck look that was all the rage in America. He went on to build a sportier version, based on the Triumph 2000 chassis. Conceived as a show car, it became the genesis of the Stag.

Development was changed and delayed several times and the Stag almost reached production using the TR5 fuel-injected engine. The decision to use a V-8 and United States safety regulations held things up until June 1970, when the new car debuted. Starting in the spring of 1971, the Stag became available in the U.S.

The Stag had a full-width grille with horizontal bars. Two round headlights were placed on either side, sitting inboard of rubber-faced bumper overriders. The Triumph name was spelled out just above the license plate holder and a Triumph badge sat in the center of the grille.

The fast, high-quality Stag was the first Triumph to carry a V-8. It

*This is the Stag roadster, the first Triumph sports car to be powered by a V-8.*

was designed to compete with the Mercedes-Benz 230SL, at about half the price. The Stag was a convertible, although it originally could be ordered with both tops or a hardtop instead of the soft top. Later, both tops were standard. The hardtop coupe model carried a $5,805 East Coast Port-of-Entry price and tipped the scales at 2,807 lbs.

Triumph designed a large T-bar, positioned just behind the front seats, to stiffen the body structure and meet rollover standards. A high-quality fabric convertible top was available. It lowered into a well, behind the rear seats, where it hid under a lift-up metal tonneau cover.

The T-bar was fixed and remained in place even when the heavy, detachable hardtop was installed. This snug-fitting hardtop made the car look much more like a coupe. The car was luxurious and modern, but the front bucket seats did not have headrests. Electric window lifts were standard equipment.

A 90-degree V-8 with five main bearings, a cast iron block, and an aluminum head was used only in the Stag. A complicated power plant, the V-8 had an overhead camshaft for each cylinder bank. With an 86 x

64.5-mm bore and stroke, it displaced 2997 cc. Other specifications included an 8.8:1 compression ratio and twin Stromberg CD175 carburetors. It was rated for 145 hp at 5500 rpm and 170 lbs.-ft. of torque at 3500 rpm.

Later, the same V-8 used 9.25:1, 8.00:1 and 7.75:1 compression ratios and slightly different 175 CDS (E) V carburetors. The Stag had a top speed of 116 mph and did 0-to-60 mph in 9.3 seconds. The stick-shift version could do the standing-start quarter mile in 17.1 seconds at 82 mph. With automatic transmission, the top speed was around 112 mph. This V-8 had many teething problems, including a marked tendency to easily overheat.

The timing chains were also prone to stretching. Such reliability issues lead to many customers making numerous warranty claims.

Riding a 100-in. wheelbase, the Stag measured 173.7 in. end-to-end. It was 49.5-in. high and 63.5 in. wide. The front tread width was 52.5 in. and the rear tread width was 52.9 in. It had a four-speed manual transmission as standard equipment, although most Stags were fitted with automatic transmission. Overdrive was optionally available with the manual gearbox.

The steering was rack-and-pinion type. Up front was an independent suspension with coil springs, MacPherson struts and an anti-roll bar. The rear suspension incorporated coil springs and semi-trailing arms. For stopping chores, Lockheed hydraulic servo-type brakes were installed, with discs up front and drums in the rear. Rostyle wheel trims were used. Wire wheels were optional in the Colonies, but not in England.

Minor changes were made in the first three years. The 1970 models had a thermal sensor on the air cleaner to enhance warm ups. During the model run, a new 6-bolt crankshaft flange was adopted. In 1971, the dash-mounted bonnet release was moved. A coolant recovery system appeared in 1972 and the cylinder head temperature warning switch was deleted.

In February 1973, a Mk 2 edition of the Stag had about 20 noticeable changes. They included the addition of double body side stripes, flat-black rocker panels with bright metal strips, a flat-black-finished rear body panel, and a beefed-up front bumper system. Wheel trim treatments were revised and alloy rims were optional.

The hardtop no longer had rear quarter windows. Inside, the instrument panel had changes to the gauges and a courtesy light was built into the T-bar. A tinted, laminated windshield became an option.

The design of the combustion chambers and pistons was revised and a distributor with an internal voltage regulator was adopted.

Technical changes included overdrive becoming standard equipment on stick-shift cars. The Mk 2 version also incorporated solutions for many of the engine problems experienced in the first-generation cars. Bad feedback—especially from U.S. buyers and the American press—ruined the model's chances of survival.

About the only significant production modification for 1974 was a newly designed rear half-shaft that could be dismantled. Although it was still selling reasonably well in England, the Stag was taken off the U.S. market.

The Triumph Stag remained available in England through 1977. In 1975, it received alloy wheels, tinted glass, and polished aluminum rocker sill moldings as standard equipment. The trip odometer knob was relocated to the face of the instrument, a high-efficiency radiator was added, a seat-belt warning light appeared, Saginaw power steering was adopted, and the rear-end panel got body-color finish. The carburetors could no longer be owner-adjusted.

Triumph made 740 Stags, 700 for England. A total of 3,901 were made the next year and 1,911 were exported. The total was 4,504 in 1972, of which 3,505 were sold in England. Peak production was 5,508 in 1973 and most (3,194) went to British buyers. Output dropped to 3,442 the next season, with only 836 exported. In 1975, the UK buyers took 1,986 of the 2,898 Stags built. Production for 1976 wasn't released. The 1977 total was 1,836, of which 464 were delivered outside of England and the U.S.

Colors offered for 1971 included Damson Maroon, Laurel Green, Royal Blue, Saffron Yellow, Signal Red, and white. In 1972, Sienna was added and Royal Blue was dropped. Most 1973 colors—Carmine Red, Emerald Green, French Blue, Magenta, Mallard Blue, Pimento Red, Sapphire Blue, Sienna Brown and white—were new. In 1974, five colors were added including Maple, Mimosa Yellow, Pimento Red, Sapphire Blue and White. For 1975, there were 10 colors: Carmine, British Racing Green, French Blue, Delft Blue, Java Green, Maple, Mimosa, Pimento, Topaz (orange-yellow), and white. The last eight 1975 colors were retained for 1976, plus Carmine.

The final year of production, 1977, holds the title for most colors available at 14. They were Carmine, French Blue, Delft, Inca Yellow, Java, Leyland White, Maple, Mimosa, Pageant Blue, Pimento, Russet Brown, Tahiti Blue, Topaz, and white.

OCW Archive

# 1975-1981 TR7

"The shape of things to come" was British Leyland's theme for the Triumph TR7 coupe. The car was conceived as a replacement for both the Triumph TR6 and the MGB. Both of these marques were now a part of the British Leyland family, but the ranks of corporate management were dominated by former Triumph executives. They decided the new sports model should carry the Triumph name.

The design work on the car was done at the British Leyland facility in Longbridge, England. The company said that this new "corporate" sports car, styled by Harris Mann, offered "the bold wedge line of the great international sports-racers." The TR7 was an all-new vehicle and it abandoned all of the traditional "TR" trademarks such as an open body, separate body, and frame construction and independent rear suspension.

British Leyland decided to make it a coupe, as it was felt that open cars would soon be outlawed in the important United States market. Though earlier TR models had used a four-cylinder engine, the return to a four after the six was viewed as a step backward. In breaking so many marque traditions, the TR7 upset Triumph purists right from the start. But it still managed to outsell many other models.

The interior of the TR7 featured two bucket seats, a convenient center console, and a bulky dashboard that ate up some space. It had a conventional luggage compartment in the rear with a locking boot lid.

The closed coupe featured unibody construction and a rigid rear axle. Under the bonnet was a 1998-cc overhead-cam four-cylinder engine, the same one used in the Triumph Dolomite sedan. In essence, the new model was really a Dolomite coupe, but British Leyland called it the TR7 in hopes that such an identity would boost its U.S. sales figures.

The TR7 was first introduced as a U.S.-market-only model for 1975 and had an East Coast P.O.E. price of $5,100. It weighed in at 2,241 lbs. It wasn't made available in Great Britain until a year later. Approximately 112,368 were produced over the full model run between 1975 and 1981.

The in-line, overhead-cam engine, which was nicknamed the "slant-four," had five main bearings, a cast-iron cylinder block and a light alloy cylinder head. With a 90 x 78-mm bore and stroke, it displaced 1998 cc. The engine had an 8.0:1 compression ratio and two Stromberg carburetors were mounted. The U.S. specifications listed 85.5/90 hp at 5000 rpm and 102.5/105 lbs.-ft. of torque at 3000/3250 rpm. In England, this engine was rated at 105 hp.

The Dolomite four made the TR7 a brisk performer with more get-up-and-go than the four-cylinder TR4A, but it was, of course, sluggish compared to the 150-hp TR5s and TR6s. Road testers found that the TR7 could do 0-to-60 mph in as little as 9.1 seconds – or as many as 11

*The Triumph TR7 featured wedge styling packaged in coupe form.*

seconds. Its top speed was in the 100 to 105 mph bracket.

A four-speed manual gearbox was standard equipment. Unfortunately, the overall gearing used with the four-speed transmission was much too low, which tended to make the car seem noisy and temperamental. A British-built three-speed Borg-Warner automatic transmission was a rare option. In 1977, a five-speed manual gearbox became available. This five-speed gearbox, adapted from the Rover SDI saloon, came with a higher rear axle ratio and made the TR7 much more pleasant to drive.

This gearbox was produced in limited quantities and was it pulled off Triumph's Home Market options list (until 1978) to make sure that the available units could be installed in U.S.-bound cars.

The Triumph TR7 chassis had an 85-in. wheelbase. From bumper-to-bumper, the car measured 164.5 in. long. The body was 49.9 in. high and 66.2 in. wide. Tread widths were 55.5 in. up front and 55.3 in. at the rear. MacPherson struts with coil springs and an anti-roll bar made up the front suspension. A rigid axle with radius arms, trailing arms, coil springs, and an anti-roll bar was used in the rear suspension. Front disc/rear drum brakes were fitted.

In March 1977, the TR7 interior was restyled and the new seats introduced at that time had tartan plaid trim, as did the interior door panels. The suspension settings were revised and this change resulted in a lower ride height. There were plans for a V-8-powered TR7 (which became the TR8) as well as a Sprint version with a 127-hp Dolomite four in 1977, which never materialized, except in prototype form.

In November 1977, workers at the Speke factory, in Liverpool, where TR7s were built, staged a strike. The plant was closed for 14 weeks, during which time British Leyland decided to move all TR7 assembly work to its Canley factory. A Pressed Steel Fisher plant in Swindon was commissioned to build the bodies.

Wider tires were installed for 1978, along with a new front air dam. A TR7 convertible arrived in America in 1979 and finally came out in England in March 1980. It incorporated various structural modifications to enhance its rigidity. These included bracing behind the seats, across the cowl, across the firewall, and at the rear of the chassis. In appearance, the convertible was a most pretty car. The 1979 coupe sold for $7,695, and the new convertible cost $8,395.

In 1980, British Leyland decided to close the Canley assembly plant and TR7 manufacturing was again moved, this time to the Rover factory at Solihull. This change was phased in between April 1980 and the following August, and the cars made in Solihull earned a reputation for having the best build quality of all TR7s. These cars included the Premium interior introduced in 1979 and also had a round emblem on the front in place of the old laurel wreath decal.

The 1980 TR7 prices climbed to $8,465 for the 2,487-lb. coupe and $9,235 for the 2,505-lb. convertible. In 1981, American references listed only the TR7 convertible at a price of $10,995. These later TR7s carried different engine output ratings: 88.5 hp at 5250 rpm and 100 lbs.-ft. of torque at 2500 rpm. The last TR7s—and the last Triumph sports cars—were built on October 5, 1981 in the Solihull factory.

OCW Archive

# 1980-1981 TR8

The TR8–introduced in 1981–was technically the "last" new sports model that Triumph produced, although it shared the title of "final Triumph sports-car" with the TR7. That's because the TR8 was based on the TR7 and both went to their grave when sports-car production concluded on October 5, 1981.

Creating the new Triumph TR8 as a last-ditch attempt to recapture lost sales in the United States (this model was not offered to sports car buyers in Great Britain), Triumph slipped Rover's all-aluminum V-8 into the two TR7 bodies. Both the coupe and convertible were offered in the TR8 series.

The closed car sold for $11,150 East Coast Port-of-Entry and tipped the scales at 2,650 lbs. The ragtop was priced at $11,900 and weighed 22 lbs. more than the coupe. A small number of right-hand drive cars (about 18 to 22 convertibles and less than 50 coupes) were constructed and show up in factory photographs. It is thought that some of these cars were built to serve as factory rally cars.

Both TR8 body styles had the wedge-shaped appearance of their TR7 counterparts and looked very much like them, except for a bulge in the bonnet put there to accommodate the higher V-8 engine, a TR8 decal at the center of the nose panel, and a similar decal on the right-hand side of the boot lid. In the center of the rear deck lid was a round badge. The TR8 also carried "3.5-liter" lettering behind the front wheel openings. The black plastic rear bumper had matching black overriders and the dual exhaust pipes exited below them

Inside the car was a TR7-style interior with tartan plaid seating surfaces, bucket seats with separate headrests, a wide center console, a bulky cabinet-style glove box, and a large hooded instrument panel that extended over the center console. The padded steering wheel was a small-diameter type with three wide aluminum-look spokes. An upscale upholstery package substituted velour seat facings and interior door panels for the plaid type. Power rack-and-pinion steering was standard, as were cast alloy wheels, tinted glass, an AM/FM stereo and metallic body paint. Air conditioning was the only option.

The aluminum V-8 engine under the TR8's bonnet had its origins at General Motors' Buick Division in the early 1960s. It was used as standard equipment in the 1961-1963 Buick Special and Oldsmobile F-85 compacts, and was also a rare option used in one percent of all

*While the Triumph TR8 resembled the TR7, it was powered by a Rover V-8 engine.*

1961-1962 Tempests. When the compacts grew into mid-size cars, GM sold the engine tooling to Rover. (Later, the engine would come back to America for use in the Jeep.)

Equipped with dual Stromberg carburetors, the 3528-cc V-8 developed 133 hp at 5000 rpm in U.S. "Federal" spec form. The torque output was 174 lbs.-ft. at 3000 rpm. It had an 89 x 71-mm bore and stroke, hydraulic valve lifters and an 8.1:1 compression ratio.

A Bosch L-Jetronic fuel-injection system was required in California—and later installed on all 1981 TR8s. This induction system added four more horsepower.

Either a five-speed manual gearbox or three-speed automatic transmission was available in the TR8. These were the same units that were optional in the TR7. The TR8 used a higher (numerically lower) 3.08:1 rear axle ratio instead of the TR7's 3.90:1 ratio.

The Triumph TR7 chassis had the same 85-in. wheelbase as the TR7. It was 165.4 in. long overall. The body was 49.5 in. high and 66.2 in. wide. Tread widths were 55.5 in. up front and 55.3 in. at the rear. As in the TR7, MacPherson struts with coil springs and an anti-roll bar made up the front suspension.

All components were beefed-up for the V-8 application. The same was true of the rear suspension, with its rigid axle, radius arms, trailing arms, coil springs, and anti-roll bar. The front disc/rear drum brakes were also a bit meatier to stop the more powerful V-8 model.

With an 8.5-second 0-to-60-mph time, the TR8 was quicker than the TR7 and its higher final drive ratio made it noticeably quieter. On the plus side, it benefited from the TR7's more outstanding design features like its interior, its handling, and its high comfort and convenience level.

On the downside, it reflected the same spotty build quality and inconsistent workmanship and had some problems with structural integrity. But it was the fastest sports car to ever carry a Triumph badge and the last new sports car the company brought out. That makes it a historical milestone.

# TRIUMPH *Spitfire & GT Series*

Greg Hertel

# 1963-1964 *Spitfire 4*

A lick Dick, the managing director of Standard-Triumph, dreamed of turning his mid-sized company into a giant. He knew he would need a business partner to take this step and spent much of the 1950s looking for one.

During the fall of 1960 and winter of 1961, Dick's company suddenly found itself in dire financial straits, largely due to a credit crunch in England. Although its sports cars were selling well in the United States, the company sold only a handful of TR3As in England. Merger talks with British Leyland started on Nov. 14, 1960. On December 5, Leyland announced it was taking over Triumph in a stock swap deal.

Plans for a new sports car, based on the Triumph Herald saloon, had been discussed at Triumph during 1956 and 1957. A year later, Austin-Healey issued the diminutive Sprite and showed there was demand for a small, cheap sports car. MG already had a foothold in this niche since it had produced "Midgets" for decades. A boxy new MG Midget appeared in 1962.

To compete with its marketplace rivals, Leyland wisely moved Triumph's small sports car project to the front burner. The Spitfire 4 was made available for sale in late 1962 and wound up selling more copies than its two British rivals combined. Italian stylist Giovanni Michelotti, who did the Herald, was credited with the Spitfire's design.

The name of the new car came from the famed World War II British fighter plane. According to one account, Air Marshall Tedder, chairman of Standard-Triumph, was responsible for obtaining an OK from Vickers aircraft company to use the Spitfire name. Supposedly, the use of the Vickers and Vanguard names was exchanged.

*Car & Driver* magazine took a cover photo showing the new sports car with one of the vintage military planes and Triumph later made it into a poster. The four-wheeled version was actually called the Spitfire 4 at first.

**The Triumph Spitfire 4 was the creation of Italian stylist Giovanni Michelotti.**

Michelotti was well regarded by Standard-Triumph management and had restyled the Vanguard Vignale. He then designed the Herald and moved on to the small sports car concept. Based on conversations he'd had with Triumph executives, Michelotti's studio turned out a great-looking prototype of a small sports car known as the "Bomb." Unfortunately, it was delivered when Triumph was just on the verge of bankruptcy.

The prototype was pushed into a corner of the company's experimental workshop, where it sat until Leyland came on the scene. Sales director Donald Stokes saw the car as a path to increased export sales and profits. Work began again with minor changes carried over 18 months.

The new car was introduced at the Earl's Court Motor Show, in London, in the fall of 1962. Up front were two small, rectangular split grilles. The headlights were partially recessed and the doors were just slightly cut-down. The suspension was the same fully-independent design used in the Herald, but mounted on a new backbone-style chassis with a shorter (83-in.) wheelbase. Welded monocoque (unibody) construction was employed. The hood and front fenders tilted upward as a unit, for excellent engine bay access.

Unibody construction made the Spitfire 4 a very sturdy car. The doors were made larger than Michelotti's original design so they could completely hide the wind-down windows when lowered. The Spitfire 4's unusual exterior body seams were covered with chrome finishing strips. This made it much easier and cheaper to weld up the bodies.

Inside, the early Spitfire 4 had the gauges housed in a panel in the center of the dashboard. Two large dials closest to the center housed the speedometer and the tachometer. The fuel and temperature gauges were inside smaller round circles flanking the larger ones. There were warning lights for oil pressure and the generator. Four control knobs ran across the dashboard below the center panel. Most Spitfire 4s featured left-hand drive for the North American market.

A rubber floor mat was provided and there was a stowage space behind the seats. Two open glove boxes were on either side of the dash. The bucket seats had low seatbacks and body-hugging contours.

Inside that bay was a modified Triumph Herald overhead-valve engine. This in-line four cylinder had a cast-iron block. With a 69.3 x 76-mm bore and stroke, it displaced 1147 cc. It featured three main bearings, solid valve lifters, an 8.5:1 compression ratio and twin S.U. carburetors. It was rated for 63 hp at 5750 rpm and 67 lbs.-ft. of torque at 3500-3750 rpm. Contemporary road tests put top speed at about 92-93 mph. The 0-to-60 mph acceleration time was in the 15.5 to 16.5 second range.

The Spitfire 4 drive train layout was a conventional front-engine, rear-drive design with a four-speed manual transmission. Overdrive was optional. Rack-and-pinion steering was fitted as were unequal-length A-arms with coil springs in front.

The rear suspension featured swing axles with radius arms and transverse leaf springs. Disc brakes were used aft, with drums at the stern end.

The Spitfire 4 had an 83-in. wheelbase and 145-in. overall length.

It was 47.5 in. high, 57 in. wide, and had a 49-in. front tread and 48-in. rear tread. The standard 5.20 x 13 tires were mounted on disc wheels. Centre-locking wire wheels were available for slight extra cost in 1963.

Triumph put the Spitfire 4 on sale from autumn 1962 until December 1964. It was introduced to Americans at the 1962 Chicago Auto Show. The East Coast Port of Entry price was $2,199 and it weighed 1,474 lbs. Approximately 45,753 Triumph Spitfire 4s were produced from 1962-1964. During the car's first year, American Triumph sales climbed 25 percent, and with overall sales up 30 percent!

In September 1963, a good-looking Spitfire 4 hardtop with a rounded roofline and curved back window was made available. Both the roadster and the hardtop carried a $2,349 East Coast price. Otherwise, the sports car was mechanically unaltered.

Strong sales continued, and in April 1964 monthly sales records were set for several months running. In April, more than 1,000 Spitfire 4s were sold.

Race drivers David Hobbs and Rob Slotemaker drove a competition version of the Spitfire 4 at Le Mans and took a third in class. Their car had an aerodynamic fiberglass fastback roof. Slotemaker teamed with Terry Hunter to take a class win in the Tour De France.

Valerie Pirie, a female driver on the Stirling Moss Auto Racing Team, campaigned another Spitfire 4 and Spitfires also won three SCCA divisionals. Today, many enthusiasts refer to the Spitfire 4 as the Spitfire MK 1.

David Gooley

# 1965-1966 Spitfire MK2

**B**y 1964, production of the Triumph Spitfire 4 had hit 500 units per week. As a result, Triumph actually became the highest-volume sports car maker in England. With such a huge success on its hands, the automaker felt no pressing need to alter the car and the Spitfire 4 (or Spitfire MK 1) remained on sale until December 1964. The Spitfire MK 2 followed and would remain in production into 1967. The second edition of Triumph's smaller sports car was introduced at the end of 1964 as a 1965 model. Triumph decided to make a few changes and improvements to maintain the sales momentum. The only exterior difference was a slightly different front grille, but the car was made more comfortable and had a few, slight mechanical upgrades.

*Cosmetic changes to the Triumph Spitfire Mk II included a different grille.*

A vinyl-covered dashboard was new and made the interior look a bit dressier. More luxurious deep-pile carpeting replaced the former rubber mat that covered the floor and transmission tunnel of the Spitfire 4. The seats were also new and more comfortable than those used in the original version.

The Spitfire MK 2's engine was the same 1174-cc. in-line, overhead-valve four-cylinder used in the Spitfire 4 with a little more power. Everything was pretty much the same, specifications-wise, right down to the 8.5:1 compression ratio. The engine was now rated for 67 hp at 6000 rpm and 67 lbs.-ft. of torque at 3750 rpm.

Owners who were interested in going faster could order three different extra-cost engine tuning kits. The basic or "interim" kit included a Solex downdraft carburetor with modified manifolds. It was good for 70 hp. A Stage I kit stepped up the power. A Stage III kit went "all the way" with a pair of Weber carburetors, a higher-lift camshaft and exhaust headers. Few Spitfires MK 2s with the Stage III package were sold. Other drive train changes included a new camshaft and a diaphragm-type clutch.

By this time, the hardtop model—which had originally been priced the same as the roadster—pulled ahead of the soft-top model in price. For 1965-1966, the open car listed for $2,155 East Coast Port of Entry. The hardtop was an additional $144. The weight of the base model was only 1,474 lbs. and the hardtop was a bit heavier. In 1967, the price of both models was hiked by $44 apiece. Approximately 37,409 Triumph Spitfire MK 2s were produced between 1964 and 1967.

In the United States, the Spitfire MK 2 took its first bow in Ft. Lauderdale, Florida, along with Triumph's TR4A. By the time of the International Auto Show in New York City in April, the readers of *Car & Driver* had selected the Spitfire as "Best GT/Sports Car Under $2,500." The Automotive Council for Women picked it as "The Pussycat Car."

*Car & Driver* said, "Maybe it's the independent rear suspension, maybe it's the slightly better performance than its rivals, but for some reason or another, the Triumph Spitfire was a clear-cut choice for honors among the Sports/Grand Touring cars under $2,500. The Spitfire won with surprising ease over the Austin-Healey Sprites, receiving 32.3 percent of the vote while its rival polled 20.4 percent. Many automotive journalists tend to lump cars in this class together, reasoning that the price, quality and performance of the Spitfire, Sprite, Morgan 4/4 and the MG Midget are so similar that one can only make a subjective choice.

You, the readers, must disagree."

In *Mechanix Illustrated*, the great automotive scribe Uncle Tom McCahill said, "Any way you approach the Triumph Spitfire MK 2, it's a real fun bucket and a true sports car.

One thing is certain, if you're a sports car buff and the Spitfire meets your budget, you can't possibly go wrong putting one of those in your barn ... It's worth every foolish dime you can't afford."

Spitfire sales continued to rise during 1965, a year in which a pair of fastback coupes took first and second in class wins at Le Mans.

Overall sales were 10 percent higher than in 1964. In racing and rallying events, Spitfires took many checkered flags and prizes.

McCahill tested one Spitfire at Daytona International Speedway and rated it above the Austin-Healey Sprite and MG Midget.

There were no trim or mechanical changes in the Spitfire MK 2 for 1966, but the list of factory accessories kept growing longer every year.

By this time, buyers could order special grilles, bumper overriders, wheel covers, radios, wood-grained steering wheels, custom gearshift knobs, tonneau covers, luggage racks, and many other items.

Racing equipment was also available and Spitfires took top honors in four different Sports Car Club of America (SCCA) divisions.

Other examples came in second and third in the American Road Race of Champions in Riverside, California.

Bob Harrington

# *1966-1968 GT-6*

I talian car designer Giovanni Michelotti was commissioned to build a Spitfire fastback prototype in 1963-1964. Instead of producing it immediately, Triumph used it as a model for racing versions of the Spitfire and sports car fans watched with interest as Triumph Spitfire 4s with add-on fiberglass fastbacks were raced successfully.

The racing cars did well at big-name events like Le Mans and Sebring, generating lots of publicity and demand for a look-alike

***The Triumph GT-6 combined Spitfire styling with a handsome fastback top.***

production model. This gave Triumph engineers ammunition ompany's sales department and the fastback GT-6 evolved. The sales people insisted the new car be different from the roadster, so the car wouldn't have a negative effect on the open-car marketing program.

The GT-6 was introduced in the fall of 1966, although pre-production "pilot" models were photographed as early as July of that year. Some enthusiasts saw the GT-6 as an affordable, pint-sized version of the E-Type Jaguar and even called it the "Mini-E-Type."

In his Tab Book called *The Triumph Spitfire,* former public relations manager Michael Cook explained the GT-6's creation. "Decision time came in 1965 when another model, priced between the Spitfire and the TR4A and directly competitive with the about-to-be-announced MGB-GT, seemed to be a better idea. The (Michelotti-designed) prototype coupe was there and it remained only to decide on the power train."

In the original plan, the new car was going to use the 1596-cc six-cylinder that powered the Vitesse sedan and convertible. However, those cars were already in line to share common use of the Triumph 2000 engine, so the GT-6 was also given the same 1998-cc six in order to keep things simple.

Cook says, "The GT-6 thus received a power increase before the first car was built."

The GT-6's clean styling was similar to that of the Spitfire, but the fastback top and a large glass hatch gave the GT-6 a distinct personality of its own, which was exactly according to plan. It was decorated with a few top-of-the-line trim bits on the outside and inside, to give customers the impression that it was fancier than the four-cylinder Spitfire and to make it competitive with the MGB GT. However, it did not carry nearly as much adornment as later versions of the car.

In England, the first-generation models were even equipped with "dog dish" hubcaps and wheel trim rings, but in the United States, where most sales were expected to be made, the GT-6 came with wire wheels, at least in the 1966-1968 period.

Inside, the car was a snug—but not an impossible—fit for large drivers. "I could get inside," said R. W. Kastner, Triumph's competition director. "Now, that might not sound like much until you remember that I am 6-ft. 4-in. and weigh 200 lbs. ... When no cranial contact was made after several minutes on New York streets, I completely forgot about the low roof-line and started paying attention to wringing out the GT-6." A popular option was a sun roof, which helped fight off sensations of claustrophobia.

The interior was fully trimmed with plush-looking bucket seats, a headliner and floor carpeting. The walnut-trimmed dashboard was similar to that of the current Spitfire, but it had the instruments grouped in front of the driver, instead of at the center. There was no divider used between the passenger compartment and the luggage compartment. A large lift gate could be opened to stow things in the carpeted luggage area. Under the load floor was the spare tire and gas tank, the latter being larger than the roadster version.

Modifying the Spitfire chassis for the fastback coupe coachwork and the in-line six wasn't terribly difficult. The GT-6 utilized the same 83-in. wheelbase, but was two inches shorter at 145 in. It stood 47 in. high to the roof (a half-inch shorter than the roadster) and had the same 57-in. overall body width. The 49-in. front and 48-in. rear treads were the same as the Spitfire's, although the GT-6 used 155 x 13 radial tires instead of the Spitfire's 5.20 x 13 bias-plies.

The all-synchromesh four-speed manual transmission, also pirated from the Vitesse, was well-suited to the torquey engine and overdrive was optional at extra cost. Many test drivers pointed out Triumph's excellent choice of gear ratios for the GT-6.

R.W. Kastner said, "The ratios are delightfully close and give the feeling of constant flowing power." The 3.27:1 ratio rear axle was a beefed-up version of the Spitfire type that handled the extra power well. It had a different axle case and stronger half shafts. Beefier U-joints were also employed. The high (numerically low) axle ratio contributed to a reputation for good fuel economy.

The GT-6 had softer suspension settings, a nose-heavy attitude (due to having two spare cylinders up front) and the swing-axle rear suspension was not fully up to its increased power. As a result, European road testers criticized its handling, but it proved to do better on American highways. *Road & Track* explained, "We approach any car with conventional swing axles with a little apprehension, but we found the GT-6 could not be faulted on its handling ... for ordinary-to-brisk driving, the car steers neutrally and simply goes where it's steered with great apparent stability." But in England, *Autocar* said, "We feel it is a pity that the limitations from the continued use of swing axles should detract so much from what is basically such a good car and we urge Standard-Triumph to make improvements without delay."

The overhead-valve six had a cast-iron block, cast-iron head and a 74.7 x 76-mm bore and stroke. Other specifications included four main bearings, solid valve lifters and a 9.5:1 compression ratio. With twin Stromberg carburetors mounted, it cranked up 95 hp at 5000 rpm and 117 lbs.-ft. of torque at 3000 rpm. The GT-6 had a 106-mph top speed and moved from a standstill to 60 mph in 12.0 to 12.3 seconds.

When introduced at the Earl's Court Show in London, the car was an instant hit with the public. The automotive press remained skeptical at first, but the GT-6 won many praises from scribes as time went by.

Only the one body style was issued (Michael Cook says that a six-cylinder-powered Spitfire roadster was never considered) and it was sold at an East Coast Port-of-Entry price of $2,895. The car's weight was 1,900 lbs. Over the full model run, from 1966 to 1968, about 15,818 first-generation GT-6s were produced. First-year sales were over 8,000 units. Today, these cars are often called GT-6 MK 1s.

The GT-6 was soon making its way to races and rallies everywhere. It was campaigned in Class EP competition, where it ran very well against a variety of cars including MG Midgets some older Triumph TR3s.

Bob Harrington

# 1969-1970 Spitfire MK3

I n six years, the Triumph Spitfire had come out of nowhere to evolve into a giant success story. Some 85,000 had been manufactured and nearly 77 percent were sold into export markets, which brought money into the British economy. At several points along the way, the Spitfire held the title of "best-selling sports car" in one market or another.

The Triumph factory in Coventry had the MK 3 edition of its popular Spitfire ready for introduction in the spring of 1967. This version was refined along lines that made it quicker, faster, more comfortable, more convenient, better equipped, safer and easier to stop.

Sacrificing none of the performance and handling features of the earlier models, Triumph kept prices affordable: $2,235 for the open car (now called the convertible) and $2,385 for the hardtop version (now called the coupe).

Styling was similar to the prior edition, except for the addition of a thick wraparound bright metal bumper directly ahead of the grille. This raised bumper had been engineered to meet a newly proposed safety standard in the United States and made the Spitfire look like it had a "bone in its teeth." The parking lamps and winkers (signal lights) ended below the bumper. New bumper guards were faced with rubber. The hood hinge brackets were also now uncovered.

The Spitfire MK 3 had new-style door handles, and back-up lights were made standard equipment. Rear quarter-bumpers were installed as they had been before, but with a modified shape.

Inside were more cushiony seats, a restyled dashboard with walnut-veneer trim around the instruments, padded rails and a padded top. Vinyl trim now hid many metal interior areas that had previously been painted. Plusher carpets were installed and attachment points for a shoulder harness were added, although lap belts only were standard equipment.

The Spitfire MK 3's hood (soft top) was one of the biggest advances for 1968. The previous style—often referred to as the "build-it-yourself" or "do-it-yourself" top—was a rather complicated affair with a frame made of light steel tubing that fit into sockets at the rear of each door.

The hood had to be stretched over the frame and fastened to the

***The Triumph Spitfire MK3 included a more powerful 1296cc power plant.***

rear and the sides of the car with snaps. A steel strip hooked over the upper windshield frame. While actually better than some earlier sports cars, this system seemed archaic to American buyers.

Triumph based the construction of the new soft top on its Herald convertible top, which used a pair of bright metal latches to secure the front bow to the windshield and four nylon snaps to attach the sides. A tonneau cover was provided to hide it from sight when it was folded.

Under the Spitfire MK 3's bonnet was a larger (1296-cc) engine used in the front-drive 1300 sedan. The inline, overhead-valve four-cylinder had a cast-iron block and head. A new anti-pollution item was a Smiths positive crankcase ventilation control valve mounted just above the rear carburettor. The engine had a 73.7 x 76-mm bore and stroke, which upped displacement to 1296 cc.

Carried over were a crank supported in three main bearings, solid valve lifters and the use of twin S.U. carburettors, but the compression ratio was boosted to 9.0:1. The engine's output climbed to 75 hp at 6000 rpm and 75 lbs-ft. of torque at 4000 rpm. The Spitfire MK 3 had a top speed of about 95 mph and could move from 0-to-60 mph in 14.0 seconds.

Other mechanical advances included a water-heated intake manifold and a larger clutch to handle the additional torque. Front disc brakes were also beefed up and DeCarbon fluid/gas shocks were added at the rear. The overall length of the car was up two inches, to 147 in., due to the larger new "safety" bumpers.

The Spitfire continued to feature a four-speed manual transmission (with overdrive available), rack-and-pinion steering, unequal-length A-arms with coil springs up front, and swing axles with radius arms and a transverse leaf spring at the rear.

Starting in 1969, Spitfire MK 3s got a revised dashboard, with the instruments mounted directly ahead of the driver, not centered in the dash. A matte-finish walnut veneer panel surrounded the instruments. A leather-trimmed padded steering wheel was fitted. The car also had new wheel covers, totally new seats (with adjustable backrests) and headrests mandated by new U.S. safety regulations.

Horsepower dropped to 68 hp, due to new pollution system hardware. Only the convertible was offered. The East Coast Port-of-Entry price declined to $2,295 and the car also lost 18 lbs. West Coast prices were $50 higher. Popular options included wire wheels for $118 extra and overdrive for $175 extra.

The price of the 1970 Spitfire increased by $100. Side marker lights were a new safety feature. The 1970 MK 3 also got new full wheel covers, a matte black grille and new body badging. The red, white and blue logo on the hood badge closely matched the RAF (Royal Air Force) symbol.

Inside, a matte-black trim panel replaced the previous wood veneer on the dashboard. New seats and a zip-out rear window were included. Federal regulations now required a buzzer to warn when the key was in the ignition switch.

New emissions regulations allowed only a single S.U. carburetor. While still rated at 68 hp, the engine wasn't really as powerful. California's evaporative emission standards meant all 1970 Triumphs were equipped with sealed gas tanks vent systems and a charcoal canister.

*Car & Driver* magazine described the Spitfire MK 3 as a "jouncy, feisty little item" and added, "There is some danger that cars may become too good to be interesting or maybe just too good to be fun. The Triumph Spitfire MK 3 has not yet fallen into that characterless condition." In 1970, the magazine picked the Spitfire as one of "The 13 Best Cars in the World."

*Road & Track* compared the Spitfire to the MG Midget MK III and found the Triumph faster, more comfortable, and better handling on rough surfaces. The magazine also preferred the Spitfire's heating and ventilation system.

During the lifespan of the Spitfire MK 3, Rover Motor Company and Standard-Triumph merged after Leyland acquired Rover. In 1968, Leyland and British Motor Holdings merged to form British Leyland. The Leyland Motor Corporation was established to sell cars in the U.S.

First quarter 1968 sales were up over 80 percent. The March sales were an all-time record for Triumph. Later that year, the 100,000th Spitfire was assembled. About 65,320 Triumph Spitfire Mk IIIs were produced between 1967 and 1970.

# 1969-'70 GT-6 Plus/ GT-6 MKII

Introduced in the fall of 1968, the second-generation Triumph GT-6 fastback coupe was known as the GT-6 Plus in the United States, but called the GT-6 MK II in England. It was mainly characterized by its front-end styling changes and by the use of a completely different independent rear suspension. The latter was designed to improve on the original swing-axle system, which was often criticized for its "finicky" handling and was not really appreciated by those interested in racing.

The styling of the new GT-6 was similar to that of the prior edition, except for the addition of a thick wraparound bright metal bumper ahead of the grille. This raised bumper had been engineered to meet a newly proposed safety standard in the United States. Its "bone-in-the-teeth" look was also seen on the Spitfire.

The parking/directional lights were now repositioned below the bumper front. New bumper guards with rubber facings were also seen. The hood hinge brackets were now uncovered. New door handles were used and back-up lights were made standard equipment.

In the rear suspension, a transverse leaf spring was still utilized, but the axles or half-shafts were of a new double-jointed design. Normal U-joints were used at the inner end of the axles. At the outer end, next to the hubs, were metalastic rubber doughnuts that acted like U-joints and also absorbed sudden torque-twist impulses. The outer axles ran in a carrier fixed at the top by the spring and at the bottom by a cast wishbone. Angled radius rods also held the axles in place. This setup was unique to the GT-6 Plus/GT-6 MK II. The Spitfire MK III used swing axles with radius rods and a transverse leaf spring.

The GT-6 Plus/GT-6 MK II model's suspension changes were greatly appreciated by drivers navigating the twisting, curvy roads of England and Europe, although they had less impact on American highway drivers. Triumph's U.S. Competition Department saw the improvements as a way to offset the GT-6's front-heavy bias by keeping the rear wheels lined up better and solidly grounded on the track.

When the dust cleared after the 1969 racing season, the first three spots at the Sports Car Club of America Championships were held by Triumph GT-6 Plus/GT-6 MK II drivers.

Inside the car were more comfortable seats with headrests and a restyled leather steering wheel. The dashboard had walnut-veneer trim around the instruments and revised heater/defroster controls. A flow-through ventilation system with new air exhaust grilles on the long C-pillars was featured and an electric defroster was added to the hatchback window glass. A three-point safety harness was provided as part of the upgraded standard safety equipment package.

Under the bonnet of the GT-6+/GT-6 Mk II was the same 1998-cc six-cylinder engine used in the 1967-1968 models, with a number of modifications including a new cylinder head and a revised camshaft design. The revised engine's compression ratio dropped from 9.5:1 to 9.25:1. In Europe, the engine was rated for 104 hp, but U.S.-spec cars had new anti-pollution hardware and were advertised as producing just 95 hp at 4700 rpm and 117 lbs.-ft. of torque at 3400 rpm. Twin side-draft carburettors were used again, but they were Zenith models instead of Strombergs.

The 1969 GT-6 Plus/GT-6 MK II had an East Coast Port-of-Entry price of $2,995. On the West Coast, the 1,792-lb. car cost $50 more. There were only detail changes for 1970, most of which were related to the addition of new safety features such as sidemarker lights, revised taillights and a safety catch on the magnetic fuel filler cap. The upper front fender feature line now carried a pinstripe. With all of these improvements, the price climbed only $10 and the shipping weight went up to 1,904 lbs.

In 1969, *Car and Driver* magazine selected the Triumph Spitfire as the Best Sports/GT model in its class. In 1970, the Spitfire had to share the same honor with the GT-6 Plus/GT-6 MK II. Such positive reviews helped the car's sales popularity, and production over the two model years came to 12,066 units. This was down from the 15,818 of the original version produced in 1966-1968, but it was still a nice contribution to Triumph's coffers.

Greg Hertel

# 1971-1972 Spitfire MKIV

Arriving in late 1970 for the 1971 model year, the new Triumph Spitfire MK IV was a much-refined version of the earlier car using the same famous name. In addition to solving almost all shortcomings of the Spitfire MK 3, the MK IV satisfied the ever-stricter federal standards required to meet new safety and anti-pollution regulations applicable in the United States. It was the start of the most popular and enduring Spitfire design, which was carried forward in the identical-looking Spitfire 1500.

While the German coachbuilder Karmann was commissioned to update the TR6 in 1969, Italian designer Giovanni Michelotti was once again tapped to facelift Triumph's smaller sports car, which he did with his usual expertise. Retaining the now-considered-classic Spitfire styling theme, Michelotti gave the car a more contemporary flavor, along with some very practical improvements like a revised cowl that looked the same, but added two inches of depth to the windshield.

Marketed as a convertible priced at $2,649 and weighing in at 1,620 lbs., the Spitfire MK IV had single-unit front fenders and a wider grille opening with a matte-black-finished insert. A large, full-width chrome bumper wrapped around each front body corner. In retooling the Mark IV's front end, the panel joints were eliminated, giving the car's nose an overall cleaner appearance. A spoiler was now mounted low on the front end.

Spitfires built for the U.S. market had black-finished bumpers with gigantic black polycarbonate underriders that protected the new, combined parking and directional lights. A new chrome-plated hood badge replaced the original RAF-style badge.

A more comfortable and quieter restyled interior greeted Spitfire lovers. Reclining seats with headrests became standard equipment. Both of the bucket seats tilted up to give access to the luggage stowage compartment. The dashboard featured flat-black finish and full instrumentation. An optional new removable hardtop was taller and provided added headroom. The hardtop incorporated rear quarter windows that greatly improved air flow and interior ventilation.

Following a theme used on the TR6 and other early 1970s Triumphs, the Spitfire got a new squared-off rear end that provided more room for luggage. The multi-functional taillights were new, as was the rear bumper. The trunk lid had a new safety lock and was decorated

*The Spitfire Mk IV featured design refinements that gave the car a cleaner look.*

with the Triumph name spelled out in block letters. On the rear fenders, the seams were decorated with black-chrome moldings.

Spitfire MK IVs initially used a carryover 1296-cc engine. Two Zenith-Stromberg carburetors were fitted to the hotter European models, while cars sold in the U.S. had a single carburetor. In Europe the output rating was 75 hp at 6000 rpm and 75 lbs.-ft. of torque at 4000 rpm, while U.S. market cars advertised 58 hp at 5200 rpm and 72 lbs.-ft. of torque at 4000 rpm. The engine had a heavier crankshaft and longer-life bearings. Also new was an eight-blade cooling fan and a redesigned air cleaner.

Body dimensions showed only minor changes with an 83-in. wheelbase, 147-in. overall length, 47.5-in. height, 57-in. width, 49-in. front tread, and 48-in. rear tread. The most noteworthy chassis modification was the installation of a revised independent rear suspension. This system replaced the familiar swing-axle setup with a configuration that allowed the transverse leaf springs to pivot at the same time. After many years of availability, wire wheels departed from the optional equipment list.

The Spitfire MK IV had a brand new all-synchromesh four-speed manual transmission. Overdrive was available as an extra-cost option. The final drive ratio was changed to 3.98:1 from 4.11:1. As was typical with Triumph sports cars, rack-and-pinion steering was provided. The front suspension featured unequal-length A-arms with coil springs. The rear had the new swing axles with radius arms and a pivoting transverse leaf spring. Front disc/rear drum brakes were standard.

The press loved the styling of the 1971 Spitfire MK IV, even if the performance of this heavier, less-powerful sportster left much to be desired. The buying public liked it, too, with Triumph enjoying a 60 percent increase in total sales. U.S. sales were 8,226 units. Spitfire production jumped from 17,041 units in 1970 to 20,577 in 1971.

For 1972, Spitfires got a higher compression ratio (8.0:1) and returned to using a lower (numerically higher) 4.1:1 rear axle ratio.

The engine had only 48 hp at 5500 rpm and 60.8 lbs.-ft. of torque at 2900 rpm, but the car felt a bit snappier.

Outwardly, the rear body panel took on satin-black finish to make the taillights stand out better.

During the model run, shoulder harnesses were made standard equipment, along with a warning light/buzzer to force you to use the shoulder belts.

Production for 1972 was 17,746 Spitfires, which brought total MK IV production to 45,035 units. U.S. sales rose to 9,685.

In 1973, Triumph launched a new version of the Spitfire, which was essentially the MK IV design with a larger 1493-cc engine.

This car looked identical to its predecessor, but carried Spitfire 1500 badges. In this book, the "1500" is covered separately.
s

Bob Harrington

# 1971-1973 GT-6 MKIII

Like the Spitfire MK IV, the third-generation Triumph GT-6 that bowed in 1971 gained a fresh look with much cleaner-looking frontal treatment. New single-unit front fenders replaced the previous two-piece style. A wider new grille opening with a matte-black-finished insert decorated the nose.

Slightly flared wheel openings were one new styling feature, along with recessed door handles and rear quarter windows that reached farther back. A large chrome front bumper was used. Models sold in the United States wore smooth black wraparound bumpers with gigantic bumper guards. The power blister on the hood was smoothened out to compliment the cleaner styling. The car had an overall sleeker appearance.

The tail end was redesigned to look more like that of the Triumph TR6. At the rear end, the gas filler cap was moved to a new position. Instead of exiting at the rear end panel, it was mounted on the left rear fender. A larger rear bumper was seen and a more integrated taillight treatment was a nice improvement.

The seats were wider and reclining seats became standard equipment. The windshield was also increased in size and an improved interior-ventilation system was featured. It had a quieter fan and newly-designed air intakes and ducting. Disc wheels (4-1/2-in. in diameter) were again standard, but wire wheels were no longer on the options list.

This time, both European and U.S. models took the same name. They were designated GT-6 MK III models. In America, the East Coast Port-of-Entry price for the 1,936-lb. fastback was $3,374. Perched on an 83-in. wheelbase, the GT-6 MK III measured 149 in. end to end, which was up two inches. It was 47 in. high and 57 in. wide. The front/rear tread dimensions were a uniform 49 in.

A four-speed manual transmission was standard in the Triumph GT-6 MK 3 and overdrive was available. Overdrive could now be selected at the gearshift lever, instead of via a switch on the dashboard. Other technical features included rack-and-pinion steering and front disc/rear drum brakes. The front suspension featured unequal-length A-arms with coil springs. The rear suspension continued to use double-jointed half-shafts with lower A-arms and transverse leaf springs.

**The Triumph GT-6 Mk III made a dashing presence wherever it raced.**

Under the bonnet once again was the 1998-cc (74.7 x 76-mm bore and stroke) in-line six with overhead valves, a cast-iron block and head, solid valve lifters, four main bearings and a new pollution-friendlier 8.0:1 compression ratio. Two Zenith-Stromberg side draft carburetors were fitted as usual. The engine again produced 95 hp.

Horsepower ratings of U.S.-market models were constantly reduced throughout the early 1970s and in 1972 the rating for the GT-6 MK III dropped to 79 hp. It should be noted that the smaller number was due to a change to SAE net horsepower rating figures instead of the old (numerically higher) gross horsepower ratings. Nevertheless, the popularity of the fastback had always been based on the image of the early prototype Le Mans race cars and the drop off in performance hurt sales considerably. A jump in price, to $3,523, was certainly not a sales incentive, either.

In 1973, the GT-6 MK III reverted to a swing-axle-type rear suspension—using the same setup introduced on the '73 Spitfire 1500. The rear track was widened by two inches. The swing-axle arrangement made the car cheaper to manufacture, but a new $3,955 price tag increased profits and reduced sales even further.

The GT-6 MK III was produced until just before the 1974 model year began. At that point, it became the last member of the GT-6 series. Approximately 13,042 of these coupes were produced over the full model run, which was down from the previous version and followed the overall trend of declining sales for the fastback model.

As the GT-6's sales fell, British Leyland realized that the model was no longer profitable. With U.S. federal safety and emissions standards becoming so tight, it was discovered, based on tests of the 2.5-liter TR6 engine, that the GT-6's 2.0-liter six-cylinder engine could not be certified for sale in the American market.

Triumph didn't need the extra expense of making this low-volume car conform to the stricter regulations and decided that dropping the fastback was the best course of action. The GT-6 was actually phased out of the market, with the last units being produced midway through the 1975 model year.

Norbert Bries/Northshore Imports

# *1973-1980 Spitfire 1500*

I n January 1973, Triumph announced its new Spitfire 1500 model. It retained all the styling upgrades and other refinements introduced with the 1971 MK IV model, but the "1500" badges on its rear flanks called out the biggest change — a new engine. This and other changes brought the East Coast Port of Entry price up to $2,995.

Other than the added identification badges, there were few exterior changes, but the interior was restyled to include new seats with individual headrests. The instruments were redesigned, genuine walnut paneling was used to highlight the dashboard and a smaller three-spoke steering wheel was provided, mainly to increase knee room.

A steel hardtop was again an option. One item that made many buyers think something was broken was the use of a "vehicle-sensitive" safety belt system with tensioners that permitted users to move around, but locked-up on sudden motions, a system took some getting used to back in 1973.

The new solid-lifter engine was an in-line, overhead-valve four with a cast-iron block and cylinder head. It had a 73.7 x 87-mm bore and stroke and 1493-cc displacement. A 7.5:1 compression ratio it the U.S.-spec version produced 57 hp at 5000 rpm and 71 lbs.-ft. of torque at 3000 rpm. A single Zenith-Stromberg side-draft carburetor was fitted. The Home Market version of this engine had a 9.0:1 compression ratio that generated 71 hp at 5500 rpm and 82 lbs.-ft. of torque at 3000 rpm.

To handle the 10 extra foot-pounds of torque, Triumph engineers installed a large diaphragm clutch. In addition, a 3.89:1 final gear ratio was used to allow high-speed cruising with less rear axle noise.

The rear track was widened two inches to make the 1500 handle better and the rear spring arrangement was improved to reduce roll stiffness and eliminate most swing-axle tuck under. A larger diameter front sway bar aided high-speed cornering and counter-acted the reduced roll stiffness at the rear

The Spitfire 1500 retained the same dimensions as the previous

**The 1973 Triumph Spitfire 1500 was powered by a new 1493cc engine.**

MK IV model. Standard tires were 5.20 x 13 tubeless bias-ply models and 1.55R-13 radials were optional. Also available was the Laycock de Normanville overdrive that operated on third and fourth gears and provided a 0.802:1 ratio. Steering was rack-and-pinion type with 3.75 turns lock to lock and an impact-absorbing steering column with an anti-theft locking device.

These early Spitfire 1500s drew good reviews. *Road & Track* noted "a marked improvement over the past model" and liked the handling and performance.

"Of the cars in its class, the Spitfire is probably the best," said the magazine. The 1973 Spitfire 1500 could accelerate from 0-to-60 mph in 15.4 seconds and had a top speed of 94 mph.

For 1974, Triumph made only a few changes to the Spitfire 1500. New bumper guards were fitted all around, a front spoiler was installed, a new day/night mirror was used and a new dash light dimmer was incorporated. The price increased to $3,195. In 1975, a new single-rail manual transmission was used and the transmission tunnel, clutch, shift lever and drive shaft were modified. Improved gear spacing eliminated the need for racers to switch to close-ratio gears.

New "Federal" bumpers were seen on the 1975 model, along with a new license plate holder and new body badges. A center armrest, a folding map light, and a trunk light were added equipment. Radial tires now became a no-cost option. In California, a catalytic converter was required anti-smog equipment.

Outside of California, you could get your 1976 Spitfire 1500 with a 9.0:1 compression ratio, which improved performance and increased fuel economy to 37 mpg. California cars got just 33 mpg by comparison. New slotted wheel rims replaced the previous style.

Production continued until August 1980 using the 1493-cc

"1500" engine. An improved version of that engine arrived in 1977. It included a new carburetor, a different intake manifold design, an improved cylinder head, a redesigned exhaust manifold, and a higher-performance distributor.

Also new in 1977 were multi-function stalk-type controls mounted on the steering column. They replaced dashboard-mounted knobs and switches. The seats had a deeper contour and new Nylon houndstooth upholstery. A new 13.5-in. steering wheel was used and the steering column also carried the ignition switch. The Spitfire 1500 was now a $4,500 machine.

The mostly unchanged 1978 version of the Spitfire 1500 raised the window sticker to $5,150. One way to spot a '78 model is by the change from a chromed outside rearview mirror and door handles to black-finished ones.

A number of the Spitfire 1500's details were revised in 1979. A padded three-spoke steering wheel replaced the previous type and 155SR-13 radial tires (mounted on new five-inch-wide rims) were made standard equipment. Several changes were made to the front and rear bumper systems to make them comply to new federal regulations in the U.S.

Both bumpers were positioned away from the body and the rear bumper overriders were made longer. Both bumpers were the rubbery, charcoal-gray-colored, impact-resistant plastic. In 1979, Triumph boasted the Spitfire had racked up 32 Sports Car Club of America national championships.

Triumph made few, if any, changes to the 1500 in 1980, when all Spitfires had the black plastic bumper and large overriders. These safety features made the cars heavier and reduced performance. The horsepower rating dropped to 52.5. The added weight, reduced performance, and disappearance of chrome trim were some of the reasons for the Spitfire's departure.

British-Leyland's balance sheet was full of red ink. Triumph couldn't get the development time and money it needed to redesign its products. The last Spitfire 1500s were produced in August 1980.

The Spitfire 1500 still was a big sales success with 13,011 cars made in 1973, 13,942 in 1974, 13,362 in 1975, 23,026 in 1976, 17,716 in 1977, 21,187 in 1978, 10,276 in 1979, and 7,503 in the final year, 1980. U.S. sales were 7,796 in 1973, 7,373 in 1974, 8,857 in 1975, 6,846 in 1976, 9,463 in 1977, 10,231 in 1978, 8,344 in 1979, and 3,561 in 1980. In all, 89,942 Spitfire 1500s were built.

*The Triumph factory was busy assembling TR7 cars in this publicity photo.*

OCW Archive

# TURNER

Stephen Agins

## 1951-1966 Turner

Turner Sports Cars, founded in 1949 by British racing driver and engine builder John H. Turner, originally focused on engines. John Turner entered the competition car business as early as 1951 in Great Britain, producing a handful of 1400-lb., 96-in. wheelbase sports roadster models and racing specials powered by MG, Ford Zephyr, Vauxhall, and Lea-Francis engines. They used large 5.25 x 16 tires fitted to Turner-designed Elektron Magnesium wheels.

Early in the 1950s, Turner also produced a midget-sized 500-cc Formula III engine with twin overhead camshafts. It delivered half its weight in horsepower and peaked at about 9500 rpm. Each air-cooled cylinder was deeply finned and the cylinder head was water-cooled. Four Amal-type carburettors were used.

The Turner 803 model, introduced in 1955, was more standardized than the earlier roadsters. It had the Austin A30 engine, an 803-cc four-cylinder with a 7.2:1 compression ratio, and 30 hp output rating. Its wheelbase shrunk to 80.5 in. and the car measured only 138 in. end-to-end with a 54-in. body width. The coachwork weighed just 1,200 lbs. It had coil springs at the front, a torsion-bar rear suspension, 5.25 x 15 tires and was capable of 80-mph-plus speeds.

When Austin moved up to a 948-cc four-cylinder engine for its A35 model in 1956, Turner also adopted the larger power plant. This overhead-valve engine produced 34 hp with a Zenith carburettor or up to 40 with S.U. carburetion. The price in the United States was nearly $2,000. A second series, introduced in 1958, boosted output to 43 bhp. With twin carburettors, the top speed went up close to 90 mph. A Coventry Climax FWA 1098-cc engine also was available. A four-speed gearbox was used. Turners were intended to mix street operation with Class H production racing and quite a few of these handcrafted sports cars were sold to U.S. customers who wanted to get into sports car racing.

In 1957, a Turner roadster won its class at the Six-Hour Sam

*A rare site on a street or in a park, the Turner has always been at home on race courses.*

Collier Memorial Trophy race in Florida, then raced again in 1958 and placed second. Also in 1958, Turners won the Team Challenge Trophy at the Autosport Series Production Sports Car Championship in Britain, taking first and second place in the 1100-cc class. Turner's 1960 models were introduced in the U.S. on August 1, 1959.

"Easy to drive—easy to look at—easy to keep," was the slogan used by Turner for its 950 Sports roadster. It had a 43-hp 948-cc engine with twin S.U. carburettors and sold for $2,245 East Coast Port-of-Entry. The Turner tipped the scales at just 1,175 lbs. and could move from 0-to-60 mph in 21.3 seconds. It did the quarter mile in 21.8 seconds at 61 mph. Tri-City Sports Cars of Massillon, Ohio, and Nemet Imported Cars of Jamaica, New York were prime U.S. distributors along with A.J. Pierson of Orlando, Florida. Later, Fergus Automobile Imports of New York City and Los Angeles-based Euroauto were Turner outlets.

*Motor Trend* was critical of the "easy to look at" portion of the company's slogan, and the fact that the center bow of the soft top rode against the driver's head, but the magazine otherwise praised the tiny two-seater as "a real goer."

A semicircular opening with flat base characterized the Turner roadster's cast aluminum grille, which contained a square crosshatch pattern. Slightly protruding round headlights stood directly above round parking lights at the ends of the front panel.

In addition to the base 950 Sports, a 60-hp SPR60 was offered for U.S. sales. It appeared to be the same as the basic model, but its engine's compression was boosted from the usual 8.3:1 to 9.5:1. A more radical camshaft, exhaust header and heavy-duty cadmium-bronze bearing inserts were used. The brake drums were enlarged from 7 to 8 in. in diameter for 1959, but the rear drums remained at 7 in. Either bolt-on disc or Dunlop wire wheels were available.

Inside Turner roadsters, leather upholstery was standard fare. So was a telescopic-adjustment feature for the multiple spring-spoke steering wheel. The leatherette-covered dashboard held a 6-in.-diameter 120-mph speedometer and a matching 8,000-rpm tachometer, along with individual gauges for oil pressure, fuel level, battery current and water temperature. Side curtains were included with the folding soft top, which contained wedge-shaped side windows.

Turner's next model, which had both BMC and Coventry Climax engine choices, went on sale in export form in 1960 before being offered in Britain. Designed for racing, its British race victories attracted both export and home-market customers. Turner also developed a new Alexander model (tuned by Alexander Engineering) and urged 80 hp out of its twin-carb, ultra-high-compression version of the 948-cc BMC engine. Production was limited to about 10 cars per month by Alexander Engineering of Haddenham, Bucks, England.

In 1962, Turner announced a prototype fiberglass-bodied GT coupe, the company's first model with a solid top. Turner experts say 10 were built, powered either by a 1340-cc Ford "Kent" or 1499-cc Ford 122E engine. The latter engine powered the last Turners, the Mk III 1500. A limited number (11) of Turner Mk III Speciales were offered by Ferguson Automotive in New York and a $2,789 Turner Super Sprint model also was sold, according to Turner experts.

A total of about 600 Turner Sports models were produced. Most Turners were exported. British sales usually were kit cars rather than fully-assembled vehicles.

By 1966, the *Car and Driver Yearbook* reported Ford-powered Turners were battling Czechoslovakia's Skoda for 68th place in U.S. imported-car registrations—and were sold mainly via classified ads from service stations. The *Yearbook* dubbed the tiny, but sure-footed Turners "unholy terrors in SCCA production-car racing."

*This photo shows an impressive gathering of Turners at the Mossport race track.*

# TVR
## 1959 Grantura MKI

TVR started small and, unlike most British marques of the past, has managed to hang on into the modern era. Trevor Wilkinson started it all in 1947 by building a modification of an Alvis Firebird with light-alloy two-seat body. He named his creation TVR (a shortening of his first name). By 1949, TVR Engineering was producing tubular chassis that were used in local race events.

Before long, Wilkinson was selling both kit cars and fully-assembled models from his headquarters at Blackpool, England. Following the appearance of a fiberglass-bodied one-off in 1954, the scene shifted to America. A replica of that first example wound up in the hands of car dealer Ray Saidel, who promptly ordered half a dozen chassis from England. Those were marketed in the United States under the Jomar name and distributed from Manchester, New Hampshire. The idea was for aluminum sports-racing bodies to be produced in New Hampshire, while the chassis and fiberglass bodies were made in Great Britain. By 1957-1958, Jomars were ready for the road (and road racing courses) in the U.S.

Ray Saidel exhibited the first TVR coupes at the 1957 New York Auto Show. The stubby profile of the fastback body was thought by some to resemble that of a Lotus Elite. The fiberglass body rode a tubular backbone chassis with an 84-in. wheelbase. The recessed headlights sat in low-positioned nacelles. Small parking lights went slightly inboard and below, alongside the very low, small, wide oval grille opening. Saidel's TVR coupes soon evolved into what became known as the Grantura line.

The first British-built TVR—a Mk I Grantura—was made available for sale around the same time. The Grantura model name stemmed from Grantura Plastic, a company owned by Bernard Williams, who joined with Wilkinson in 1956.

The Mk I model was offered as either a fully-assembled car or in kit form. It featured a fiberglass body constructed over a tubular backbone chassis. Like Jomars, TVRs were designed to accept a variety of engines and suspensions. Early Grantura models came with the choice of engines.

The base engine was the Ford 100E, an in-line, L-head four-cylinder, which was offered with a supercharger. It had a cast-iron block, solid valve lifters and a Solex carburetor. The 1172-cc power plant used a 63.5 x 92.5-mm bore and stroke. With a 7.0:1 compression ratio, it was good for 36 hp. The famous 1098-cc Coventry Climax four was also available as an option. This power plant was an overhead-cam in-line four with a cast-iron block, solid valve lifters and twin S.U. carburettors. It had a 72.4 x 66.6-mm bore and stroke and 9.8:1 compression ratio, good for 85 hp at 7000 rpm.

The 1,455-lb. Grantura was built on an 84-in. wheelbase. It was 138 in. long, 64 in. wide and had a 52-in. front/rear track width. Size 5.00 x 15 tires were standard. The four-wheel independent suspension system consisted of transverse torsion bars and trailing links at both ends. Though hard riding, the lightweight TVRs soon became known for their superior handling and roadholding abilities.

Road tests in car magazines like *Autocar* put the Grantura name on the map. The TVRs drew favorable ratings for their performance and road handling, although they had few real creature comforts.

Production difficulties prevented the company from filling the orders it received. A total of only 100 Mk I Granturas were built by 1960. TVR was unable to supply enough cars to meet the strong demand and slid slowly into debt. In the 1960s, the company was rescued by Layton Sports Cars, Ltd. of Blackpool, England.

Andrew Morland

# 1960-1966 Grantura Mk II/Mk III

**M**odified Mk II and IIA Granturas arrived in 1959, followed by a Mk III during 1962. The introduction of the MGB brought a change in engine usage and the designation Mk III 1800. Financial troubles ran rampant in the early 1960s, leading to three stages of corporate reorganization. Layton Sports Cars Ltd., of Blackpool, England, owned TVR in 1960-1961. The firm changed hands again in 1962, to become Grantura Engineering Ltd. Trevor Wilkinson, whose name continued to adorn the sports cars he'd created, left the firm in 1962. Another name change, to TVR Cars Ltd., came in 1964. It lasted only a year. After its 1965 liquidation, TVR was acquired by Martin Lilley (a TVR dealer) and Arthur Lilley (his father). They reorganized the company as TVR Engineering Ltd.

The Mk II and Mk IIA were marketed starting in 1960. Modifications were modest for these models. They were available with a choice of two different engines: a 1588-cc BMC (MG) four rated at 80 hp or a 1216-cc four with 83 hp. The base engine was the basic MG 1600 mill of the day fitted with twin S.U. caburettors and using an 8.3:1 compression ratio. It produced the same horsepower in the Grantura that it did in the MG. The optional in-line, overhead cam four had a 76.2 x 66.7-mm bore and stroke, solid lifters, a 10.0:1 compression ratio and twin S.U. carburettors. With the bigger engine, the car had a top speed of 101 mph and moved through the quarter mile in 18.3 sec.

There was no change in dimensions or standard equipment tires from earlier Grantura models, but 5.60 x 15 tires were now factory optional. A four-speed manual transmission was again fitted and a choice of 4.1:1, 4.7:1, or 5.1:1 final drive ratios was offered. The front suspension was made up of trailing links with transverse torsion bars. The rear suspension used trailing links with transverse torsion bars.

The Grantura Mk III was offered in 1962-1963. Production of this model began in September 1962, some months after it was first announced. *The Motor* (in Britain) said the Mk III's "deceptively good road holding, allows the T.V.R. to cover cross-country journeys remarkably quickly." *Autocar* described it as "A car for the person who drives for the sheer fun of it," one that was "extremely comfortable" and "eminently controllable."

A 1622-cc MGA four-cylinder engine powered this version of the TVR coupe, which also had front disc brakes. A fully-independent coil-spring suspension from the Triumph Herald replaced the former transverse torsion bars. The wheelbase grew to 85.5 inches, but the overall length was the same as before.

Standard Grantura body colors were British Racing Green, Pippin

*The 1960 to 1966 TVR Grantura Mk II and Mk III cars were powered by various MG engines.*

Red, Cirrus White, Charcoal Grey, Ambassador Blue, Signal Red, Riviera Blue, Imperial Crimson, Lichen Green, Powder Blue, Sunburst Yellow, Opalescent Silver Blue, Opalescent Silver Grey, and Opalescent Bronze. Upholstery (standard vynide) came in Cherry Red, Steel Grey, Forest Green, Saxe Blue, or Finnish Black. TVR provided what it described as a "sumptuous sound-insulated interior." Competition-type bucket seats were standard, with the driver's seat being adjustable.

The coupe's doors held wind-up windows and the dashboard held a tachometer, trip odometer, and gauges for oil pressure, charging, water temperature, and fuel. As before, the Grantura rode a multi-tube chassis, but it was stiffened up a bit. It had rack-and-pinion steering

As before, two engines were offered for the base model. A 1622-cc cast-iron in-line four was standard. It had a 76.2 x 88.9-mm bore and stroke, three main bearings, solid valve lifters, a 9.0:1 compression ratio and two S.U. carburetors. This power plant generated 90 hp at 5500 rpm. The optional engine was the same size, but it had a light-alloy HRG head, a 9.5:1 compression ratio, and twin Weber carburetors to help it develop 108 hp at 6000 rpm and 109 lbs.-ft. of torque at 4500 rpm.

A larger 1798-cc version of the MG engine was installed in the Grantura Mk III 1800, which was introduced in 1963. By this time, Granturas had a larger back window and a chopped-off tail that was soon to become a trademark.

The larger in-line, overhead-valve four stuck with a cast-iron block and head. It had an 80.3 x 88.9-mm bore and stroke and an 8.8:1 compression ratio. Fitted with twin S.U.s, as usual, the 1800 developed 95 hp at 5500 rpm. Top speeds for the 1800 model were in the 107-mph bracket and it was tested through the quarter mile at 18 seconds.

In England, the Grantura Mk III was priced at 862 pounds sterling with disc wheels or 888 pounds sterling with wire wheels, plus purchase tax. Production of the base model reached 90 units and the 1800 version (Mk III and Mk IV series) reached an additional 206 customers.

The final version of the Grantura coupe, introduced in 1966, was the Grantura IV 1800S. It was powered by the 1798-cc four-cylinder engine, now rated 88 hp. It had a top speed of nearly 108 mph and did the quarter mile in 18 seconds. Production of the Mk IV began in fall 1966. Subsequent TVR models followed up on the original theme, but carried the Griffith, Vixen, and Tuscan model names.

Andrew Morland

# 1963-1966 Griffith

TVR's Griffith 200 (a fastback coupe introduced in 1963) qualifies as a semi-imported car, with its British-built body and U.S.-manufactured engine. The body was made by TVR Engineering Ltd., in Blackpool, England. The cars were completed in Great Britain and shipped to America without an engine. Griffith Motors then installed a 289-cid Ford V-8 and a Ford four-speed manual transmission at its New York facility.

The small-block Ford V-8 was offered in standard tune (195 hp) and high-performance tune (271 hp), either one hooked to Ford's own four-speed manual gearbox. The wire wheels were stronger than TVR used before, with wider rims.

Blending stunning performance with excellent handling, Griffith 200s also rode hard. They had a tight cockpit, miniature luggage space and no trunk lid. Griffith 200s also suffered overheating and quality-control problems, particularly the earliest ones.

Introduced at the April 1964 New York Auto Show, the Griffith 400 looked identical to the Grantura Mark III 1800, except for its hood bulge, sharply cut-off tail and massive wraparound back window. An open, horizontal air vent was on the cowl.

The protruding nose held a fairly wide but low grille opening that contained small parking lights at its ends. The headlights sat in low, recessed nacelles. Small horizontal bumperettes stood at each side of the front end.

TVR coupe bodies had no rear quarter windows, but the doors contained vent wings. Some of TVR's earlier mechanical and quality-

*Ford V-8 engines made the TVR Griffith of the 1960s a hot racing car.*

control problems were corrected in the Griffith 400 version, thanks to the installation of a larger radiator and Kenlowe thermostatically-controlled fans. Large, round, tri-section taillights came from the Ford Consul.

The Griffith 200 coupe listed for $3,893 and tipped the scales at 1,905 lbs. The 400 was nearly $998 more and weighed the same. Before long, TVR was sending five engineless cars per week to Griffith in the U.S. Ultimately, some 300 Griffiths of both types were produced.

An overhead-valve Ford small-block V-8 was the base engine. It had a cast-iron block and cylinder head. With a 101.6 x 72.9-mm bore and stroke, it displaced 4727 cc. The engine featured five main bearings, a Holley carburetor, and 9.0:1 compression ratio. Its output was 195 hp at 4400 rpm and 282 lbs.-ft. of torque at 2400 rpm.

The hotter engine produced 271 hp at 6500 rpm and 314 lbs.-ft. at 3400 rpm. Power moved to the 3.89:1 rear axle via a four-speed manual gearbox. The Griffith had a top speed of 125-135 mph and did 0-to-60 in 5.7 seconds.

Quality control problems and a lengthy dock strike harmed Griffith sales in the U.S. After a liquidation in 1965, TVR was acquired by Martin Lilley (a TVR dealer) and Arthur Lilley (his father). The company reorganized as TVR Engineering Ltd.

Andrew Morland

# 1967-1971 Tuscan

After being liquidated in 1965, TVR was saved by Arthur Lilley and his son Martin, who re-established the company and called it TVR Engineering, Ltd. Martin Lilley knew the cars had a good foundation with their space-frame chassis. He appreciated the fact they were designed to accept either the MG four-cylinder engine or a small-block Ford V-8 and realized this opened up all kinds of interesting possibilities. Martin pushed the creation of a variety of different models over the next decade or so, and the Tuscan was one of the most interesting ones.

The Tuscan represented a high-performance evolution of the TVR Griffith 1800S. Like other TVRs, it carried a lightweight fiberglass body on the tube-steel chassis and had four-wheel independent suspension. As a hand-built car, the Tuscan package could be configured a number of different ways. Britain's *Motor* magazine said the Tuscan was "Designed to a large extent for fun, for the sheer uninhibited enjoyment of performance. Even stationary it has the hint of power which makes it look restless."

With a long, low snout, heavily-sculpted wheelhouse feature lines front and rear, chrome-trimmed front fender air extractors, front fender vent doors, and a truncated fastback cabin with a huge glass window, the Tuscan was a pure sports car built for going fast. A huge bulge at the rear of the bonnet emphasized the raw power parked below it and the car's speediness.

Built from January 1967 through the following autumn, the original Tuscan V-8 was a rare car with just 28 examples being built. Of these, 22 cars were exported out of England. The engine used in both models was the famous 289-cid Ford V-8 (101.6 x 72.9-mm bore and stroke and 4727-cc displacement), but two versions of it were made available. The standard edition had a 9.0:1 compression ratio and a single Holley four-barrel carburetor. This setup was good for 195 hp at 4400 rpm and 282 lbs.-ft. of torque at 2400 rpm.

Also available at additional cost was the so-called "hi-po" version of the Ford V-8, which was advertised to have 271 hp at 6500 rpm and 314 lbs.-ft. of torque at 3400 rpm. This engine was available as part of the Special Equipment package, and cars equipped with it were called Tuscan V-8 SE models.

With the lower-powered engine, the Tuscan V-8 could do 0-to-60 in six seconds and had a top speed of 130 mph. The hotter version accelerated to 60 mph in one less second and had a maximum velocity of 160 mph. It was considered an incredibly fast car back in the 1960s —not that 160 mph is slow today!

Both Tuscan V-8s had the same 85.5-in. wheelbase and measured

*The TVR Tuscan series was described as a combination of fun and performance.*

140 in. long from end-to-end. (You can't say "bumper-to-bumper," as TVRs did not have full bumpers, although there were bright-metal protective bars at each corner of the body.) The fastback coupe was 48 in. high and 64 in. long. Front/rear track widths were 52.5 and 53.5 in. Power front disc/rear drum brakes were fitted and 5K x 15-in. 72-spoke Dunlop wire wheels were standard equipment. Prices for built-up Tuscans in England were 1967 British pounds for the 195-hp edition and 2364 British pounds for the more powerful SE variation. The cars tipped the scale in the 1,900-lb. range.

Starting in April 1967, and continuing through early 1968, a slightly larger Tuscan SE model was offered in several variations, not all of which were well documented. About 27 of these cars were made and most sources say that 11 were exported. The majority had the 271-hp version of Ford's small-block V-8, but a few had a 306-hp engine that could power the Tuscan to 175 mph.

These longer cars are known as long-wheelbase (or LWB) models and had a 90-in. stance. They were 145 in. long overall. The LWB models switched to 6L x 15 in. wire-spoke wheels, but most other specs were unchanged, except for an increase in weight to about 2,200 lbs. The Tuscan V-8 SE LWB coupe was tested to run 160 mph flat out and needed only five seconds to scat from 0-to-60 mph. It had a price of $2,364 British pounds.

In April 1968, a run of 21 special "wide-body" Tuscan V-8 SE LWBs was produced primarily for sale in the United States, although three of these cars managed to remain in the hands of enthusiasts in the United Kingdom. These cars were an inch longer and four inches wider than the regular long-wheelbase coupes, but were otherwise the same with the exception of weight.

After a brief absence, the standard 60-in. wide Tuscan coupe returned with a new engine below its bonnet. This Tuscan V-6 model was available in kit form for 1,492 British pounds or in assembled form for 1930 British pounds. Manufacturing began in mid-1969. It used the 90-in. wheelbase, 145-in. long chassis.

The engine found under the bonnet was the 2994-cc V-6 from the English Ford Zodiac. It was hooked to an all-synchro four-speed gearbox. This was the most popular Tuscan, especially in Great Britain, with 101 copies being built and only seven being exported. Production of this model continued all the way thru November 1971.

Jonathan Stein

# 1967-1972 Vixen

TVR announced its new "Vixen" family of small sports coupes in 1967. The car was constructed on the company's standard short-wheelbase chassis and was technically a Grantura Mk 4 1800S with a Ford engine replacing the regular MG power plant.

The first Vixen was designated the S1. It was introduced in October 1967 and lasted one year. Under the bonnet of the 1627-lb. Vixen was a longitudinally-mounted Ford Cortina GT "crossflow" engine. This in-line, overhead-valve four had 81 x 77.6 mm bore and stroke dimensions. Other specifications included a five-main-bearings crankshaft, solid valve lifters, a 9.0:1 (or 9.2:1) compression ratio and a Weber carburetor. It developed 88 hp at 5400 rpm and 96 lbs.-ft. of torque at 3600 rpm. A 108.7-mph top speed was reported.

Hooked behind the engine was the excellent Ford four-speed manual gearbox, which had "friendlier" ratios than the MG gearbox used in the 1800S. Since some buyers preferred the old MG engine, and since TVR needed all the buyers it could find, the MG engine returned as a no-cost option in early-production Vixen S1s. It was installed in just 12 cars, which also had the MG transmission, of course.

The Vixen had the same styling as the Grantura 1800S, but could be spotted by its distinctive larger bonnet vent. Its fiberglass body was set on a multi-tubular chassis made up of 1-1/2-in. diameter 18-gage tubing. In kit form, the S1 sold for 998 British pounds. It was 1,216 British pounds in assembled form.

The front suspension was made up of coil springs and unequal-length wishbones. Steering was rack-and-pinion. Girling front disc/rear drum brakes were fitted. The car had an 85-1/2-in. wheelbase and was 138 in. long. The body was 48 in. high and 64 in. wide. The S1 was the only Vixen to use a factory bonded-on body. The front track was 52-1/2 in. and the rear track was 53-1/2 in.

After assembling 117 Vixen S1s, TVR Engineering moved on to the Vixen S2, which was marketed from October 1968 to the same month in 1970. The S2 switched to a bolted-on body, which makes the job of restoring the car much easier. The body was virtually the same as that used on the long-wheelbase Tuscan model, but had longer doors. New trim vents decorated the front fenders, but perhaps the easiest way to spot an S2 was by its upside-down Ford Cortina Mk 2 taillight clusters. A single exhaust pipe exited from the rear.

Early S2s had a sausage-like bulge in their bonnets to fit the anti-pollution hardware required in the United States into the engine bay. In

*The 1970 TVR Vixen used Ford engines to propel this great road car.*

England, this design proved unpopular and a Tuscan-type bonnet was soon substituted for the "sausage" type. A total of 438 Vixen S2s were built and only 144 were sold into the export market.

The S2's tubular frame was made of heavier 16-gage tubing and output from the 1599-cc Cortina GT engine was boosted to 92 hp at 5400 rpm. The wheelbase was stretched to 90 in. making the length 145 in. The S2 could do 0-to-60 mph in 9 seconds, two seconds faster than the S1. Its top speed was about 115 mph. The extra performance brought the kit price up to 1,250 British pounds and the assembled car to 1,583 British pounds. Servo brakes were added in 1969. With new fender vents pirated from the Ford Zodiac/Mk IV Zephyr, the Vixen S3 arrived on the scene in October 1970. It survived until late in 1971. New cast-alloy wheels—the same type seen on the Tuscan V-6—were also used on the S3. The third Vixen model found a total of 168 buyers.

Under the bonnet of the S3 was a 1599-cc four-cylinder "crossflow" engine that came from the Ford Capri, instead of the Cortina GT. This engine was rated for 86 hp and was capable of propelling the car to about 100 mph. A 10-seconds 0-to-60-mph time was reported. The engine was linked to an all-synchro gearbox.

Introduced early in 1972, the Vixen S4 (only 23 built) brought some additional improvements to the series. It was much the same as the S3, except it used the new M chassis that was introduced in 1971.

Many sources indicate that Vixens disappeared around 1971 or 1972, but we have seen an advertisement dated as a 1975 ad that promotes the Vixen as "A hand-built sports car for $7,295." The ad reads, "We build our cars by an unusual process. By hand. Every TVR multi-tube space-frame chassis is hand-welded. And protected by undercoating and Inner-Coating®. Every TVR has an unstressed fiberglass body with a hand-rubbed lacquer finish. Every TVR has a hand-upholstered and hand-fitted interior. And every TVR is hand-built with front mid-engine design, 4-wheel independent suspension, rack and pinion steering and power-assisted front disc brakes. The TVR. A car that's put together by hands, for the price of a car that's put together by machines."

Alex Le Barre

# 1972-'79 2500, 1300 M Series

**B**etween 1972 and 1979, TVR offered four- and six-cylinder coupes and a few six-cylinder convertibles. Two four-cylinder models—the 1300 and the 1600M—were sold. The six-cylinder offerings included the 2500, the 2500M and the 3000M. The 1600M, the 2500M, and the 3000M were true M Series cars, which means they shared a new M Series tubular chassis.

This chassis was developed by Martin Lilley and Mike Bigland. Lilley was the TVR dealer who had taken over the company in 1965 and reorganized it as TVR Engineering, Ltd. Bigland was a dealer from the Midlands region of England, who had built a V-8-powered TVR Tuscan. His numerous modifications were then put in the M Series chassis. It was constructed of round and square tubing made from 14- and 16-gauge metal.

TVRs in these years weren't 100 percent standardized. Some had new chassis and old bodies and some had new chassis and new bodies. Models such as the 1300 didn't last long. The M Series lasted until 1979 and went through several updates.

TVR's 2500 was released early in 1971 in the U.S. only and wasn't released in England until August 1971. A total of 385 were made through Spring 1972. The 2500 used the Triumph 2498-cc in-line, overhead-valve six, the TR6's four-main-bearings engine, with a 74.7 x 95-mm bore and stroke. The engine had an 8.5:1 compression ratio, solid valve lifters, twin S.U. carburetors, and was rated at 104 hp at 4500 rpm.

The 2500 was capable of 10-sec. 0-to-60-mph runs and had a top speed of 118 mph. "A real sports car," said Britain's *Hot Car* magazine. "It's what driving is all about – fast and fun." The 2500 sold for 1,482 pounds in kit form and 1,927 pounds fully assembled.

Only 15 1300s were manufactured from August 1971 until the fall of 1972. Fourteen of these cars had the same body as the six-cylinder 2500. The 1300 was identical to the 2500, but weighed about 200 lbs. less. It came with a four-speed manual gearbox and optional overdrive.

The TVR 1300 engine was Triumph's in-line, overhead-valve four-cylinder, which had solid lifters, a 9.0:1 compression ratio and twin S.U. carburetors. With a 73.7 x 76-mm bore and stroke, it displaced 1296 cc. and produced 63 hp at 3500 rpm.

The 1300 had a fiberglass body mounted on a tubular backbone. The front and rear suspensions combined coil springs and unequal-length wishbones. Rack-and-pinion steering and Girling front disc/rear drum brakes were fitted. It sold for 1295 pounds in kit form. With a 90-in. wheelbase, was 145 in. long, stood 48 in. high and was 64 in. wide. Track widths were 53 in. up

*The red 1974 TVR 2500M seems like fun even at rest.*

front and 54 in. at the rear. Weighing 1,765 lbs., the 1300 did 0-to-60-mph in 12.5 seconds with a top speed in excess of 100 mph. One TVR 1300 used a new M series body, a narrower version of the limited-production 1968 Tuscan SE V-8. The M body had a longer front end with a larger air intake and a lengthened bonnet that allowed the spare tire to be stored up front. That allowed room for a behind-the-seats luggage compartment. Grilles pirated from the Ford Zodiac decorated the air extractors on each front fender. Early production units had air vents in the bonnet, Ford Cortina taillights and Vixen-style black alloy wheels. TR6 taillights were found on the later M Series cars.

The four-cylinder 1600M originally was produced from July 1972 until April 1973 in kit form only. After a disastrous mid-1975 fire at the TVR factory, it was re-introduced as an assembled car priced at 2,895 pounds. The 1600M used the M Series body on the 90-in. wheelbase M Series chassis. TVR intended to replace the Vixen with the 155 in. long, 47 in. high coupe. Only 68 TVR 1600Ms were made with the last having some of the later M Series appearance upgrades.

Tucked under the 1600M's bonnet was Ford's 1.6-liter (1588-cc) "Kent" crossflow four-cylinder engine, which generated 86 hp at 5500 rpm. Linked to an all-synchro gearbox and heavier than the 1300, the 1600M was faster. It could manage 0-to-60 mph in 10.5 seconds and topped out at about 110 mph.

"The 1600 M [has] a unique personality," stated *Motor Sport* magazine. "The performance is quite respectable, handling and road holding very safe. Best of all, this car returned 34-35 mpg."

The 2500M was produced from April 1972 until 1977. It cost 1,560 pounds in kit form. A total of 947 were built. The 2500M used the 2.5-liter Triumph six with twin S.U. carburetors, but was rated for 106 hp at 4950 rpm and 133 lbs.-ft. of torque at 3000 rpm. Dimensionally and technically, the 2500M was similar to the 2500 but sat an inch lower.

After 1973, 6JK x 14-in. alloy wheels were used on 2500Ms, in place of the 5-1/2J x 15-in. aluminum wheels used on other TVR models. The 2500M was a bit heavier but tested out slightly quicker. *Road & Track* published a 9.3-sec. 0-to-60-mph time and a top speed of 104 mph.

The third M Series car, the 3000 M, entered production in August 1972 and was introduced at the London Motor Show that fall. Initially offered exclusively in Europe, it was offered in the U.S. after California-based Olsen Laboratories prepared its engine with smog and pollution equipment. It remained in production through 1979.

The main difference between the 3000M and the 2500M was the

2994-cc 142-hp Ford "Essex" V-6.

The 3000M engine resulted in a fast car that could do 0-to-60 mph in just 7.5 seconds with a top speed of above 120 mph. TVR made 654 of them.

Later M Series models included TVR Turbos, the Taimar, the 3000S and a handful of SEs.

The TVR Turbo was introduced in 1975 and carried a turbocharged Ford V-6 developed by Broadspeed. It generated 230 hp at 3000 rpm, did 0-to-60 mph in six seconds with a top speed of 150 mph.

Initially priced at 6,903 pounds, the Turbo featured a full luxury-equipment package, including the buyer's choice of body finish.

The turbocharged engine was technically an option that went into 20 TVR 3000Ms, 30 Taimers, and 13 convertibles. The cars carried "TVR Turbo" graphics.

The Taimar bowed at Earls Court in 1976, essentially a 3000M with a lift gate. The model was produced until the end of the M Series and was fairly popular, with 395 sold. Except for the rear-opening panel, the Taimar and 3000M looked identical. The hatchback release button was hidden in the driver's door jamb.

The 3000S convertible was based on a special car for Martin Lilley. This open model was a derivation of the 3000M/Taimar chassis and running gear with convertible coachwork.

All body panels except the bonnet were redesigned. Only 258 of these cars were created through 1979.

Four cars with the SE ("Special Equipment") option were sold. Three were Taimar Turbo SEs and one was a Turbo SE convertible built for Martin Lilley.

The SEs had a special bonnet, enlarged wheel openings, special alloy rims, leather interior trimmings and air conditioning.

Andrew Morland

# 1980-1989 Tasmin V-6

The all-new TVR Tasmin hatchback coupe debuted in January 1980, after it drew rave reviews at the Brussels Motor Show. This dramatic wedge-shaped automobile replaced the M-Series models and the Taimar. This Tasmin (called the 280i after 1984) started a family of cars. It came with the choice of a Rover or Ford engine.

A convertible, a coupe, and 2+2 coupe were available in the original Tasmin line. Buyers had a choice of manual or automatic transmissions. A variety of models—identified by dozens of alpha-numerical designations—were marketed in different countries. Since TVR models were hand-built from different combinations of engines, transmissions, chassis and fiberglass bodies, their features, equipment and design elements weren't standardized.

No TVRs were sold in the United States in the early 1980s. By 1982, the company had changed hands again, with Peter Wheeler taking over. He was interested in the U.S. market and in increasing the power of the cars. He went looking for larger, more powerful engines to put in the Tasmin family of cars. He installed a turbocharged V-6, then a V-8. By 1983, the TVR had been turned into an exotic, ultra-high-performance machine, and American sales resumed.

Despite their lack of standardization, TVRs built in this era were awesome, high-performance sports cars. They were the highest-quality products the automaker had ever turned out.

Tasmin convertibles featured a fold-down, Targa-style rollover bar. All of the models were pricey for their day. A 1984 price list shows that prices in the United Kingdom ranged from 13,254 pounds for the lowest-priced model to 15,500 pounds for the most expensive.

**The wedge-shaped 1982 TVR Tasmin series was powered by a 2.8 liter Ford V-6 engine.**

The coupe weighed 2,345 lbs., the convertible was 13 lbs. lighter and the 2+2 coupe was a pound heavier than the open model. TVR's annual production totals varied widely. Factory output was at a low of 121 cars in 1982 and rose to 472 units by 1985, when additional sales were made. Following TVR tradition, the Tasmin bodies were laid up from fiberglass moldings. A long nose and hide-away headlights characterized the front end. A composite black bumper with horizontal ribbing extended the frontal length of the car and incorporated parking lamps and turn signals. Rectangular fog lights could be mounted below the bumper.

A conventional trunk was provided. Multi-color taillight lenses (red-amber-white) were placed in rectangular openings in horizontally ribbed panels on either side of the license plate recess. A black rear bumper wrapped around the body corner at each end. Two exhausts pipe tips jutted out, one below each taillight unit.

Tasmin upholstery came in Suede Velour and Ambla. The passenger-side sun visor held a vanity mirror and doors disguised the ashtrays. Power windows were standard equipment. An AM/FM stereo radio with cassette player was standard.

The chassis was used to carry all the different body styles and had the same wheelbase. This gave the 2+2 coupe a very small rear passenger compartment. Tasmin family models sold in the U.S., the majority of which were convertibles, used a 2.8-liter German Ford engine, at least through 1986. This 60-degree overhead-valve V-6 had four-main bearings.

A cast-iron, block-and-head engine, it had a 93.0 x 68.5-mm bore and stroke for 2792-cc displacement.

Other specifications included a 9.2:1 compression ratio and a Bosch K-Jetronic fuel-injection system. The V-6 produced 145 hp and 150 lbs.-ft. of torque at 4300 rpm. The new TVR's top speed was well over 108 mph (the factory claimed 133 mph). The U.S. version was tested at 125 mph. Hitting 60 mph from a standstill took 7.5 seconds and the quarter mile took 16 seconds.

Other engines were found in some Tasmins sold in America. A lower-priced model, powered by a Ford 2.0-liter (1993-cc) four-cylinder engine, was available with the 280i. This car was marketed as the Tasmin 200 and only 61 examples were built. In 1987, the V-6-powered Tasmin models actually used a new 2.9-liter engine to replace the 2.8-liter German Ford power plant.

All Tasmin models used the same multi-gauge-tube "space frame" as the M-Series models and the Taimar. A 94.0-in. wheelbase was a common trait of all models. The coupe and convertible were 158 in. long and the 2+2 had an overall length of 161 in. All models were 47 in. high and 68 in. wide with a 56.5-in. front tread and a 56.7-in. rear tread. The standard 205/60VR14 tires (205/60VR15 on the 350i) were mounted on cast alloy wheels.

Tasmin models featured four- or five-speed manual gearboxes, as well as a three-speed automatic transmission. Gear ratios for the four speed manual gearbox were 3.16:1 in first, 1.94:1 in second, 1.41:1 in third and 1.00:1 in fourth. A 3.07:1 final drive ratio was standard. The

steering was a rack and pinion design, with optional power assist. The running gear was largely the same as that used on previous TVRs, but the use of all-wheel disc brakes as standard equipment was new.

In the late 1980s, different engines were installed in TVRs, including a turbocharged V-6. Then, a V-8 model appeared. Called the 350i, it bowed in August 1983. Britain's *CAR* magazine said it had "more appeal than a Ferrari." It had an all-aluminum 3.5-liter Rover engine that was based on an early 1960s design built by Buick and also used by Pontiac and Oldsmobile.

With an 88.8 x 71-mm bore and stroke, the five-main-bearings V-8 displaced 3228 cc. It had hydraulic valve lifters, fuel injection and a 9.8:1 compression ratio. Engine output was 190 (DIN) hp at 5300 rpm and 220 lbs.-ft. of torque at 4000 rpm. The 350i's top speed was in the 135-140-mph range and 0-to-60 mph took 5.6 to 11.8 seconds. The 1984 Tasmin 350i convertible sold for 14,000 pounds.

At the October 1984 Motor Show in Birmingham, England, a bigger V-8 debuted in the new TVR 390SE model. Only a handful of these cars were made during the mid-1980s. They had a 3.9-liter 257-hp Rover V-8. Road tests recorded a top speed of 150 mph for the 390SE and found the car could accelerate from 0-to-60 mph in five to five-and-a-half seconds.

Next was the 420SEAC, priced at 45,000 pounds in England. The SEAC designation stood for "Special Equipment Aramad Composite," which indicated the use of a lightweight Kevlar body. This model was powered by a 4.2-liter (4228-cc) 300-hp V-8.

Andrew Morland

# 1990-2003 TVR

**T**he last of the "wedge" cars rolled off the assembly line in 1991. Another new series TVR bodies had been on the market for several years. The new S2 model entered production in 1987 and was available in North America starting in 1990.

With a more rounded styling theme, the S2 looked like the M Series on the surface, but was actually all new, powered by a fuel-injected 2933-cc V-6 rated 168 hp (DIN) at 6000 rpm. The S2 model's convertible top was designed to be fully open, closed or targa-style. The car could reach 98 mph in a quarter-mile run and with a 140 mph top speed.

With prices beginning at $48,280, the S2 quickly became very popular. It transformed TVR's fortunes and doubled production.

*The 1988 TVR S captured all the fun of a British sports car and added modern refinements.*

The S2 contributed mightily to TVR's coffers, but a new Griffith model inspired TVR's real renaissance. By 1990, customers were asking for more power. Several prototypes, like the ES and the Speed 8, were created and pointed the way to the new Griffith. The first cars were delivered to customers early in 1992 and was overwhelmingly successful. An order was taken on average every eight minutes at the 1990 NEC Motor Show, where it was first exhibited. By the end of the show, TVR had 350 deposits for cars.

*Autocar* (June 17, 1992) said, "With the Griffith, TVR might just have rewritten the rule book on sports cars for all time, just as Jaguar did with the E-type more than 30 years ago. The car's tangible assets—thundering performance, fabulous looks, a $27,000 price tag and its build quality…reads even more like a fairy tale than Alice in Wonderland ever did.'

The Griffith had a 4280-cc 280 hp pushrod V-8 that gave it a top speed of 161 mph. It did 0-to-60 mph in 4.7 seconds. That was faster than a Porsche 911 Turbo or a Ferrari Testarossa.

"The Griffith is so much better than any previous TVR in terms of its general cabin ergonomics that it's sometime hard to believe it originates from the same source," said *Autocar*. The magazine praised the car in all categories except handling and economy.

With the introduction of the 1993 500 model, the TVR Griffith achieved true classic status. It had a 4988-cc V-8 that produced 320 hp at 5500 rpm. It did the 0-to-60 mph sprint in 4.6 seconds. A 2000 Griffith 500 SE was produced to close the series on a high note and keep sales going until the very end. Only 100 of these 5.0-liter collectibles, introduced at the Birmingham Motor Show, were ever made.

The TVR Chimaera went into production in 1993. The name of this car came from mythology. Chimaera was a beast with a lion's head, the body of a goat, and a serpent's tail. Buyers got a choice of a 4.5-liter 285-hp V-8 or a 5.0-liter 320-hp V-8. The milder version of the car did 0-to-60 mph in 4.7 seconds and had a 160-mph top speed. Comparable figures for the hotter version were 4.1 seconds and 167 mph. Over 10,000 Chimaeras were built.

Also new in 1993 was a handsome 2 + 2 coupe called the Cerbera, the first model ever to have a TVR-designed engine. Its high-tech, light Speed 8 engine resulted from five years of research and two years of road testing.

The Cerbera grand touring coupe shared styling cues with the Chimaera, but was a different car with new brakes, a new chassis, a new suspension and completely different construction. The car came in three variations. The Speed Six featured an in-line six-cylinder engine. The 4.2 V-8 produced 350 hp. The Cerbera 4.2 did 0-to-60 in 4.4 seconds and had a top speed of 170 mph. Also available was the Cerbera 4.5 with 420 hp. It could do 0-to-60 in 3.9 seconds and had a 180-mph top speed.

Every TVR is still hand-built to the customer's specifications and every engine has the engine builder's initials on it. Everything—body, chassis and engine—is designed and crafted in-house. TVR claims to have "probably more employees per car" than anyone else. The latest series of TVR models include the Tuscan Speed Six, the Tuscan R, and the Tamora.

The TVR Tuscan Speed Six is probably TVR's most significant new model since the Chimaera. It is powered by TVR's own 360-hp Speed Six.

sIts unique roof looks like a fixed-head coupe, but the roof and rear window can be removed and stored in the boot, leaving room for luggage.

The TVR Tuscan R is manufactured to order by the TVR Motorsport Division. Variations range from a fast 2+2 street car to a full-race GT. All body panels are new.

The body is a composite blend of carbon and kevlar making the Tuscan R remarkably light. The engine is a super-high-performance 200-mph-plus version of TVR's own straight six with options up to 450 hp.

The chassis uses stressed aluminum honeycomb panels. The "R" is 8 in. longer than the Tuscan Speed Six.

Seating options range from leather to carbon-kevlar competition seats. Two or four seats are possible. Rs can be fitted with roll cages. Top speed is over 200 mph.

The Tamora is named after a Queen of the Goths. This stylish TVR will become a popular model in the sports car market. The Tamora is to the Tuscan what the Chimarea was to the Griffith—a more affordable car sharing the same platform. It represents an "entry-level" two-seat roadster. It uses a slightly smaller 3.6-liter version of the in-line six found in the Tuscan that generates "only" 350 hp.

The Tamora is shorter and lighter with different styling—and smaller wheels and tires. It can out-accelerate a Porsche 911.

TVR uses the latest technology to solve the problem of building its cars in small volumes.

"If TVR ever had accountants in positions of authority, they would make sure cars like the Tuscan and Tamora would never make it off the drawing board just because of the cost of switchgear."

Fortunately, TVR Chairman Peter Wheeler is an engineer who, in his own words, "just likes designing and building things ..."

*This yellow 1973 TVR 2500M invites an adventurous driver to get behind the wheel.*

# BRITISH CAR CLUBS & ORGANIZATIONS

This is selected list of some of the many fine organizations supporting these wonderful cars. Clubs referred to here were helpful in preparation of this book. Contact the club nearest you or the national or international organization of your favorite British car.

**A.C.** . . . . . . . . . . . . . . . . A.C. Owners Club Ltd. (North America)
11955 S.W. Faircrest St., Portland, OR 97225-4615
Jim Feldman, Registrar

A.C. Owners Club Ltd. PO Box 112, Saffron, Walden, UK CB10 2ZJ www.racecar.co.uk/acoc

**Alvis** . . . . . . . . . . . . . . North American Alvis Owners Club
Wayne Brooks, PO Box 46, Bainbridge, PA 17502

**Austin-Healey** . . . . . . . . . Austin Healey Club of America
606 East Euclid Ave., Arlington Heights, IL 60004

**Bristol** . . . . . . . . . . . . . Bristol Owners Club
Vesutor Ltd., Marringdean Road, Billingshurst, UK RH14 9RH

**Daimler** . . . . . . . . . . . . . Daimler Enthusiasts Club
Stamford Lodge, Ickburgh, Thetford, UK IP25 6HX

Daimler SP250 Owners Club
15 Broom Mead, Bexleyheath, Kent, UK DA6 7NZ

**Dellow** . . . . . . . . . . . . . . The Dellow Register
davehaley@btinternet.com

Dellow Developments
dellowdevelopments@btopenworld.com

**Doretti** . . . . . . . . . . . . . . The Swallow Doretti Page
www.doretti.co.uk

**Elva** . . . . . . . . . . . . . . . . Elva Courier Home Page
www.96trees.com

Elva Racing Components Ltd.
Roger Dunbar, 8 Liverpool Terrace, Worthing, West Sussex, UK
BN11 1TA
www.elvacourier.com

**Fairthorpe** . . . . . . . . . . . . The Fairthorpe Registry
Charles Armstrong-Wilson
FthorpeReg@aol.com

**Frazer-Nash** . . . . . . . . . . . The Frazer-Nash Archives
James Trigwell, Coxon House, Reading Road
Henley on Thames, UK RG9 1HG

Frazer Nash of United States
www.Frazer-Nash-USA.com

**Gordon-Keeble** . . . . . . . . . Gordon-Keeble Owners Club
Enco Mezzo 7 Bridgewater Road, Brackley, Northants, UK NN13 6BY

**Jaguar** . . . . . . . . . . . . . . . Jaguar Clubs of North America
Nelson Roth, 1000 Glenbrook, Anchorage, KY 40223

1-888-CLUB JAG (258-2524)
(Helps you find local clubs)

**Jensen and Jensen-Healey** . . Jensen-Healey Preservation Society
Greg Fletcher, 2950 Airway Ave., Apt. 9, Costa Mesa, CA 92626

Jensen Owners Club
Keith Andrews, 2 Westgate, Fullshaw Park, Wilmslow, Cheshire, UK SK9 1QQ

**Jowett Jupiter** . . . . . . . . . . Jupiter Owners Auto Club
319 Markfield Lane, Markfield, Leicester, UK LE67 9PR

**Lea Francis** . . . . . . . . . . . Lea Francis Owners Club
Frenchs, Long Wittenham, Abingdon, Oxford, UK OX14 4QQ

**Lotus** . . . . . . . . . . . . . . . Lotus Owners Club
90 Coppell Lane, Stanstead Abbots, Ware, Hertsfordshire, UK SG12 8BY

Lotus Limited
PO Box L, College Park, MD 20741
301-982-4054
hq@lotuscarclub.org

**Marauder** . . . . . . . . . . . . . The Rover P 4 Drivers' Guild
Barry Kensett, 32 Arundel Road, Luton, Bedfordshire, UK LU4 8DY

**Marcos** . . . . . . . . . . . . . . Club Marcos International
26 Blackberry Close, Chippenham, Wiltshire, UK SN14 6RG

Marcos Owners Club
Larry Killick, Grove Lodge, 11 Thundersley Grove, Thundersley, Benfleet, Essex, UK SS7 30B

Mini Marcos Owners Club (Mini Marcos, Mini Jem, Kingfisher) Ian Hayward, 7 Ecclestone Close, Seddens Farm, Bury, Lancashire, UK BL8 2JF

**MG** . . . . . . . . . . . . . . . . . American MGB Association
P. O. Box 11401
Chicago, IL 60611

American MGC Register
Tom Boscarino
34 Park Avenue
Asheville, NC 28803-2056

British Motor Trade Association
c/o Eclectic Motorworks LLC
422 Diekema Ave.
Holland, MI 49423
MG Car Club Ltd.
PO Box 251, Abingdon, Oxfordshire, UK OX14 3FA
www.mgcars.org.uk/mgcc

MG Drivers Club (MG DC)
Richard Miller, 18 George's Place, Clinton, NJ 08809-1334
www.mgclub.com 908-735-5417
(There are numerous model-based and regional MG car clubs.)

# BRITISH CAR CLUBS & ORGANIZATIONS

MGT
New England MGT Register
NEMGTR
Drawer #220
Oneonta: NY 13820
Richard Knudson

MG Vintage Racers
Mark Palmer, editor
253 Bridlepath Road
Bethlehem, PA 18017

MG ZA & ZB Magnette
Z Magnette Group
Jeff Powell
910 Hirsch
Melrose Park, IL. 60160

MMM (Midget, Magna and Magnette cars)
North American MMM Register
Tom Metcalf, registrar
1532 St. Rt. 60 South
Ashland, Oh 44805

North American MGA Register
Don Holle
P.O. Box 11746
Albuquerque, NM 87192-0746

The North American MGB Register
MGB, Midget, 1100/1300
PO Box MGB
Akin, IL 62805-0447

**Morgan** . . . . . . . . . . . . . . The Morgan Registry
www.morganville.org
(There are many regional Morgan car clubs
around the world.)

**Nash-Healey** . . . . . . . . . . . Nash Car Club of America (NCCA)
1N274 Prairie Road, Glen Ellyn, IL  60137
www.nashcarclub.org

**Panther** . . . . . . . . . . . . . . Panther Enthusiasts Club UK
George Newell, 91 Fleet Road, Cove,

Farnborough, Hants, UK GU14 9RE
George.Newell@purely-panther.freeserve.co.uk

**Peerless** . . . . . . . . . . . . . . The Peerless and Warwick Register
registrar@peerless-gt.co.uk

**Reliant** . . . . . . . . . . . . . . Reliant Sabre and Scimitar Owners Club
PO Box 67, Teddington, Middlesex, UK  TW11
8QR

**Riley** . . . . . . . . . . . . . . . Riley Motor Club
Treelands, 127 Penn Road, Wolverhampton, UK
WV3 0DU

The Riley Motor Club of South Australia
Meets at Parkside School, Parkside, South
Australia
Mail to PO Box 267, Fullarton, South Australia
(S.A.) 5063

**Singer** . . . . . . . . . . . . . . North American Singer Owners Club
. . . . . . . . . . . . . . . . . . . Peter McKercher, 370 First Ave.,
. . . . . . . . . . . . . . . . . . . Ottawa, ON, Canada www.singercars.com

**Sunbeam** . . . . . . . . . . . . . Alpine
Sunbeam Alpine Owners Club of North America
www.saoca.org
www.sunbeamalpine.org

Tiger
Sunbeam Tiger Owners Association
Jennifer Guerra, Pleasanton, CA  94566   925-
462-9383

Sunbeam-Talbot Alpine
Sunbeam-Talbot Alpine Register (STAR)
D. Cook, 47 Crescent Wood Road, Sydenham,
London, UK SE26 6SA

**Triumph** . . . . . . . . . . . . . The Vintage Triumph Registry
PO Box 665, Howell, MI  48844-0655
www.vtr.org

**Turner** . . . . . . . . . . . . . . Turner Registry
c/o Russell Filby, 5 Claremont Gardens, Nailsea,
Bristol, UK BS48 2HY

Pete Amsler

# TRANSLATING THE TERMS

*"The water impeller comes with a leakproof self-adjusting gland."*
*"The inbuilt spare wheel compartment has a quick action clamp."*
*"The sound-insulated bodies are free from objectionable drumming and creaking."*
*"The car has a double-scuttle bulkhead."*

British cars can be a lot of fun. However, British car terms often lose something in translation to American audiences. Here is a comparison of British and American auto terms.

| British | American |
|---|---|
| **Accumulator** | Battery |
| **Actuator** | Switch |
| **Air strangler** | Older type air vent |
| **Bonnet** | Hood |
| **Boot** | Trunk |
| **Bulkhead** | Firewall |
| **Bullnose** | Radiator that looked like a bull's nose |
| **Cam follower** | Valve lifter |
| **Chummy** | Open-topped two-seat car in 1920s |
| **Clevis pin** | Cotter pin |
| **Coffin box** | Eight-sided valve cover |
| **Companion box** | Built-in storage area |
| **Crosshead** | Phillips head |
| **Crown wheel** | Ring gear |
| **Cubby box or parcel tray** | Glove box/ tray |
| **Damper** | Shock absorber |
| **Dashpot** | Part of carburetor |
| **Decoke** | Removing carbon buildup |
| **Dickey seat** | Rumble seat |
| **Dip and switch mechanism** | High beam headlight switch |
| **Draught excluder** | Vent window |
| **Draught welt** | Door and window sealant material |
| **Dress** | Smoothing an area of metal with a file |
| **Drop-head coupe** | Convertible |
| **Dumpy screwdriver** | Short screwdriver |
| **Dynamo** | Generator |
| **Estate or estate wagon** | Station wagon |
| **Fascia** | Dashboard |
| **Fairing panel** | Front apron |
| **Fencer's mask** | Type of 1930s radiator grille |
| **Fixed-head coupe** | Two-door sport coupe |
| **Five-stud fixing** | Wheel rim with five holes |
| **Flush-type runners** | Seat rails |
| **Foot dipping switch** | Foot-mounted dimmer switch |
| **Full chat** | At top speed |
| **Fume discharge** | Exhaust |
| **Gearbox** | Transmission |
| **Gudgeon pin** | Wrist pin |
| **Hackney carriage** | Formal or traditional taxi |
| **Hills and dales** | Uneven wear on a clutch |
| **Hood** | Convertible top |
| **Hood sticks** | Convertible top bows |
| **Horn push** | Horn button |
| **Joint** | Gasket |
| **Landcrab** | Nickname for BMC series such as Austin 1800 and MG 1100 |
| **Marque** | Car maker |
| **Mini** | Very small or subcompact car such as the Mini Marcos or Morris/ustin Mini Minors |
| **Mole wrench** | Vice grip wrench |

# TRANSLATING THE TERMS

| | |
|---|---|
| Monocoque | Unibody |
| Nacelle | Housing for a switch |
| Nave plate | Hubcap |
| Overriders | Bumper guards |
| Paraffin | Kerosene |
| Perspex | Type of transparent plastic |
| Petrol | Gasoline |
| Pinking | Knocking |
| Positive earth wiring | Electrical grounding |
| Prop shaft | Drive shaft |
| Proud | Above or raised |
| Pumpkin | Differential unit |
| Quarterlight | Vent window |
| Rear or back light | Rear window |
| Rev counter | Tachometer |
| Road wheel embellishers | Full wheel covers |
| Rocker box | Valve cover |
| Roof guttering | Drip molding |
| Roof stretchers | Landaulet bars |
| Roundabout | Traffic circle |
| RoStyle | Type of steel wheel |
| Saloon | Two or four-door sedan |
| Scuttle | Cowl |
| Shooting brake | A two-door sports car-based station wagon |
| Side curtains | Removable side windows |
| Silencer | Muffler |
| Sill | Rocker panel |

| | |
|---|---|
| Spanner | Wrench |
| Split pin | Cotter pin |
| Splutter | Engine running too lean |
| Spring eyes | Hole drilled to accept bolts |
| Spring washer | Lock washer |
| Squab | Part of car seat |
| Stove enameled wings | Oven-baked painted fenders |
| Striking dog | Sliding hub that moves with gear shift |
| Suction advance | Vacuum advance |
| Sump | Oil pan |
| Tail locker | Trunk |
| Thrust bearing | Throwout bearing |
| Tickover | Idle |
| Torch | Flashlight |
| Tommy bar | Small bar used to turn a socket |
| Trunnion | Sliding/ rotating suspension joint |
| Trafficators | Semaphore-style signal units |
| Tunk | Freeplay in suspension |
| Waist rail | Padded rail at top of door |
| Wheel nut | Lug nut |
| Whitworth | British thread measurement |
| Windscreen | Windshield |
| Wing | Fender |
| Winkers | Turn signals |

### And some British and American spelling differences:

| | |
|---|---|
| Aluminium | (aluminum) |
| Tyres | (tires) |
| Colour | (color) |
| Centre | (center) |

# BRITISH CAR PRICING

The prices listed here represent a sample of British sports cars imported to North America, taken from the 2004 Old Cars Price Guide. If you do not see your car here, check the 2005 edition of Cars and Prices published by Krause Publications or contact the club for your British car.

### Vehicle Condition Scale:

1. Excellent. Restored to current maximum professional standards of quality in every area or perfect original with components operating and appearing as new. A 95-plus point show car that is not driven.
2. Fine. Well-restored or a combination of superior restoration and excellent original parts. An extremely well-maintained original vehicle showing minimal wear.
3. Very good. Completely operable original or older restoration. A good amateur restoration, or a combination of well-done restoration and good operable components or partially restored car with parts necessary to complete and/or valuable NOS parts.
4. Good. A driveable vehicle needed no work or only minor work to be functional. A deteriorated restoration or poor amateur restoration. All components may need restoration to be "excellent" but the car is useable "as is."
5. Restorable. Needs complete restoration of body, chassis, and interior. May or may not be running. Isn't weathered or stripped to the point of being useful only for parts.
6. Parts car. May or may not be running but it weathered, wrecked and/or stripped to the point of being useful primarily for parts.

## AC

| | 6 | 5 | 4 | 3 | 2 | 1 |
|---|---|---|---|---|---|---|
| **1953-54 Ace, 6-cyl., 90" wb** | | | | | | |
| 2d Rds | 2,800 | 8,400 | 14,000 | 28,000 | 49,000 | 70,000 |
| **1955-56 Aceca, 6-cyl., 90" wb** | | | | | | |
| 2d FBk Cpe | 2,300 | 6,950 | 11,600 | 23,200 | 40,600 | 58,000 |
| **1957 Ace, 6-cyl., 90" wb** | | | | | | |
| 2d Rds | 2,800 | 8,400 | 14,000 | 28,000 | 49,000 | 70,000 |
| **1958 Aceca, 6-cyl., 90" wb** | | | | | | |
| 2d FBk Cpe | 2,300 | 6,950 | 11,600 | 23,200 | 40,600 | 58,000 |
| **1960 Ace, 6-cyl., 90" wb** | | | | | | |
| 2d Rds | 2,800 | 8,400 | 14,000 | 28,000 | 49,000 | 70,000 |
| **1960 Aceca, 6-cyl., 90" wb** | | | | | | |
| 2d FBk Cpe | 2,300 | 6,950 | 11,600 | 23,200 | 40,600 | 58,000 |
| **1962 Ford/AC Shelby Cobra, 260/289 V-8, 90" wb** | | | | | | |
| 2d Rds | 8,600 | 25,800 | 43,000 | 86,000 | 151,000 | 215,000 |
| **1963 Ford/AC Shelby Cobra Mk II, 280 V-8, 90" wb** | | | | | | |
| 2d Rds | 8,600 | 25,800 | 43,000 | 86,000 | 151,000 | 215,000 |

NOTE: Add 20 percent for 1956-63 Ace or Aceca with Bristol engine.

| | 6 | 5 | 4 | 3 | 2 | 1 |
|---|---|---|---|---|---|---|
| **1964 Ford/AC Shelby Cobra Mk II, 289 V-8, 90" wb** | | | | | | |
| 2d Rds | 9,000 | 27,000 | 45,000 | 90,000 | 158,000 | 225,000 |
| **1965 Ford/AC Shelby Cobra Mk II, 289 V-8, 90" wb** | | | | | | |
| 2d Rds | 9,000 | 27,000 | 45,000 | 90,000 | 158,000 | 225,000 |
| **1965 Ford/AC Shelby Cobra Mk III, 427-428, V-8, 90" wb** | | | | | | |
| 2d Rds | 13,400 | 40,200 | 67,000 | 134,000 | 234,000 | 335,000 |
| **1965 Ford/AC 428, 428 V-8, 96" wb** | | | | | | |
| 2d Conv | 2,800 | 8,400 | 14,000 | 28,000 | 49,000 | 70,000 |
| 2d Cpe | 2,500 | 7,550 | 12,600 | 25,200 | 44,100 | 63,000 |

| | 6 | 5 | 4 | 3 | 2 | 1 |
|---|---|---|---|---|---|---|
| **1966 Ford/AC Shelby Cobra Mk III, 427/428 V-8, 90" wb** | | | | | | |
| 2d Rds | 13,400 | 40,200 | 67,000 | 134,000 | 234,000 | 335,000 |
| **1966 Ford/AC 289, 289 V-8, 90" wb** | | | | | | |
| 2d Rds | 8,200 | 24,600 | 41,000 | 82,000 | 144,000 | 205,000 |
| **1966 Ford/AC 428, 428 V-8, 96" wb** | | | | | | |
| 2d Conv | 2,800 | 8,400 | 14,000 | 28,000 | 49,000 | 70,000 |
| 2d Cpe | 2,500 | 7,550 | 12,600 | 25,200 | 44,100 | 63,000 |
| **1967 Ford/AC Shelby Cobra Mk III 427/428 V-8, 90" wb** | | | | | | |
| 2d Rds | 13,400 | 40,200 | 67,000 | 134,000 | 234,000 | 335,000 |
| **1967 Ford/AC 289, 289 V-8, 90" wb** | | | | | | |
| 2d Rds | 8,600 | 25,800 | 43,000 | 86,000 | 151,000 | 215,000 |
| **1967 Ford/AC 428, 428 V-8, 96" wb** | | | | | | |
| 2d Conv | 2,800 | 8,400 | 14,000 | 28,000 | 49,000 | 70,000 |
| 2d Cpe | 2,500 | 7,550 | 12,600 | 25,200 | 44,100 | 63,000 |
| **1968 Ford/AC 289, 289 V-8, 90" wb** | | | | | | |
| 2d Rds | 8,600 | 25,800 | 43,000 | 86,000 | 151,000 | 215,000 |

## Allard

| | 6 | 5 | 4 | 3 | 2 | 1 |
|---|---|---|---|---|---|---|
| **1946-49 J1, V-8, 100" wb** | | | | | | |
| 2d Rds | 5,700 | 17,200 | 28,600 | 57,200 | 100,000 | 143,000 |
| **1946-49 K1, V-8, 106" wb** | | | | | | |
| 2d Rds | 6,100 | 18,400 | 30,600 | 61,000 | 107,000 | 153,000 |
| **1950-51 J2, V-8, 100" wb** | | | | | | |
| 2d Rds | 4,900 | 14,800 | 24,600 | 49,200 | 86,000 | 123,000 |
| **1950-51 K2, V-8, 106" wb** | | | | | | |
| 2d Rds | 5,300 | 16,000 | 26,600 | 53,200 | 93,000 | 133,000 |
| 2d Spt Sed | 2,750 | 8,300 | 13,800 | 27,600 | 48,300 | 69,000 |
| **1952-54 K3, V-8, 100" wb** | | | | | | |
| 2d Rds | 5,550 | 16,700 | 27,800 | 55,600 | 97,500 | 139,000 |
| **1952-54 J2X, V-8, 100" wb** | | | | | | |
| 2d Rds | 6,100 | 18,400 | 30,600 | 61,000 | 107,000 | 153,000 |
| 2d LeMans Rds | 6,100 | 18,400 | 30,600 | 61,000 | 107,000 | 153,000 |
| **1952-54 JR, V-8, 96" wb** | | | | | | |
| 2d Rds | 6,500 | 19,600 | 32,600 | 65,000 | 114,000 | 163,000 |
| **1952-54 Palm Beach, 4-cyl., 96" wb** | | | | | | |
| 2d Rds | 2,900 | 8,750 | 14,600 | 29,200 | 51,100 | 73,000 |
| **1952-54 Palm Beach, 6-cyl., 96" wb** | | | | | | |
| 2d Rds | 3,150 | 9,500 | 15,800 | 31,600 | 55,300 | 79,000 |

| | 6 | 5 | 4 | 3 | 2 | 1 |
|---|---|---|---|---|---|---|

## Aston-Martin

**1948-50 DB1, 4-cyl., 1970cc, 108" wb**
2S Rds (14 made)  value not estimable

**1950-53 DB2, 6-cyl., 2580cc, 99" wb**

| | 6 | 5 | 4 | 3 | 2 | 1 |
|---|---|---|---|---|---|---|
| DHC | 6,000 | 18,000 | 30,000 | 60,000 | 105,000 | 150,000 |

**1953-55 DB2/4, 6-cyl., 292cc, 99" wb**

| | 6 | 5 | 4 | 3 | 2 | 1 |
|---|---|---|---|---|---|---|
| DHC | 6,000 | 18,000 | 30,000 | 60,000 | 105,000 | 150,000 |

**1953-56 DB3S, 6-cyl., 2922cc, 87" wb**

| | 6 | 5 | 4 | 3 | 2 | 1 |
|---|---|---|---|---|---|---|
| Cpe | 8,000 | 24,000 | 40,000 | 80,000 | 140,000 | 200,000 |

**1955-57 DB2/4, 6-cyl., 2922cc, 99" wb**

| | 6 | 5 | 4 | 3 | 2 | 1 |
|---|---|---|---|---|---|---|
| Mk II DHC | 6,000 | 18,000 | 30,000 | 60,000 | 105,000 | 150,000 |
| Mk II FHC | 3,600 | 10,800 | 18,000 | 36,000 | 63,000 | 90,000 |

**1958-60 DB4, 6-cyl., 3670cc, 98" wb, Series 1**

| | 6 | 5 | 4 | 3 | 2 | 1 |
|---|---|---|---|---|---|---|
| Saloon | 3,040 | 9,120 | 15,200 | 30,400 | 53,200 | 76,000 |

**1959-63 DB4GT, 6-cyl., 3670cc, 93" wb**

| | 6 | 5 | 4 | 3 | 2 | 1 |
|---|---|---|---|---|---|---|
| Saloon | 5,040 | 15,120 | 25,200 | 50,400 | 88,200 | 126,000 |
| Cpe by Zagato  value not estimable |

**1962-63 DB4, 6-cyl., 3670cc, 98" wb, Series 5**

| | 6 | 5 | 4 | 3 | 2 | 1 |
|---|---|---|---|---|---|---|
| Saloon | 3,040 | 9,120 | 15,200 | 30,400 | 53,200 | 76,000 |
| DHC | 5,600 | 16,800 | 28,000 | 56,000 | 98,000 | 140,000 |

**1963-65 DB5, 6-cyl., 3995cc, 98" wb**

| | 6 | 5 | 4 | 3 | 2 | 1 |
|---|---|---|---|---|---|---|
| Saloon | 3,200 | 9,600 | 16,000 | 32,000 | 56,000 | 80,000 |
| DHC | 6,000 | 18,000 | 30,000 | 60,000 | 105,000 | 150,000 |
| Volante (37 made)  value not estimable |

**1965-69 DB6, 6-cyl., 3995cc, 102" wb**

| | 6 | 5 | 4 | 3 | 2 | 1 |
|---|---|---|---|---|---|---|
| Saloon | 3,440 | 10,320 | 17,200 | 34,400 | 60,200 | 86,000 |
| Volante | 6,000 | 18,000 | 30,000 | 60,000 | 105,000 | 150,000 |

**1969-70 DB6, 6-cyl., 3995cc, 102" wb**

| | 6 | 5 | 4 | 3 | 2 | 1 |
|---|---|---|---|---|---|---|
| Mk II Saloon | 3,200 | 9,600 | 16,000 | 32,000 | 56,000 | 80,000 |
| Mk II Volante | 6,000 | 18,000 | 30,000 | 60,000 | 105,000 | 150,000 |

**1973-78 AMV8, V-8, 5340cc, 103" wb, Series III**

| | 6 | 5 | 4 | 3 | 2 | 1 |
|---|---|---|---|---|---|---|
| Saloon | 2,360 | 7,080 | 11,800 | 23,600 | 41,300 | 59,000 |

**1983 AMV8, V-8, 5340cc, 103" wb**

| | 6 | 5 | 4 | 3 | 2 | 1 |
|---|---|---|---|---|---|---|
| 2d Vantage Cpe | 2,800 | 8,400 | 14,000 | 28,000 | 49,000 | 70,000 |
| 2d Volante Conv | 3,920 | 11,760 | 19,600 | 39,200 | 68,600 | 98,000 |

**1985 V-8**

| | 6 | 5 | 4 | 3 | 2 | 1 |
|---|---|---|---|---|---|---|
| 2d Vantage Cpe | 528 | 1,584 | 2,640 | 5,280 | 9,240 | 13,200 |
| 2d Volante Conv | 552 | 1,656 | 2,760 | 5,520 | 9,660 | 13,800 |

**1987 V-8**

| | 6 | 5 | 4 | 3 | 2 | 1 |
|---|---|---|---|---|---|---|
| 2d Vantage Cpe | 3,760 | 11,280 | 18,800 | 37,600 | 65,800 | 94,000 |
| 2d Volante Conv | 4,000 | 12,000 | 20,000 | 40,000 | 70,000 | 100,000 |

**1988 V-8**

| | 6 | 5 | 4 | 3 | 2 | 1 |
|---|---|---|---|---|---|---|
| 2d Vantage Cpe | 3,840 | 11,520 | 19,200 | 38,400 | 67,200 | 96,000 |
| 2d Volante Conv | 4,080 | 12,240 | 20,400 | 40,800 | 71,400 | 102,000 |

## Austin-Healey

**1953-56 "100", 4-cyl., 90 hp, 90" wb**

| | 6 | 5 | 4 | 3 | 2 | 1 |
|---|---|---|---|---|---|---|
| Rds | 1,240 | 3,720 | 6,200 | 12,400 | 21,700 | 31,000 |

**1956 "100-6", 6-cyl., 102 hp, 92" wb**

| | 6 | 5 | 4 | 3 | 2 | 1 |
|---|---|---|---|---|---|---|
| Rds | 1,280 | 3,840 | 6,400 | 12,800 | 22,400 | 32,000 |

**1958 Sprite Mk I, 4-cyl., 43 hp, 80" wb**

| | 6 | 5 | 4 | 3 | 2 | 1 |
|---|---|---|---|---|---|---|
| Rds | 720 | 2,160 | 3,600 | 7,200 | 12,600 | 18,000 |

**1960 "3000" Mk I, 6-cyl., 124 hp, 92" wb**

| | 6 | 5 | 4 | 3 | 2 | 1 |
|---|---|---|---|---|---|---|
| Rds | 1,320 | 3,960 | 6,600 | 13,200 | 23,100 | 33,000 |

Aston-Martin Media

| | 6 | 5 | 4 | 3 | 2 | 1 |
|---|---|---|---|---|---|---|
| **1961 "3000" Mk II, 6-cyl., 132 hp, 92" wb** | | | | | | |
| Rds | 1,240 | 3,720 | 6,200 | 12,400 | 21,700 | 31,000 |
| **1961 Sprite Mk II, 4-cyl., 46 hp, 80" wb** | | | | | | |
| Rds | 640 | 1,920 | 3,200 | 6,400 | 11,200 | 16,000 |
| **1964 "3000" Mk II, 6-cyl., 132 hp, 92" wb** | | | | | | |
| Conv | 1,280 | 3,840 | 6,400 | 12,800 | 22,400 | 32,000 |
| **1964 "3000" Mk III, 6-cyl., 150 hp, 92" wb** | | | | | | |
| Conv | 1,320 | 3,960 | 6,600 | 13,200 | 23,100 | 33,000 |
| **1964 Sprite Mk II, 4-cyl., 56 hp, 80" wb** | | | | | | |
| Rds | 600 | 1,800 | 3,000 | 6,000 | 10,500 | 15,000 |
| **1964 Sprite Mk III, 4-cyl., 59 hp, 80" wb** | | | | | | |
| Conv | 620 | 1,860 | 3,100 | 6,200 | 10,850 | 15,500 |
| **1965 "3000" Mk III, 6-cyl., 150 hp, 92" wb** | | | | | | |
| Conv | 1,320 | 3,960 | 6,600 | 13,200 | 23,100 | 33,000 |
| **1965 Sprite Mk III, 4-cyl., 59 hp, 80" wb** | | | | | | |
| Conv | 620 | 1,860 | 3,100 | 6,200 | 10,850 | 15,500 |
| **1966 "3000" Mk III, 6-cyl., 150 hp, 92" wb** | | | | | | |
| Conv | 1,320 | 3,960 | 6,600 | 13,200 | 23,100 | 33,000 |
| **1966 Sprite Mk III, 4-cyl., 59 hp, 80" wb** | | | | | | |
| Conv | 620 | 1,860 | 3,100 | 6,200 | 10,850 | 15,500 |
| **1967 "3000" Mk III, 6-cyl., 150 hp, 92" wb** | | | | | | |
| Conv | 1,320 | 3,960 | 6,600 | 13,200 | 23,100 | 33,000 |
| **1968 Sprite Mk IV, 4-cyl., 62 hp, 80" wb** | | | | | | |
| 2d Rds | 640 | 1,920 | 3,200 | 6,400 | 11,200 | 16,000 |
| **1970 Sprite MK IV, 4-cyl., 62 hp, 80" wb** | | | | | | |
| 2d Rds | 640 | 1,920 | 3,200 | 6,400 | 11,200 | 16,000 |

## Jaguar

| | 6 | 5 | 4 | 3 | 2 | 1 |
|---|---|---|---|---|---|---|
| **1950 XK-120, 6-cyl., 160 hp, 102" wb** | | | | | | |
| Rds | 2,750 | 8,300 | 13,800 | 27,600 | 48,300 | 69,000 |

NOTE: Some XK-120 models delivered as early as 1949 models, use 1950 prices.

| | 6 | 5 | 4 | 3 | 2 | 1 |
|---|---|---|---|---|---|---|
| **1952 XK-120S (modified), 160 hp, 102" wb** | | | | | | |
| Rds | 3,400 | 10,200 | 17,000 | 34,000 | 59,500 | 85,000 |
| Cpe | 2,250 | 6,700 | 11,200 | 22,400 | 39,200 | 56,000 |
| **1953 XK-120, 6-cyl., 160 hp, 102" wb** | | | | | | |
| Rds | 3,250 | 9,700 | 16,200 | 32,400 | 56,700 | 81,000 |
| Cpe | 2,100 | 6,250 | 10,400 | 20,800 | 36,400 | 52,000 |
| Conv | 2,500 | 7,450 | 12,400 | 24,800 | 43,400 | 62,000 |
| Conv | 2,500 | 7,450 | 12,400 | 24,800 | 43,400 | 62,000 |

Robert Simansky

Kris Kandler

| | 6 | 5 | 4 | 3 | 2 | 1 |
|---|---|---|---|---|---|---|
| **1955 XK-140, 6-cyl., 190 hp, 102" wb** | | | | | | |
| Cpe | 1,900 | 5,650 | 9,400 | 18,800 | 32,900 | 47,000 |
| Rds | 3,100 | 9,250 | 15,400 | 30,800 | 53,900 | 77,000 |
| Conv | 2,500 | 7,450 | 12,400 | 24,800 | 43,400 | 62,000 |
| **1955 XK-140M, 6-cyl., 190 hp, 102" wb** | | | | | | |
| Cpe | 2,100 | 6,250 | 10,400 | 20,800 | 36,400 | 52,000 |
| Rds | 3,400 | 10,200 | 17,000 | 34,000 | 59,500 | 85,000 |
| Conv | 2,900 | 8,750 | 14,600 | 29,200 | 51,100 | 73,000 |
| **1955 XK-140MC, 6-cyl., 210 hp, 102" wb** | | | | | | |
| Cpe | 2,300 | 6,850 | 11,400 | 22,800 | 39,900 | 57,000 |
| Rds | 3,550 | 10,700 | 17,800 | 35,600 | 62,500 | 89,000 |
| Conv | 3,150 | 9,500 | 15,800 | 31,600 | 55,300 | 79,000 |
| **1956 XK-140MC, 6-cyl., 210 hp, 102" wb** | | | | | | |
| Cpe | 2,300 | 6,850 | 11,400 | 22,800 | 39,900 | 57,000 |
| Rds | 3,550 | 10,700 | 17,800 | 35,600 | 62,500 | 89,000 |
| Conv | 3,150 | 9,500 | 15,800 | 31,600 | 55,300 | 79,000 |
| **1957 XK-140** | | | | | | |
| Cpe | 2,000 | 6,000 | 10,000 | 20,000 | 35,000 | 50,000 |
| Rds | 2,700 | 8,050 | 13,400 | 26,800 | 46,900 | 67,000 |
| Conv | 2,200 | 6,600 | 11,000 | 22,000 | 38,500 | 55,000 |
| **1957 XK-150, 6-cyl., 190 hp, 102" wb** | | | | | | |
| Cpe | 2,200 | 6,600 | 11,000 | 22,000 | 38,500 | 55,000 |
| Rds | 2,900 | 8,750 | 14,600 | 29,200 | 51,100 | 73,000 |
| **1961 XK-150, 6-cyl., 210 hp, 102" wb** | | | | | | |
| Cpe | 1,900 | 5,750 | 9,600 | 19,200 | 33,600 | 48,000 |
| Conv | 2,100 | 6,250 | 10,400 | 20,800 | 36,400 | 52,000 |
| **1961 XKE, 6-cyl., 265 hp, 96" wb** | | | | | | |
| Rds | 2,400 | 7,200 | 12,000 | 24,000 | 42,000 | 60,000 |
| Cpe | 1,800 | 5,400 | 9,000 | 18,000 | 31,500 | 45,000 |
| **1966 XKE 4.2, 6-cyl., 265 hp, 96" wb** | | | | | | |
| Rds | 2,400 | 7,200 | 12,000 | 24,000 | 42,000 | 60,000 |
| Cpe | 1,500 | 4,550 | 7,600 | 15,200 | 26,600 | 38,000 |

| | 6 | 5 | 4 | 3 | 2 | 1 |
|---|---|---|---|---|---|---|
| **1967 XKE 4.2, 6-cyl., 265 hp, 96" wb** | | | | | | |
| Rds | 2,500 | 7,450 | 12,400 | 24,800 | 43,400 | 62,000 |
| Cpe | 1,750 | 5,300 | 8,800 | 17,600 | 30,800 | 44,000 |
| 2 plus 2 Cpe | 1,400 | 4,200 | 7,000 | 14,000 | 24,500 | 35,000 |
| **1971 Model XKE, 246 hp, 96" wb** | | | | | | |
| Rds | 2,400 | 7,200 | 12,000 | 24,000 | 42,000 | 60,000 |
| Cpe | 1,700 | 5,150 | 8,600 | 17,200 | 30,100 | 43,000 |
| V-12 2 plus 2 Cpe | 1,550 | 4,700 | 7,800 | 15,600 | 27,300 | 39,000 |
| V-12 Conv | 2,600 | 7,800 | 13,000 | 26,000 | 45,500 | 65,000 |
| **1974 Model XKE V-12, 272 hp, 105" wb** | | | | | | |
| Rds | 2,850 | 8,500 | 14,200 | 28,400 | 49,700 | 71,000 |
| **1975 Model XJ6** | | | | | | |
| C Cpe | 1,250 | 3,700 | 6,200 | 12,400 | 21,700 | 31,000 |
| 4d L Sed | 1,050 | 3,100 | 5,200 | 10,400 | 18,200 | 26,000 |
| **1977 Model XJS** | | | | | | |
| GT 2 plus 2 Cpe | 1,100 | 3,350 | 5,600 | 11,200 | 19,600 | 28,000 |

Jaguarv

Richard Gaspar

| | 6 | 5 | 4 | 3 | 2 | 1 |
|---|---|---|---|---|---|---|
| **1980 Model XJS** | | | | | | |
| 2d XJS 2 plus 2 Cpe | 1,100 | 3,350 | 5,600 | 11,200 | 19,600 | 28,000 |
| **1987 Model XJS** | | | | | | |
| 2d Cpe | 1,250 | 3,700 | 6,200 | 12,400 | 21,700 | 31,000 |
| 2d Cpe Cabr | 1,650 | 4,900 | 8,200 | 16,400 | 28,700 | 41,000 |
| **1994 XJS** | | | | | | |
| 2d Cpe, 6-cyl. | 900 | 2,650 | 4,400 | 8,800 | 15,400 | 22,000 |
| 2d Cpe, V-12 | 1,150 | 3,500 | 5,800 | 11,600 | 20,300 | 29,000 |
| 2d Conv, 6-cyl. | 1,300 | 3,850 | 6,400 | 12,800 | 22,400 | 32,000 |
| 2d Conv, V-12 | 1,500 | 4,550 | 7,600 | 15,200 | 26,600 | 38,000 |
| **1995 XJS, 6-cyl. & V-12** | | | | | | |
| 2d Cpe, 6-cyl. | 900 | 2,650 | 4,400 | 8,800 | 15,400 | 22,000 |
| 2d Cpe, V-12 | 1,150 | 3,500 | 5,800 | 11,600 | 20,300 | 29,000 |
| 2d Conv, 6-cyl. | 1,300 | 3,850 | 6,400 | 12,800 | 22,400 | 32,000 |
| 2d Conv, V-12 | 1,500 | 4,550 | 7,600 | 15,200 | 26,600 | 38,000 |
| **1996 XJS, 6-cyl.** | | | | | | |
| 2d Conv | 1,250 | 3,700 | 6,200 | 12,400 | 21,700 | 31,000 |

## MG

| | 6 | 5 | 4 | 3 | 2 | 1 |
|---|---|---|---|---|---|---|
| **1947-48 MG-TC, 4-cyl., 94" wb** | | | | | | |
| Rds | 1,200 | 3,600 | 6,000 | 12,000 | 21,000 | 30,000 |
| **1950 MG-TD, 4-cyl., 54.4 hp, 94" wb** | | | | | | |
| Rds | 1,050 | 3,100 | 5,200 | 10,400 | 18,200 | 26,000 |
| **1951 Mk II, 4-cyl., 54.4 hp, 94" wb** | | | | | | |
| Rds | 1,100 | 3,350 | 5,600 | 11,200 | 19,600 | 28,000 |

| | 6 | 5 | 4 | 3 | 2 | 1 |
|---|---|---|---|---|---|---|
| **1952 Mk II, 4-cyl., 62 hp, 94" wb** | | | | | | |
| Rds | 1,100 | 3,350 | 5,600 | 11,200 | 19,600 | 28,000 |

*NOTE: Add 20 percent for Inskip 4 place Roadster.*

| | 6 | 5 | 4 | 3 | 2 | 1 |
|---|---|---|---|---|---|---|
| **1954 MG-TF, 4-cyl., 57 hp, 94" wb** | | | | | | |
| Rds | 1,050 | 3,100 | 5,200 | 10,400 | 18,200 | 26,000 |
| **1955 MG-TF, 4-cyl., 68 hp, 94" wb** | | | | | | |
| Rds | 1,080 | 3,240 | 5,400 | 10,800 | 18,900 | 27,000 |
| **1956 MG-"A", 4-cyl., 68 hp, 94" wb** | | | | | | |
| 1500 Rds | 960 | 2,880 | 4,800 | 9,600 | 16,800 | 24,000 |
| **1958 MG-"A", 4-cyl., 72 hp, 94" wb** | | | | | | |
| 1500 Cpe | 900 | 2,750 | 4,600 | 9,200 | 16,100 | 23,000 |
| 1500 Rds | 950 | 2,900 | 4,800 | 9,600 | 16,800 | 24,000 |

Richard Brown

Jaguar

|  | 6 | 5 | 4 | 3 | 2 | 1 |
|---|---|---|---|---|---|---|
| **1959-60 MG-"A", Twin-Cam, 4-cyl., 107 hp, 94" wb** | | | | | | |
| Rds | 1,200 | 3,600 | 6,000 | 12,000 | 21,000 | 30,000 |
| Cpe | 1,100 | 3,250 | 5,400 | 10,800 | 18,900 | 27,000 |
| **1961 MG-"A", 4-cyl., 79 hp, 94" wb** | | | | | | |
| 1600 Rds | 880 | 2,640 | 4,400 | 8,800 | 15,400 | 22,000 |
| 1600 Cpe | 840 | 2,520 | 4,200 | 8,400 | 14,700 | 21,000 |
| 1600 Mk II Rds | 920 | 2,760 | 4,600 | 9,200 | 16,100 | 23,000 |
| 1600 Mk II Cpe | 880 | 2,640 | 4,400 | 8,800 | 15,400 | 22,000 |
| **1962 MG Midget, 4-cyl., 50 hp, 80" wb** | | | | | | |
| Rds | 400 | 1,200 | 2,000 | 4,000 | 7,000 | 10,000 |
| **1962 MG-"A", 4-cyl., 90 hp, 94" wb** | | | | | | |
| 1600 Mk II Rds | 960 | 2,880 | 4,800 | 9,600 | 16,800 | 24,000 |
| 1600 Mk II Cpe | 920 | 2,760 | 4,600 | 9,200 | 16,100 | 23,000 |

*NOTE: Add 40 percent for 1600 Mk II Deluxe.*

|  | 6 | 5 | 4 | 3 | 2 | 1 |
|---|---|---|---|---|---|---|
| **1963 MG Midget, 4-cyl., 56 hp, 80" wb** | | | | | | |
| Rds | 400 | 1,200 | 2,000 | 4,000 | 7,000 | 10,000 |
| **1963 MG-B, 4-cyl., 95 hp, 91" wb** | | | | | | |
| Rds | 700 | 2,100 | 3,500 | 7,000 | 12,300 | 17,500 |
| **1965 MG Midget Mk II, 4-cyl., 59 hp, 80" wb** | | | | | | |
| Rds | 440 | 1,320 | 2,200 | 4,400 | 7,700 | 11,000 |
| **1966 MG Midget Mk III, 4-cyl., 59 hp, 80" wb** | | | | | | |
| Rds | 440 | 1,320 | 2,200 | 4,400 | 7,700 | 11,000 |
| **1966 MG-B, 4-cyl., 95 hp, 91" wb** | | | | | | |
| Rds | 700 | 2,050 | 3,400 | 6,800 | 11,900 | 17,000 |

|  | 6 | 5 | 4 | 3 | 2 | 1 |
|---|---|---|---|---|---|---|
| **1967 MG Midget Mk III, 4-cyl., 59 hp, 80" wb** | | | | | | |
| Rds | 440 | 1,320 | 2,200 | 4,400 | 7,700 | 11,000 |
| **1967 MG-B, 4-cyl., 98 hp, 91" wb** | | | | | | |
| Rds | 700 | 2,050 | 3,400 | 6,800 | 11,900 | 17,000 |
| GT Cpe | 650 | 1,900 | 3,200 | 6,400 | 11,200 | 16,000 |
| **1969 MG-C, 6-cyl., 145 hp, 91" wb** | | | | | | |
| Rds | 700 | 2,100 | 3,500 | 7,000 | 12,300 | 17,500 |
| GT Cpe | 550 | 1,700 | 2,800 | 5,600 | 9,800 | 14,000 |
| **1970 MG-B/GT, 4-cyl., 78.5 hp, 91" wb** | | | | | | |
| Rds | 650 | 2,000 | 3,300 | 6,600 | 11,600 | 16,500 |
| GT Cpe | 600 | 1,850 | 3,100 | 6,200 | 10,900 | 15,500 |

*NOTE: Add 10 percent for wire wheels. Add 5 percent for overdrive.*

|  | 6 | 5 | 4 | 3 | 2 | 1 |
|---|---|---|---|---|---|---|
| **1973 MG Midget, 4-cyl., 54.5 hp, 80" wb** | | | | | | |
| Conv | 400 | 1,200 | 2,000 | 4,000 | 7,000 | 10,000 |

Daniel Donahue Jr.

John Gunnell

| | 6 | 5 | 4 | 3 | 2 | 1 |
|---|---|---|---|---|---|---|
| **1973 MG-B/GT, 4-cyl., 78.5 hp, 91" wb** | | | | | | |
| Conv | 600 | 1,850 | 3,100 | 6,200 | 10,900 | 15,500 |
| GT Cpe | 550 | 1,700 | 2,800 | 5,600 | 9,800 | 14,000 |

NOTE: Add 10 percent for wire wheels. Add 5 percent for overdrive.

| | 6 | 5 | 4 | 3 | 2 | 1 |
|---|---|---|---|---|---|---|
| **1974 MG-B, 4-cyl., 78.5 hp, 91" wb** | | | | | | |
| Conv | 600 | 1,850 | 3,100 | 6,200 | 10,900 | 15,500 |
| GT Cpe | 550 | 1,700 | 2,800 | 5,600 | 9,800 | 14,000 |
| **1974 Interim MG-B, 4-cyl., 62.9 hp, 91.125" wb** | | | | | | |
| Conv | 600 | 1,750 | 2,900 | 5,800 | 10,200 | 14,500 |
| GT Cpe | 350 | 1,100 | 1,800 | 3,650 | 6,350 | 9,100 |

NOTE: Add 10 percent for wire wheels. Add 5 percent for overdrive.

| | 6 | 5 | 4 | 3 | 2 | 1 |
|---|---|---|---|---|---|---|
| **1978 MG-B, 4-cyl., 62.5 hp, 91.13" wb** | | | | | | |
| Midget Conv | 400 | 1,200 | 2,000 | 4,000 | 7,000 | 10,000 |
| B Conv | 560 | 1,680 | 2,800 | 5,600 | 9,800 | 14,000 |
| **1979 MG-B, 4-cyl., 62.5 hp, 91.13" wb** | | | | | | |
| Midget Conv | 400 | 1,200 | 2,000 | 4,000 | 7,000 | 10,000 |
| B Conv | 560 | 1,680 | 2,800 | 5,600 | 9,800 | 14,000 |
| **1980 MG-B, 4-cyl., 62.5 hp, 91.13" wb** | | | | | | |
| B Conv | 560 | 1,680 | 2,800 | 5,600 | 9,800 | 14,000 |

# *Morgan*

| | 6 | 5 | 4 | 3 | 2 | 1 |
|---|---|---|---|---|---|---|
| **1945-50 4/4, Series I, 4-cyl., 1267cc, 92" wb** | | | | | | |
| 2d Rds | 1,200 | 3,600 | 6,000 | 12,000 | 21,000 | 30,000 |
| 2d Rds (2 plus 2) | 1,150 | 3,500 | 5,800 | 11,600 | 20,300 | 29,000 |
| 2d DHC | 1,350 | 4,100 | 6,800 | 13,600 | 23,800 | 34,000 |

| | 6 | 5 | 4 | 3 | 2 | 1 |
|---|---|---|---|---|---|---|
| **1951-54 Plus Four I, 4-cyl., 2088cc, 96" wb** | | | | | | |
| 2d Rds | 1,100 | 3,350 | 5,600 | 11,200 | 19,600 | 28,000 |
| 2d Rds (2 plus 2) | 1,100 | 3,250 | 5,400 | 10,800 | 18,900 | 27,000 |
| 2d DHC | 1,200 | 3,600 | 6,000 | 12,000 | 21,000 | 30,000 |
| 2d DHC (2 plus 2) | 1,250 | 3,700 | 6,200 | 12,400 | 21,700 | 31,000 |
| **1955-62 Plus Four Super Sports 4-cyl., 2138cc, 96" wb** | | | | | | |
| 2d Rds | 1,200 | 3,600 | 6,000 | 12,000 | 21,000 | 30,000 |
| **1955-62 4/4 II (1955-59) L-head, 4-cyl., 1172cc, 96" wb** | | | | | | |
| 2d Rds | 1,100 | 3,350 | 5,600 | 11,200 | 19,600 | 28,000 |
| **1955-62 4/4 III (1960-61) 4-cyl., 997cc, 96" wb** | | | | | | |
| 2d Rds | 1,100 | 3,250 | 5,400 | 10,800 | 18,900 | 27,000 |
| **1955-62 4/4 IV (1961-63) 4-cyl., 1340cc, 96" wb** | | | | | | |
| 2d Rds | 1,100 | 3,250 | 5,400 | 10,800 | 18,900 | 27,000 |
| **1963-67 Plus Four Plus (1963-66) 4-cyl., 2138cc, 96" wb** | | | | | | |
| 2d Cpe | value not estimable | | | | | |
| **1963-67 4/4 Series V (1963-68) 4-cyl., 1498cc, 96" wb** | | | | | | |
| 2d Rds | 1,200 | 3,600 | 6,000 | 12,000 | 21,000 | 30,000 |
| **1968-69 Plus 8, V-8, 3528cc, 98" wb** | | | | | | |
| 2d Rds | 1,250 | 3,700 | 6,200 | 12,400 | 21,700 | 31,000 |
| **1968-69 4/4 Series V (1963-68) 4-cyl., 1498cc, 96" wb** | | | | | | |
| 2d Rds | 1,150 | 3,500 | 5,800 | 11,600 | 20,300 | 29,000 |
| **1970-90 Plus 8 (1972-90) V-8, 3528cc, 98" wb** | | | | | | |
| 2d Rds | 1,200 | 3,600 | 6,000 | 12,000 | 21,000 | 30,000 |

Andrew Morland

| | 6 | 5 | 4 | 3 | 2 | 1 |
|---|---|---|---|---|---|---|

**1970-90 4/4 1600 (1970-81) 4-cyl., 1599cc, 96" wb**

| | 6 | 5 | 4 | 3 | 2 | 1 |
|---|---|---|---|---|---|---|
| 2d Rds | 1,200 | 3,600 | 6,000 | 12,000 | 21,000 | 30,0002d |
| Rds (2 plus 2) | 1,150 | 3,500 | 5,800 | 11,600 | 20,300 | 29,000 |

**1970-90 4/4 1600 (1982-87) 4-cyl., 1596cc, 96" wb**

| | 6 | 5 | 4 | 3 | 2 | 1 |
|---|---|---|---|---|---|---|
| 2d Rds | 1,100 | 3,350 | 5,600 | 11,200 | 19,600 | 28,000 |
| 2d Rds (2 plus 2) | 1,300 | 3,850 | 6,400 | 12,800 | 22,400 | 32,000 |

## Sunbeam

**1953-55 4-cyl., 2267cc, 97.5" wb, Sunbeam Alpine**

| | 6 | 5 | 4 | 3 | 2 | 1 |
|---|---|---|---|---|---|---|
| Rds | 560 | 1,680 | 2,800 | 5,600 | 9,800 | 14,000 |

**1960 4-cyl., 1494cc, 86" wb, Sunbeam Alpine Series I**

| | 6 | 5 | 4 | 3 | 2 | 1 |
|---|---|---|---|---|---|---|
| Conv | 540 | 1,620 | 2,700 | 5,400 | 9,450 | 13,500 |

**1962 4-cyl., 1592cc, 86" wb, Sunbeam Alpine Series II/III**

| | 6 | 5 | 4 | 3 | 2 | 1 |
|---|---|---|---|---|---|---|
| Conv | 540 | 1,620 | 2,700 | 5,400 | 9,450 | 13,500 |

**1962 Sunbeam Herrington LeMans**

| | 6 | 5 | 4 | 3 | 2 | 1 |
|---|---|---|---|---|---|---|
| Cpe | 620 | 1,860 | 3,100 | 6,200 | 10,850 | 15,500 |

**1963 4-cyl., 1592cc, 86" wb, Sunbeam Alpine Series II/III**

| | 6 | 5 | 4 | 3 | 2 | 1 |
|---|---|---|---|---|---|---|
| Conv | 580 | 1,740 | 2,900 | 5,800 | 10,150 | 14,500 |
| Conv GT | 620 | 1,860 | 3,100 | 6,200 | 10,850 | 15,500 |

**1963 Sunbeam Herrington LeMans**

| | 6 | 5 | 4 | 3 | 2 | 1 |
|---|---|---|---|---|---|---|
| Cpe | 660 | 1,980 | 3,300 | 6,600 | 11,550 | 16,500 |

**1964 4-cyl., 1592cc, 86" wb, Sunbeam Alpine Series III/IV**

| | 6 | 5 | 4 | 3 | 2 | 1 |
|---|---|---|---|---|---|---|
| Conv | 580 | 1,740 | 2,900 | 5,800 | 10,150 | 14,500 |
| Conv GT | 620 | 1,860 | 3,100 | 6,200 | 10,850 | 15,500 |

**1964 V-8, 260 cid, 86" wb, Sunbeam Tiger Series I**

| | 6 | 5 | 4 | 3 | 2 | 1 |
|---|---|---|---|---|---|---|
| Conv | 680 | 2,040 | 3,400 | 6,800 | 11,900 | 17,000 |

**1966 4-cyl., 1725cc, 86" wb, Sunbeam Alpine Series V**

| | 6 | 5 | 4 | 3 | 2 | 1 |
|---|---|---|---|---|---|---|
| Conv | 580 | 1,740 | 2,900 | 5,800 | 10,150 | 14,500 |

**1966 V-8, 260 cid, 86" wb, Sunbeam Tiger Series I/IA**

| | 6 | 5 | 4 | 3 | 2 | 1 |
|---|---|---|---|---|---|---|
| Conv | 840 | 2,520 | 4,200 | 8,400 | 14,700 | 21,000 |

**1967-68 4-cyl., 1725cc, 86" wb, Sunbeam Alpine Series V**

| | 6 | 5 | 4 | 3 | 2 | 1 |
|---|---|---|---|---|---|---|
| Conv | 580 | 1,740 | 2,900 | 5,800 | 10,150 | 14,500 |

**1967-68 V-8, 289cc, 86" wb, Sunbeam Tiger Series II**

| | 6 | 5 | 4 | 3 | 2 | 1 |
|---|---|---|---|---|---|---|
| Conv | 880 | 2,640 | 4,400 | 8,800 | 15,400 | 22,000 |

John Gunnell

Andrew Morland

|  | 6 | 5 | 4 | 3 | 2 | 1 |
|---|---|---|---|---|---|---|

# Triumph

**1946-48 1800, 4-cyl., 63 hp, 100" wb**

| Rds | 900 | 2,750 | 4,600 | 9,200 | 16,100 | 23,000 |

**1953 TR-2, 4-cyl., 90 hp, 88" wb**

| Rds | 760 | 2,280 | 3,800 | 7,600 | 13,300 | 19,000 |

**1955 TR-2, 4-cyl., 90 hp, 88" wb**

| Rds | 650 | 1,900 | 3,200 | 6,400 | 11,200 | 16,000 |

**1955 TR-3, 4-cyl., 95 hp, 88" wb**

| Rds | 680 | 2,040 | 3,400 | 6,800 | 11,900 | 17,000 |

**1958 TR-3, 4-cyl., 100 hp, 88" wb**

| Rds | 650 | 2,000 | 3,300 | 6,600 | 11,600 | 16,500 |
| HT Rds | 700 | 2,050 | 3,400 | 6,800 | 11,900 | 17,000 |

**1962 TR-3, 4-cyl., 100 hp, 88" wb**

| Rds | 650 | 1,900 | 3,200 | 6,400 | 11,200 | 16,000 |
| HT Rds | 650 | 2,000 | 3,300 | 6,600 | 11,600 | 16,500 |

**1962 TR-4, 4-cyl., 105 hp, 88" wb**

| Rds | 700 | 2,050 | 3,400 | 6,800 | 11,900 | 17,000 |
| HT Rds | 700 | 2,100 | 3,500 | 7,000 | 12,300 | 17,500 |

**1962 Spitfire, 4-cyl., 100 hp, 83" wb**

| Conv | 700 | 2,050 | 3,400 | 6,800 | 11,900 | 17,000 |

**1963 TR-3B, 4-cyl., 100 hp, 88" wb**

| Rds | 600 | 1,850 | 3,100 | 6,200 | 10,900 | 15,500 |
| HT Rds | 650 | 1,900 | 3,200 | 6,400 | 11,200 | 16,000 |

**1964 TR-4, 4-cyl., 105 hp, 88" wb**

| Conv | 700 | 2,050 | 3,400 | 6,800 | 11,900 | 17,000 |
| HT Cpe | 600 | 1,850 | 3,100 | 6,200 | 10,900 | 15,500 |

**1965 TR-4 and TR-4A, 4-cyl., 105 hp, 88" wb**

| Conv | 750 | 2,200 | 3,700 | 7,400 | 13,000 | 18,500 |
| HT Cpe | 650 | 1,900 | 3,200 | 6,400 | 11,200 | 16,000 |

**1966 TR-4A, 4-cyl., 105 hp, 88" wb**

| Conv | 750 | 2,200 | 3,700 | 7,400 | 13,000 | 18,500 |
| HT Cpe | 600 | 1,850 | 3,100 | 6,200 | 10,900 | 15,500 |

**1966 Spitfire Mk II, 4-cyl., 100 hp, 83" wb**

| Conv | 550 | 1,700 | 2,800 | 5,600 | 9,800 | 14,000 |

**1968 TR-250, 6-cyl., 104 hp, 88" wb**

| Conv | 650 | 1,900 | 3,200 | 6,400 | 11,200 | 16,000 |

**1968 Spitfire Mk III, 4-cyl., 68 hp, 83" wb**

| Conv | 600 | 1,750 | 2,900 | 5,800 | 10,200 | 14,500 |

**1968 GT-6 Plus, 6-cyl., 95 hp, 83" wb**

| Cpe | 300 | 950 | 1,600 | 3,200 | 5,600 | 8,000 |

NOTE: Add 10 percent for wire wheels and factory hardtop. Add 5 percent for overdrive.

**1970 TR-6, 6-cyl., 104 hp, 88" wb**

| Conv | 650 | 1,900 | 3,200 | 6,400 | 11,200 | 16,000 |

**1970 Stag, 8-cyl., 145 hp, 100" wb**

| Conv | 700 | 2,150 | 3,600 | 7,200 | 12,600 | 18,000 |

NOTE: Add 10 percent for wire wheels and for factory hardtop. Add 5 percent for overdrive.

|  | 6 | 5 | 4 | 3 | 2 | 1 |
|---|---|---|---|---|---|---|

**1972 Spitfire Mk IV, 4-cyl., 48 hp, 83" wb**

| Conv | 600 | 1,750 | 2,900 | 5,800 | 10,200 | 14,500 |

**1972 GT-6 Mk III, 6-cyl., 79 hp, 83" wb**

| Cpe | 300 | 950 | 1,600 | 3,200 | 5,600 | 8,000 |

**1972 Stag, 8-cyl., 127 hp, 100" wb**

| Conv | 700 | 2,100 | 3,500 | 7,000 | 12,300 | 17,500 |

NOTE: Add 10 percent for wire wheels and for factory hardtop. Add 5 percent for overdrive.
NOTE: Add 10 percent for factory hardtop. Add 5 percent for overdrive.

**1975 TR-6, 6-cyl., 106 hp, 88" wb**

| Conv | 600 | 1,800 | 3,000 | 6,000 | 10,500 | 15,000 |

**1975 TR-7, 4-cyl., 92 hp, 85" wb**

| Cpe | 450 | 1,300 | 2,200 | 4,400 | 7,700 | 11,000 |

**1975 Spitfire 1500, 4-cyl., 57 hp, 83" wb**

| Conv | 450 | 1,400 | 2,300 | 4,600 | 8,050 | 11,500 |

NOTE: Add 10 percent for factory hardtop. Add 5 percent for overdrive.

**1978 TR-7, 4-cyl., 92 hp, 85" wb**

| Cpe | 350 | 1,000 | 1,700 | 3,400 | 5,950 | 8,500 |

**1978 Spitfire 1500, 4-cyl., 57 hp, 83" wb**

| Conv | 450 | 1,300 | 2,200 | 4,400 | 7,700 | 11,000 |

NOTE: Add 10 percent for factory hardtop. Add 5 percent for overdrive.

**1980 TR-7, 4-cyl., 86 hp, 85" wb**

| Conv | 450 | 1,350 | 2,250 | 4,500 | 7,850 | 11,200 |
| Spider Conv | 450 | 1,400 | 2,300 | 4,650 | 8,100 | 11,600 |
| Cpe | 350 | 1,000 | 1,650 | 3,300 | 5,800 | 8,300 |

**1980 TR-8, 8-cyl., 133 hp, 85" wb**

| Conv | 700 | 2,050 | 3,450 | 6,900 | 12,000 | 17,200 |
| Cpe | 600 | 1,850 | 3,100 | 6,200 | 10,900 | 15,500 |

**1980 Spitfire 1500, 4-cyl., 57 hp, 83" wb**

| Conv | 450 | 1,350 | 2,300 | 4,550 | 8,000 | 11,400 |

NOTE: Add 10 percent for factory hardtop. Add 5 percent for overdrive.

**1981 TR-7, 4-cyl., 89 hp, 85" wb**

| Conv | 500 | 1,450 | 2,400 | 4,750 | 8,350 | 11,900 |

**1981 TR-8, 8-cyl., 148 hp, 85" wb**

| Conv | 750 | 2,200 | 3,700 | 7,400 | 13,000 | 18,500 |

Alex LeBarre